ANTITRUST

ANTITRUST
Third Edition

By

HERBERT HOVENKAMP
Ben V. & Dorothy Willie Professor
University of Iowa College of Law

BLACK LETTER SERIES®

WEST GROUP

ST. PAUL, MINN.
1999

TEXT IS PRINTED ON 10% POST
CONSUMER RECYCLED PAPER

to my sons Arie & Erik

HERBERT HOVENKAMP is the Ben V. and Dorothy Willie Distinguished Professor of Law at the University of Iowa College of Law. He received his Ph.D. and J.D. at the University of Texas School of Law. He is a former member of the Executive Committee, Antitrust Section, of the AALS and held the chair for the Antitrust Section, AALS. Professor Hovenkamp has received many academic honors including University of Iowa Regents Award for Distinguished Faculty Scholars. He has written numerous articles on Antitrust as well as several publications for West Publishing Company, including *Federal Antitrust Policy: The Law of Competition and Its Practice, Black Letter on Antitrust, Cases and Materials on American Property Law,* and *The Law of Property, An Introductory Survey* with Boyer and Kurtz. He has also delivered lectures on federal antitrust, property and legal history.

*

PUBLISHER'S PREFACE

This "Black Letter" is designed to help a law student recognize and understand the basic principles and issues of law covered in a law school course. It can be used both as a study aid when preparing for classes and as a review of the subject matter when studying for an examination.

Each "Black Letter" is written by experienced law school teachers who are recognized national authorities in the subject covered.

The law is succinctly stated by the authors of this "Black Letter." In addition, the exceptions to the rules are stated in the text. The rules and exceptions have purposely been condensed to facilitate quick and easy recollection. For an in-depth study of a point of law, citations to major student texts are given. In addition, a Text Correlation Chart provides a convenient means of relating material contained in the Black Letter to appropriate sections of the casebook the student is using in his or her law school course.

If the subject covered by this text is a code or code-related course, the code section or rule is set forth and discussed wherever applicable.

FORMAT

The format of this "Black Letter" is specially designed for review. (1) **Text.** First, it is recommended that the entire text be studied and, if deemed necessary, supplemented by the student texts cited. (2) **Capsule Summary.** The Capsule Summary is an abbreviated review of the subject matter which can be used both before and after studying the main body of the text. The headings in the Capsule Summary follow the main text of the "Black Letter." (3) **Table of Contents.** The Table of Contents is in outline form to help you organize the details of the subject and the Summary of Contents gives you a final overview of the materials. (4) **Practice Examination.** The Practice Examination in Appendix B gives you the opportunity of testing yourself with the type of questions asked on an exam and comparing your answer with a model answer.

In addition, a number of other features are included to help you understand the subject matter and prepare for examinations:

Short Questions and Answers: This feature is designed to help you spot and recognize issues in the examination. We feel that issue recognition is a major ingredient in successfully writing an examination.

Perspective: In this feature, the authors discuss their approach to the topic, the approach used in preparing the materials, and any tips on studying for and writing examinations.

Analysis: This feature, at the beginning of each section, is designed to give a quick summary of a particular section to help you recall the subject matter and to help you determine which areas need the most extensive review.

Examples: This feature is designed to illustrate, through fact situations, the law just stated. This, we believe, should help you analytically approach a question on the examination.

Glossary: This feature is designed to refamiliarize you with the meaning of a particular legal term. We believe that the recognition of words of art used in an examination helps you to better analyze the question. In addition, when writing an examination you should know the precise definition of a word of art you intend to use.

We believe that the materials in this "Black Letter" will facilitate your study of a law school course and assure success in writing examinations not only for the course but for the bar examination. We wish you success.

THE PUBLISHER

SUMMARY OF CONTENTS

APPENDICES

TABLE OF CONTENTS

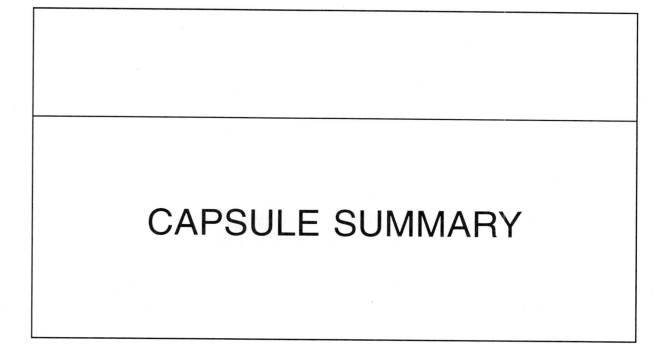

CAPSULE SUMMARY

Editor's Note: References to pages in the text are to the printed version of **Antitrust, Second Edition**, by Herbert Hovenkamp.

I. ANTITRUST ECONOMICS: PRICE THEORY AND INDUSTRIAL ORGANIZATION

A. AN OVERVIEW OF BASIC PRICE THEORY FOR ANTITRUST

Price theory is the theory concerning how a firm decides how much of a product or service to produce, and what price to charge.

1. Supply and Price Under Perfect Competition

Perfect competition exists when a large number of firms produce the same product, and no single firm has the power to reduce total market output by reducing its own output. If a firm in perfect competition did reduce its own output, its competitors would simply increase their output by the same amount.

In order to understand the individual firm's output and pricing decisions when the firm faces perfect competition, you should know the meaning of the following terms:

(1) A *"Reservation Price"* is the highest price that a customer is willing to pay for a certain product.

(2) The *Supply Curve* is a line on the price-output graph that shows the total costs of production in an industry at every level of output. The supply curve generally slopes upward, because as output in an industry increases, costs increase. This is so because the market makes use of the best materials first, then the next best, etc.

(3) *The Demand Curve* is a line on the price-output graph that shows how much of a product or service will be sold at a given price. The demand curve generally slopes downward, because as output in an industry increases, the good must be sold to buyers with lower reservation prices. Thus the rule that as supply goes up, price goes down.

(4) *Equilibrium* is a state that exists when a market is not changing and is not being affected by any changes imposed from outside.

(5) *Consumers' Surplus* is the difference between a consumer's reservation price and the price that he or she must pay for a product.

(6) *Producers' Surplus* is the difference between a firm's costs and the price it obtains for a product.

(7) *Market Elasticities of Supply and Demand* describe the rate at which supply and demand change in response to a change in the price, or vice-versa. If the demand for a good drops dramatically when the price rises, then elasticity of demand is said to be high. Likewise, if the supply of a good increases dramatically when the price rises (but costs do not rise proportionately), then elasticity of supply is said to be high.

(8) *Marginal Cost* is the additional cost that a firm incurs when it produces an additional unit of output.

a. Market Price and Output Under Perfect Competition

In perfect competition the market price and market output will be determined by the intersection of the market demand curve and the market supply curve.

b. The Output Decision of the Individual Firm In Perfect Competition: Marginal Cost

An individual firm in perfect competition must accept the market price as given—i.e., it is a "price taker." However, such a firm does make its own output decision. It will produce at the rate at which its marginal cost equals the market price. If it produces any more or less than that amount, it will earn less than it could when P=MC. Thus marginal cost pricing is consistent with perfect competition, and is an important goal of the antitrust laws.

2. Monopoly

A monopoly is a market dominated by a monopolist. A monopolist is technically a firm that produces all of the output in a particular market. For antitrust purposes, however, a firm may be considered a monopolist when it produces a very high percentage—say, 75% or more—of a particular market.

a. The Monopolist's Price and Output Decisions

Unlike the perfect competitor, the monopolist has the power to reduce total market output by reducing its own output. This is so because there are no competitors (or not enough competitors) to respond to the monopolist's output decrease with an offsetting output increase. As a result, the market price goes up when the monopolist's output goes down.

1) The Marginal Revenue Curve

The marginal revenue curve is a line on the price-output graph that shows how much additional revenue the monopolist makes when it produces one additional unit of output. The marginal revenue curve slopes downward, and for the monopolist it slopes downward more steeply than the demand curve does.

2) The Monopolist's Profit–Maximizing Price

The monopolist's profit-maximizing price is the price that will maximize the monopolist's net revenues (i.e., the difference between the monopolist's total revenues and its costs). Assuming that the monopolist controls 100% of its market and that it is unconcerned about entry by competitors, its profit-maximizing price is determined by the intersection of its marginal cost and marginal revenue curves. For most monopolists the profit-maximizing price is higher and output lower than would exist in the same market under perfect competition.

b. The De Facto Monopolist in the Real World

Unlike the absolute monopolist described above, the *de facto* monopolist in the real world may not control 100% of its market, and it may have to be concerned about entry by competitors. Such a monopolist will often charge a price lower than the price determined by the intersection of its marginal cost and marginal revenue curves. It does this in order to make the market relatively less attractive to potential competitors who might want to enter.

c. The Social Cost of Monopoly

The *social cost* of monopoly is the amount by which society is worse off as a result of the existence of a monopoly.

1) The Monopoly Wealth Transfer

One effect of monopoly is that it makes the monopolist wealthier and customers poorer, because they must pay a higher price for the monopolized product. This is a wealth *transfer*, however, and not a social cost. Society as a whole is not poorer because of this overcharge: the monopolist is better off by exactly the same amount that the customers are worse off.

2)   The Deadweight Loss of Monopoly

The deadweight loss of monopoly represents value that is lost to society because some customers who would have purchased a product at the competitive price decide not to purchase it at the monopoly price. This deadweight loss is a true social cost. The customers who substitute another product take something that would not have been their first choice in a competitive market. At the same time, however, the monopolist is no better off, for it does not make any profits from unmade sales.

B.   INDUSTRIAL ORGANIZATION: ECONOMIES OF SCALE AND THE DILEMMA OF ANTITRUST POLICY

Industrial organization is the study of how the structure of the market and of the individual business firm are determined.

1.   Economies of Scale

An economy of scale exists whenever the costs of producing some product or service decrease as output increases. Probably all industries are subject to *some* economies of scale; however, in some industries economies of scale are far more substantial than they are in others.

2.   Natural Monopoly

A natural monopoly is a market that can be served most efficiently by a single firm, provided that the firm does not charge monopoly prices. More technically, a natural monopoly is a market in which costs decline continuously as output increases, right up to the point that demand in the market is saturated.

3.   The Dilemma of Antitrust Policy: Coping With Bigness

The existence of economies of scale poses a difficult problem for antitrust policy. High output and low prices are important goals of the antitrust laws. However, in many industries economies of scale are substantial and only very large firms with large market shares will be able to take advantage of all scale economies. As firms obtain larger market shares, however, the danger of monopolization and other anticompetitive activities increases. Antitrust policy faces the very difficult task of permitting firms to grow large enough to take advantage of available economies of scale, but at the same time forcing such firms to perform competitively. This task is complicated enormously by the fact that neither economies of scale nor competitive performance (marginal cost pricing) can easily be quantified.

II. CARTELS, TACIT COLLUSION, JOINT VENTURES AND OTHER COMBINATIONS OF COMPETITORS

A. HOW AND WHEN PRICE FIXING WORKS

A cartel is a group of firms who should be competitors, but who have agreed with each other to "fix" their prices. Cartels are analyzed under § 1 of the Sherman Act, and "naked" price fixing (i.e., price fixing not accompanied by any integration of the firms' other business) is illegal *per se* under that Act.

1. The Cartel Market

Price fixing does not work well in all markets. The following characteristics make a market conducive to price fixing.

(a) *Market Concentration.* The smaller the number of firms in a market, the easier price fixing will be.

(b) *Barriers to Entry.* If entry into a market is easy, the firms within the market will not be able to earn monopoly profits for long. New competitors will come in. Therefore high entry barriers are conducive to cartelization. "Mobility barriers"—i.e., a long period of time required for new entry—also facilitate cartelization.

(c). *Sales Methods.* Some market sales methods facilitate cartelization by making it easy for the cartel to detect cheating members. Price fixing is easiest in "auction" markets with publicly announced prices; it is most difficult in markets where individual sales are large and prices are negotiated in secret.

(d) *Product Homogeneity.* Cartels work best in markets containing fungible products, for then the cartel members will find it easiest to agree on a cartel price. Product differentiation tends to frustrate cartelization, because some cartel members' products are perceived as superior to the products of other members.

(e) *Facilitating Devices.* Firms can facilitate cartelization by standardizing products, by vertically integrating in order to turn their sales into small, public, unnegotiated retail sales, or by using other devices such as advance price announcements and basing-point pricing.

2. The Cartel Members

Certain characteristics of the cartel members themselves may make a market more conducive to cartelization:

(a) *Firm Size.* In order for the cartel to operate, each member must reduce its output. The allocation of each member's output reduction will be easiest if the firms are all about the same size.

(b) *Efficiency.* Cartels work best if all members are equally efficient. If efficiency varies widely, the less efficient (higher cost) members will want to set a higher cartel price than the more efficient members.

(c) *Level of Participation.* The cartel will work best if 100% of the firms in the market participate.

(d) *Incentives to Cheat and Cartel Countermeasures.* Because every cartel sale is highly profitable, individual members have a strong incentive to cheat on the cartel by making secret sales at a lower price than that agreed to by the cartel. The cartel may have to take elaborate precautions against such cheating.

3. Variations on Horizontal Collusion

Cartels sometimes use these variations on price fixing. All of them are *per se* illegal:

(a) *Horizontal Territorial or Customer Division* occurs when the cartel members agree that each will make sales only in a certain territory, or only to a certain class of customers. By using such an agreement the cartel can reduce the problem of deciding and monitoring the output of each cartel member. In *Palmer v. BRG of Georgia* the Supreme Court recently re-affirmed the per se rule against horizontal market definition.

(b) *Market Share Agreements* are agreements that each firm will maintain its sales at an agreed-upon percentage of total sales in the market. Firms which exceed their quotas are penalized.

(c) *Output Reduction Schemes* are formulas by which the cartel reduces output. Once output is lowered, the market will determine the cartel price. The *Socony-Vacuum* case involved such an arrangement.

B. EXPRESS AND TACIT COLLUSION: AN INTRODUCTION TO THE OLIGOPOLY PROBLEM

An oligopoly is a market containing only a few firms. These may be able to arrive at a consensus about price and output without explicitly agreeing about anything.

1. Oligopoly and the Sherman Act

Section one of the Sherman Act requires the existence of a contract, combination, or conspiracy. Courts have been virtually unanimous in holding that, in the absence of an *explicit* agreement, no violation of § 1 has occurred.

2. Possible Approaches to the Oligopoly Problem

a. The Structural Approach

One possible approach to the oligopoly problem is new legislation that would break up the firms in highly concentrated markets. However, such an approach might cost more in lost economies of scale than it would gain in increased competition.

b. The Conduct Approach

Another approach would be to use the existing antitrust laws to control oligopoly by attacking various facilitating devices, such as basing point pricing and most-favored nation clauses, that make tacit collusion easier. This approach has the advantage that it would permit firms to be as large as necessary to attain scale economies. So far, courts have not been receptive to this approach.

3. The Agreement Requirement and the Antitrust Laws

a. Circumstantial Evidence of Express Collusion

Although § 1 of the Sherman Act requires an "agreement," the agreement may be established by circumstantial evidence. This may include evidence that several firms were invited to participate in an illegal scheme, and that each one responded affirmatively in a way that would have been irrational but for the assumption that other firms would do the same thing. This was the holding of the *Interstate Circuit* case.

The Supreme Court's decision in *Matsushita Electric Indust. Co. v. Zenith Radio Corp.* has made it much more difficult for plaintiffs to create a jury issue on collusion. In order to avoid summary judgment they must produce evidence that tends "to exclude the possibility" that the defendants acted alone.

b. Detecting and Challenging Tacit Collusion

Before tacit collusion can be challenged it must be detected.

1) Evidence of Markets Conducive to Tacit Collusion

Only certain markets are conducive to tacit collusion. These are characterized by high concentration on the sellers' side, a large number of poorly informed buyers, economies of scale, barriers to entry, and fungible or homogeneous products.

2) Evidence that Collusion Is Occurring

(a) *Very Stable Market Shares* are generally inconsistent with competition. In competition, the fortunes of various firms rise and fall over time. Rigid stability suggests that the firms in the market have reached an understanding about the output of each.

(b) *A Rigid Price Structure* also suggests that the market is not performing competitively. In a competitive market, prices will fall in response to a decline in demand.

(c) *Industry-Wide Use of Facilitating Devices* also suggests collusion, whether tacit or express. These devices include:

(1) *Standardization of Products and Terms,* which permits each firm in a market to monitor the prices and output of the other firms, and prevents firms from competing with one another by offering more favorable credit terms, etc.

(2) *Delivered and Basing Point Pricing* can facilitate both express and tacit collusion by permitting the firms to quote identical delivered prices to the same buyer. Basing point pricing is illegal under the Sherman Act when it is undertaken by agreement of the firms engaged in it. However, if there is no evidence that the firms agreed to engage in basing point pricing, then it is generally legal.

3) Tacit Collusion and the FTC Act

Section 5 of the Federal Trade Commission Act condemns "unfair methods of competition." Unlike § 1 of the Sherman Act, it contains no agreement requirement. Theoretically, it seems that § 5 of the FTC Act could be used to challenge tacit collusion that cannot be reached by the Sherman Act. So far, however, most courts have been hostile toward expansive use of the FTC Act to reach tacit collusion, most recently in the *DuPont* (Ethyl) case.

C. JOINT VENTURES AND MARKET FACILITATING AGREEMENTS

A joint venture is any association of two or more firms for carrying on some activity that each firm might otherwise perform alone.

1. Joint Ventures: the Threat to Competition

When the firms engaged in a joint venture are competitors, the possibility of express or tacit collusion cannot be ignored. This is likely to be the case only if the members of the joint venture collectively have a large market share. Likewise, the threat of competition is greatest when the joint venture's activities affect the price or output decisions of the participating firms. For example, a joint venture created exclusively to facilitate research and development is *not* generally conducive to collusion. Finally, the threat to competition is greatest when the venture is exclusive—that is, when the members are forbidden to make sales outside the venture.

2. Joint Ventures: Economic Rationales

Most firms engage in joint ventures in order to reduce their costs. Joint ventures can create economies in the following ways:

(a) *Economies of Scale.* Sometimes a joint venture can enable an association of smaller firms to attain scale economies unavailable to each firm acting alone.

(b) *Economies of Distribution.* Sometimes firms acting together can market their products more efficiently. The *Appalachian Coals* case involved such a joint venture.

(c) *Joint Ventures and Free Rider Problems.* A free rider is someone who takes advantage of a good or service without paying for it. Sometimes joint ventures are organized in order to force all firms in a market to pay their fair share of the costs of a certain activity. Such joint ventures are common in research and development, and in advertising.

(d) *Joint Ventures in Network Industries.* Certain markets perform efficiently only if the firms in them engage in substantial cooperation. For example, the *NCAA* case involved college athletic teams, which must agree with one another on output (the number of games to be played per year). Joint ventures in network industries receive rule of reason treatment.

(e) *Joint Ventures and the Problem of Market Information.* Among the most controversial joint ventures are those that involve competitor exchanges of price information. On the one hand, markets in which price and output information are freely available to all participants operate very efficiently. On the other hand, competitor exchanges of price information can be used to facilitate collusion. Today competitor exchanges of price information are analyzed under the rule of reason created by the Supreme Court in the *Container* case. They are generally condemned if 1) concentration in the market is high; and 2) there is evidence that the information exchange had some effect on price or output. Competitor exchanges of non price information are generally legal.

(f) *Joint Ventures as Market Facilitators.* Many joint ventures either create a market or make it operate much more efficiently than it would in the absence of the joint venture. For example, the "Call" rule in the *Chicago Board of Trade* case tended to force market transactions into a setting where all buyers and sellers could rely on the same information and bid competitively for the commodities exchanged there. Likewise, the blanket licensing arrangement at issue in the *Broadcast Music* case substantially reduced the transaction costs of using the market for performance rights to music.

D. HORIZONTAL AGREEMENTS AND THE PER SE RULE: THE PROBLEM OF CHARACTERIZATION

Conduct analyzed under the *per se* rule is condemned without elaborate judicial analysis into the purpose or effects of the conduct in the particular case before the court. However, conduct must be "characterized" as falling inside or outside the *per se* rule. This problem of characterization can be very complex. Generally, the Supreme Court will not apply the per se rule to a certain activity until it has had substantial experience with the activity, and knows that it is virtually always anticompetitive. Today price fixing, horizontal territorial division, certain concerted refusals to deal (boycotts), certain tying arrangements, and resale price maintenance are analyzed under the per se rule.

The following guidelines are useful in determining when the *per se* rule ought to be applied to a certain activity:

(1) *Agreement Among Competitors.* Courts are inherently more suspicious of agreements between competitors than of agreements among noncompetitors.

(2) *Price-Affecting Conduct.* The court has traditionally been most suspicious of conduct designed to affect price or market output. Unfortunately, they have carried this concern too far. For example, the holding of the Supreme Court in the *Maricopa County Medical Society* case condemning maximum price fixing by physicians has been widely criticized because the effect of the agreement was to reduce medical costs.

(3) *Public Conduct.* Public conduct is generally public because the actors regard it as being legal. By contrast, the fact that people do something in secret is stronger evidence that they want to avoid being detected. Clandestine conduct is inherently more suspicious than public conduct.

(4) *Network Industries.* According to the holding in the *NCAA* case, agreements in network industries (i.e., industries in which agreements among market participants are necessary to make the market work) will be governed by the rule of reason.

(5) *Efficiency Producing Agreements.* Even if an agreement affects price or output, it may qualify for rule of reason treatment if there is a *very strong* argument that the result of the agreement is increased efficiency and thus lower costs.

(6) *The Quick Look.* A small number of highly suspicious restraints are exposed to a "quick look," which is a little more elaborate than the per se rule in that the defendants will be given an opportunity to show either that the restraint produces a substantial benefit or that the defendants lack power. If the defendants fail in this showing the per se rule is applied; if they succeed, the restraint is assessed under the rule of reason. The "quick look" is generally reserved for restraints that look like per se violations but where judicial experience is sufficiently lacking that a slightly deeper examination is appropriate.

E.　THE DEATH OF THE INTRA–ENTERPRISE CONSPIRACY DOCTRINE

In the *Copperweld* case the Supreme Court held that a parent and its wholly-owned subsidiary could not be "conspiring entities" under § 1 of the Sherman Act. As a result, single-firm conduct cannot generally be brought within the *per se* prohibitions of § 1. It remains to be seen how the court will treat the problem of agreements between a parent corporation and a subsidiary that is less than wholly owned. Courts continue to find a conspiracy in situations where the agents or employees of a corporation have separate businesses of their own, and the affect on competition in the latter motivates their decision. For example, the medical staff of a hospital, which ordinarily is treated as agents of the hospital, may be capable of "conspiring" to deny a physician staff privileges if the staff is fearful of threats to their own separate medical practices.

III. MONOPOLIZATION, ATTEMPT TO MONOPOLIZE AND PREDATORY PRICING

A. SINGLE–FIRM MONOPOLIZATION

Illegal conduct undertaken by a firm that is already a monopolist, designed to enable the firm to preserve its monopoly position, is called monopolization. Monopolization is condemned under § 2 of the Sherman Act.

1. Introduction: The Modern Formulation of the Monopolization Offense

According to the *Grinnell* decision, the offense of monopolization consists of two parts: 1) the possession of monopoly power in a relevant market; and 2) the commission of one or more impermissible exclusionary practices, designed by the monopolist to strengthen or perpetuate its monopoly position. In order to convict a firm of monopolization, both elements must be established. Today there is no law against "no fault" monopolization: that is, being a monopolist is legal as long as one does not engage in impermissible exclusionary practices.

2. Monopoly Power In a Relevant Market

"Market power" is a firm's power to reduce output and raise prices above marginal cost, and to make a profit by doing so. "Monopoly power" is simply a very large amount of market power.

(a) *Measuring Market Power Directly,* as a function of the relationship between a firm's marginal cost and its profit-maximizing price, is *theoretically* possible. However, such measurement is not frequently used in court, because the court cannot easily measure marginal cost.

(b) *The Market Share Proxy.* Because of these measurement difficulties the court uses market share of some "relevant market" as a proxy, or surrogate, for market power. A relevant market consists of a relevant product market and a relevant geographic market. In order to meet the monopoly power requirement, a defendant must generally have a market *share* of 70% or more. The defendant's market share is equal to its percentage of the sales made in the relevant product and geographic market.

(c) *Measuring the Relevant Product Market.* A relevant product market is some grouping of sales for which the elasticity of demand and the elasticity of supply are sufficiently low that a firm with 100% of this market could profitably reduce output and raise price substantially.

Elasticity of Demand is low when a large number of customers will not turn to substitute products produced by other firms in response to a firm's non-costjustified price increase.

In measuring elasticity of demand it is important not to commit the fallacy the Supreme Court committed in the *DuPont* (Cellophane) case, of looking at the elasticity of demand at *current* market prices. Elasticity of demand is always high at current market prices, for the monopolist is charging as high a price as it can without losing customers to substitutes.

Elasticity of Supply is low when manufacturers of the same product or close substitutes cannot quickly respond to a non-cost-justified price rise by increasing their own output and restoring it to the competitive level. In measuring elasticity of supply it is important to consider:

(1) The *time* that it will take other firms to enter the monopolist's market (the longer the time, the more profitable a monopoly price increase will be).

(2) The easily diverted *excess capacity* of competitors, for they can quickly increase their own output out of excess capacity. For example, in the *Alcoa* case Judge Hand probably should have included the entire output of the foreign aluminum producers in the relevant market, rather than merely the amount they actually imported into the United States.

(d) *Measuring the Relevant Geographic Market.* A relevant geographic market is some area in which a firm can increase its price *without*

(1) large numbers of customers immediately turning to alternative supply sources outside the area (i.e., elasticity of demand is low); and

(2) producers outside the area quickly flooding the area with substitute products (i.e., elasticity of supply is also low).

One way to determine the geographic market is to look at pricing behavior over a long period of time. If price in Area A consistently and quickly rises and falls in response to price changes of the same product in Area B, then the two areas should be grouped together in the same market.

(e) *How big a share of the Relevant Market is Required?* Courts consistently find that market shares in excess of 80%–90% are sufficient to support a finding that the defendant is a monopolist. Most find that market shares of less than 50% are insufficient. In between, the question is more ambiguous. In any case, the question of market power is generally one of fact.

(f) *Entry Barriers.* Before monopolization is plausible, a market must be subject to high entry barriers. Otherwise new firms will come into the market as soon as the intending monopolist attempts to raise the price above the competitive level.

3. Conduct Requirements

a. The Rule of Reason in Monopolization Cases

The rule of reason in monopolization cases is designed to enable the court to distinguish between exclusionary conduct that should be condemned and conduct which, while "exclusionary," is efficient and should be approved.

1) Injury to Competition and Injury to Competitors

   Competitors can be injured by the monopolist's efficiency. For example, the monopolist that engages in aggressive research and development win exclude *competitors* by making it more difficult for them to compete. This is injury to competitors, however, and not injury to competition. Injury to competition occurs when a practice is exclusionary and it produces no efficiency gains to the monopolist.

2) Intent

   In the *Grinnell* case the Supreme Court stated that the offense of monopolization requires some showing of intent. However, the intent may be inferred from the exclusionary practices themselves.

b. Illustrative Exclusionary Practices

The following exclusionary practices have been alleged by plaintiffs or found by courts to be sufficient to condemn a defendant of monopolization:

(1) *Predatory Pricing,* which is discussed below.

(2) *Mergers to Monopoly*

(3) *Purchase and Shutdown of Rivals' Plants*

(4) *Expansion of Output or Capacity;* however, the rationale for regarding this as an unlawful exclusionary practice is dubious.

(5) *Price Discrimination,* which is equally dubious.

(6) *Vertical Integration,* although recent courts have been skeptical about such claims and most instances of vertical integration by the monopolist (generally manifested as a refusal to deal with vertically related independent firms) have been found to be legal.

(7) *Price and Supply "Squeezes",* which occur when a vertically integrated monopolist sells to vertically related firms at a high price, but suppresses the output price in the market in which those firms sell.

(8) *Tying Arrangements*

(9) *"Predatory" Research and Development and Failure to Predisclose Developments in Progress* have been alleged by plaintiffs to be illegal, but courts have not yet condemned them.

(10) *Patent "Abuse",* including obtaining a patent by fraud, and perhaps the accumulation and *non* use of patents. The mere accumulation of patents by the monopolist is generally legal.

(11) *Raising Rivals' Costs*—that is, engaging in activity that makes it more expensive for the rival to do business and thus forces it to charge a higher price.

(12) *Refusal to Deal With a Competitor* can be illegal, according to the *Aspen Highlands* decision, if a dominant firm's motive in so doing is to injure the competitor substantially or drive it from the market. The court reiterated this position in the *Kodak* case, which involved an alleged attempt to monopolize by a tying arrangement that excluded competitors from the market for servicing Kodak photocopiers.

(13) *Essential Facility Doctrine*—the owner or operator of an essential facility, such as a scarce resource or a natural monopoly facility may have an antitrust obligation to share the facility with a rival.

B. ATTEMPT TO MONOPOLIZE

1. The Formulation of the Offense

The offense of attempt to monopolize includes three elements: 1) specific intent to control prices or eliminate competition in some market; 2) predatory or anticompetitive conduct directed at accomplishing this unlawful purpose; 3) a "dangerous probability of success"—that is, a realistic danger that the conduct, if permitted to run its course, would have created a monopoly.

2. Specific Intent

Much evidence of specific intent is ambiguous, and consistent with hard competition as well as attempt to monopolize. The effect of the ambiguity has been to reduce the relative importance of the intent element in the attempt offense. However, courts continue to require a showing of intent, generally manifested as 1) an intent to achieve monopoly power; or 2) an intent to drive competitors out of business so that the defendant could later charge monopoly prices.

3. "Dangerous Probability of Success"

The purpose of the "dangerous probability" requirement is to analyze the market as well as the defendant and its conduct, in order to determine if the conduct was likely to create a monopoly. Many markets are simply not conducive to monopolization. In that case, there is no dangerous probability that a monopoly will be created. Today many courts hold that the requirement is not met unless the defendant has a certain amount of market power; however, the market power requirement is substantially less than it is for monopolization cases. The requirement cannot be met unless the a relevant market is defined and the defendant shown to have a certain amount of power in that market.

4. Conduct Requirements

The offense of attempt to monopolize has narrower and more specific conduct requirements than does the offense of monopolization. In any case, the conduct must be capable of giving the defendant a monopoly.

C. PREDATORY PRICING AS AN ATTEMPT TO MONOPOLIZE

1. Antitrust Policy and the Problem of Predatory Pricing

Predatory pricing is the offense of charging a low price today in order to drive rivals from the market, so that the predator can charge monopoly prices later. The offense is problematic because low prices are such an important goal of the antitrust laws. In a predatory pricing case the plaintiff is complaining that the defendant's prices are illegal because they are too low.

2. How Often Does Predatory Pricing occur?

At one time courts believed that predatory pricing was very common. Today, however, many people believe that predatory pricing is rare because it is so expensive and the chances of success are very small.

3. The Areeda–Turner Test for Predatory Pricing

a. The Orthodox Formulation of the Areeda–Turner Test

The Areeda–Turner test for predatory pricing begins with the premise that a price lower than marginal cost is irrational unless it is predatory.

1) The Average Variable Cost (AVC) Surrogate

Since courts cannot measure marginal cost, Areeda and Turner proposed a surrogate: average variable cost (AVC). Average variable cost is equal to the sum of a firm's variable costs, or those costs that vary with output, divided by the number of units produced.

2) The Basic Presumptions of the Areeda–Turner Test

(a) A price above "full cost" (which is the same as average total cost, or all of a firm's costs, divided by its output) is nonpredatory, and therefore legal. Such a price is fully profitable for the firm.

(b) A price at or above average variable cost is presumed to be legal, even though it may be lower than average total cost.

(c) A price lower than average variable cost is conclusively presumed to be predatory.

3) The Areeda–Turner Test and the Elements of the Attempt Offense

The pricing element of the Areeda–Turner test described above constitutes the *conduct* part of the three-element attempt to monopolize test. The Areeda–Turner test virtually eliminates the specific intent requirement. Finally, the Areeda–Turner test satisfies the "dangerous probability of success" element by requiring that the market be conducive to monopolization *and* that the defendant already be the dominant firm in the market. In fact, as formulated, the Areeda–Turner test applies only to firms that are already monopolists.

b. The Areeda–Turner Test in the Courts

Although courts were initially enthusiastic about the Areeda–Turner test, they subsequently rejected parts of the test. However, all courts that have considered the test have retained the basic AVC framework. In addition, the plaintiff in a predatory pricing case must show "recoupment"—which is structural conditions sufficient to warrant an inference that the predatory period of below-cost prices will be followed by a monopoly or oligopoly period of high prices sufficient to pay off the investment in predation. This requires (a) a well defined market, (b) high entry barriers, and (c) rivals that have been destroyed or cannot readily expand their output.

D. PREDATORY PRICING UNDER THE ROBINSON–PATMAN ACT

The Robinson–Patman Act condemns the sale of the same product at two different prices, where the effect may be to injure competition. The predatory pricing theory of the Robinson–Patman Act, called "primary-line" injury, is that the defendant charges a low, predatory price in the target market, but subsidizes this predation with higher priced sales in other markets. A serious problem of the Robinson–Patman Act is that sales of the same product at different prices in different markets is consistent with *both* predation and healthy competition. For that reason, some additional test must be used to determine whether the price in the low price market is predatory or competitive. The trend in recent cases is for courts to use a variation of the Areeda–Turner test: that is, to determine whether the sale in the low price market was below the defendant's AVC.

The Supreme Court has held that the basic principles of predation are the same under the Sherman Act and the Robinson–Patman Act, with one difference: the Sherman Act requires a dangerous probability of monopoly, while the Robinson–Patman standard can be met by proof of likely oligopoly. In any event, prices under both statutes must be shown to be below relevant costs, and the plaintiff must show the likelihood of sufficient post-predation profits to "recoup" the investment in predation.

E. CONSPIRACY TO MONOPOLIZE

The offense of conspiracy to monopolize contains four elements:

(1)   the existence of a conspiracy among two or more participants;

(2)   specific intent to monopolize some part of trade or commerce;

(3)   some overt act carried out in furtherance of the conspiracy;

(4)   an effect on interstate commerce.

Unlike the offense of attempt to monopolize, the conspiracy offense does not require a showing of dangerous probability of success.

IV.   VERTICAL INTEGRATION AND VERTICAL MERGERS

A. INTRODUCTION: THE NATURE OF VERTICAL INTEGRATION

A firm is "vertically integrated" whenever it performs for itself some function that could otherwise be purchased in the marketplace.

1. **Three Methods of Vertical Integration and Why Firms Choose Them**

   Firms can integrate vertically in three different ways: 1) by new entry; 2) by merger; or 3) by a long-term contract, such as a franchise or exclusive dealing contract with another firm.

   Which of these three methods a firm chooses depends on a host of factors, such as firm size and nature of the product. It also depends on the relevant antitrust laws. For example, a monopolist might not be legally able to integrate vertically by merger.

2. **Antitrust Treatment of the Forms of Vertical Integration**

   Vertical integration by new entry is of least concern to the antitrust laws, and is illegal, if at all, only when the integrating firm is a monopolist. Traditionally, vertical integration by merger has fared most harshly under the antitrust laws. However, the 1984 Justice Department Merger Guidelines would approve most vertical mergers. Vertical integration by contract is treated under the law of tie-ins, exclusive dealing, and vertical price and nonprice restraints. Some vertical integration by contract, including resale price maintenance and some tying arrangements, is illegal *per se*.

B. **VERTICAL INTEGRATION, EFFICIENCY AND ANTITRUST POLICY**

1. **Vertical Integration and Efficiency**

   Simple economic analysis indicates that most vertical integration is efficient in that it reduces the costs of the integrating firm.

   a. **Production Cost Savings from Vertical Integration**

      Sometimes vertically integrated firms can achieve production costs savings by taking advantage of technologies that are not available to firms that are not vertically integrated. The steel mill combined with the rolling mill (which forms hot steel into sheets) is an example of such savings.

   b. **Transaction Cost Savings from Vertical Integration**

      Transactions costs are the costs of using the market. The vertically integrated firm can reduce these costs by eliminating the need for market transactions. The potential for vertical integration to reduce transaction costs is generally greater than its potential to reduce production costs.

   c. **The Problem of Market Power Held by Other Firms**

      A firm is always better off if the firms with which it deals behave competitively. Often a firm will integrate vertically in order to avoid dealing with a monopolist or perhaps a cartel at a different level of production or distribution. By vertically integrating the monopolist can eliminate a monopoly output reduction in another part of the distribution chain. Otherwise it can transfer someone else's monopoly profits to itself.

d. Vertical Integration and Optimum Product Distribution

Finally, a firm can use vertical integration to ensure that its product is distributed in the best way. By vertically integrating to the retail level, for example, a manufacturer may obtain the best control over how its product is marketed and priced.

2. Perceived Dangers to Competition from Vertical Integration

a. Increased Market Power

Vertical integration seldom increases the market power of the integrating firm. This is so because a monopolist of any level in a distribution chain can generally obtain all the profits available from that chain.

For Further Discussion and Example, See pp. 139–140

b. Barriers to Entry

Vertical integration can make it more difficult for new firms to enter a market, particularly if the vertical integration is undertaken by a monopolist or if all firms in the market become vertically integrated. In that case the prospective entrant must come in at two levels rather than one. Such integration will impede new entry, however, only if it makes costs higher for the entering firm than they are for firms already in the market.

c. Price Discrimination

Vertical integration can facilitate price discrimination by enabling a monopolist to segregate groups of customers who have different reservation prices for its product.

d. Rate Regulation Avoidance

A rate regulated firm can use vertical integration into an *un*regulated market to "cheat" on the rate regulation by hiding monopoly profits in sales of the unregulated product or service.

e. Vertical Integration by Cartels

Cartels sometimes integrate vertically in order to make it more difficult for cartel members to cheat. For example, if cartel members integrate vertically to the retail level, their sales will be small, and at publicly announced prices. Cheating will be relatively unprofitable and easily detected.

C. VERTICAL MERGERS

1. The Law of Vertical Mergers Before 1950

Before 1950 most vertical mergers were analyzed under § 1 of the Sherman Act, because § 7 of the Clayton Act had been held not to apply to them. In 1950,

however, § 7 was amended by the Celler–Kefauver amendments, which made it
clear that the statute applies to vertical mergers.

2. The Law of Vertical Mergers Since 1950

Since 1950 vertical mergers have been condemned under two different theories.

(a) *The Foreclosure Theory* holds that vertical mergers are bad because they
deprive firms that are not vertically integrated of access to necessary inputs or
outlets. Such foreclosure will generally not occur unless the vertically
integrating firm is a monopolist or vertical integration is widespread in the
market. In the *Brown Shoe* case, however, the Supreme Court condemned a
vertical merger that foreclosed only 1% or perhaps 2% of the market. Although
Brown Shoe has never been overruled, courts today would almost certainly
insist on much higher foreclosure percentages.

(b) *The Entry Barriers Theory* is similar to the foreclosure theory, except that it
focuses on the ability of new firms to enter the market, rather than the ability
of existing firms to find inputs or outlets. The entry barrier theory suggests
that vertical mergers create entry barriers because they require new firms to
enter a market at two levels instead of one. Vertical integration will not create
such an entry barrier, however, unless a high percentage of sales in the
market are made by vertically integrated firms.

Today the case law tends to condemn vertical mergers under both these theories if
the transactions between the merging firms account for 15% or more of the market.

3. Vertical Mergers and the 1984 Justice Department Merger Guidelines

The 1984 Justice Department Merger Guidelines cite three circumstances under
which the Justice Department might challenge vertical mergers.

(a) *Increased Barriers to Entry.* The Department will challenge mergers under
this theory, but only if the market is concentrated, having an HHI of 1800 or
more (see the discussion of the Herfindahl–Hirschman Index below).
Furthermore, there must be evidence that the existence of entry barriers is
preventing the market from performing competitively.

(b) *Vertical Mergers and Collusion.* The Department will challenge a merger
under this theory if a market is conducive to collusion and has an HHI of 1800
or higher.

(c) *Rate Regulation Avoidance.* The Department will challenge a vertical merger
by a price regulated firm if it presents substantial opportunity for rate
regulation avoidance.

V. TIE–INS, RECIPROCITY, EXCLUSIVE DEALING AND THE FRANCHISE CONTRACT

A. INTRODUCTION

A tying arrangement is a sale or lease of one product (the "tying" product) on the condition that the buyer or lessee take a second product (the "tied" product) as well. Tying arrangements are analyzed under § 1 of the Sherman Act and § 3 of the Clayton Act.

B. JUDICIAL TESTS FOR THE ILLEGALITY OF TIE–INS

The Supreme Court has never articulated a complete test for tie-ins, and the circuit court tests differ from each other. Perhaps the most well known test for tying arrangements is this one:

(1)   The scheme involves two distinct products and provides that one (the tying product) may not be obtained unless the buyer or lessee takes the second product (the tied product) as well;

(2)   The seller possess sufficient market power in the market for the tying product to restrain competition in the market for the tied product;

(3)   A "not insubstantial" amount of commerce in the tied product market is affected by the arrangement. Sales of $50,000 to $60,000 have been found to satisfy this requirement.

C. THE AMBIGUOUS PROBLEM OF TIE–INS AND CONSUMER WELFARE

Many tying arrangements are efficient, in that they enable a firm to reduce the costs of production or distribution. These tying arrangements make consumers better off. Antitrust policy has the difficult problem of distinguishing efficient from anticompetitive tying arrangements.

D. TIE–INS, MARKET POWER AND THE *PER SE* RULE

1. The Difference Between the Sherman Act and Clayton Act Tests

In the *Times-Picayune* case the Supreme Court said that tie-ins should be analyzed under § 3 of the Clayton Act by a rule of reason, and condemned if the seller had market power in the tying product market or the arrangement affected a not insubstantial amount of commerce. The Court also said that a tie-in could be condemned as a *per se* violation of § 1 of the Sherman Act if *both* these requirements were met.

2. The Consequences of a Two-fold Test

a. Rule of Reason Tie-ins in the Absence of Market Power

One consequence of the *Times-Picayune* decision was that tie-ins could sometimes be condemned under a rule of reason when the defendant had no market power in the market for the tying product. It is difficult to see how such a tie-in could be anticompetitive. Today most courts (not all) ignore this rule. In recent years few tying arrangements have been condemned unless the defendant was found to have *some* market power in the market for the tying product.

b. *Per Se* illegal Tie-ins

The *Times-Picayune* case also held that tying arrangements could be illegal *per se* if the seller had market power in the tying product market and the arrangement affected a not insubstantial amount of commerce. In the *Jefferson Parish Hospital* case in 1984 a bare majority of the Court (five justices) stated that there is still a *per se* rule of tying arrangements. However, the Court appeared to require a market share in the tying product market of 30% or more before the *per se* rule would apply. However, in the *Kodak* case the Court appeared to say that sufficient market power could be found in Kodak's own brand of replacement parts, provided that there was other evidence of its power to exclude competitors or increase prices above the competitive level.

3. Market Power in Markets for Intellectual Property

Courts historically presumed market power in the market for the tying product when the product is patented or copyrighted. A few courts gave the same presumption when the tying product is trademarked. As a matter of economics, the presumptions make little sense, are widely criticized, and recent decisions have expressed skepticism about them.

4. Separate Products

Two products are "separate" for tying purposes if the tying product is regularly sold in both bundled and unbundled form under ordinary competitive market circumstances. For example a new car and its tires are a single product, because new cars are rarely sold without their tires. By contrast, computers are sold both with and without pre-installed word processing programs; so a tie of the two would involve distinct products.

E. WHY DO COURTS CONDEMN TIE–INS AND WHY DO FIRMS USE THEM?

1. The Leverage and Entry Barrier Theories

The oldest and most common theories under which tying arrangements are condemned are the leverage theory and the entry barrier theory. The leverage theory suggests that a monopolist can increase its monopoly profits by tying an unmonopolized product to its monopolized product. This theory is implausible. If the monopolist is already charging its profit-maximizing price for the tying product, it cannot earn additional monopoly profits by tying.

The entry barrier theory suggests that the monopolist can use a tying arrangement to deter or delay competitive entry by forcing potential competitors to enter the market at two levels rather than one. This theory is marginally more plausible than the leverage theory. It is quite plausible when the seller has a legally protected monopoly in the tying product. For example, if a statutory telephone line monopolist forces all lessees of lines to lease its telephones as well, there will be no independent market for telephones.

2. Evasion of Statutory Price Regulation

A tying arrangement can enable a price regulated firm to evade the price regulation by transferring available monopoly profits to an *un*regulated tied product. For example, the telephone company which is required by law to charge a certain price for its lines, might require all lessees of its lines to lease a telephone as well, and charge a monopoly price for the telephone.

For Further Discussion and Example, See pp. 155–156

3. Tie-ins as Price Discrimination and Metering Devices

a. Price Discrimination

Today it is well known that *variable proportion* tying arrangements can be used as price discrimination devices. For example, a lessor of photocopy machines might require all its lessees to purchase their copy paper requirements from it as well. By charging a monopoly price for the paper, the lessor will obtain a higher overall rate of return from lessees who make many copies than from lessees who make only a few. Note: a firm must have a certain amount of market power in the tying product market before this scheme will work.

b. Tie-ins as Metering Devices

A firm might also use a scheme similar to the one above to meter the costs of leasing out a particular machine. For example, if maintenance costs are directly proportional to use of a photocopy machine, the lessor of the machine might require lessees to purchase its paper and build the maintenance costs into the price of the paper.

4. Tie-ins and Efficiency: The Two–Product Test

Many tying arrangements are used by firms because the arrangement lowers the firms' costs of manufacturing or distribution. Courts *sometimes* recognize this by holding that in a particular case the alleged tying arrangement did not involve separate tying and tied "products."

5. Coercion

"Coercion" is a term of art in the law of tying arrangements that can have several meanings:

(a) *Coercion as Conditioning.* All courts agree that there is no tying arrangement unless the defendant *requires* the buyer to take the tied product. If the buyer is free not to take the product, there is no coercion in this sense. Some courts hold, however, that in class action tie-in cases, coercion in this sense will be inferred if all class members received contracts that stipulated the purchase of both tying and tied products.

(b) *Market Power.* A few courts have used the word coercion simply to refer to the fact that the defendant had market power in the tying product market.

(c) *Restriction of Buyer Choice.* Some courts use the word "coercion" to consider whether the buyer was forced to take a product that it would not have taken anyway. The *Jefferson Parish Hospital* case appears to *require* coercion in this sense: it held that tying arrangements should be condemned when the defendant has enough market power "to force a purchaser to do something that he would not do in a competitive market."

F. TYING ARRANGEMENTS AND THE FRANCHISE CONTRACT

Many litigated tying arrangement cases have involved franchises in various industries, such as fast foods. In most of those cases the tying arrangement was used by the franchisor as a price discrimination device. As a result, the franchisor made more money from highly successful franchisees than from relatively less successful ones. The trend in recent cases has been for courts to approve such franchise tie-ins.

G. RECIPROCITY

Reciprocity occurs when someone conditions the purchase of one product on the sale of another product, or vice versa. For example, "I will purchase this from you only if you will purchase that from me." Courts have generally analyzed reciprocity in the same way that they have analyzed tying arrangements, often by the leverage theory.

The test for illegal reciprocity is that the plaintiff must show that the defendant had market power in the market for one of the products, and refused to sell (buy) that product unless the other party agreed to sell (buy) something in return. Because the two products are moving in the market in opposite directions, there is no distinct "separate products" requirement.

H. EXCLUSIVE DEALING

An exclusive dealing arrangement is a contract under which a buyer promises to purchase all its requirements of a particular product from a particular seller. Exclusive dealing is analyzed under both § 1 of the Sherman Act and § 3 of the Clayton Act.

1. Exclusive Dealing and the Foreclosure and Entry Barrier Theories

Exclusive dealing has often been condemned by courts on foreclosure and entry barrier theories similar to those discussed above concerning vertical mergers and tying arrangements. In general, the same criticisms apply. Exclusive dealing will not foreclose anyone or create an entry barrier (i.e., the requirement of two-level entry) unless the firm engaging in exclusive dealing is a monopolist or unless exclusive dealing is widespread in the industry. Even in that case, exclusive dealing is unlikely to result in higher prices. However, exclusive dealing by the monopolist may sometimes *delay* competitive entry if two-level entry is riskier or more costly than entry at a single level.

2. Exclusive Dealing and Cartels

Exclusive dealing can facilitate cartelization by isolating buyers from one another. That is, if a particular buyer is forced by contract to deal with a particular seller, the buyer is not in a good position to force the sellers to bid against each other for sales.

3. Exclusive Dealing and Efficiency

Most exclusive dealing is efficient. Sometimes it enables firms to reduce the risks, and thus the costs, of relying on the market by guaranteeing them outlets or sources of supply. Other times exclusive dealing can prevent "interbrand free riding," which occurs when a dealer sells two different brands of a product, and gives customers of Brand B amenities provided by the supplier of Brand A.

4. The Judicial Test for Exclusive Dealing

Exclusive dealing is evaluated by courts almost entirely on the foreclosure theory. The court looks at the percentage of the market foreclosed. In the *Standard Stations* case the court condemned exclusive dealing when the defendant's contracts covered about 7% of the market for gasoline; however, most other suppliers in the market were using exclusive dealing as well, and this was a factor in the court's decision. In the *Tampa Electric* case the Supreme Court appeared to approve a more open-ended rule of reason approach. Today most courts require a foreclosure of at least 30%. If foreclosure is greater than 30%, the court will generally apply a rule of reason and consider other factors, such as the degree to which the contracts actually appear to be hindering new entry, the duration of the contracts, and the number of other firms in the market who are using exclusive dealing.

I. TIE–INS AND EXCLUSIVE DEALING UNDER THE JUSTICE DEPARTMENT VERTICAL RESTRAINTS GUIDELINES

In 1985 the Justice Department issued Guidelines concerning its enforcement policy against vertical nonprice restraints, including tying arrangements and exclusive dealing. The Guidelines acknowledge that tie-ins and exclusive dealing might be anticompetitive when they 1) facilitate collusion, 2) exclude rivals from the market (foreclosure), or 3) permit a rate regulated firm to cheat on its regulated rates. In any case, the Justice Department is not likely to challenge such arrangements unless market concentration is very high and the arrangements cover a large percentage of the market.

VI. RESALE PRICE MAINTENANCE AND VERTICAL NONPRICE RESTRAINTS

A. INTRODUCTION

1. Vertical Price Restraints

Vertical price restraints, sometimes called vertical price fixing or resale price maintenance (RPM) are supplier or manufacturer regulation of the price at which its product can be resold. Since the *Dr. Miles* decision in 1911, minimum RPM has been *per se* illegal under § 1 of the Sherman Act. However, supplier regulation of dealer's *maximum* prices is addressed under the rule of reason, and is ordinarily legal.

2. "Fair Trade"

For almost forty years Congress permitted states to enact so-called "fair trade" legislation that permitted RPM. However, the Congressional enabling act was repealed in 1975. The 1975 legislation appears to show Congressional approval for continued application of the *per se* rule to RPM.

3. Vertical Nonprice Restraints

Vertical nonprice restraints are a variety of mechanisms by which a manufacturer or supplier regulates the way its product is distributed or sold. These include:

(a) *Vertical Territorial Division,* which is supplier assignment of the territories in which dealers can operate.

(b) *Location Clauses,* which are supplier designation of the location of the stores from which the reseller can sell the supplier's product.

(c) *Vertical Customer Division,* which is supplier assignment of the classes of customers with which a particular reseller can deal.

(d) *"Air Tight" Restraints* are restraints that permit one and only one dealer to make sales in an assigned territory.

(e) *Areas of Primary Responsibility* are restraints that permit a dealer to make sales in other territories, provided that it is doing well in its own assigned territory.

(f) *Exclusive Territories* are territories to which only one dealer is assigned. *Nonexclusive Territories* are territories that are assigned to more than one dealer.

Since 1977 all vertical nonprice restraints have been governed by a rule of reason, and most have been upheld by the courts.

4. The Ongoing Controversy over Antitrust Policy Toward Vertical Restraints

There are broad differences of opinion respecting antitrust policy concerning vertical restrictions. Some people think all should be *per se* illegal. Others think all should be legal. Equally controversial is the fact that the two kinds of restraints are governed by two different rules, *per se* illegality for price restraints and rule of reason treatment for nonprice restraints.

B.   WHY DO SUPPLIERS USE RESTRICTIONS ON DISTRIBUTION?

1.   Vertical Restrictions and Market Power

Today the prevailing economic theory suggests that most vertical restrictions are efficient rather than anticompetitive. In any case, it seems clear that a firm that has no market power cannot acquire any by the simple device of regulating resale prices or assigning territories to its dealers.

2.   Vertical Restrictions and Supplier Collusion

Vertical restrictions can facilitate supplier collusion. For example, RPM can change the supplier cartel's output prices to retail prices fixed by the cartel. Such prices are publicly announced and nonnegotiable. Thus incentives to cheat on the cartel are reduced. Vertical territorial division can also facilitate horizontal collusion, particularly if the suppliers are engaged in horizontal territorial division.

Vertical restrictions facilitate cartelization, however, only if all cartel members agree to use them. As a result, such restrictions are evidence of supplier collusion only if all, or almost all, of the suppliers in the market are employing the restrictions. In the vast majority of litigated antitrust cases this has not been so.

3.   Vertical Restrictions and Dealer Collusion

Vertical restrictions can also facilitate dealer collusion. The dealers might succeed in convincing the suppliers to participate in their cartel and "impose" the restrictions on the dealers. If the suppliers in a market have no market power, then the only dealers' cartel that will work is an "interbrand" cartel (i.e., a cartel consisting of the dealers of the various brands in the market). In that case the restrictions are evidence of a cartel only if all these suppliers are employing the restrictions. If a supplier is a monopolist, however, its own dealers might be able to create an "intrabrand" cartel.

In any case, it is difficult to see why a supplier would want to participate in such a dealer cartel. It is not likely that this explanation explains very many vertical restrictions.

4. Control of "Free Rider" Problems

A "free rider" is someone who takes advantage of a good or service offered by someone else without paying for it. It is likely that vertical restrictions are often used by suppliers in order to combat free rider problems. For example, the "discount" automobile dealer may rely on *other* dealers of the same brand to give test drives, do warranty maintenance, and keep a staff of trained salespersons. The discounter simply sells the product at a lower price.

Free riding injures the supplier, because it forces all dealers to cut their level of services in order to compete with the discounter. When that happens, customers will begin buying from someone else. The manufacturer or supplier can avoid free rider problems by forcing all dealers to charge the same price (RPM), so that discounting is impossible; or by separating dealers by means of territorial restrictions.

5. Using Vertical Restrictions to Purchase Retail Services

Suppliers may also use vertical restrictions to "purchase" retail services from retailers who are attractive to customers. Such retailers naturally give their best shelf space and put their strongest promotional efforts into products that they believe are most profitable. RPM and vertical nonprice restraints can guarantee such stores a relatively high markup by eliminating price competition with other nearby stores.

C. RESALE PRICE MAINTENANCE IN THE COURTS

1. The Colgate exception for "unilateral" RPM

RPM is generally illegal *per se*. However, if a supplier merely announces that it will not deal with resellers that charge less than its stipulated prices, and then later refuses to deal with such a reseller, there is no violation of § 1 of the Sherman Act because, according to the *Colgate* decision, there is no "agreement" between the two parties.

The traditional *Colgate* exception is a narrow one: the supplier may not threaten or warn price cutters. It may simply announce its policy, and then refuse to deal with the price cutter.

a. The Continuing Vitality of *Colgate*

In the *Russell Stover* case, decided in 1983, the Federal Trade Commission had held that once a supplier terminated a dealer who cut price, it had by its action communicated a message to other dealers that they had better "agree" to abide by the stipulated prices. This took the activity out of the *Colgate* doctrine. However, the Eighth Circuit vacated the FTC's decision, and in the process declared that the orthodox *Colgate* doctrine was still the law.

b. An Important, Recent Variation on the Colgate Doctrine

In the *Monsanto* case, decided in 1984, the Supreme Court held if a supplier terminated one dealer in response to a second dealer's complaint about the first dealer's prices, the termination could be *per se* illegal resale price maintenance. However, under *Colgate*, the terminated dealer must show that there was actually an agreement between the supplier and the second dealer. The mere fact that the second dealer had complained and that the supplier subsequently terminated the first dealer was not sufficient to establish an agreement. Further, it must be shown that the rationale for the termination was the dealer's price cutting, not its violation of a nonprice restriction.

2. The Exception for Consignment Agreements

In the *General Electric* case the Supreme Court created an exception to the per se rule against RPM for consignment arrangements, in which title to the product remains with the supplier. In *Simpson v. Union Oil* the Court held, in essence, that the exception would apply only to *bona fide* consignment arrangements in which risk of loss remained with the seller, and not to large distribution schemes that were merely disguised to look like consignment arrangements.

3. Maximum Resale Price Maintenance

In its *Albrecht* decision in the 1960s the Supreme Court held that even manufacturer setting of a dealer's *maximum* prices is unlawful per se. But in 1997 *Albrecht* was overruled by *State Oil v. Khan*, and maximum RPM is now addressed under the rule of reason.

In *Atlantic Richfield v. USA Petroleum*, the Supreme Court held that maximum resale price maintenance may not be challenged by a *competitor* of the firm upon whom it is imposed; presumably, the only permissible private plaintiff challenger is the firm upon which the maximum RPM is imposed.

D. VERTICAL NONPRICE RESTRAINTS AND THE RULE OF REASON

1. "Interbrand" Competition v. "Intrabrand" Competition

In the *Sylvania* case (1977), the Supreme Court adopted a rule of reason for vertical nonprice restraints. Such a rule was necessary, the court explained, because vertical nonprice restraints can simultaneously improve "interbrand" competition (i.e., competition among all sellers of a product) while they injure "intrabrand" competition (i.e., competition among the dealers of a particular brand of the product). A rule of reason was necessary to balance these against one another.

2. Vertical Nonprice Restraints Since the Sylvania Case

A vertical restriction can injure competition (i.e., result in lower output and higher prices) only if the firm imposing the restriction has market power. Although the Supreme Court has not spoken on the issue, many lower courts have now held that vertical nonprice restrictions are legal if the firm imposing them has no market power.

Even if the supplier has market power, however, its vertical nonprice restrictions might well be competitive. (For example, the monopolist suffers from free rider problems just as much as the competitor). As a result, even if the supplier has market power, some anticompetitive explanations for the restrictions must be found. So far courts have not been successful in finding such explanations, and the vast majority of such restrictions have been upheld.

In *Business Electronics v. Sharp Electronics*, the Supreme Court held that a complaint by one dealer about another dealer's price cutting, and the supplier's termination of the second dealer, did not involve a "price" agreement. The plaintiff must show that the complaining dealer and the supplier specifically agreed on a price (or minimum price) that other dealers must charge. Otherwise the agreement will be treated as a non-price agreement and the rule of reason will be applied. In practice, this generally means that the agreement is legal.

VII.   REFUSALS TO DEAL

A.   ANTITRUST POLICY AND REFUSALS TO DEAL

As far as the antitrust laws are concerned, a firm is generally free to deal or not to deal as it pleases. A refusal to deal raises antitrust concerns only:

(1)   when it is concerted—that is, two or more firms agree not to deal with someone; or

(2)   when it is an attempt by a firm to create or maintain a monopoly.

Concerted refusals to deal are generally analyzed as combinations in restraint of trade under § 1 of the Sherman Act. Unilateral refusals to deal are dealt with as monopolization or attempt to monopolize under § 2 of the Sherman Act.

B.   CONCERTED REFUSALS TO DEAL

It has been widely said that concerted refusals to deal are *per se* violations of § 1 of the Sherman Act. However, that rule is so full of exceptions that it applies far less than half the time. In fact, the rule to be applied to concerted refusals varies with the nature of the refusal. The trend in recent cases is to apply the rule of reason in cases where the defendants jointly have no market power.

1.   Concerted Refusals and Cartels

Concerted refusals to deal are sometimes used by cartels to pressure nonparticipants or vertically related firms that are trying to undermine the cartel by making noncartel sales in the cartel's market. *Eastern States Lumber* probably involved such a situation. If the statement that concerted refusals are illegal *per se* has any general application, it is to this kind of concerted refusal.

Recently, in the *Superior Court Trial Lawyers* case, the Supreme Court re-affirmed that concerted refusals designed to facilitate naked price fixing are illegal *per se*. In the *Indiana Federation of Dentists* case it stated that it was applying a rule of reason to an agreement among dentists not to participate in a health insurer's cost reduction scheme; but the restraint was condemned.

2. Concerted Refusals and Cartels: Some Variations

a. Concerted Refusals and Free Rider Problems

Suppose that a manufacturer has three dealers, A, B, and C. A is a discounter and takes a free ride on the distribution efforts of B and C (see the discussion of vertical price and nonprice restraints above). B and C complain to the manufacturer, who responds by terminating A. Perhaps there was an "agreement" that A be terminated. If so, A has been the victim of a concerted refusal to deal. Under the Supreme Court's holding in the *Monsanto* case, this agreement will be governed by the *per se* rule if A was terminated for a reason pertaining to *price*. It will be governed by the rule of reason if the reason does not pertain to price. The Supreme Court recently so held in *Business Electronics v. Sharp*.

b. Concerted Refusals and "Free Riding" in Intellectual Property: The *FOGA* Case

The *Fashion Originators' Guild* case also involved a concerted refusal to deal directed at free riders (the design pirates). In this case, however, the *per se* rule was appropriate, because the defendants had no legal right to deprive the pirates of access to their designs, which were not protected by the copyright or patent laws.

c. Concerted Refusals by Noncompetitors

When a concerted refusal to deal involves only noncompetitors—for example, a single supplier agrees with a single dealer to cut off a second dealer—the per se rule does not apply. This was the Supreme Court's holding in *NYNEX v. Discon*.

3. Noncommercial Boycotts

A *bona fide* noncommercial boycott, established in furtherance of some political goal, is generally exempt from the antitrust laws, even though it might be anticompetitive. However, if the boycotters are selling something, the mere fact that their boycott is a type of speech and is addressed to the government will not relieve them of per se liability. The Supreme Court so held in the *Superior Court Trial Lawyers* case.

4. Concerted Refusals and Efficiency

Many joint ventures involving refusals to deal are themselves efficient. Nevertheless, a court may have to consider whether the refusal to deal is necessary to the efficiency goals of the venture, or whether it is unnecessary and affords some opportunity for collusion.

a. Efficient Joint Ventures With Efficient Refusals to Deal

Some efficient joint ventures *need* refusals to deal or they will not work properly. For example, a risky joint venture to develop a new product or process cannot be placed under an obligation to admit new members to the venture *after* it has proved successful. If every firm knew that it could avoid the risk now and join the venture only after it became a success, all would wait and the venture would never come into being.

b. Efficient Joint Ventures With Inefficient Refusals to Deal

Several litigated concerted refusal cases involved joint ventures that were efficient. However, the participants' refusal to admit new members to the venture was inefficient, and could have created the opportunity for collusion. In these cases the correct response of the court is to permit the joint venture to exist, but to throw it open to new members. This is the approach the Supreme Court took in the *Terminal Railroad* case and the *Associated Press* case.

Under the holding in the *Pacific Stationery* case, such refusals to deal will always be treated under the rule of reason, unless the defendants have market power. They may be treated under the rule of reason even if the defendants have market power, but the refusal to deal was efficient, or at least harmless, to competition.

5. Standard Setting and Rule Making

Refusals to deal are often the mechanism by which associations of manufacturers or professionals engage in setting standards or making rulers,. In *Silver v. New York Stock Exchange* the court permitted such rule making, but held that Silver had a right to be informed of the reasons for the discipline taken against him.

Standard setting by associations of competitors is generally analyzed under the rule of reason. The court will have to look at the standards themselves for reasonableness and will have to determine whether they have been applied fairly. In the absence of such evidence, the court may have to look at the intent of the parties engaged in the standard setting. In a few cases, such as the *Radiant Burner* case, the court may apply the per se rule, if the standards that are set appear to be completely arbitrary and the defendants put undue pressure on other people to deny the excluded person access to a market.

6. Proof of Agreement in Concerted Refusal Cases

Since concerted refusals are analyzed under § 1 of the Sherman Act, an "agreement" among the participants must be established. For example, in the *Cement Manufacturer's Protective Ass'n* case the Supreme Court held that the defendants could exchange the names of undesirable customers, as long as they did not agree with one another to refuse to deal with the customers.

C. UNILATERAL REFUSALS TO DEAL

Unilateral refusals to deal are illegal, if at all, when they constitute illegal monopolization or an attempt to monopolize. For example, in the *Lorain Journal* case, the Supreme Court condemned as an attempt to monopolize a newspaper's refusal to deal with advertisers who purchased from a competing radio station.

Even the monopolist may refuse to deal as long as the refusal is not part of a scheme to enlarge its monopoly power or extend its duration. The Eighth Circuit so held in *Paschall v. Kansas City Star Co.*

However, according to the *Aspen* case, the refusal to deal may be evidence of a monopolist's anticompetitive intent, which, if the other elements of the offense are present, will condemn the defendant of monopolization or attempt to monopolize. Likewise, a monopolist's refusal to share a properly defined "essential facility" may be illegal under § 2 of the Sherman Act.

VIII. HORIZONTAL MERGERS

A. HORIZONTAL MERGERS AND COMPETITION

1. Mergers and § 7 of the Clayton Act

A merger occurs whenever two firms that had been separate come under common ownership or control. Mergers today are most generally analyzed under § 7 of the Clayton Act. Until that Act was broadened in 1950, they were also frequently analyzed under § 1 of the Sherman Act.

2. Identifying Horizontal Mergers

A merger is "horizontal" when it involves the union of two firms that manufacture the same product *and* sell it in the same geographic market—that is, the firms were competitors before the merger occurred. After the merger the market contains one fewer firm than it did before the merger, and the post-merger firm is usually larger than either of the pre-merger firms. This means that horizontal mergers raise the concentration level in the market.

3. The Dangers of Horizontal Mergers: Collusion and Unilateral Price Increases

Horizontal mergers threaten competition when they increase the likelihood of collusion in the post-merger market. In extreme cases, a merger may create a monopolist. A merger may also facilitate a unilateral price increase when two firms making relatively similar products in a product differentiated market merge, thus eliminating competition among relatively close rivals and relegating customers to more remote choices.

4. The Rule of Reason and the Efficiencies Produced by Mergers

Mergers also can create substantial economies for the post-merger firm. For this reason, horizontal mergers are not illegal *per se*. In fact, most are legal. These economies include:

(a) *Economies of Plant size*, which result when a merger permits the post-merger firm to engage in more specialized production in a single plant.

(b) *Multi-plant Economies*, which occur because firms that run large numbers of plants can often coordinate purchasing or production in ways that are unavailable to the single-plant firm. This is particularly true of advertising and research and development.

(c) *Economies of Distribution*, which are economies in the way a product or service is distributed or marketed.

5. Efficiency and Merger Policy

Today the law of mergers has the difficult task of balancing the efficiency gains that can be created by mergers against the increased likelihood of collusion. This was not always so. During the 1960's horizontal mergers were frequently condemned *because* they created efficiencies, and thereby injured competitors of the post-merger firm. Today, however, the emerging policy is that horizontal mergers should be permitted when the danger to competition is small, so that any available efficiencies can be realized.

a. An Efficiency Defense in Merger Cases?

Even today, however, there is no well developed "efficiency defense" in merger cases—i.e., a defense that would exonerate an otherwise illegal merger because the merger obviously produces substantial efficiencies. The efficiency defense does not exist because courts are incapable of identifying and quantifying the amount of available efficiencies, and balancing this against the losses that might come from collusion or monopolization.

b. The Efficiency Defense in the 1992 Merger Guidelines

The 1992 Horizontal Merger Guidelines, issued by the Justice Department and the Federal Trade Commission, state that those agencies will consider evidence that a merger will help the post-merger firm achieve substantial efficiencies, and that these efficiencies could not have been attained by less anticompetitive means.

B. THE BASIC TESTS FOR LEGALITY IN HORIZONTAL MERGER CASES

Mergers are generally analyzed by the courts in two stages:

(1) First, the court examines the market structure and the size of the merging firms to establish *prima facie* legality or illegality.

(2) Secondly, it looks at various non-market share factors that might make the merger more likely or less likely to be anticompetitive.

This approach was approved by the Supreme Court in the *Philadelphia Bank* case. A few recent decisions have called *Philadelphia Bank* into question, suggesting that the challenger must prove the structural prerequisites and likelihood of anticompetitive activity separately.

1. **Market Structure, Post–Merger Market Share and Prima Facie Illegality**

   Market structure can be measured in a variety of ways, but the following are most used by courts:

   (a) *The Four–Firm Concentration Ratio (CR4)*, which consists of the sum of the market shares of the four largest firms in the market. A market in which the CR4 exceeds 75 or 80 is considered to be highly concentrated, and probably conducive to collusion. The CR4 was the measure of market concentration used in the 1968 Justice Department Merger Guidelines.

   (b) *The Herfindahl–Hirschman Index (HHI)*, which consists of the sum of the squares of the market shares of all firms in the market. Today many economists believe that the HHI is a more reliable indicator of market concentration than the CR4 is. A market with an HHI of 1800 or above is considered to be highly concentrated. The HHI is employed by the 1992 Merger Guidelines.

2. **Market Definition Under the 1992 Horizontal Merger Guidelines**

   Before a merger can be characterized as "horizontal" it must be determined that both premerger firms sell in the same relevant market. The Merger Guidelines define a relevant product market as "a grouping of products such that a … firm that was the only present and future seller of those products … could profitably impose a 'small but significant and nontransitory' increase in price." The definition of a relevant geographic market is similar. In determining a relevant market the government will begin with the output of one of the merging companies and its closest competitors and ask how many customers would substitute away or how many new firms would enter the market in response to a "small but significant and nontransitory increase in price," usually understood to be a 5% increase. If a large number of customers would substitute away or if a large number of suppliers of similar products, or of the same product in a different area, could flood the market with substitutes in response to this price increase, the Department will include these alternatives in the relevant market. It will repeat this process until it has identified a grouping of sales for which the elasticity of supply and elasticity of demand are sufficiently low that the price increase would be profitable.

   If both firms are included in the relevant market as thus defined, the merger is horizontal. Next the government will compute market concentration and each firm's share of the market. The government will generally include the excess capacity of other firms in the market in its computation of market concentration.

3. **Merger Standards under the Merger Guidelines: Market Share Thresholds**

   Once the government has defined the market, it applies the following market concentration standards for evaluating the legality of the merger.

   (a) A market in which the *post*-merger HHI is less than 1000 is a safe harbor, in which the government is "unlikely" to challenge the merger;

(b) If the post-merger HHI falls between 1000 and 1800, the government will probably not challenge a merger that produces an *increase* in the HHI of less than 100 points. However, if the increase is greater than 100 points it may challenge the merger, depending on the presence of non-market share factors.

(c) The government will challenge most mergers where the post-merger HHI exceeds 1800 and the merger adds more than 50 points to the HHI.

Note: in order to compute the *increase* in HHI that results from a horizontal merger, multiply the market shares of the merging firms together and double the product.

4.   Non–Market Share Factors Under Existing Law and the Merger Guidelines

In considering the legality of a merger, both the government and the courts have examined the following factors:

(a) *Barriers to Entry.* According to the Merger Guidelines, if barriers to entry are so low that no firm in the market could profitably raise price to monopoly levels, the government will not likely challenge the merger. This statement came back to haunt the government in *Waste Management* and other cases, where the courts cited low barriers to entry as a reason for not condemning a merger that had been challenged by the government. Courts have also considered barriers to entry in merger cases. However, they have cited high barriers as a reason for condemning mergers far more often than they have cited low barriers as a reason for approving them. The 1992 Guidelines analyze entry barriers under a three-part test that finds low entry barriers only if entry is shown to be (a) likely, (b) timely, and (c) sufficient to counter collusive pricing.

(b) *Adequacy of Irreplaceable Raw Materials.* Sometimes a firm's current output overstates its market position, particularly if it is in short supply of an irreplaceable natural resource. For this reason the Supreme Court refused to condemn the *General Dynamics* merger.

(c) *Excess Capacity.* A market containing a great deal of excess capacity, held by all firms, is not conducive to monopolization, and generally is less conducive to cartelization.

(d) *Degree of Product Homogeneity.* The more homogeneous the product, the easier cartelization will be. The 1992 Guidelines note that the government will be less likely to challenge mergers in markets for differentiated, specialized products.

(e) *Marketing and Sales Methods.* Collusion is most likely to occur in markets in which buyers are poorly informed, final output sales are small and are made at prices that are publicly announced and cannot be negotiated. Courts have generally ignored such factors in considering mergers. The Merger Guidelines state that the government is more likely to challenge mergers in such markets.

(f) *The Significance of a "Trend" Towards Concentration.* In the 1960's many Supreme Court merger decisions, such as *Brown Shoe and Von's Grocery*, cited a trend toward concentration in those industries as a rationale for condemning the merger. In those cases and many others, the trend toward concentration existed because larger firms could take advantage of economies of scale. Overall, the trend probably benefitted consumers by yielding lower prices. The Merger Guidelines ignore the issue.

5. The Problem of Characterization In Merger Law: When is a Merger "Horizontal"?

A merger is truly "horizontal" only if it involves two firms that produce exactly the same product and sell it in exactly the same geographic area. Most real world mergers are not perfectly horizontal in this sense. On the other hand, even products that are physically quite different from one another—such as glass bottles and aluminum can—scompete for sales. In considering whether a merger is horizontal, courts look at the following factors:

(1) *The Degree to Which the Firms Bid for the Same Sales.* The more often the two firms attempt to compete for the same customers, the more likely the court will call the merger horizontal.

(2) *Elasticity of Supply.* The more easily one firm can increase production of the other firm's product, or ship into the other firm's primary market areas, the more likely the merger will be called horizontal.

(3) *Responsiveness of one Product's Price to Price Changes in the Other Product.* A close relationship between changes in the prices of the two firms' products suggests that customers view the products as substitutes for one another.

The "Fix it First" Rule. If a merger involves two firms that manufacture overlapping products, or sell them in overlapping geographic areas, then the merger is horizontal only in the overlapping segment of the market. The government may approve the merger contingent on the acquiring firm's sale of assets in the overlap. The result will be that the final merger is not horizontal at all.

6. The "Failing Company" Defense

The failing company defense can make it legal for a firm to acquire a qualifying "failing company" even though market structure and other indicators suggest that the merger is illegal. In the *Citizen Publishing* case the Supreme Court held that before the defense can be used the defendant must show 1) that the acquired firm was almost certain to go bankrupt and unlikely to be reorganized; and 2) that no less anticompetitive acquisition was available. The Merger Guidelines generally assess the same requirement.

7. Partial Acquisitions and Acquisitions "Solely for Investment"

Section 7 of the Clayton Act applies to partial as well as total acquisitions. In such cases, the issue is not necessarily whether the acquiring firm obtains "control" of the acquired firm, but rather whether the merger has an adverse impact on competition. As a result partial acquisitions of competitors are closely scrutinized. As a general rule, partial asset acquisitions are less injurious than partial stock acquisitions. In a partial asset acquisition, the asset changes hands. In a partial stock acquisition, on the other hand, one firm acquires an ongoing interest in the other firm's well-being.

Section 7 contains an exception for acquisitions that are "solely for investment." Today, however, the exception is almost meaningless. If a merger has any adverse impact on competition, the exception will not apply.

C. PRE–MERGER NOTIFICATION

Since 1976 firms have had to give the government advance notice concerning large mergers. The notice period is generally thirty days, but may be reduced to fifteen days for tender offers.

D. INTERLOCKING DIRECTORATES OR OFFICERS UNDER § 8 OF THE CLAYTON ACT

Section 8 of the Clayton Act prohibits the same person from serving as a director or officer on two corporations if the firms meet certain minimum threshold requirements for size and volume of sales, and if the two firms are competitors, such that the elimination of competition between them would violate *any* antitrust law.

IX. CONGLOMERATE MERGERS

A. ANTITRUST POLICY AND THE CONGLOMERATE MERGER

1. Conglomerate Mergers and § 7 of the Clayton Act

A conglomerate merger is any merger that is neither horizontal nor vertical. Although the legislative history of § 7 is ambiguous on the question of conglomerate mergers, today it is clearly established that they can be reached by § 7.

2. Conglomerate Mergers and Efficiency

Conglomerate mergers generally do not create as many opportunities for efficiency as horizontal and vertical mergers do. Nevertheless, certain efficiencies are possible. For example:

(1) If the firms produce complimentary products, such as laundry soap and bleach, the post-merger firm may achieve efficiencies in distribution and marketing.

(2) Many conglomerate mergers, particularly by tender offer, are efficient in that they transfer productive assets from inefficient managers to more efficient ones.

(3)   The conglomerate firm can frequently raise capital internally, by transferring it from divisions that produce a surplus to divisions that require large infusions of capital. The smaller firm must raise its capital by entering the capital market, which can be quite costly.

3. Efficiency and Antitrust Policy Toward Conglomerate Mergers

There is no generalized "efficiency defense" in conglomerate merger cases, just as there is none in horizontal merger cases. The available efficiencies simply cannot be quantified. Rather, courts try to establish a threshold of legality that will permit mergers that are not harmful to competition to proceed, so that any available efficiencies can be realized. However, mergers that threaten competition are condemned, even though they might produce some efficiencies as well.

B. COMPETITION AND CONGLOMERATE MERGER POLICY

Conglomerate mergers have been condemned by courts on a variety of theories. In recent years, however, only the potential competition doctrines have been widely used.

1. Reciprocity

Reciprocity occurs when one firm purchases from another firm only on the condition that the second firm purchase something in return. Reciprocity is discussed in more detail in the section on tying arrangements, above. Conglomerate mergers are conducive to reciprocity, if only for the reason that the post-merger firm operates in more markets than it did before the merger. In the *Consolidated Foods* case the Supreme Court held that if a firm commands a substantial share of some market, a finding that reciprocity is likely to occur warrants condemnation of the merger. This rule has been widely criticized for condemning efficient mergers on very bare evidence that anything anticompetitive will happen. Today the enforcement agencies appear to have abandoned reciprocity as a concern in merger cases, and there have been few such cases.

2. Leverage and Tie-ins

A few conglomerate mergers have also been condemned on the theory that they might facilitate tying arrangements—i.e., the post-merger firm might attempt to tie its newly-acquired product to some product it had produced before. The law of tying arrangements is probably a much better way to deal with such possibilities than the law of mergers. In recent years few mergers have been analyzed under this theory.

3. Predatory Pricing

Some conglomerate mergers have been condemned on the theory that they might facilitate predatory pricing, because the post-merger firm has a deeper pocket than it did before the merger. Such allegations are generally dealt with much more forthrightly under the law of predatory pricing. Few recent mergers have been condemned under this theory.

4.   The Potential Competition Doctrines

Today most conglomerate mergers are analyzed under two different "potential competition" theories. "Potential" competition is really competition viewed from the supply side rather than the demand side—i.e., two firms are potential competitors if one firm is easily able to enter a second firm's market in response to the second firm's monopoly price increase.

a.   The Line Between Actual Competition and Potential Competition

The line between "actual" and "potential" competition is hard to locate. For example, in the *El Paso Natural Gas* case the court condemned a merger as horizontal, even though only one of the firms had actually made sales in the geographic market. However, both firms had actively bid for such sales.

A true "potential" competitor has never actually made bids in the target market (i.e., the market where the effect on competition is being assessed), but is clearly in a position to do so if the market becomes profitable enough. For example, in the *Procter & Gamble* case the Supreme Court noted that P & G, a manufacturer of household products including laundry detergent, had frequently *thought* about manufacturing bleach, but had never actually entered the market. Thus it was a potential competitor in the bleach market.

b.   The Perceived Potential Entrant Theory

The perceived potential entrant theory begins with a target market with high concentration and high barriers to entry. The market is conducive to collusion. However, the firms in the market perceive that a large firm sitting on the "edge" of the market will enter if profits in the target market become too high. As a result, the firms in the market restrain their pricing. Once the large firm on the edge acquires a firm in the market, however, it is no longer there as a perceived potential entrant and collusion will be much more likely in the target market. The Supreme Court applied this theory in the *Falstaff* case.

The theory works only if:

(1)   The target market is highly concentrated;

(2)   The target market contains high entry barriers, but not so high that they also effectively deter entry by the perceived potential entrant;

(3)   There are only a small number (one to three) of perceived potential entrants;

(4)   The acquisition does not itself *increase* competition in the target market.

c.   The Actual Potential Entrant Theory

The actual potential entrant theory is more speculative than the perceived potential entrant theory. This theory also begins with a target market that is highly concentrated and conducive to express or tacit collusion. Under the theory the acquiring firm is not perceived as a potential entrant. Rather, the merger is challenged because the acquiring firm *could have* entered the market in a way that would have made the market more competitive— perhaps by new entry, or perhaps by acquiring a very small firm in the market. Instead, it came in by merger. Thus the merger is actually condemned under this doctrine, not because it "lessened" competition, but rather because it failed to increase competition. Most courts and the FTC have expressed extreme skepticism about the theory, although a few courts have used it.

In any case, courts now require that there be hard evidence that the acquiring firm would have entered the market *de novo* or by acquisition of a fringe firm had it not entered by acquisition of a larger firm.

d.   Potential Competition Mergers Under the 1984 DOJ Merger Guidelines

The 1984 Merger Guidelines reiterate that the DOJ will challenge mergers under both the perceived potential entrant and the actual potential entrant theories, in appropriate cases. Other theories of conglomerate mergers are ignored.

X.   PRICE DISCRIMINATION AND DIFFERENTIAL PRICING UNDER THE ROBINSON–PATMAN ACT

A.   THE ECONOMICS OF PRICE DISCRIMINATION

1.   Differential Pricing and Price Discrimination

Price discrimination occurs whenever a seller has two different rates of return on two different sales, or more technically, has two different ratios of price to marginal cost on two different sales. *Differential pricing* occurs whenever a seller sells the same product at two different prices.

2.   Price Discrimination in Competitive Markets

Within the perfect competition model price discrimination does not exist. Every purchaser is able to obtain the product at marginal cost. If any seller attempts to charge more than marginal cost, customers will go elsewhere.

In real world competitive markets, however, *sporadic* price discrimination occurs all the time. This is so because such markets change constantly. Prices rise and fall, and some buyers purchase at more favorable times than others.

3.   Persistent Price Discrimination by the Firm With Market Power

Price discrimination is *persistent* when a seller establishes a policy of obtaining a higher rate of return from one group of buyers than from another. Only a firm with market power can engage in persistent price discrimination. This is so because the sales to disfavored purchasers (those who pay the higher price, or who give the seller the higher rate of return) produce a certain amount of monopoly profits. Otherwise the sales to the favored purchasers would be made at a loss.

a.   Perfect Price Discrimination

Perfect price discrimination occurs when a seller can identify every buyer's reservation price (the highest price that buyer is willing to pay) and make the sale to that buyer at that price. In perfect price discrimination output is the same as it would be under perfect competition.

b.   Imperfect Price Discrimination

In imperfect price discrimination, which is the only kind that exists in the real world, the seller identifies different categories of buyers and attempts to charge a price that will maximize its profits for each category. Output under imperfect price discrimination varies with the circumstances, but it is always less than output under perfect price discrimination, or perfect competition.

c.   The Social Cost of Price Discrimination

Real world (imperfect) price discrimination always produces a certain monopoly deadweight loss, because output is less than it would be under perfect competition. In addition, schemes for facilitating price discrimination can be expensive to set up and operate. These expenses are a social loss. As a result, the antitrust laws are properly concerned with at least some instances of price discrimination.

B.   THE ROBINSON–PATMAN ACT

1.   The Legislative History of the Robinson–Patman Act

The Robinson–Patman Act, a Depression Era statute passed in 1936, was *not* designed to reduce the social cost of true price discrimination. Rather, it was designed to protect small stores from larger, more efficient rivals who could buy and sell at lower prices.

2.   The Meaning of "Price Discrimination" Under the Robinson–Patman Act

Although the Robinson–Patman Act uses the term "price discrimination," the term *means* "price difference." That is, the Act is aimed at differential pricing, not at true price discrimination.

3.   Primary–Line and Secondary–Line Violations

The Robinson–Patman Act recognizes two kinds of violations. Primary-line violations are a form of predatory pricing. They are discussed in chapter III.D. above. Secondary-line violations result when one buyer must pay a higher price for a particular commodity than another buyer paid. As a result, the first (disfavored) buyer is placed at a competitive disadvantage vis-a-vis the second (favored) buyer.

4.   The Coverage of the Robinson–Patman Act

(a) *Commerce Requirement.* The Robinson–Patman Act applies only to sales that are in the stream of commerce. This generally means that at least one of the sales must cross a state line.

(b) *The "Sales of Commodities" Requirement.* The statute applies only to sales, not to leases. Further, it applies only to sales of commodities, not to sales of services.

(c) *The "Like Grade and Quality" Requirement.* The Robinson–Patman Act applies only to sales of commodities of "like grade and quality." The products involved in the two sales need not be identical, but they must be very similar. However, an advertised national brand and an unadvertised "house" brand have been held to be products of "Like Grade and Quality."

(d) *The "Competitive Injury" Requirement.* The theory of the Act is that the disfavored purchaser, who pays a higher price, is placed at a competitive disadvantage vis-a-vis the favored purchaser. This requires that the two purchasers *compete* with one another in the resale market.

(e) *"Direct" and "Indirect" Discrimination.* The Act is also directed at "indirect" discrimination, which arises when a seller gives buyers different treatment in the provision of certain services, such as delivery, stocking, credit, etc. If such services are offered, they must be made "functionally available" to all buyers on equal terms.

(f) *Allowances for Brokerage and Services.* Under the Act sellers are forbidden to give buyers "allowances" for brokerage or other services unless such services were actually performed. However, in the *Henry Broch* case the Supreme Court found it illegal for a broker to reduce his commission in order to complete a sale, if the customer who benefitted from the reduction received a lower price than other customers did.

In *Texaco, Inc. v. Hasbrouck*, the Supreme Court adhered to the traditional view that functional discounts can be given only to buyers who actually perform some function normally provided by the seller.

(g) *Violations by Buyers.* The Robinson–Patman Act makes it illegal for a buyer knowingly to receive a price discrimination which is prohibited by the Act. However, in the *A & P* case the Supreme Court held that the buyer could not be in violation of this provision unless the seller were also in violation. If the seller *believed* it was meeting competition and thus could use the "meeting competition" defense (see below), the buyer could not be in violation of the statute, even if the seller had such a belief because the buyer had lied.

(h) *Affirmative Defenses.* The Act contains two affirmative defenses. In both, the burden of proof is on the defendant-seller:

(1) *The Cost Justification Defense* theoretically permits a defendant to show that sales at two different prices were "cost justified," because the seller incurred proportionately higher costs with respect to the higher price sale. However, the Supreme Court has set unrealistic accounting requirements that have made this defense unavailable to most sellers.

(2) *The "Good Faith Meeting Competition" Defense* permits a seller to show that it made a low price sale in a good faith effort to meet a competing bid. Only good faith, not actual knowledge of a lower bid from a competitor, is necessary. Furthermore, the seller need not "meet" competition on an individual bid-by-bid basis. It is sufficient if the seller merely meets the lower prevailing price structure in a particular market.

(i) *Damages for Secondary–Line Injuries.* For many years successful plaintiffs in Robinson–Patman actions (usually the disfavored purchasers) were entitled to "automatic" damages, equal to treble the difference between the prices charged to the favored and disfavored purchasers, multiplied by the number of units the plaintiff purchased. However, in the *J. Truett Payne* case the Supreme Court held that a plaintiff is entitled only to damages that reflected the injury caused by the decreased competition. It gave little guidance as to how these damages should be computed.

XI. JURISDICTIONAL, PUBLIC POLICY AND REGULATORY LIMITATIONS ON THE DOMAIN OF ANTITRUST

A. THE JURISDICTIONAL REACH OF THE ANTITRUST LAWS

1. Domestic (Interstate) Commerce

Today the jurisdictional reach of most of the federal antitrust laws extends to the full limit of Congress' power to regulate interstate commerce. The only exceptions are the Robinson–Patman Act and perhaps § 3 of the Clayton Act, which apply only to activities in the stream of commerce. All activities "affecting commerce" are reachable by the other antitrust laws. This means that those laws will reach highly localized activities, such as restraints in the real estate industry, the local trash collection industry, and local hospitals.

2. Foreign Commerce

Most of the antitrust laws also reach activities that affect foreign commerce. However, the reach of the antitrust laws to such activities is limited by the Act of State doctrine, which prohibits an American court from interfering in the policy of foreign nations; the Foreign Sovereign Compulsion doctrine, which exonerates antitrust violations compelled by foreign sovereigns; and the doctrine of Foreign Sovereign Immunity, which exempts the noncommercial activities of foreign sovereigns from the antitrust laws.

B.   LEGISLATIVE AND CONSTITUTIONAL LIMITATIONS ON ANTITRUST ENFORCEMENT

1.   Statutory and Judicially Created Exemptions

Certain markets have received qualified statutory exemptions from the antitrust laws. These include:

(a)   *Labor.* The activities of labor unions are generally exempt from the antitrust laws, provided that the union acts in its own self-interest and does not combine with non-labor groups.

(b)   *Insurance.* The McCarran–Ferguson Act permits states to regulate the "business of insurance," and exempts the insurance business from the federal antitrust laws, insofar as such state regulation exists.

(c)   *Agricultural Associations and Fisheries.* Agricultural cooperatives and cooperative fisheries have a qualified exemption.

(d)   *Export Associations.* The Webb–Pomerene Act permits American firms to join together into export associations, provided that they do not restrain trade inside the United States or engage in unfair methods of competition.

(e)   *Baseball and Other Professional Sports.* Since 1922 baseball has been exempt from the antitrust laws as the result of a Supreme Court decision. The exemption does not apply to other professional or collegiate sports.

2.   First Amendment and Related Defenses

The *Noerr-Pennington* doctrine holds that the antitrust laws do not prohibit people from associating together in order to petition a branch of the government to take some action, even if the desired action is anticompetitive. The doctrine is grounded in the First Amendment.

In the *Columbia* case the Supreme Court held that *Noerr-Pennington* protected a private person even if the allegation was that the private person somehow "conspired" with the government in order to obtain favorable legislation. But in *Superior Court Trial Lawyers* the Court refused to extend *Noerr-Pennington* to protect a boycott directed at the government where the boycotters were themselves selling their product to the government.

In *Allied Tube* the Supreme Court suggested that *Noerr-Pennington* might even extend to private standard-setting bodies that strongly influence governmental decisions, but that there would be no exemption for a private firm that "captured" standard setting body and manipulated its rule-making.

However, there is a "sham" exception to the *Noerr-Pennington* doctrine for "baseless and repetitive" judicial or administrative actions brought with the intent of excluding a rival from the market. The "sham" exception will not apply to a lawsuit unless it is objectively baseless and thus intended to harass the rival rather than obtain a favorable decision.

C. ANTITRUST IN FEDERALLY REGULATED INDUSTRIES AND THE DOCTRINE OF PRIMARY JURISDICTION

1. Exclusive Agency Jurisdiction

Some regulated markets exist in which oversight of competition has been delegated exclusively to one or more regulatory agencies. The antitrust laws do not apply in these industries, except insofar as the agency is itself authorized to apply them.

2. "Primary" Jurisdiction

In other regulated markets the regulatory agency has the "primary" obligation to protect competition, but there is a certain amount of room for the antitrust laws, particularly if the agency has not carefully evaluated the effects on competition of a certain activity which it has approved. For example, if a rate regulator approves requests for rate changes without a thorough investigation of their effect on the market, a private plaintiff might still be able to allege that the new rate constitutes predatory pricing or some other antitrust violation.

D. FEDERALISM AND THE PROBLEM OF MUNICIPAL ANTITRUST LIABILITY

1. The "State Action" Doctrine and State–Imposed Regulation

In *Parker v. Brown* the Supreme Court held that the federal antitrust laws were not intended to interfere too substantially with decisions by the states to eliminate competition in a particular market.

a. Compulsion

As a general rule, the "state action" doctrine applies only to activities that are *compelled* by the state. However, in the *Southern Motor Carriers* case the Supreme Court held that compulsion is not necessary if mere authorization, rather than compulsion, would produce a more competitive result. Furthermore, compulsion is not required when the defendant is not a private party, but rather a municipality or other governmental subdivision.

b. The *Midcal* Test

In the *Midcal* case the Supreme Court held that the "state action" exemption would apply to *private* activity when state legislation displacing competition was

(1) part of a "clearly articulated and affirmatively expressed" state policy of displacing competition with some regulatory scheme; *and*

(2) the state "actively supervises" the activity in question.

Under *Hoover v. Ronwin*, when the activity is not private but rather the action of the state itself, these two requirements are unnecessary.

In *Patrick v. Burget* the Supreme Court held that the "active supervision" requirement is met only when a governmental agency has the authority to review the merits of private decision making, and disapprove those found to be anticompetitive. In *FTC v. Ticor Title Co.*, the Supreme Court additionally held that this authority must be exercised; that is, the regulatory agency must actually review such things as rate change requests and not merely rubber stamp them or let them take effect without review. The fact that the agency was staffed and funded, and that it had the authority to disapprove a rate change request, was not sufficient to meet the "active supervision" requirement.

2. The "State Action" Doctrine and Municipal Antitrust Liability

Municipalities and other governmental subdivisions cannot claim the "state action" exemption on their own. It must be given to them by the state.

a. The Consequences of Failing to Qualify for the "State Action" Exemption

If a municipal price regulation or restriction on entry does not qualify for the "state action" exemption it may be found to *violate* the antitrust laws. Until 1984 this meant that a municipality could be liable for treble damages. The 1984 Municipal Government Antitrust Act now limits the remedy to injunctive relief. However, the Act says nothing about when the "state action" exemption will apply to municipalities, or about how to determine whether a municipality has violated the antitrust laws.

b. The "State Action" Exemption as Applied to Municipalities

1) *State Authorization to Regulate in a Particular Market*

   Before the "state action" exemption will apply to municipal activities the municipality must have "market specific" authority from the state to regulate a particular market. For example, if the market at issue is taxicabs, the municipality must have express state authority to regulate taxicabs. In the *Boulder* case the Supreme Court held that a Home Rule provision, which gives a municipality blanket authority to regulate within its borders, was not specific enough to exempt the city's regulation of cable television from antitrust enforcement. But in *Hallie* the Court held that authorization would be found adequate if the municipality's action was a "foreseeable" consequence of state legislation.

   In *Columbia*, the Supreme Court held that, once a municipality qualifies for the "state action" exemption, the exemption applies no matter what the motive of the city decision makers, nor how anticompetitive the consequences.

2) *Active Supervision*

   Under the *Hallie* decision, the active supervision requirement does *not* apply to municipalities.

XII. ENFORCEMENT, PROCEDURE AND RELATED MATTERS

A. PUBLIC ENFORCEMENT

1. Enforcement by the Department of Justice

The United States Department of Justice has exclusive authority to enforce the *criminal* provisions of the federal antitrust laws. In addition, the DOJ can obtain civil remedies, and may sue for damages in behalf of the United States.

2. Enforcement by the Federal Trade Commission (FTC)

The FTC has express authority to enforce § 5 of the FTC Act (which forbids unfair methods of competition) as well as the Clayton Act. However, the scope of § 5 of the FTC Act covers any antitrust violation. Thus the Commission effectively has the authority to enforce all the antitrust laws. Only the FTC may enforce § 5 of the FTC Act.

B. PRIVATE ENFORCEMENT

1. Standing to Sue

Section 4 of the Clayton Act requires that before a private plaintiff has standing to sue under the antitrust laws, she must be able to show injury to her "business or property." In *Reiter v. Sonotone*, the Supreme Court held that a retail customer who pays a monopoly price for a cartelized product has suffered such an injury.

In addition to the "business or property" requirement, courts have developed other complex rules for standing. Once effect of these rules is that only a small percentage of the people who are in fact injured by an antitrust violation have standing to sue. For example, if a corporation is the target of an antitrust violation, the corporation may sue in its own name. However, its shareholders, employees who lost their jobs, landlord and creditors who no longer receive payment have no standing.

Courts have formulated two widely used tests for private plaintiff standing in antitrust cases:

(a) The *"Direct Injury" Test* purports to measure whether a particular plaintiff's injury was a "direct" or only an "indirect" consequence of the violation.

(b) The *"Target Area" Test* purports to measure whether the plaintiff was in the "target area" of the violation.

Both tests are highly inconclusive and often give little guidance on standing issues. The Supreme Court itself has shown considerable skepticism about the tests. In the *Blue Shield* case it granted standing to a plaintiff who was not in the target area of a boycott, on the theory that 1) the plaintiffs injury was a foreseeable result of the violation; and 2) the plaintiff's injury was "inextricably intertwined" with the injury that the defendants had intended to cause. But in *Associated General Contractors* the court held that a union could not sue on the theory that its employee members were injured by an alleged boycott directed against their employers.

By statute, a state has authority to sue as *parens patriae* in behalf of its resident consumers. The state may not represent business firms in its *parens patriae* capacity. Any damages awarded in such suits must be reduced by the amount awarded in private plaintiff suits on the same cause of action.

2. The Indirect Purchaser Rule

In the *Illinois Brick* case the Supreme Court decided that indirect purchasers (i.e., buyers two or more transactions removed from a monopolist or cartel member) may not maintain a damages action under the federal antitrust laws. Under that rule the direct purchaser is entitled to the *entire* monopoly overcharge, even though the direct purchaser likely "passed on" much of the overcharge to its own customers. The Supreme Court recently re-affirmed the rule in the *Utilicorp* decision.

The *Illinois Brick* rule is subject to three exceptions created by lower courts:

(a) *Pre-Existing, Fixed–Cost, Fixed–Quantity Contract.* If an indirect purchaser had a contract, entered into before the monopoly or cartel came into existence, and which specified *both* the quantity and the markup, we can be assured that the entire monopoly overcharge was passed on to the indirect purchaser. In that case the indirect purchaser, rather than the direct purchaser, will have the damages action with respect to the sales covered by the contract.

(b) *Co-Conspirator in the Middle.* If the direct purchaser is really a part of the conspiracy, then the indirect purchaser will have an action against both the cartel member who made the sale and the direct purchaser. Likewise, if the direct purchaser is a subsidiary of the cartel member or is otherwise controlled by it, the indirect purchaser may pursue an action against the cartel member.

(c) *Actions for an Injunction.* The rationale for the *Illinois Brick* rule is that pass-on injuries are very difficult to compute. However, such computation is not necessary in actions for an injunction. Most courts have held that the indirect purchaser limitation applies only to damages actions.

3. Antitrust Injury

The "antitrust injury" doctrine requires that a plaintiff show, not merely that it was injured by an antitrust violation, but rather that it was injured by the *anticompetitive consequences* of the violation. For example, in the *Brunswick* case the court held that a plaintiff could not pursue a damages action for an illegal merger if the plaintiff's injury was that the merger made a rival a more efficient competitor than it had been before. Likewise, in the *Cargill* case the Supreme Court held that a competitor could not challenge a merger of its rivals on the theory that the post-merger firm would reduce its price, at least not as long as there was no good reason for thinking that the price reduction would be predatory.

The antitrust injury doctrine applies to all types of antitrust violations. In the *USA Petroleum* case the Supreme Court held that it prevented a competitor from challenging maximum resale price maintenance imposed on a rival. Thus it seems clear that the doctrine even applies to *per se* violation.

4.   Contribution Among Joint Violators

A right of contribution exists when one co-conspirator can force a fellow co-conspirator to pay a share of the damages. In the *Texas Industries* case the Supreme Court held that there is no right of contribution under the federal antitrust laws. Contribution legislation has been pending in Congress for several years, but as of the time this is being written, none has passed.

5.   Damages and Attorneys' Fees

The antitrust laws provide for treble damages plus attorney's fees to prevailing plaintiffs. Juries are not told about the trebling. Rather, the judge multiplies the jury award by three. Damages are computed in two different ways, depending on the nature of the violation and injury:

(a) *Overcharge Injuries*. Direct purchasers from a monopolist or cartel, purchasers in some tying arrangement cases, and others who prove that they paid a monopoly price as a result of an antitrust violation, are entitled to "overcharge" injuries. These are equal to the difference between the competitive price and the price that the plaintiff was forced to pay as a result of the violation. This amount is then trebled.

(b) *Lost Profits*. Competitors of antitrust violators and other businesses who have not purchased from the violator are generally entitled to damages based on their lost profits. These damages are likewise trebled.

6.   Other Private Remedies—Injunction and Divestiture

A private plaintiff may also obtain an injunction against the occurrence or continuation of an antitrust violation. Section 16 of the Clayton Act provides that the defendant must pay the attorney's fees of a plaintiff who successfully obtains an injunction.

In *California v. American Stores* the Supreme Court held that private plaintiffs may also obtain divestiture of illegally merged firms, under § 16 of the Clayton Act.

7.   Class Actions

Plaintiff class actions in antitrust litigation are common, especially in cases alleging price fixing. In such actions the violation and the amount of the overcharge per unit are generally established by proof that is common to the entire class. After that, each individual class member must establish the amount of its individual purchases.

8. *In Pari Delicto* and "Unclean Hands"

The common law defense of *In Pari Delicto* bars a plaintiff from recovering damages as a result of unlawful activities in which the plaintiff also participated. In the *Perma Life* case the Supreme Court held that the defense is not *generally* available in antitrust cases. However, today some lower courts hold that the defense is available if the plaintiff was a leading participant in the violation.

The defense of "unclean hands" applies when the defendant alleges that the plaintiff committed a different violation than the one that the defendant is accused of committing, and that this should bar recovery. The defense is not generally available in antitrust litigation.

9. Summary Judgment

In *Matsushita* the Supreme Court held that an antitrust defendant is entitled to summary judgment if, after discovery, the record shows that the plaintiff has failed to establish an element essential to its claim. However, in *Kodak* the Court additionally said that a defendant is not entitled to summary judgment merely because economic theory is on its side, if there are facts that tend to support the plaintiff's claim.

10. Statute of Limitations

Section 4B of the Clayton Act creates a four-year statute of limitations for antitrust damages actions. The statute does not begin to run until damages can be ascertained. This generally means that it will not run until a secret violation has been discovered.

11. The "Prima Facie Evidence" Rule and Offensive Collateral Estoppel

Section 5(a) of the Clayton Act provides that a final judgment in an antitrust proceeding brought by the United States shall be "prima facie" evidence against the defendant in a subsequent private action. The rule does not apply to consent decrees or to judgments obtained before any testimony is taken.

Private plaintiffs can also take advantage of offensive collateral estoppel in cases where an earlier plaintiff has prevailed against the same defendant on the same cause of action. The general requirements of the collateral estoppel doctrine apply to such cases.

PERSPECTIVE

This Black Letter surveys the coverage of all the federal antitrust laws. It is designed for use in a law school course on federal antitrust law, typically one of three or four semester units.

The approach taken in this Black Letter is moderately "economic." On the one hand, it assumes no prior knowledge of economics. On the other, it attempts to be sophisticated enough in its treatment of antitrust economics to deal in a realistic way with the most important issues in antitrust policy today. However, not all antitrust teachers emphasize economic theory to the same degree. If your antitrust professor takes a strongly economic approach to antitrust, you will find all parts of this Black Letter to be useful. If your antitrust professor avoids economics, however, you may want to omit chapter one, as well as the occasional section or subsection that is expressly designated "economic."

The author of this Black Letter believes that it is impossible to understand the antitrust laws today without at least a modicum of simple economics. Antitrust has gone through an economics revolution in the last two decades, and that revolution is strongly reflected in the current case law. One purpose of this Black Letter is to present this rather specialized subject of "antitrust economics" in a way that is simple, and that explains the rationales (and sometimes the errors) of federal antitrust policy. The most important purpose of the Black Letter, however, is to tell you what the cases say, how the statues have been interpreted, and what are the enforcement positions of the Department of Justice and the Federal Trade Commission.

PREPARING FOR EXAMINATIONS

This Black Letter has been designed to be a valuable study aid for use with all of the major antitrust casebooks. All those casebooks are structured differently, but you should find it quite easy tp track the development of your own antitrust course through the table of contents of this Black Letter. Further, Appendix C is a chart that correlates the chapters of this Black Letter with the pages of the major antitrust casebooks.

The author recommends that when you study for your antitrust examination you follow the course structure laid down by your own professor. Most antitrust courses are analytic; that is, they require you to study and analyze facts and to make policy arguments, rather than to memorize facts about cases. For this reason the author suggest that you *not* use this outline simply to look up the facts or the holding of a particular case. Rather, read an entire section or chapter from beginning to end. That will give you a feel for how the law works in a particular area and what the special problems are. That will also prepare you best for an analytic antitrust exam.

This Black Letter attempts to distinguish clearly between what economic analysis suggest the law *ought* to be, and what the law in fact is. You should try to keep the same distinctions in mind. Today many of the existing judge-made antitrust rules are under broad attack, not only by academic professors and economists, but also by the Federal Trade Commission and the Department of Justice. You can almost be sure that in an analytic antitrust examination you will be asked to offer some criticisms of antitrust law. This Black Letter will prepare you to do that.

ADDITIONAL READING MATERIAL

The antitrust literature is particularly rich. However, most of it is unnecessary for the law student taking his or her first antitrust class. There is no Restatement of the law of antitrust. The standard multi-volume treatise is P. Areeda & H. Hovenkamp, Antitrust Law (20 volumes, 1980–2000). Useful legal texts include:

H. Hovenkamp, Federal Antitrust Policy: the Law of Competition and its Practice (West Hornbook Series, 2d ed. 1999).

E.T. Sullivan & J. Harrison, Understanding Antitrust and Its Economic Implications, 39–70 (3d ed. 1998).

Stephen F. Ross, Principles of Antitrust Law (1993)

References in this Black Letter such as "Hovenkamp § 12.5" are to *Federal Antitrust Policy,* supra.

ANTITRUST ECONOMICS: PRICE THEORY AND INDUSTRIAL ORGANIZATION

Analysis

In order to understand modern antitrust policy, you need at least a nodding acquaintance with two basic areas of economics: price theory and industrial organization. Price theory is the theory of firm decisionmaking about how much to produce and what price to charge. Industrial organization is the theory of how the structure of the business firm and the market are determined.

A. AN OVERVIEW OF BASIC PRICE THEORY FOR ANTITRUST

1. SUPPLY AND PRICE UNDER PERFECT COMPETITION

A perfectly competitive market has the following characteristics:

(a) All sellers make an absolutely homogeneous product, so that customers do not care which seller they purchase from, provided that price is the same;

(b) Each seller in the market is so small in proportion to the entire market that the seller's increase or decrease in output, or even its exit from the market, will not noticeably affect the decisions of other sellers in the market;

(c) All participants in the market have perfect knowledge of price, output and other information about the market.

The perfect competition model also generally assumes "constant returns to scale"— that is, that it costs the same amount per unit to purchase a product, no matter how many the producer makes. "Economies of scale," which are efficiencies that obtain only when production reaches a certain volume, can undermine the perfect competition model, particularly in extreme cases; they are discussed below in B.1.

a. The Value of the Perfect Competition Model

Perfect competition exists nowhere in the real world. Nevertheless, the perfect competition model is useful because it predicts the behavior that we would expect to see in real world competitive markets, even though that behavior may be manifested only imperfectly. For example, in the perfect competition model, price equals marginal cost (see § 1.c. below). In the real world price may often be higher than marginal cost; however, as real world markets become more competitive, price tends to approach marginal cost.

b. Supply and Demand in Perfect Competition

For every product there are different customers willing to pay different amounts. For example, both artificial hearts and whiffle balls are made from plastic. However, the manufacturers of artificial hearts place a much higher value on the plastic than the whiffle ball makers do, because the cost of the plastic is such an insignificant part of the cost of producing an artificial heart. If whiffle balls and artificial hearts both use one unit of plastic and the price of one unit rises by $100, the price of a whiffle ball would rise from 89 to $100.89. Demand for whiffle balls would drop precipitously. However, the price of artificial hearts would rise from $175,000.00 to $175,100.00, and demand would change very little.

1) The "Reservation Price"

If only a small amount of plastic were produced in a given year, the artificial heart manufacturers would bid the price of it up very high, with the result that no whiffle balls would be manufactured. This is so because the price of plastic would be higher than the "reservation price" of the whiffle ball manufacturers. *A reservation price is the highest price a particular customer is willing to pay for a product.* As more and more plastic is manufactured, however, the markets for people with very high reservation prices (such as artificial heart manufacturers) will become saturated. Then the plastic will have to be sold to people whose reservation prices are lower. In order to reach the whiffle ball manufacturers, the price of one unit of plastic may have to drop to 50¢.

Importantly, when the price drops all buyers in the market—even those with very high reservation prices—will be able to purchase the product at the lower price. This is generally true because the seller will not be able to segregate different groups of customers and will not be able to prevent "arbitrage." Arbitrage occurs when purchasers who pay a low price resell the product to purchasers asked to pay a higher price.

Example: Assume that the plastic supplier asked whiffle ball manufacturers to pay 50¢ per unit for plastic, and artificial heart manufacturers $1000 per unit. The whiffle ball manufacturers would respond by purchasing more plastic than they needed and reselling it to the artificial heart manufacturers at some price between 50¢ per unit and $1000 per unit.

2) The Supply Curve

Manufacturers and other sellers have costs. "Cost," in economic terms always includes competitive profits (which are enough profits to maintain investment in the industry). *As a general rule, costs rise when output increases.* This is so because the first production in a market will take advantage of the cheapest and best raw materials. As production increases, increasingly marginal materials will be used.

Example: A farmer who has 1000 acres and intends to plant 100 will choose the 100 most fertile, where the cost of production per unit is lowest. If the farmer decides to plant a second 100 acres, she will choose the 100 most fertile of the 900 remaining acres, etc.

3)   Equilibrium

Figure One illustrates how a market arrives at "equilibrium"—the point where supply of a good and demand for it are perfectly balanced. Figure One illustrates the demand curve (D) and the supply curve (S) facing an entire market for a single product. The vertical axis represents price, which increases from zero as one moves upward. The horizontal axis represents output (or quantity), which increases from zero as one moves to the right.

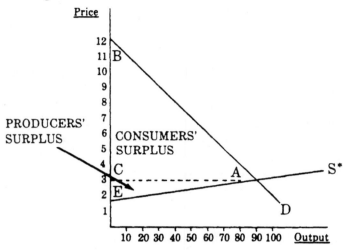

* Supply Curve = Industry Cost Curve = Sum of Marginal Costs of Individual Firms

FIGURE ONE

At low levels of output the cost of production, indicated by the supply curve (S), is quite low. Demand, illustrated by the demand curve (D) is very high, for the good will be sold only to buyers with very high reservation prices. At such price and cost levels, sellers will be earning enormous profits on their output. *Remember, "cost" includes normal, or competitive profits. Since the supply curve represents costs, a price equal to the supply curve gives the firm a competitive rate of profit, which is defined as a rate of profit sufficient to maintain investment in the industry. Any vertical distance between the supply curve and the demand curve represents "excessive" or "monopoly" profits.*

Monopoly profits naturally attract increased output. As long as the profits earned in a market are very high, two things will happen:

(a)   Firms already in the market will produce more, so they can earn more of the large profits;

(b)   New firms will enter the market.

This will continue to happen until output reaches a level where the supply curve and demand curve intersect. From that point any further increase in production would generate higher additional costs (shown by the supply curve) than it would produce additional revenues (shown by the demand curve). The competitive market reaches "equilibrium" at the point where the supply curve and demand curve intersect.

Two things are important to know about competitive equilibrium:

(a) When a market is in equilibrium supply and demand will not change unless the market is shocked by some kind of *external* change, such as a war, famine, weather, a new invention that creates new competition or decreases production costs, new entry by a large firm, changes in customer taste, etc.;

(b) Competitive equilibrium is determined by the "marginal" buyer and the "marginal" seller in the market. That is, the buyer located at the intersection of the supply and demand curves in Figure One is the buyer who has the *lowest reservation price and is still able to purchase in the market.* Anyone with a lower reservation price will be unwilling to purchase at the competitive price. Likewise, the seller located on the supply curve at the same intersection is the seller *with the highest costs who is still capable of staying in the market.* Any seller with higher costs would lose money at the competitive price.

4) Consumers' Surplus and Producers' Surplus

As noted above, in a competitive market all buyers pay the "market price," determined by the intersection of the supply and demand curves, even though their individual reservation prices may be much higher. Triangle ABC in Figure One represents "consumers' surplus," or the difference between what customers were willing to pay and what they were required to pay in a competitive market. At the same time, some firms in the market will have lower costs than others, perhaps because they have better access to resources, or perhaps because they are more efficient. They are also able to sell at the market price, even though they have lower costs. For them, the competitive price yields high profits in the form of "producers' surplus." Producers' surplus is the difference between a firm's costs and the price it obtains for a product.

5) Market Elasticities of Supply and Demand

The supply and demand "curves" illustrated in Figure One are generally *not* linear in the real world. They can assume a wide variety of shapes. The shapes generally reflect the responsiveness of buyers and sellers to changes in price.

Elasticity of Demand is a relationship between the change in the price of a product and the amount of consumer demand for it. As a fraction, it is equal to the percentage change in demand for a product, divided by the percentage change in price necessary to cause that change in demand. This fraction is generally a negative number (demand goes down as price goes up, and vice-versa), but it is expressed positively.

> ***Example:*** At a price of $1.00 per unit, demand for a product equals 1000 units. When the price rises to $1.25, demand falls to 800. In this case a 25% price increase caused a 20% demand decrease. The elasticity of demand in the market is $^{20}/_{25}$ or .8.

When customers are highly sensitive to changes in price, we say demand in that market is "elastic." As a general rule, elasticities of demand greater than one are considered elastic. Elasticities of demand less than one are considered inelastic.

Elasticity of supply is a ratio between the change in the amount of a product produced and the corresponding price change. It is expressed as a fraction, with the change in the amount produced as the numerator and the corresponding price change as the denominator. For example, if a 10% increase in price causes a 30% increase in the amount produced, the elasticity of supply is $^{30}/_{10}$, or 3. Elasticity of supply is a positive number.

c.   The Output Decision of the Individual Firm in Perfect Competition: Marginal Cost

1)   The Perfect Competitor's Price Decision

The individual firm in perfect competition is a "price taker"—that is, it has no price decision to make. It can sell all it pleases at the market price, but it will sell nothing if it attempts to charge more, for some other firm will always be there to make the sale. We say, therefore, that *the firm in perfect competition faces a horizontal* individual *demand curve.* This is sometimes called the "residual" demand curve, to distinguish it from the demand curve of the market as a whole. The curve is said to be "residual" because it describes the demand that is left over for the firm after all other firms have made their sales at the going price.

2)   The Perfect Competitor's Output Decision

Although the perfect competitor accepts the market price as given, it *does* have to decide how much to produce. Even a perfectly competitive market contains firms of different sizes, and each one makes its own output decisions.

The individual firm in perfect competition always produces at that level of output at which the market price equals its marginal costs. Marginal cost is the additional cost that a firm incurs in the production of one additional unit of output. A firm's marginal costs usually rise as output increases in the relevant range because, just as the market as a whole, the individual firm must use its best resources first, its second best resources second, etc. As a result the relationship between the horizontal demand curve and the marginal cost (MC) curve of the individual firm in perfect competition looks like Figure Two:

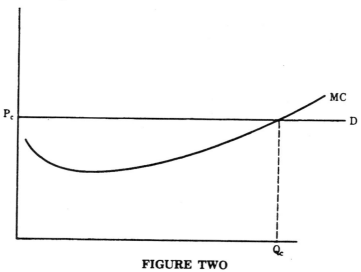

FIGURE TWO

Note that in the perfectly competitive market the *individual firm* faces a horizontal demand curve, D, which is equal to the market, or competitive price, P_c. For the individual perfect competitor that price cannot be varied.

Suppose that price is $1.00, and that at the lowest point on the marginal cost curve, MC equals about 60 From that point, if the firm produced one additional unit of output, the MC curve tells us that it would incur 60in additional costs. Since the market price is $1.00, this unit could be sold for a 40profit. The firm will increase output. How long will the increases continue? Once the firm has reached output level Q_c on the curve in Figure Two, it will no longer make additional money by increasing output, but will begin losing money. For example, if output is to the right of Q_c, an additional increase in output of one unit will generate additional revenues of $1.00, the market price, but it will generate additional costs of more than $1.00. The firm will maximize its profits if it can control its production at precisely the rate at which its marginal costs equal the market price. From that point it will make less money if it produces one unit more, or one unit less. Thus we can say that price under competition equals marginal cost.

2.   MONOPOLY

The monopolist, which is the *only* firm selling in a particular market, makes different price and output decisions than those made by the perfect competitor. The analysis that follows makes two assumptions about the monopolist that generally do not apply to the *de facto* monopolist in the real world. (The *de facto* monopolist is a monopolist that achieved its position by its own doing, and does not have statutory monopoly protection.) The assumptions are:

(1) The monopolist is the only firm in the market;

(2) The monopolist does not need to be concerned about new entry from a competitor.

In the real world we often consider firms to be "monopolists" for antitrust purposes even though they control only 90% or perhaps even only 70%–80% of their markets. Furthermore, in the real world the de facto *monopolist generally faces the threat that another firm will come in and challenge its monopoly position.*

a. The Monopolist's Price and Output Decisions

Because our monopolist is the only firm in its market, it faces the same demand curve as the *market* demand curve illustrated in Figure One above. However, we have redrawn that curve, together with some others, in Figure Three below.

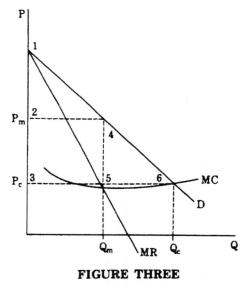

FIGURE THREE

Even the monopolist cannot charge an infinite price for its product, because the monopolist's customers have reservation prices, and they will not pay more. On the other hand, the monopolist is not a price taker. *Unlike the perfect competitor, the monopolist has the power to obtain a higher price for its product by reducing output.* As Figure Three reveals, the less the monopolist produces, the higher will be the "market clearing price" (i.e., a price sufficiently low to sell all units produced).

1) The Marginal Revenue Curve

Note the marginal revenue (MR) curve in Figure Three. *The MR curve represents the additional revenue that the monopolist obtains when it increases output.* For the perfect competitor the MR curve is horizontal and identical with the demand curve that the perfect competitor faces, because the market price remains constant. However, the monopolist's MR curve slopes downward more sharply than the monopolist's demand curve, because when the monopolist increases output it must reduce the price of every unit that it sells. For example, suppose that at an output of one unit the monopolist's price is $20. When output increases to two units, the market price drops to $18. However, the monopolist must sell both the first and second units for $18.00, so its total revenue increases to $36.00. This is an increase of $16.00 over the revenue that was obtained when output was one unit. In short, when the price fell $2, from $20.00 to $18.00, marginal revenue (the *additional* revenue earned) fell $4, from $20.00 at an output of one unit, to $16.00 at an output of two units.

2)   The Monopolist's Profit–Maximizing Price

The monopolist will produce and set a price at the point at which its marginal revenue (MR) curve intersects its marginal cost (MC) curve. As long as the monopolist is producing less than this amount, an output increase will result in more additional revenues than additional costs. As soon as the monopolist increases output to the right of the intersection of MR and MC, however, the additional costs will increase more rapidly than the additional revenues. *For this reason the intersection of the MR and MC curves determine the monopolist's "profit-maximizing price" and profit-maximizing rate of output.* Output at that point is designated by Q_m in Figure Three and price at that point by P_m. This is sometimes called the "monopoly price."

> ***Note 1:***   The difference between a monopolist's profit-maximizing price and its marginal cost (which would be the price in a competitive market) tells us something about the amount of market power that a firm has. If a firm's profit-maximizing price is $1.02 and its marginal cost at that point is $1.00, the firm has a small amount of market power. However, if the firm's profit-maximizing price is $2.00 and its marginal cost at that point is $1.00, then the firm has a substantial amount of market power.

> ***Note 2:***   A "monopsonist" is a monopoly buyer rather than a seller. Just as a monopolist reduces output and raises the price of the goods that it sells, a monopsony buyer reduces output and *lowers* the price of the things that it purchases.

b.   The *De Facto* Monopolist in the Real World

In the preceding discussion we assumed that the monopolist controlled 100% of its market and was unconcerned about new entry by competitors. When those two assumptions are relaxed, the monopolist may not charge the price dictated by the intersection of its MR and MC curves. *Rather, the real world monopolist may behave "strategically"—i.e., it may set a somewhat lower price designed to make output increases by competitors, or potential entry by new firms, somewhat less attractive.* The effect of such a price decrease will be to reduce the monopoly price for a single unit of the monopolist's product; however, it may greatly increase the *duration* of the monopoly.

c. The Social Cost of Monopoly

The social cost of monopoly is the *net loss to society* caused by the existence of monopoly in the economy. *You should distinguish a social cost from a wealth transfer. For antitrust purposes, a transfer of wealth—the mere payment of money from one person to another—is assumed to make society no richer or poorer than it was before: one person is wealthier but another person is poorer by exactly the same amount.*

Reconsider Figure Three above. In a competitive market, where price equals P_c and output equals Q_c, purchasers would enjoy a consumers' surplus equal to triangle 1–3–6. The monopolist, however, will reduce output to Q_m and increase price to P_m. In that case two things will happen:

(1) Buyers located along the demand curve between points 1 and 4 will pay a higher price;

(2) Buyers located along the demand curve between points 4 and 6 will not purchase the monopolized product at all, for the monopoly price is higher than their reservation price.

1) The Monopoly Wealth Transfer

Under monopoly consumers' surplus has been reduced to triangle 1–2–4. Rectangle 2–3–5–4 represents a "wealth transfer" to the monopolist—that is, the monopolist has "robbed" consumers of this amount of consumers' surplus. Because it is merely a wealth transfer it does not make society as a whole worse off—the monopolist is merely richer and the customers poorer by the same amount.

2) The Deadweight Loss Triangle

Triangle 4–5–6 is a different story. It represents people who would have purchased the product at the competitive price, but substitute away at the monopoly price. As a result, the consumers' surplus is lost to consumers; however, the monopolist gains nothing from this area either, for it makes no profit on unmade sales. *As a result, triangle 4–5–6 is a net social loss. Because of this monopoly society as a whole is poorer by the area of triangle 4–5–6. This triangle is called the "deadweight loss" of monopoly, or the "social cost" of monopoly.*

> *Note:* It seems clear today that triangle 4–5–6 in the above illustration *under*states the true social cost of monopoly.

That is, although the triangle represents the social cost of monopoly *pricing* it does not measure the social cost of monopoly *conduct*. The *de facto* monopolist may spend a great amount of money in various "exclusionary" practices in order to preserve its monopoly position. Chapter III.A.3. below is concerned with such practices. Many of these practices, such as predatory pricing and raising the costs of rivals may be inefficient and thus increase the social cost of monopoly. At the extreme, the monopolist may spend most of the anticipated profits from its monopoly position (i.e., rectangle 2–3–5–4) in maintaining its monopoly. In that case a substantial part of rectangle 2–3–5–4 should not be considered a wealth transfer at all, but part of the social cost of monopoly.

B.   INDUSTRIAL ORGANIZATION: ECONOMIES OF SCALE AND THE DILEMMA OF ANTITRUST POLICY

Industrial organization is the study of firm structure. A knowledge of industrial organization can be important to antitrust analysis for two reasons:

(a)   It can help us distinguish markets in which the perfect competition model has some application from those in which it does not;

(b)   It can help us understand why firms engage in certain practices, such as vertical integration or mergers, and what are the consequences of such practices for competition.

1.   ECONOMIES OF SCALE

An economy of scale exists whenever the cost of some input declines as volume increases. *The result of economies of scale is that the cost of production decreases on a per unit basis as the amount being produced increases.* Economies of scale are widespread in most markets. Consider the following examples:

(a)   To drive a truck from point A to point B costs $100, whether the truck is full or half empty. As a result the full truck carries its cargo at a lower cost per pound.

(b)   To set up a metal lathe to turn out a particular machine part costs $100 in labor. Once the lathe is set up, the costs of turning out the parts is $1.00 each. If the lathe is set up to turn out a single part, the cost of that part will be $101.00. If the lathe turns out 10,000 parts, their cost will be $1.01 each.

(c)   A manufacturer of essential medical supplies must always keep one production machine in reserve, so that a breakdown will not interrupt production. If he produces with a single machine operating at a time, he must therefore maintain capacity equal to twice his actual output. If he produces with eight machines, however, he needs to maintain only nine machines, a capacity equal to 12% more than his output.

(d) A thirty-second television commercial advertising automobiles costs $100,000, whether the manufacturer produces 10,000,000 automobiles per year, or 90,000 automobiles per year. As a result, advertising costs are far lower per unit for the larger manufacturer.

a.   Economies of Scale and Technology

Economies of scale are largely a function of technology, which both creates and destroys economies of scale. Scale economies can generally be divided into economies of scale that can be attained by a single plant and multi-plant economies that make it cheaper to operate multiple plants than it is to operate only one.

b.   Minimum Optimal Scale

The term Minimum Optimal Scale (MOS) or Minimum Efficient Scale (MES) refers to the smallest production unit capable of achieving all relevant economies of scale. If a firm or plant operates at MOS, no other firm or plant can be more efficient because of its scale of operation. (Keep in mind, however, that firms can be inefficient for reasons that have nothing to do with economies of scale; for example, even the very large firm may be poorly managed.)

2.   NATURAL MONOPOLY

At the extreme, economies of scale in a market may be so substantial that the market will operate most cheaply if a single firm controls the entire market. Such markets are called natural monopolies. *Technically, a market is a natural monopoly if costs decrease as output increases all the way to the point that the market is saturated.*

Unfortunately a natural monopolist, just as any other monopolist, maximizes its profit by engaging in monopoly pricing. This creates a problem for those concerned with efficient market behavior: "competition" among multiple firms will require that the market operate inefficiently because the relatively small firms will have higher costs. By contrast, the monopoly will operate inefficiently because the monopolist will charge a monopoly price. *The traditional solution in cases involving recognized natural monopoly is to establish a regulatory agency that will permit a single firm to occupy the market, but regulate its prices in order to maintain them at the competitive level.* See Hovenkamp § 1.4b.

3.   THE DILEMMA OF ANTITRUST POLICY: COPING WITH BIGNESS

The existence of economies of scale can create extraordinary dilemmas for antitrust policy. On the one hand, antitrust policy has traditionally expressed a concern with bigness in business. Furthermore, bigness can incline businesses toward anticompetitive behavior. For example, price fixing is much more likely to occur in "concentrated" markets—i.e., markets that contain only a few large firms (see chapter II.A. below). On the other hand, any *unqualified* attack on bigness or high business concentration can produce higher consumer prices because the antitrust laws will prevent firms from attaining Minimum Optimal Scale.

If antitrust policy is to be guided by the "consumer welfare principle"—that is, if its overriding goal should be to maximize output and minimize consumer prices—then a certain tolerance of large firms is necessary. *Finding the proper balance between the efficiencies that result from scale economies on the one hand, and our distrust of bigness and some of its anticompetitive consequences on the other, is a problem that is pervasive in antitrust policy today.*

C.   THE ECONOMIC MODEL AND REAL WORLD MARKETS

The economic models presented in the preceding discussion are somewhat simplistic in comparison with the situation that exists in the real world. It is a good idea to be aware of the most important differences between the models and the markets that can be found in antitrust litigation. Antitrust policy must deal with each of these real world deviations from the basic economic models:

1.   PRODUCT DIFFERENTIATION

In the perfect competition model, you will recall, the products sold by all sellers were fungible. As a result, customers were sensitive only to price. In the real world, however, many products, particularly manufactured products, are differentiated from one another. For example, although IBMS and Apples are both computers and both compete in the same market, some customers prefer one to the other, and may even be willing to pay a higher price in order to have their preference. The result of product differentiation is that many firms face a slightly downward sloping demand curve and may charge a price somewhat higher than their marginal cost. *More importantly for antitrust analysis, product differentiation may explain why many firms employ various restrictions on distribution, such as those discussed in chapters V and VI.*

2.   PRICE DISCRIMINATION

In the perfect competition model price discrimination never occurs and all buyers pay exactly the same price for a product. In the real world, however, price discrimination occurs daily. The topic of price discrimination will come up frequently in this discussion of antitrust law, but it is discussed systematically in chapter X. below.

3.   TRANSACTION COSTS

Transaction costs are the costs of using the marketplace. The perfect competition model outlined above assumes that transaction costs are nonexistent. In the real world, however, transaction costs can be substantial, and they can explain many aspects of business behavior, particularly vertical mergers, tying arrangements, exclusive dealing, and restrictions on distribution.

4. BARRIERS TO ENTRY

In economic models of competitive behavior we generally assume that entry by competitors will occur instantly when price rises above marginal cost. In the real world, however, various barriers to entry may prevent or delay such entry. In general, an entry barrier is some factor that makes the cost of doing business higher for the newcomer than for the incumbents. Certain parts of antitrust analysis, particular of mergers and monopolization by predatory pricing, begin with the premise that anticompetitive results are likely only if entry barriers into the market at issue are high.

D.   REVIEW QUESTIONS

1. What is the Relevance of Economies of Scale for Antitrust Policy?

2. T or F   The monopolist has the power to force customers to pay more than their reservation price for the monopolist's product.

3. T or F   The supply curve is really a cost curve.

4. T or F   Under monopoly consumers' surplus is reduced to zero.

5. T or F   Any firm would naturally prefer to face a low elasticity of demand.

6. T or F   A wealth transfer is the same thing as a social cost.

7. T or F   Marginal cost pricing should be an important goal of antitrust policy.

*

II

CARTELS, TACIT COLLUSION, JOINT VENTURES AND OTHER COMBINATIONS OF COMPETITORS

Analysis

A. HOW AND WHEN PRICE FIXING WORKS

A cartel is a group of firms who *should* be competitors, but who have agreed with each other to "fix" their prices in order to earn monopoly profits. *Cartels are analyzed under Section 1 of the Sherman Act, which prevents contracts, combinations, and conspiracies in restraint of trade. Price fixing is said to be "naked" when it is unaccompanied by any joint venture or other integration of the participants' business activities. Naked price fixing is per se illegal under § 1.* This was established in an important series of price fixing decisions. U.S. v. Trans–Missouri Freight Ass'n, 166 U.S. 290, 17 S.Ct. 540 (1897); U.S. v. Trenton Potteries Co., 273 U.S. 392, 47 S.Ct. 377 (1927); U.S. v. Socony–Vacuum Oil Co., 310 U.S. 150, 60 S.Ct. 811 (1940).

1. THE CARTEL MARKET

Price fixing works much better in some markets than in others, and in some it probably cannot work at all. This is important to know, because price fixing agreements are usually clandestine and often very difficult to detect. It makes good economic sense to spend law enforcement dollars in those markets that are most conducive to price fixing.

The following characteristics suggest that a market is conducive to price fixing.

a. Market Concentration

The smaller the number of firms in a market, the more conducive a market is to cartelization. This is so for two reasons. First, the firms must meet in secret (at least, in those parts of the world that have laws against price fixing) and communicate their ideas to one another. The more firms there are, the more difficult secret meetings will be to arrange, and the easier they will be to detect. Secondly, the firms must reach price and output agreements that will take all of their individual preferences and differences into account. The more firms the market contains, the harder it will be to arrive at compromise agreements that account for all the differences.

Economists generally agree that cartelization is likely to occur in markets containing from two to perhaps seven or eight firms. Once a market exceeds, say, fifteen or twenty firms, cartelization becomes extremely difficult. It is not likely to occur in such relatively unconcentrated markets.

b. Barriers to Entry

A "barrier to entry" is some factor in a market that makes the cost of doing business higher for new entrants than it is for firms already established in the market. High barriers to entry are essential to effective cartelization, because when the cartelized market becomes highly profitable more firms will want to enter it. If every attempt by the cartel to raise prices is met by a flood of new firms entering the market, the cartelization scheme will not work. Barriers to Entry may include:

(1) The large cost of entering a market, particularly (a) if the new entrant must pay higher rates for capital than existing firms are paying; or (b) these costs are irreversible, or "sunk,"—which means that the entrant will lose the investment if entry fails.

(2) Licensing by the government that makes it difficult or impossible for people to enter new businesses (yes, the government actually encourages price fixing by protecting some markets from outsiders);

(3) "Mobility barriers"—that is, a long period of time between the decision to enter and actual sales in the market.

> ***Example:***   From the time that a firm decides to become an automobile manufacturer until the time that it can actually be producing cars takes ten or more years. A plant must be designed, contracted and built; a product must also be designed and built. During that ten year period the firms already in the market need not worry about sales by outsiders. Cartelization could be very profitable during that time. If the incumbent firms can delay the entry even more by legal actions or other exclusionary practices, the cartel may be even more profitable. Entry will be particularly unpromising if the automobile plant is highly specialized and cannot be converted to other uses in the event of failure. In that case the entire investment will be lost.

c.   Sales Methods

Some sales methods are far more conducive to cartelization than others. The cartel will be concerned about "cheating" by its members. That is, cartel members will try to make additional sales at a price lower than the cartel price, but which is nevertheless profitable. *For this reason cartels work best in markets in which the incentives to cheat are small and cheating can easily be detected.* Incentives to cheat are small when individual sales are small, there are a large number of sales, and prices must be publicly communicated, such as through consumer advertising. Cheating is easiest to detect when prices are publicly announced and "non-negotiable"—that is, the market is not characterized by individual, secret buyer-seller haggling over price.

Cartels work best of all in auction markets, in which a seller asks for bids and the cartel members "bid" against each other for the sale. In such a market, the cartel members can agree in advance who will submit the winning bid, and all other firms will submit higher bids. If a firm cheats and wins the bid, the other firms will know immediately.

d.   Product Homogeneity

Cartels work best in markets containing perfectly "fungible" products—i.e., products that do not bear any important, unique characteristics supplied by the firm that produced them. As a result, customers are indifferent as to which producer's product they buy, as long as price is the same.

The problem of heterogeneous or "brand specific" products is that consumers distinguish among them and may prefer one over the other. As a result, arriving at a suitable cartel price may be very difficult.

Example: Three manufacturers of stereo equipment decide to form a cartel. However, one firm makes relatively expensive equipment that is perceived by the public as high quality. Another firm manufactures a product perceived as being of medium quality. The third manufactures a cheaper product perceived by consumers as cut-rate. If the firms decided to fix the *same* price for their stereo systems, nearly all customers would buy the output of the first firm. The three firms will have to guess at some compromise, and will probably have to create a complex price *scale,* rather than a single cartel price, so that each firm will be able to retain its share of the stereo market. Computation of that scale will be very difficult. If there is an error one firm may lose market share to the others.

e. Facilitating Devices

Sometimes cartel members can intentionally change the nature of the market in order to make cartelization more profitable. For example,

(1) *Product Standardization* agreements may solve the problem of product heterogeneity described above and make the determination of a cartel price easier. However, product standardization can also be very efficient, because it gives consumers reliable information about what they are purchasing. Unfortunately, it is often difficult to determine whether a particular instance of product standardization is being used to facilitate cartelization or to benefit consumers by providing information about standard product quality.

(2) *Vertical Integration and Resale Price Maintenance may help the cartel members enforce their cartel by ensuring that all cartel sales are public, small (if the members vertically integrate to the retail level) and non-negotiable (again, if the members vertically integrate to the retail level).*

(3) Other facilitators, such as advance price announcements, and delivered and basing-point pricing schemes, are discussed below in chapter II.B. on tacit collusion. However, these facilitators can generally benefit an express cartel as much as an oligopoly.

2. THE CARTEL MEMBERS

a. Firm Size

In order for the cartel to succeed, it must reduce total market output to monopoly levels. (See the discussion of monopoly above at chapter I.A.) The firms will have the easiest time agreeing about the reduction in output each firm must accept if they are all of roughly the same size. If the firms are of widely differing sizes, they may have a much more difficult time allocating the output reduction. Traditionally, large cartel members have had to take a disproportionately large share of the output reduction in order to make the cartel work. This difficulty is exacerbated if the market is subject to scale economies, for larger firms may then have lower costs than smaller firms.

b.   Efficiency

If the firms operate at different levels of efficiency, they will have different costs, even though they manufacture identical (fungible) products. In general, firms with higher costs want to set higher cartel prices than firms with lower costs.

Note: The reason why a firm with higher costs will want to set higher cartel prices is illustrated by Figure Three in chapter I.A.2. above. Each firm will want to equate its own marginal costs with its anticipated marginal revenue. For the firms with higher marginal costs, this intersection will occur at a higher price than for firms with lower marginal costs. The wider the variation in firm efficiency, the harder it will be for the cartel members to agree on a cartel price.

c.   Extent of Participation

The cartel will work best if 100% of the firms in the market participate. By contrast, the existence of a substantial number of outsiders can undermine the effectiveness of the cartel. For example, the outsiders may increase output in response to the cartel's attempt to reduce market output. If that happens the cartel will be unsuccessful in raising the market price level, and they will reap nothing but a loss of market share. On the other side, one of the best positions for a firm to be in is to be a nonmember of a cartel in a cartelized market. The outsider can raise its price to a highly profitable level somewhat lower than the cartel price. Furthermore, it is not bound by the cartel's restrictions on output: it can make all the sales it wants.

d.   Incentives to Cheat and Cartel Countermeasures

When the cartel is working properly, two things are true:

(1)   Because of the cartel output reduction, each cartel member is selling less than its pre-cartel level, and probably less than its capacity.

(2)   Each cartel sale is highly profitable.

This gives each cartel member a strong incentive to cheat by making secret, additional sales at a price somewhat lower than the cartel price. The cartel must stop such cheating or it will fall apart. To do so, it may use the facilitating devices described above. However, it may act more coercively—for example, by engaging in concerted refusals to deal, predatory pricing or other exclusionary practices directed at cheaters.

The cartel may also direct such practices against firms that refuse to participate in the cartel. Allegations of concerted refusals to deal are often based on the theory that the victim was undermining the activities of a cartel by refusing to participate and expanding its own output in response to the cartel's output reduction.

Finally, the cartel may take very specific measures to prevent cheating in the particular market in which the cartel is located.

Example 1: In U.S. v. Addyston Pipe & Steel Co., 85 Fed. 271 (6th Cir. 1898), modified and affirmed, 175 U.S. 211, 20 S.Ct. 96 (1899), the cartel used a complex internal bidding scheme to determine who would submit the winning bid for a particular cartel sale. The cartel member who agreed to pay the largest part of its revenues as a "bonus" to the other cartel members won the bid. Once the bid was assigned to a particular cartel member, all members of the cartel would know immediately if another member won a bid.

Example 2: In U.S. v. Trenton Potteries Co., 273 U.S. 392, 47 S.Ct. 377 (1927), the cartel members had to agree to destroy all "seconds"—i.e., presumably defective merchandise that was not sold subject to the cartel's output limitations. If seconds could be sold for more than their marginal cost of production, a cartel member who wanted to cheat on the cartel would simply classify first quality merchandise as "seconds" and offer it to the higher bidder, without reporting these sales to the cartel.

3. VARIATIONS ON HORIZONTAL COLLUSION

Sometimes cartels find it easier to accomplish their purpose by varying the traditional agreement to reduce output and raise price.

a. Horizontal Territorial or Customer Division

In a horizontal territorial division scheme firms that would otherwise be competitors divide the market into territories, and each agrees that it will make sales only in its assigned territories. In a horizontal customer division scheme, firms divide the market by classifications of customers—e.g., one chemical manufacturer will sell only to hospitals, another only to schools, another only to factories, etc.

Territorial and customer division *can* enable firms to solve some of the problems of cartelization—for example, under them each firm may make its own price and output decisions. But only a few markets are conducive to such schemes. For example, territorial division will work only if the market can easily be divided into discrete territories, with one cartel member in each region.

When horizontal territorial division is used simply to eliminate competition among rivals it is illegal per se. The Supreme Court re-affirmed that long-standing rule in Palmer v. BRG of Georgia, 498 U.S. 46, 111 S.Ct. 401 (1990), which condemned such a territorial division agreement between two schools offering bar review courses: "One of the classic examples of a per se violation of § 1 is an agreement between competitors at the same level of the market structure to allocate territories in order to minimize competition." (Quoting United States v. Topco Associates, Inc., 405 U.S. 596, 92 S.Ct. 1126 (1972)).

b.   Market Share Agreements

In a market share agreement firms make their own pricing decisions, but they agree that each will make a certain percentage of the sales in the market. Penalties will be imposed upon firms that exceed their agreed-upon percentages. Such an agreement may permit individual firms more flexibility in making price and output decisions, and the penalty may operate to discourage cheating.

c.   Output Reduction Schemes

Sometimes the cartel will merely devise a way to reduce output, and then let each cartel member establish its own price. *For example, the scheme condemned by the Supreme Court in U.S. v. Socony–Vacuum Oil Co., 310 U.S. 150, 60 S.Ct. 811 (1940) involved each of the defendant major oil companies buying up the production of one or more independent oil producers. In the process, the major producers could reduce their own production proportionately, and total production on the market would decline.*

For more on the economics of price fixing, see Hovenkamp § 4.1.

B.   EXPRESS AND TACIT COLLUSION: AN INTRODUCTION TO THE OLIGOPOLY PROBLEM

An oligopoly is a highly concentrated market, containing only a few firms. The firms may be able to arrive at a consensus about price and output without explicitly agreeing with each other about anything. For example, if a market contains one very large firm and two or three smaller ones, the smaller ones may have to watch the larger firm's pricing decisions very closely. If the larger firm sets a high, relatively profitable price, the smaller firms will be invited to follow and participate in the monopoly profits. But if they refuse to follow, the dominant firm will lose market share and may have ways of retaliating. Under such circumstances the firms may reach an "understanding" about price even though they do not formally communicate with each other.

In extreme cases, oligopoly pricing may be just as anticompetitive as explicit price fixing. As a general rule, however, the kind of "silent communication" that goes on in oligopoly is less effective than the explicit communication that occurs in price fixing. For this reason, most oligopoly markets probably have lower prices and higher output than they would have under express collusion; however, they have higher prices and lower output than they would have under real competition. This makes oligopoly an antitrust problem. Many of the prevailing economic models of monopoly conclude that (1) prices under oligopoly are higher than competitive prices but lower than monopoly prices; and (2) the price tends to rise as the number of firms in the market decreases.

1. OLIGOPOLY AND THE SHERMAN ACT

Section 1 of the Sherman Act requires a "contract," "combination" or "conspiracy" among two or more firms. *Courts have held almost without exception that in the absence of an express agreement no violation of § 1 is possible. The few exceptions that exist have been dicta in cases which found an express agreement.*

Section 2 of the Sherman Act reaches conduct in the absence of an agreement among multiple firms, but § 2 requires that the firm engaging in the conduct either be a monopolist, or else that there be a dangerous probability that it will become a monopolist. (See the discussion of monopolization and attempt to monopolize below in chapter III.) Oligopoly markets are highly concentrated, but as a general rule no firm in them is a monopolist.

As a result, neither section of the Sherman Act deals adequately with the problem of noncompetitive behavior in highly concentrated markets in the absence of evidence of a qualifying agreement among the firms.

2. POSSIBLE APPROACHES TO THE OLIGOPOLY PROBLEM

a. The Structural Approach

One possible approach to the oligopoly problem is to acknowledge that oligopoly behavior is *inherent* in oligopoly markets—that is, it would be irrational for firms in an oligopoly market to ignore their situation and behave competitively. In this case, one solution to the problem of oligopoly may be new legislation forcing the break-up of large firms in oligopoly markets. *Such legislation has never been passed.*

This approach suffers from one enormous difficulty: most industries are highly concentrated because economies of scale in those industries are substantial. In that case, large firm size is necessary to efficient production and distribution. Although mandatory divestiture in such a market may force the firms to behave more competitively, it may also increase their costs by depriving them of economies of scale or scope. There is no telling what the overall effect would be on market price.

b.   **The Conduct Approach**

An alternative solution is to reach oligopoly conduct directly, without changing the structure of the market. This approach analogizes oligopoly behavior to collusion, and usually calls it "tacit collusion." The approach begins with the premise that it is generally unwise to change the structure of oligopoly markets, because the resulting destruction of economies of scale could hurt consumers. Secondly, the approach assumes that performance in oligopoly markets can be improved by changing various elements of conduct in the market. For example, if it is clear that oligopoly pricing is being facilitated by advance, public announcements of price changes, an injunction against such announcements could make the market perform more competitively. This approach was attempted unsuccessfully by the Federal Trade Commission in E.I. du Pont De Nemours & Co. v. FTC, 729 F.2d 128 (2d Cir.1984), discussed below.

3.   THE AGREEMENT REQUIREMENT AND THE ANTITRUST LAWS

To date, neither of the two approaches outlined above to the problem of oligopoly has met with substantial success. At best, courts have been able to reach tacit collusion only indirectly.

a.   **Circumstantial Evidence of Express Collusion**

Although it now seems well established that § 1 of the Sherman Act requires an "agreement" among the firms, the agreement may be established by circumstantial evidence. The Supreme Court has occasionally condemned multi-firm conduct under § 1 of the Sherman Act even though there was no *direct* evidence that the defendants had agreed with each other to engage in the conduct.

Example 1:   Eight distributors of motion pictures deal with a large number of exhibitors (theater operators). One of the largest exhibitors sends identical letters to each of the eight distributors naming all eight as addressees and urging that in future film licensing contracts with the exhibitors the distributors place in each contract: 1) a clause requiring the exhibitor to charge at least 40¢ admission for first run films, and 25¢ admission for subsequent run films; 2) a clause prohibiting the exhibitors from exhibiting two films together as double features. Subsequently, all eight distributors place both clauses into their film licensing contracts.

In Interstate Circuit, Inc. v. U.S., 306 U.S. 208, 59 S.Ct. 467 (1939), the Supreme Court affirmed a lower court decision based on the above facts that there was an agreement among the eight distributors to engage in the conduct. That decision rested on two premises:

(1)   There was an express invitation (the eight letters) communicated to each distributor to engage in the illegal conduct (horizontal price fixing and output reduction); furthermore, each distributor knew that the others had received the letter as well.

(2) *An affirmative response to the letter by any single distributor would have been irrational, unless the distributor had reason to believe that all other distributors were going to do the same thing. That is, if only one distributor had imposed the price maintenance and the ban on double features on its exhibitors, those exhibitors would have responded by seeking out other distributors.*

Example 2: The owner of a movie theater in a suburban area several miles from downtown asks several large film distributors to give it exclusive first runs of successful films. However, each of the distributors refuses to give such exclusive first runs to suburban movie theatres; rather, it gives them only to large downtown theatres. The owner of the suburban theatre sues, claiming that the distributors have agreed among themselves not to deal with his theatre. (*Concerted* refusals to deal can be *per se* violations of the Sherman Act; see chapter VII below.)

In Theatre Enterprises, Inc. v. Paramount Film Distrib. Corp., 346 U.S. 537, 74 S.Ct. 257 (1954), the Supreme Court affirmed a judgment for the defendant based on the above facts because there was *not* sufficient evidence of an agreement among the distributors. *In this case, each distributor acting in its own self-interest would naturally pursue a policy of giving exclusive first-run film rights to those theatres that could draw the largest audiences, and all such theatres were downtown.*

Example 3: In American Tobacco Co. v. U.S., 328 U.S. 781, 66 S.Ct. 1125 (1946) the Supreme Court cited the fact that all the major tobacco companies raised their prices during the depression era, when both demand and costs were falling, as "circumstantial evidence of the existence of a conspiracy.... " *The case is the closest the Supreme Court has ever come to permitting a conspiracy to be inferred from cost and price data alone. However, lower courts have not followed the leader in this case, and the existence of price fixing agreements is virtually never established exclusively on the basis of price or cost information.*

In any event, the Supreme Court's decision in Matsushita Electric Indust. Co. v. Zenith Radio Corp., 475 U.S. 574, 106 S.Ct. 1348 (1986) has greatly increased the burden on plaintiffs attempting to prove conspiracies on the basis of indirect evidence. Under that decision the evidence must "tend to exclude the possibility" that the defendants were acting independently; otherwise no jury issue will be created and the defendants will be entitled to summary judgment.

b. Detecting and Challenging Tacit Collusion

Theoretically, a court should be able to identify on the basis of economic evidence alone 1) markets that are conducive to collusion; and 2) markets in which tacit or express collusion is actually occurring.

1) Evidence of Markets Conducive to Tacit Collusion

   The evidence that a market is *conducive* to collusion includes evidence of

   (a) high concentration on the sellers' side;

   (b) a large number of small, poorly informed buyers;

   (c) significant barriers to entry;

   (d) significant economies of scale (which will operate as a barrier to entry in this case by deterring small firms from entering the market;

   (e) a fungible or homogeneous product.

2) Evidence that Collusion is Occurring

   Evidence that tacit or express collusion is actually occurring in a "suspect" market (i.e., a market which is determined to be conducive to collusion on the basis of the criteria mentioned above) includes:

   (a) *Very Stable Market Shares.* In competition we expect market shares of individual firms to fluctuate as their fortunes rise and fall. In a cartel, however, each member will be jealous of its own market share; cartel members will try to assign production quotas that maintain those shares.

   (b) *A Rigid Price Structure.* In competitive markets price fluctuates in response to changes in supply and demand. The cartel is likely to resist such changes, however, usually preferring to reduce market output in response to weak demand, rather than reducing the price.

   (c) *Industry-Wide Use of Facilitating Devices.* The discussion in chapter II.A.1. above suggested that sometimes firms will use vertical integration, resale price maintenance, delivered pricing or other "facilitating devices" to make tacit or express collusion easier. Such devices generally work, however, only if all firms in the market employ them. Thus the *industry-wide* use of such devices can be a signal that collusion is occurring. Two particular classes of facilitating devices are important here:

   (1) *Standardization of Products and Terms.* The more homogeneous the product of the firms in a market, and the more uniform the process by which it is marketed, the more conducive the market will be to tacit collusion.

   Courts have had no difficulty condemning horizontal "standardization" agreements, provided that the evidence of agreement was clear and that the agreement pertained to price or output.

   Example 1: In Catalano, Inc. v. Target Sales, Inc., 446 U.S. 643, 100 S.Ct. 1925 (1980), the Supreme Court condemned an agreement among beer wholesalers to eliminate short term credit and require payment on delivery. Such an agreement could easily facilitate express or tacit collusion. Without it, even though firms had agreed about price, they might compete with one another by offering longer periods of credit.

Example 2: In Sugar Institute, Inc. v. U.S., 297 U.S. 553, 56 S.Ct. 629 (1936), the Supreme Court condemned a trade association rule prohibiting the members from giving secret discounts to buyers. The anticompetitive potential of such an agreement is obvious. In a competitive market "secret" discounts are harmless. Each seller sets its own price. However, secret discounts can undermine express or tacit collusion by making sellers unsure about the prices that a competitor is actually charging.

Example 3: In American Medical Association v. FTC, 638 F.2d 443 (2d Cir.1980), affirmed by an equally divided Court, 455 U.S. 676, 102 S.Ct. 1744 (1982), the FTC condemned "ethical canons" that forbade medical doctors from advertising. The FTC held that the canons should be treated under the rule of reason on the theory that professional rules of conduct should receive a certain amount of deference under the antitrust laws. The FTC also held that the AMA had the power to discipline members for engaging in false or deceptive advertising. Both the circuit court and the Supreme Court affirmed.

Example 4: In National Macaroni Mfrs. v. FTC, 65 F.T.C. 583 (1964), affirmed, 345 F.2d 421 (7th Cir. 1965), the FTC condemned an agreement among macaroni manufacturers to standardize the content of macaroni at 50% semolina and 50% farina. Such a product standardization agreement could have three different purposes. (1) It could be a procompetitive device for ensuring that consumers obtain a product of consistently high quality. (2) It could be a mechanism for making a product more homogeneous in order to facilitate collusion. (3) In this particular case, however, it was probably an effort to reduce demand for semolina and thus suppress its price. Such a scheme would work only if the macaroni manufacturers accounted for a very high percentage of the semolina wheat grown.

(2) *Delivered and Basing Point Pricing.* Price uniformity is essential to tacit or express collusion. If products are delivered to the buyer by the seller, prices become hard to track, for delivery charges will vary

considerably from one buyer to the next. For this reason the cartel members may find it necessary to "fix" the delivery charges as well as the prices themselves.

In basing point pricing a firm charges customers a freight rate from a particular point even though the product was actually shipped from a different location. If the firms in a cartel agree with *each other* to engage in basing point pricing and use the same basing points, they can effectively produce bids that are uniform as to both price and delivery charges. This effectively eliminates "placement competition"—i.e., the competitive advantage that accrues to a particular firm because it is closer to the buyer than other firms are.

a)   Basing Point Pricing by Agreement

Basing point pricing has been consistently condemned by the courts when multiple firms agreed with each other to establish a basing point scheme. Triangle Conduit and Cable Co. v. FTC, 168 F.2d 175 (7th Cir.1948), affirmed sub nom. Clayton Mark & Co. v. FTC, 336 U.S. 956, 69 S.Ct. 888 (1949). See also FTC v. Cement Institute, 333 U.S. 683, 68 S.Ct. 793 (1948), which inferred the existence of an agreement from the absolute uniformity of "competitive" bids given by the defendants.

b)   Basing Point Pricing in the Absence of an Agreement

The more difficult question is whether basing point pricing can be condemned under the antitrust laws *in the absence of evidence that firms agreed with each other to use the basing point scheme.* The *Triangle Conduit* case mentioned above suggested that proof of an agreement was unnecessary. *However, at least one court has concluded that basing point pricing is not illegal if it is unilateral, even if all firms in the market are engaging in the practice and using exactly the same basing points.* Boise Cascade Corp. v. FTC, 637 F.2d 573 (9th Cir. 1980).

3)   Tacit Collusion and the FTC Act

Section 5 of the Federal Trade Commission Act condemns "unfair methods of competition." The statute may be enforced only by the Federal Trade Commission, and the remedy most frequently used by the FTC is an injunction, called a "cease and desist" order, instructing the defendant to stop engaging in a certain practice. Courts have held that "unfair methods of competition" include any antitrust violation, but they may also include some conduct that would not be an antitrust violation. *In short, the scope of § 5 of the FTC Act is somewhat broader than the scope of the Sherman and Clayton Acts. Importantly, nothing in the FTC ACT expressly requires proof of the existence of an "agreement" among competitors before anticompetitive multifirm conduct can be condemned.*

E.I. du Pont De Nemours & Co. v. FTC, 729 F.2d 128 (2d Cir.1984) involved an attempt by the FTC to reach oligopoly behavior in the highly concentrated market for lead antiknock compounds for gasoline. The market showed high profits and rigid price uniformity consistent with either express or tacit collusion. However, there was no evidence of any express agreement among the four sellers in the market. The FTC tried to use § 5 of the FTC Act to make the market more competitive by enjoining the use of three oligopoly facilitating devices:

(1) Advance announcements of price changes;

(2) Uniform delivered prices;

(3) Price protection, or "most favored nation," clauses in sales contracts.

A price protection clause promises a buyer that if a subsequent buyer receives a lower price than the first buyer paid (usually within a specified time period) the first buyer will be entitled to a retroactive rebate that will reduce its net price to the same level. Buyers generally like price protection clauses. However, often such clauses operate to make discounting very expensive: a seller who gives one buyer a discount will have to offer it retroactively to other buyers as well. As a result, widespread use of price protection clauses can discourage discounting.

The FTC found that all three practices were anticompetitive and issued a cease and desist order, but the circuit court vacated the Commission's order. *The court held that, even under § 5 of the FTC Act, the Commission must show 1) evidence of anticompetitive intent or purpose on the part of the defendants; or 2) the absence of any competitive justification for the practices.*

See Hovenkamp, § 4.4.

C. JOINT VENTURES AND OTHER ANCILLARY RESTRAINTS UNDER § 1 OF THE SHERMAN ACT

A joint venture is any association of two or more firms for carrying on some activity that each firm might otherwise perform alone. Not all joint ventures involve competitors; however, the ones subjected to antitrust scrutiny generally involve competing firms. As a general rule, however, to characterize an agreement among firms as a "joint venture" says nothing about its effect on competition. Some joint ventures can be anticompetitive, while others are procompetitive.

1. JOINT VENTURES: THE THREAT TO COMPETITION

The chief threat to competition that arises out of joint ventures is collusion of some form. Joint ventures can often facilitate price fixing or collusion by territorial division. Joint venturers can also engage in concerted refusals to deal. These are dealt with in chapter VII below.

If joint ventures offered only anticompetitive consequences and no competitive ones, we could justifiably condemn all of them under a *per se* rule. However, most joint ventures—even most joint ventures of competitors—are competitive. *At the same time, no court is capable of measuring the anticompetitive impact of a joint venture and "balancing" this against the efficiency savings that might result. For this reason the approach most generally followed is to condemn the venture if the threat to competition is substantial, but to leave it alone if that threat is not substantial, on the theory that in that case the only likely effect of the venture is procompetitive.*

This makes it imperative to identify some of the signs of an *anti* competitive joint venture:

a.   The Firms Participating in the Venture Are Competitors

Joint ventures involving competitors invite at least the possibility of price fixing. Those that involve noncompetitors generally do not.

b.   The Participants Control a Large Market Share

Even if the participants in a joint venture are competitors, the venture will not be anticompetitive unless the firms collectively wield some market power.

> ***Example:***   A city contains 60 grocery stores. Three relatively small stores decide that they can compete more effectively with larger stores by jointly running a newspaper advertisement showing some "sale" prices on certain products—for example, coffee at $1.89 per pound. Because the advertisement displays the prices, the firms must come to an *agreement* about the price. On balance, however, the joint venture is competitive. In its favor is the argument that the three stores have been able to reduce their advertising costs by two-thirds. Likewise, the fact that the three stores make up only a small share of the relevant market tells us there is little danger of price fixing.

c.   The Joint Venture's Activities Affect Price or Output

A joint venture's activities are most likely to be anticompetitive if the venture involves itself in the price or output decisions of its members. A pure research and development joint venture, for example, is not likely to do this. However, joint ventures engaged in marketing, product standardization, and reporting of market conditions (including the exchange of price and output information) are all more likely to create opportunities for price fixing.

d.   The Venture Is Exclusive

A venture is a bigger threat to competition if the members agree to make sales only through the venture itself. Suppose, for example, that a group of physicians set up a jointly-run clinic, but are permitted to maintain unlimited independent practices. The clinic is less likely to facilitate price fixing even if the participating physicians collectively control a large share of the market. If clinic prices are too high, the individual physicians will have an incentive to serve more customers through their independent practices.

2. JOINT VENTURES: ECONOMIC RATIONALES

Most firms engage in joint ventures in order to accomplish something more cheaply than each could do it alone. The following economies may result from joint ventures.

a. Economies of Scale and Scope

An economy of scale results from the lower per unit cost of performing a large number of similar operations. A joint venture can enable a group of firms acting together to achieve economies of scale in production, research and development or some other activity. For example, if a group of firms need a certain specialized chemical in their production processes, but manufacturing of the chemical is cheaper when large quantities are manufactured at once, the firms might more profitably manufacture the chemical jointly and distribute it to members as it is needed. These lower costs will be passed on to consumers.

b. Economies of Distribution

A joint venture might be organized in order to take advantage of economies in the distribution of a product. For example, suppose that Firm A and Firm B manufacture automobiles. A certain town is too small to support a dealer of either Firm A's automobiles or Firm B's automobiles. As a result, the town might not have a dealer of either brand. However, by acting together the two firms might be able to set up a single dealership that sold both brands, and which would make enough sales to support its existence.

Example: In Appalachian Coals, Inc. v. U.S., 288 U.S. 344, 53 S.Ct. 471 (1933), the Supreme Court approved a joint selling agency agreement among 137 coal producers. The agency classified the coal, marketed it, and distributed the proceeds to the participants. Since coal is fungible, the agent necessarily sold the coal of all the members at the same price. The Court's decision has been criticized because the agency was exclusive— i.e., its members were forbidden to make sales except through the agency. However, the Court's decision was probably correct. It is unlikely that 137 coal producers could be engaged in price fixing. Furthermore, their share of the market was too small to warrant any conclusion that they were an effective cartel.

c. Solving Free Rider Problems

A "free rider" is a firm that takes advantage of a product or service offered by someone else without paying for it. Research and development (R & D) is one area in which free riding problems are widespread, particularly if the product of the R & D cannot be patented, or if it is easy to "invent around" the patents. In that case one firm will engage in expensive R & D. Other firms will wait until the product of the R & D is made public. Then they will "reverse engineer" the product and copy it without undergoing the expense of the R & D.

If such free riding is substantial, no firm will want to take the initiative to engage in the R & D, for the initiator will suffer the higher costs but many firms in the market will obtain the benefit. One way to get around the problem is a joint venture for R & D. That way, all firms will participate in the costs (and the rewards) from the beginning.

The same arguments apply to advertising. If three firms sell Brand X toasters in a city, any single firm who advertised the qualities of Brand X toasters would find that the benefit accrued not only to itself, but to its competitors as well. An advertising joint venture might solve this problem. However, some firms have attempted to solve it by means of various territorial division schemes, designed to place firms far enough apart that such free rider problems would not be substantial.

Example: In U.S. v. Topco Assoc., Inc., 405 U.S. 596, 92 S.Ct. 1126 (1972), the Supreme Court condemned an arrangement created by about 25 small grocery chains who had collectively created "Topco" brand food products. The Association jointly purchased products, packaged them and distributed them to members. None of these activities was challenged by the government. However, the Association also assigned each member a territory in which it could sell the Topco brand. It could open additional grocery stores in other territories, but it could not market Topco brand products in those other stores. The Supreme Court characterized this as horizontal territorial division, governed by the *per se* rule.

The *Topco* case has been subject to great criticism. First of all, the market shares of the Topco members were very small. The average member had about 6% of the grocery trade in its assigned territory. This fact makes cartelization by horizontal territorial division implausible. Second, the relatively small Topco chains were attempting to compete with much larger chains. In order to do this effectively, they had to advertise. However, if a territory contained several Topco brand store owners, one's advertising would benefit all, and each would be tempted to free ride on the efforts of others. The Supreme Court finally recognized this in Continental T.V., Inc. v. GTE Sylvania Inc., 433 U.S. 36, 97 S.Ct. 2549 (1977), in which it adopted a rule of reason for *vertical* territorial division. (The *Sylvania* case is discussed below at chapter VI.D.) However, the Court has never overruled *Topco*.

At least one lower court has applied the rule of reason in a *Topco*-like situation involving a horizontal *product* division agreement among two retailers sharing the same building and parking lot, as well as its management expenses. Polk Bros. v. Forest City Enterprises, 776 F.2d 185 (7th Cir. 1985).

d. Joint Ventures in Network Industries

A network industry is one in which the business of individual firms is interrelated in such a way that certain joint activities are necessary to the functioning of the market. For example, the creation of a grain futures market such as the Chicago Board of Trade requires the market participants to agree on such things as the market's location and the hours it will be open. The first antitrust case that the Supreme Court decided on the merits concerned a joint venture in a network industry. U.S. v. Trans–Missouri Freight Ass'n, 166 U.S. 290, 17 S.Ct. 540 (1897), involved an association of railroads that coordinated freight hauling schedules, transfers of cargo from one line to another, and freight rates on behalf of its members.

More recently, in National Collegiate Athletic Ass'n (NCAA) v. Board of Regents of the Univ. of Oklahoma, 468 U.S. 85, 104 S.Ct. 2948 (1984) the Supreme Court considered a rule by the NCAA, an association which regulates collegiate athletics on behalf of its members, which limited the number of times per season that each member could have its games televised. *The Supreme Court held that the rule of reason must be applied to an industry in which agreements among competitors were "essential if the product is to be available at all." However, then the Court went on to condemn the arrangement because it reduced the output of televised college football with no apparent competitive justification.* The Tenth Circuit did the same thing in *Law v. NCAA*, 134 F.3d 1010, 1024 n. 16 (10th Cir. 1998), cert. denied, ___ U.S. ___, 119 S.Ct. 65, 142 L.Ed.2d 51 (1998), a closely watched decision that condemned the colleges' fixing of maximum salaries for certain classes of basketball coaches.

See Hovenkamp, § 5.6.

e. Joint Ventures and the Problem of Market Information

Among the most controversial of joint ventures are those that involve competitor exchange of price information. Markets vary widely in the amount of information about prices that is available. For example, the New York Stock Exchange provides daily information, available in many newspapers, about prices and volume on the exchange. At the other extreme, in markets for rare works of art or other customized products prices are often kept secret from everyone except the parties to the transaction.

1) Market Information and Efficiency

Markets generally work best when participants have good, reliable information about price. When such information is not available, people are in a position to take advantage of the ignorance of others. Furthermore, the absence of price information can increase the costs of using a market, because people negotiate longer when market price is uncertain. That explains why the price of a rare work of art may be negotiated for months, while potatoes and corn will be put on the market and sold at the going "market price."

2) Market Information and Collusion

Two extreme situations are easy to characterize: markets in which information is very bad function poorly, with considerable room for price gouging and expensive negotiation. By contrast, markets in which all parties have access to reliable information tend to function quite well. Unfortunately, there is no smooth continuum between these two extremes. It does not follow that the more information that exists, the more efficiently a market will perform. Certain exchanges of price information can facilitate collusion. This is most likely to be true in concentrated markets that are conducive to tacit or express collusion anyway.

The court must therefore distinguish information producing activities (most generally exchanges of price and output information by competitors) that make the market operate more efficiently from those that might facilitate collusion.

Example 1: In American Column & Lumber Co. v. U.S., 257 U.S. 377, 42 S.Ct. 114 (1921), the Supreme Court condemned an exchange among competitors of detailed reports concerning the production and price charged by each. On the one hand, the lumber producers were clearly concerned about "overproduction," and their motive may have been cartelization. On the other, there were 365 members, and they collectively controlled only one-third of their market. Cartelization seems implausible. Further, many of the members were isolated and had poor knowledge of market conditions. Many buyers, by contrast, were large and well informed. The price information exchange was more likely competitive than anticompetitive.

Example 2: In Maple Flooring Mfrs' Ass'n v. U.S., 268 U.S. 563, 45 S.Ct. 578 (1925), the Supreme Court refused to condemn a price information exchange agreement among members of this association. The court dwelt on the fact that the reports exchanged by the members did not identify particular customers, and reported past transactions rather than future prices. However, such reports could facilitate collusion as well as more specific reports. Furthermore, this time there were only 22 producers and they controlled 70% of the market. Even more suspicious, the association provided members with a freight rate book showing freight rates from Cadillac, Michigan. This suggests that the members were engaged in basing point pricing, and all using the same basing point. In this case, the danger to competition was far more substantial.

Example 3: In U.S. v. Container Corp. of America, 393 U.S. 333, 89 S.Ct. 510 (1969), the Supreme Court finally decided that competitor price information exchanges should be governed by the rule of reason, and that they are more threatening to competition in concentrated markets than in markets containing many small producers. The court also held that the lower court must determine whether the price information exchange affected the market price. Unfortunately, the Court gave no guidance on how to measure such an effect.

Today competitor exchanges of price information are governed by the rule of reason. Market concentration is one of the factors to be considered—the more concentrated the market, the more likely that the exchange is anticompetitive. Furthermore, the exchange will be condemned if the court determines that it affected the market price.

f. Joint Ventures as Market Facilitators

Although all joint ventures are market "facilitators" in the broadest sense, some joint ventures are peculiarly designed to "create" a market. To be sure, a market would probably exist without the venture; however, the market created by the venture performs much more efficiently than the market that would exist without it. *Such ventures are governed by the rule of reason.*

Example 1: In Chicago Board of Trade v. U.S., 246 U.S. 231, 38 S.Ct. 242 (1918), the Supreme Court applied the rule of reason and refused to condemn the "call rule" established by the Board. The Board itself was an enormous exchange of commodities set up by Board members. The exchange gathered all buyers and sellers together at one time and place and created a highly competitive, smoothly functioning market for commodities. Under the call rule, Board members were required to trade commodities at the closing price of the last exchange day. That is, although exchanges could be made off the exchange floor, all price determination had to be made during the regular sessions of the exchange. The general effect of the rule was to force all exchanges into an atmosphere where relevant information was equally available to all participants.

See Hovenkamp § 5.2–5.3.

Example 2: In Broadcast Music, Inc. v. Columbia Broadcasting System, Inc. (BMI), 441 U.S. 1, 99 S.Ct. 1551 (1979), the Supreme Court approved an arrangement under which thousands of individual artists and other performance right owners licensed their performance rights through "blanket licenses" issued by BMI, which permitted the licensee (mainly radio and television stations) to perform anything in BMI's repertoire. BMI then monitored the licensees to see how often a particular composition was performed, and paid the performance right owners in proportion to the number of uses.

The Court upheld this arrangement even though BMI controlled a commanding share of the performance right market. Furthermore, the arrangement literally involved "price fixing"—that is, all participants had to agree to accept a certain royalty for each performance of their compositions. However, the scheme reduced transaction costs of licensing performance rights so substantially that it effectively made mass marketing of performance rights feasible. The alternative would have been for individual radio and television stations to negotiate individually for each performance right they wanted. This would have required dozens of transactions per day for each licensee. Furthermore, the arrangement between each artist and BMI was *non-exclusive*—that is, each artist could engage in individual licensing if she pleased. This fact, plus the fact that the artists numbered in the thousands, made cartelization implausible.

D.   HORIZONTAL AGREEMENTS AND THE PER SE RULE: THE PROBLEM OF CHARACTERIZATION

Most restraints are analyzed for antitrust legality under the rule of reason, which requires (1) definition of a relevant market (see III.A) and (2) assessment of competitive or efficiency effects. Once market power and a facially anticompetitive restraint is found, the plaintiff has made out a prima facie case of illegality, but the defendant can rebut this showing by proving a legitimate business justification or efficiency benefit for its conduct. If the defendant succeeds, the burden shifts to the plaintiff to show that the same justification or benefit could have been attained by some less restrictive alternative.

A more dangerous subset of practices, however, is said to be illegal per se. These are condemned without an elaborate investigation into market power or the precise reasons for the conduct in the particular case. A class of conduct is brought within the per se rule only after the court has had sufficient experience with the conduct that it can be fairly certain that the conduct is almost always anticompetitive ad almost never socially beneficial. Thus the per se rule is one of administrative convenience. It permits the court to avoid a long, expensive investigation into a particular market when such an investigation is unlikely to change the court's initial evaluation. See Hovenkamp § 5.6.

The difficult question left open by this analysis is whether there are any *general* guideposts for determining when the *per se* rule should be applied to a joint activity involving competitors, and when they will be entitled to rule of reason analysis. There is no universal guidepost, but the following factors are important:

1. PRICE–AFFECTING CONDUCT

In U.S. v. Socony–Vacuum Oil Co., 310 U.S. 150, 60 S.Ct. 811 (1940) the Supreme Court applied the *per se* rule to an arrangement among major oil producers to "allocate" gasoline demand. Justice Douglas held that any "combination formed for the purpose and with the effect of raising, depressing, fixing, pegging, or stabilizing the price of a commodity ... is illegal *per se.*"

It seems clear today, however, that the *Socony-Vacuum* rule must be made subject to at least limited exceptions. For example, the *Broadcast Music* case, discussed above, certainly fell into Justice Douglas' classification of *per se* violations, but the Supreme Court applied the rule of reason. Nevertheless, application of the rule of reason to an agreement among competitors that affects price or output is rare.

In National Society of Professional Engineers v. U.S., 435 U.S. 679, 98 S.Ct. 1355 (1978), the Supreme Court condemned a rule which forbade engineers from bidding competitively for jobs. Their defense was that competitive bidding was not in the public interest, because the result would be that engineers would cut corners and design dangerous structures. The Supreme Court responded by saying that the defense that "competition" is not in the public interest is inappropriate. In order to receive rule of reason treatment the defendant must show, not that "competition" in a particular instance is bad, but rather that a particular practice is not anticompetitive. Although the Court did not use *per se* language, its analysis seems most consistent with the *per se* approach.

Thus any exception to the *per se rule* for price-affecting conduct among competitors must rest on a showing that the conduct at issue actually reduced prices or increased output in the market. This distinguishes the *Broadcast Music* case from the *Engineers* case.

In Arizona v. Maricopa County Medical Society, 457 U.S. 332, 102 S.Ct. 2466 (1982), the Supreme Court applied the *per se* rule to an arrangement among doctors and health insurors which fixed *maximum* prices that the doctors would charge. Under the arrangement, insured patients received a list of participating doctors. If the patient went to a participating doctor, all his costs would be covered by the insurance policy. If he went to a different doctor, he might have to pay the difference between the amount that doctor charged and the amount covered by the insurance policy. *The Supreme Court condemned the arrangement under the per se rule, on the theory that maximum price fixing can easily be a cover for minimum price fixing.*

The case has been widely criticized. First, the arrangement was nonexclusive—any participating doctor could make unlimited sales outside the arrangement. Second, the participation of the health insurors, who stand in a vertical relationship with the doctors, is inconsistent with a doctors' price fixing agreement. Vertically related firms are almost always injured by a cartel. See chapter IV below. Finally, there was substantial evidence that the agreement was being used to *reduce* health care costs by facilitating the matching of patients with doctors who agreed not to charge more than a certain amount for their services. See Hovenkamp § 5.6.

2. PUBLIC CONDUCT

A price affecting agreement among competitors must generally be public before it will qualify for rule of reason treatment. When an arrangement is public from its inception, then the participants have presumably calculated that it does not violate the antitrust laws, probably because it is procompetitive (although many public agreements are subjected to the *per se* rule as well). By contrast, people generally do something in secret because they suspect that what they are doing is wrong and want to avoid detection.

3. CONCLUSION: SOME GUIDELINES FOR DECIDING TO APPLY THE PER SE RULE OR THE RULE OF REASON

Be warned. The Guidelines that follow are not perfect, because the Supreme Court continues to wrestle with the problem of characterization.

(a) Does the agreement involve competitors? If yes, it is a *candidate* for *per se* treatment. If it does not, then it will receive the rule of reason (unless it involves resale price maintenance or tying arrangements. See chapters V & VI below).

(b) Does the arrangement involve a "network industry" in which cooperation of competitors is necessary to make the product at all (e.g., collegiate or professional sports, the internet, ATM cash transfer systems). If so, then the practice will receive the rule of reason.

(c) Does the arrangement *explicitly* "affect" price or output? If so, and if the agreement involves competitors, the court will most generally apply the *per se* rule, although there are some exceptions. The word "explicitly" is important. Competitor exchanges of price information may affect price or output, but they are not agreements to affect price or output, so they affect them only implicitly. They are governed by the rule of reason.

(d) If the agreement affects price or output, is it "naked," or is it ancillary to some other activity that arguably enhances the efficiency of the participants? If the agreement is naked, application of the *per se* rule is virtually automatic. If the agreement is ancillary to other joint activity, the court will consider whether the price-affecting agreement is necessary to make the joint activity work. If the agreement passes this second test, then the defendants must still show that the effect of the agreement is to reduce price or increase output by making the market operate more efficiently than it would otherwise? If this argument is very strong and convincing, the Supreme Court may apply the rule of reason even to competitors' agreements that explicitly affect price or output.

4. THE "QUICK LOOK" FOR HIGHLY SUSPICIOUS, OR "NEARLY NAKED" RESTRAINTS

In its decision in *FTC v. Indiana Federation of Dentists*, 476 U.S. 447, 106 S.Ct. 2009, 90 L.Ed.2 445 (1986), (see Ch. 7, infra, on refusals to deal) the Supreme

Court approved a truncated analysis of a highly suspicious practice, but under circumstances where the Court had only limited experience with the restraint in question (a refusal to deal by a professional organization). Under this analysis a court may take only a brief look at market power for a restraint that seems highly suspicious, or may dispense with any market power requirement at all, if the defendant cannot offer a reasonable business justification. In sum, the difference between the "quick look" for highly suspicious restraints and the per se rule is that the defendant may be entitled to show *either* lack of any power to achieve an anticompetitive result, or an adequate justification. If one of these is found, then the court usually proceeds with full rule of reason treatment.

In its decision in California Dental Assn. v. FTC, 119 S.Ct. 1604 (1999), however, a divided Supreme Court held that the "quick look" could not be applied to a dental association's rules that purported to limit deceptive advertising but were in fact so aggressive that they eliminated nearly all price and quality advertising claims. The five-member majority believed that a complex market with poorly informed consumers might function as well or better even with aggressive limitations on advertising. The four dissenters emphasized that even in a complex market truthful claims about price and quality serve to bring buyers and sellers together, thus enhancing competition.

E. THE DEATH OF THE INTRA–ENTERPRISE CONSPIRACY DOCTRINE

For many years antitrust courts condemned various "bathtub" conspiracies—i.e., conspiracies among firms or subsidiaries related by ownership—under § 1 of the Sherman Act. One of the unfortunate effects of this inter-enterprise conspiracy doctrine was that essentially single firm conduct was brought within the scope of the *per se* rule, often when the firm had no market power.

In Copperweld Corp. v. Independence Tube Corp., 467 U.S. 752, 104 S.Ct. 2731 (1984) the Supreme Court held, however, that a parent and its wholly owned subsidiary could not be "conspiring entities" for the purposes of § 1. The Court held that the existing law of inter-enterprise conspiracy gave "undue significance to the fact that a subsidiary is separately incorporated and thereby treats as the concerted activity of two entities what is really unilateral behavior flowing from decisions of a single enterprise."

Since *Copperweld* lower courts have held that two wholly-owned subsidiaries of the same parent also cannot be conspiring entities under § 1. The outcomes are mixed when the subsidiaries are not wholly-owned.

However, several lower courts have also held that if agents of a single firm have an *independent* financial interests that in fact motivated their actions, then these agents might be treated as separate actors for Sherman § 1 purposes.

Example: Five physicians act as the managing staff of a hospital and make decisions about which physicians may practice there; however, the five physicians also have independent practices. Three of the five are pediatricians. When the plaintiff, a new pediatrician, applies for staff privileges at the hospital the three incumbent pediatricians all vote no, complaining that the new pediatrician's office is open evenings and weekends, and her fees are too low. Some courts hold that both the hospital and the staff physicians have conspiratorial capacity. See, for example, Bolt v. Halifax Medical Center, 891 F.2d 810 (11th Cir. 1990). Others hold that the physicians, but not the hospital itself, can be held to be conspirators. For example, Oksanen v. Page Memorial Hosp., 945 F.2d 696 (4th Cir. 1991), cert. denied, 502 U.S. 1074, 112 S.Ct. 973 (1992).

F. REVIEW QUESTIONS

1. Five bolt manufacturers agree with each other to fix the content of "standard grade bolts" at 75% steel and 25% aluminum. Collectively, the five manufacturers produce 90% of the nation's bolts; however, bolts consume only 3% of the nation's steel and 5% of the nation's aluminum. Should the arrangement be analyzed under the *per se* rule or the rule of reason? What outcome?

2. T or F   Naked price fixing is legal if it occurs in an unconcentrated market, or in a market in which barriers to entry are low.

3. The electric radio market contains thirty manufacturers. Radios compete with one another, but they vary widely in quality, size, and individual capabilities. They are generally sold wholesale by individually negotiated orders. How much effort should the Department of Justice spend in trying to detect price fixing in this market? Why?

4. T or F   Tacit Collusion is legal under the antitrust laws.

5. T or F   Basing point pricing is irrefutable evidence of express collusion in a market, and is therefore illegal under the antitrust laws.

6. T or F   All joint ventures are *per se* illegal under the antitrust laws.

7. General Motors Corp. is divided into four divisions, Pontiac, Oldsmobile, Buick, and Chevrolet. The vice presidents of the four divisions meet one day and agree 1) to use the same engines for all models of their automobiles; 2) to set the same prices for models of a particular size. As a result there is no price competition and much less product competition among the four divisions than there had been before. Should the conduct be governed by the *per se* rule? The rule of reason? Should it be legal or illegal?

III

MONOPOLIZATION, ATTEMPT TO MONOPOLIZE AND PREDATORY PRICING

Analysis

This chapter is concerned with single-firm conduct intended by the actor to preserve or create a monopoly position in some market. Conduct undertaken by a firm that is already a monopolist, designed to enable it to preserve its monopoly position, is called monopolization. The offense of attempt to monopolize is concerned with conduct designed to give monopoly power to a firm that is not yet a monopolist in the market in which the conduct occurred (although it may already be a monopolist in a different market). Predatory pricing is a complex offense often characterized by courts as an attempt to monopolize; however, the offense is in many ways more similar to substantive monopolization.

A.   SINGLE–FIRM MONOPOLIZATION

Section 2 of the Sherman Act condemns "every person who shall monopolize.... " The offense of monopolization is aimed most directly at the evil with which the antitrust laws have historically been concerned: persistent monopoly pricing by the dominant firm in a market.

1.   THE FORMULATION OF THE MONOPOLIZATION OFFENSE

a.   The Development of the Offense

Early cases brought under § 2 of the Sherman Act almost always involved defendants who had committed violations of § 1 of the Sherman Act as well. For example, Standard Oil Co. of N.J. v. U.S., 221 U.S. 1, 31 S.Ct. 502 (1911); and U.S. v. American Can Co., 230 Fed. 859 (D. Md. 1916), appeal dismissed, 256 U.S. 706, 41 S.Ct. 624 (1921), both involved allegations that the defendants were initially formed by the union of several competing firms; that they had bought up their rivals, sometimes closing their plants; and that they had entered into various covenants not to compete. As a result, initially there was no clear line of demarcation between the combination in restraint of trade and the offense of single-firm monopolization. *Even today it is well established that a § 1 violation by a firm with monopoly power is also a violation of § 2.*

In U.S. v. United Shoe Machinery Corp., 110 F.Supp. 295 (D.Mass.1953), affirmed per curiam, 347 U.S. 521, 74 S.Ct. 699 (1954), Judge Wyzanski suggested three approaches to the offense of monopolization:

(1)   That a dominant firm violated § 2 of the Sherman Act when it had engaged in unreasonable restraints of trade condemned under § 1 of the Sherman Act.

(2)   That a firm engages in illegal monopolization when "it (a) has the power to exclude competition, and (b) has exercised it, or has the power to exercise it." Judge Wyzanski interpreted this to mean that "it is a violation of § 2 for one having effective control of the market to use, or

plan to use, any exclusionary practice, even though it is not a technical restraint of trade" in violation of § 1.

(3) That "one who has acquired an overwhelming share of the market 'monopolizes' whenever he does business ... apparently even if there is no showing that his business involves any exclusionary practices."

Today Judge Wyzanski's first definition is clearly too narrow: one need not violate § 1 in order to violate § 2. His third definition is too broad. Although there have been many proposals for an offense of "no fault" monopolization—to be directed at a firm on the mere basis of its monopoly power—no such statute has ever been passed. Today, the modern offense of monopolization most resembles Judge Wyzanski's middle approach.

b.   The Modern Formulation of the Offense

In U.S. v. Grinnell Corp., 384 U.S. 563, 86 S.Ct. 1698 (1966), the Supreme Court defined the offense of monopolization as containing two elements: "(1) the possession of monopoly power in the relevant market and (2) the willful acquisition or maintenance of that power as distinguished from growth of development as a consequence of a superior product, business acumen, or historic accident." Before a defendant can be condemned of monopolization, both of these elements must be established. In 1985, in Aspen Skiing Co. v. Aspen Highlands Skiing Corp., 472 U.S. 585, 105 S.Ct. 2847 (1985), the Supreme Court once again stated this legal test for monopolization.

2.   MONOPOLY POWER IN A RELEVANT MARKET

In U.S. v. E.I. du Pont de Nemours & Co., 351 U.S. 377, 76 S.Ct. 994 (1956) the Supreme Court defined monopoly power as "the power to control prices or exclude competition." That definition is not particularly helpful, however, and is somewhat misleading. *Monopoly power is not itself an exclusionary practice: in fact, the exercise of such power—the sale of products at a monopoly price—generally attracts new sellers into the market.* Exclusion of competitors is not market power; however, it is an important means by which a firm obtains or maintains market power.

Further, monopoly power is not a function of absolute firm size. The offense of monopolization is not directed at absolute firm size, but rather at size in relation to some market. The only movie theatre in an isolated town may be a monopolist. However, Chrysler Corp., which is more than 1000 times bigger, is not. This is so because the movie theatre may have the power to make a profit by increasing its price above the competitive level, for its customers have few good alternatives. If Chrysler Corp. attempted to do the same thing it would immediately lose most of its sales to its (even larger) competitors.

Before a firm can be convicted of monopolization it must have monopoly power in a relevant market. "Market Power" is the power to reduce output and raise prices above marginal cost, and to make a profit by doing so. "Monopoly power" is simply a large amount of market power.

a.   Measuring Market Power Directly

As the discussion of monopoly above at chapter I.A. shows, the monopolist will make a profit by reducing output to less than the competitive level and raising price to higher than the competitive level. The competitive level is marginal cost. Theoretically, one could measure a firm's market power by computing the difference between its profit-maximizing price and its marginal cost at the profit-maximizing output rate. The larger that difference, the more market power the firm has. In fact, however, courts are not capable of determining marginal cost. Rather, they must find some suitable alternative mechanism for measuring a firm's market power. Theoretically, one might also measure monopoly power from large profits, but accounting profits—which is what most profit data measure—is not the same as economic profits, which are the difference between price and marginal cost. Today apparent high profits are generally regarded as rather poor evidence of monopoly power in all but a few extreme cases.

b.   The Market Share Proxy

The alternative method is to identify a "relevant market," which is a market *capable* of being monopolized. The relevant market consists of two parts: 1) a relevant product market; and 2) a relevant geographic market. *Once such a relevant market has been determined, the court then computes the defendant's share of that market. If the defendant's market share is high enough—generally 70% or more, although the percentage may sometimes be less—then the first element of the monopolization offense has been established.*

A helpful alternative definition of a relevant market is this: A relevant market is some grouping of sales such that, if those sales were made by a single firm, that firm would have the power to raise prices above the competitive level without losing so many sales that the price increase would be unprofitable.

c.   Measuring the Relevant Product Market

If a firm controls a large percentage of a relevant product market, the inference is strong that the firm has a certain amount of market power.

1)   Identifying the Relevant Product Market

Markets are not self-defining. For example, General Motors Corp. (GM) makes 1) 100% of the market for "General Motors Automobiles" (which includes Chevrolets, Pontiacs, Buicks, and Oldsmobiles); 2) 55% of the market for "domestically-manufactured automobiles"; 3) 12% of the market for "automobiles"; 4) 1.3% of the market for "vehicles." (The percentages are hypothetical.) Which of these is a "relevant market" for antitrust purposes? If it is the first, GM is certainly a monopolist. If it is the second, it is probably not a monopolist (although some courts have suggested that a jury could find that a firm with a 55% market share is a monopolist). If it is the third or the fourth, GM is certainly not a monopolist.

A relevant product market is the smallest product market for which 1) the elasticity of demand and 2) the elasticity of supply are sufficiently low that a firm with 100% of that market could profitably reduce output and increase price substantially above the competitive level. (Elasticities of demand and supply are discussed at chapter I.A. above.)

In order to assess the relevant market in this case we begin with the smallest hypothesized market, "General Motors Automobiles." What would happen if GM increased the price of its automobiles by, say, $1000 each? Most likely, two things:

1) Large numbers of customers would choose not to buy GM automobiles, and would look to other automobile manufacturers instead; and

2) other automobile manufacturers (Ford, Chrysler, American Motors, Toyota, Nissan, Honda and others) would respond by increasing their output in order to satisfy this new demand.

In that case "General Motors automobiles" is not a relevant market for antitrust purposes. First, the *elasticity of demand* is too high: in response to GM's unilateral price increase, too many customers would choose to buy automobiles from someone else. Second, the *elasticity of supply* is too high: in response to GM's price increase, other automobile manufacturers would be able to increase their own output as demand shifted to their brands. For example, suppose GM estimated that it must reduce automobile output by 30,000 units in order to clear the market at the increased price. (Remember, when the monopolist increases price, demand goes down.) However, if the other automobile manufacturers answered by increasing their own output by 30,000 units, total output of automobiles would remain the same. GM would be stuck with unfilled orders and a loss of market share, but no monopoly profits. The proposed relevant market of "General Motors automobiles" is too small.

Note: Most, but not all, courts have concluded that a single manufacturer's brand of some good cannot be a relevant product market. However, in Eastman Kodak Co. v. Image Technical Services, 504 U.S. 451, 112 S.Ct. 2072 (1992), the Supreme Court concluded that there could be a relevant market for replacement parts and service for Kodak's photocopiers, since purchasers of these machines were "locked in" to such replacement parts and service; *and* there was independent evidence of Kodak's power to increase the price of service and parts above the competitive level.

The next step is to repeat the process, this time using the next bigger plausible market. What would happen in the American passenger car market if a single firm produced all "domestically-manufactured automobiles" and attempted to increase price by $1000? Once again, many customers would probably try to substitute away to *imported* automobiles. Here, however, the movement may be a little slower than it was for the first proposed market. Some people may be committed to larger American cars and reluctant to buy imports. On the supply side the situation is also ambiguous. Importers would certainly try to increase their supplies to the American market, but they may have a hard time meeting the increased demand, or governmental restraints on imports may prevent them from doing so. The manufacturer of all "domestically-manufactured automobiles" might profitably impose at least *some* price increase to supracompetitive levels. In that case, a jury would probably be warranted in finding that "domestically-manufactured automobiles" is a relevant market.

2)   Computing the Market Share

Once such a relevant market has been determined, the defendant's share of the market must be determined. In this case GM does not manufacture all "domestically-manufactured automobiles," but only 55% of them. We have made out a very marginal case for GM's being a monopolist (on our hypothetical figures) of the market for domestically-manufactured automobiles.

If we used an even broader market, it would be much clearer that we had a relevant market for antitrust purposes. For example, if the proposed market were "automobiles," manufactured anywhere in the world, a single firm controlling such a market would almost certainly be able to get away with a very substantial price increase. On the demand side, many people would probably be willing to pay the price increase, rather than switch to alternatives—in this case, trucks, horses, kayaks or bicycles. On the supply side, some firms would probably try to enter the market for automobiles in response to the high profits being earned there; however, such entry would take a long time (perhaps ten years to design and build a plant and begin production of automobiles). The sole manufacturer of automobiles could earn monopoly profits this entire time.

"Automobiles" is certainly a relevant market for antitrust purposes. Unfortunately for the plaintiff or prosecutor, however, GM's share of the market for "automobiles" is only 12%. GM is not even close to being a monopolist of this market.

3)   Cross Elasticity of Demand

Estimating market power by defining a relevant market works only if we have some idea about 1) the extent to which customers will substitute away from the defendant's product in response to its price increase; and 2) the degree to which this substitution limits the defendant's ability to charge a monopoly price. Elasticity of demand for a product can be quantified mathematically, but the necessary information is generally not available to a court in a monopolization case. *The concept of cross elasticity of demand enables the court to compare two relatively tangible "products" and compare the rate at which customers turn to one in response to a price increase in the other.* In the preceding example we decided that "General Motors automobiles" was not a relevant market because the cross elasticity of demand between "General Motors automobiles" and "Ford automobiles" or "Chrysler automobiles" is very high.

a)   The *Cellophane* Fallacy

The concept of cross elasticity of demand can be misused, as it probably was in the Supreme Court's decision in U.S. v. E.I. du Pont de Nemours & Co., 351 U.S. 377, 76 S.Ct. 994 (1956). DuPont was alleged by the government to have a monopoly in the market for cellophane. However, the court ultimately concluded that the relevant market was not "cellophane" but rather "flexible packaging materials." Once the market was defined this broadly, DuPont's market share was too small to warrant a finding that it was a monopolist.

In reaching this conclusion the Supreme Court relied on the fact that at current market prices many other products were considered substitutes for cellophane, and the "competition" among these products was very strong. For example, it appeared that in response to a small increase in the price of cellophane, many bakers would switch from cellophane to opaque waxed paper. The Court concluded that the relevant market must include "products that have reasonable interchangeability for the purposes for which they are produced.... "

The DuPont *Court almost certainly erred, however, by making this assessment on the basis of customer choices at current market prices.* A moment's reflection about the monopolist's calculation of its profit-maximizing price should bear this out. When the monopolist charges its profit-maximizing price, it is trying to charge as high a price as it can without losing a substantial number of customers. In that case the cross elasticity of demand will appear high, not because the monopolist has no monopoly power, but because it is *already* charging a monopoly price.

> ***Example:***   Amos invented the Gizmo, which does everything that a Widget does, except it is cheaper to produce. Widgets cost $4.75 to produce, and they sell for that price in a competitive market. The cost of producing Gizmos is $2.90. However, Amos sells Gizmos at $4.70 and makes large monopoly profits. Amos is later charged with monopolizing the Gizmo market, in which his market

share is almost 100%. He defends by arguing that the relevant market is not "Gizmos," but rather "Gizmos plus Widgets," in which his market share is only 35%. As evidence of this fact, Amos points out that at current market prices the cross elasticity of demand between Gizmos (selling at $4.70) and Widgets (selling at $4.75) is very high. In fact, if he increased the price of Gizmos by 10 thousands of customers would turn from Gizmos to Widgets.

Clearly in this case the use of current market prices to evaluate cross elasticity of demand is wrong. The cross elasticity of demand between Gizmos and Widgets appears high, because Amos is *already* charging a monopoly price of $4.70, rather than a competitive price of $2.90, at which the cross elasticity of demand with widgets would not be very high at all.

b) The Usefulness of the Concept of Cross Elasticity of Demand
Unfortunately the fact that cross elasticity of demand in monopolization cases cannot be measured at current market prices is a major impediment to the use of the concept of cross elasticity of demand. *The relevant question is what would the cross elasticity of demand be if the monopolist were charging a competitive (marginal cost) price?* However, a court cannot measure marginal cost. The chief function of the concept of cross elasticity of demand in monopolization cases should be to remind us that close, technologically similar substitutes (where we can infer that the costs are similar) should be grouped into the relevant market. For example, we can infer that the cross elasticity of demand between "General Motors Automobiles" and "Ford Automobiles" is very high *and* that the two products have about the same production costs. This tells us more reliably that the two should be grouped into the same market.

4)   Measuring Elasticity of Supply

Elasticity of supply is the rate at which competitors or potential competitors will increase their output of a product in response to the alleged monopolist's price increase. If elasticity of supply is high, a firm has no market power. At the extreme, a firm who manufactures 100% of the world's widgets today may have no market power if, as soon as it attempts to charge a monopoly price, hundreds of other firms can instantly enter the widget market.

a)   Time of Entry

In measuring elasticity of supply it is important to consider two things: 1) whether other firms will be able to enter in response to the defendant firm's price increase; 2) the time that entry will take. If entry (construction of a plant, and development and marketing of a product) takes, say, ten years, the defendant firm will have a substantial time during which it will be able to earn monopoly profits.

b)   Measuring the Output/Capacity of Competitors

One of the most obvious sources of high elasticity of supply is the excess capacity of competitors. Competitive entry comes easiest and most quickly from other firms in the market who have unused plant capacity and can quickly put it into production. *As a result, the excess capacity of competing firms should always be included in the relevant market.*

Example: Total current demand for Zerks is 100,000 units per year. Of this Firm A produces 70,000 units and Firm B produces 30,000 units. Firm A has no monopoly power, however. The industry is depressed and each firm's plants are currently producing at one-third of their capacity. B has the capability of producing 90,000 units per year. Therefore, if A attempted to reduce production to, say, 40,000 units, in order to charge monopoly prices, B could respond by immediately increasing its own production by 30,000 units. The result is that total market output and market price would stay the same, and Firm A would simply lose a large part of its market share.

When market share is measured, the fraction should generally include the defendant's current output in the numerator, and the market's output in the denominator. However, if competitors have significant excess capacity, this fraction overstates the defendant market power. In extreme cases—where it is obvious that competitors can increase output very quickly and at per unit costs no higher than current costs—it may make sense to use total market *capacity* as the denominator.

Note: In U.S. v. Aluminum Co. of America, 148 F.2d 416 (2d Cir. 1945), Judge Hand was probably mistaken to include the amount of foreign aluminum actually *imported* into the United States rather than the entire production of the foreign firms who imported the aluminum. Hand noted that if Alcoa had raised its prices "more ingot would have been imported." Nevertheless, he included in the relevant market only the aluminum actually imported.

If foreign imports are governed by a quota, only the amount that can be legally imported, rather than the foreign importers' full output, should be included in the relevant market.

c)   Judicial Recognition of Elasticity of Supply

In some more recent cases courts have properly assessed elasticity of supply in estimating the relevant market. For example, in Telex Corp. v. IBM Corp., 510 F.2d 894 (10th Cir.1975), cert. dismissed, 423 U.S. 802, 96 S.Ct. 8 (1975), the court held that "IBM plug-compatible peripherals" (that is, peripheral products, such as disk drives, that could be plugged directly into IBM computers) was not a relevant market, because other manufacturers of peripheral products could quickly and cheaply change their peripherals into IBM plug-compatible peripherals.

d.   **Measuring the Relevant Geographic Market**

A relevant geographic market is some area in which a firm can increase its price without 1) large numbers of its customers immediately turning to alternative supply sources outside the area; or 2) producers outside the area quickly flooding the area with substitute products. *The best way to assess the size of the geographic market is to look at pricing behavior over a long period of time. If price in Area A consistently and quickly rises and falls in response to price changes in Area B, then the two areas should be grouped together in the same market.*

On the demand side many markets seem to be far smaller than they appear on the supply side, particularly if the demand side is retail. For example, grocery store customers typically will not drive outside their own city to purchase groceries, and many may drive only a few blocks. However, on the supply side, many grocery chains may be able to enter a new city quickly if the profits there are high enough. Since a relevant market is one for which *both* elasticity of demand and elasticity of supply are low, in this case the relevant geographic market should include some larger area that takes into account the degree to which grocery chains compete with each other by building new stores in new areas.

Example: The Supreme Court must have been looking at elasticity of supply in U.S. v. Grinnell Corp., 384 U.S. 563, 86 S.Ct. 1698 (1966), when it decided that the market for "accredited central station protective services" (burglar/fire/hazard protection employing wires connected from the protected building to a central monitoring station) was nationwide rather than local. On the demand side, a customer in, say, St. Louis could wire her building only to a station located in St. Louis. This would suggest dozens or even hundreds of citywide markets. On the supply side, however, it is possible that one firm could enter a city in response to another firm's charging of monopoly prices there.

Unfortunately, the court did not develop the facts to warrant such a finding. In finding a nationwide market it relied on the fact that the defendant set prices from a central office that served all its cities. This fact tells us nothing, however, about the firm's monopoly power. A firm might be a monopolist in one city and an intense competitor in another city, but nevertheless make its pricing decisions for both from a central corporate headquarters.

e. How Big a Share of the Relevant Market Is Required?

In the *Alcoa* (Aluminum Co. of America) case, cited above, Judge Hand concluded that a 90% market share would be enough to characterize a firm as a monopolist. He concluded that whether 60% or 64% is enough is "doubtful," and that 33% was certainly not enough. *Although the* Alcoa *case is now nearly fifty years old, Judge Hand's statement is still a fairly accurate statement of the market share requirements.* Courts consistently find market shares of 80%–90% and higher to be sufficient to conclude that the defendant is a monopolist. They also consistently find market shares of less than 50% to be insufficient. A majority of courts are reluctant to find sufficient monopoly power when the market share is less than 70%.

In all but the most extreme cases, the question of monopoly power is a question of fact, which in a jury trial will be answered by the jury. A few courts direct a verdict for the defendant on this issue if it is established that the defendant's market share is less than 50%. However, other courts have held that even in that case the jury is entitled to decide the issue.

f. Entry Barriers

If entry into a market is so easy that no firm could successfully charge monopoly prices for an extended period, then the market is not capable of being monopolized no matter how high the defendant's market share. See U.S. v. Syufy Enterprises, 903 F.2d 659 (9th Cir. 1990); Ball Memorial Hosp. v. Mutual Hosp. Ins., 784 F.2d 1325 (7th Cir. 1986). Measurement of entry barriers is difficult, but barriers are generally found to be low if (1) there has been frequent entry in the past; (2) the firm's productive assets are non-specialized, so they can be readily converted to other uses in the event of failure.

3. CONDUCT REQUIREMENTS

The law of monopolization contains two elements: 1) proof of the defendant's monopoly power; and 2) proof that the defendant engaged in an impermissible "exclusionary practice" designed to increase the amount or duration of its monopoly. Not all exclusionary conduct warrants condemnation of the monopolist, however. In fact, some such conduct is efficient and should be encouraged.

a. The Rule of Reason in Monopolization Cases

Ever since the Supreme Court's decision in Standard Oil Co. of N.J. v. U.S., 221 U.S. 1, 31 S.Ct. 502 (1911) monopolization cases have been governed by the rule of reason. The purpose of the rule of reason in monopolization cases is to enable the court to distinguish between efficient, or competitive, exclusionary conduct; and inefficient, or anticompetitive, exclusionary conduct.

1)   Injury to Competition and Injury to Competitors

Not all behavior that injures the monopolist's competitors is anticompetitive. In fact, efficiency itself—i.e., mechanisms by which the monopolist lowers its costs or delivers a better product at the same price—is highly "exclusionary" in that it makes life more difficult for competitors or potential competitors. The rule of reason must distinguish between injury to competitors, which is not to be condemned, and injury to competition, which is illegal. Injury to competition occurs when the monopolist's practices make it more difficult for competitors to enter or operate in the market *and* the practice does not improve the efficiency of the monopolist.

2)   Intent

The intent requirement in monopolization cases is so ambiguous that it is difficult to formulate. In *Alcoa* Judge Hand purported to "disregard any question of 'intent,' "concluding that intent could be presumed because "no monopolist monopolizes unconscious of what he is doing." In U.S. v. Grinnell Corp., 384 U.S. 563, 86 S.Ct. 1698 (1966), however, the Supreme Court defined the offense of monopolization to include "the willful acquisition or maintenance of [monopoly] power.... " That definition appears to require some showing of intent.

In Aspen Skiing Co. v. Aspen Highlands Skiing Corp., 472 U.S. 585, 105 S.Ct. 2847 (1985) the Supreme Court returned to an intent requirement more similar to the one stated by Judge Hand in *Alcoa*. The Supreme Court concluded that in monopolization cases "evidence of intent is merely relevant to the question whether the challenged conduct is fairly characterized as 'exclusionary' or 'anticompetitive'.... "

a)   Specific and General Intent

In antitrust cases courts have generally adhered to a distinction commonly used in criminal law between substantive offenses and attempt offenses. *Attempt* offenses require a *specific* intent to achieve a prohibited result. In such cases the result is not completed, and evidence of specific intent is necessary to show the anticipated consequences of the act. In cases involving completed monopolization, however, intent may be inferred from evidence that the firm had monopoly power and engaged in one or more prohibited exclusionary practices.

b)   Subjective and Objective Evidence of Intent

Subjective evidence is evidence such as statements or memoranda that indicate that the defendant consciously had a certain goal in mind. Objective evidence of intent is evidence that can be inferred from the defendant's conduct. *In monopolization cases, objective evidence of intent is sufficient, although subjective evidence of intent will certainly make the plaintiff's case stronger.*

For more on the problem of determining illegitimate intent in monopolization cases, see Hovenkamp § 6–4c.

b. Illustrative Exclusionary Practices

A large number of alleged exclusionary practices have been condemned by courts under § 2 of the Sherman Act, when the defendant satisfied the monopoly power requirements. The list that follows is not exhaustive, but it includes most of the important ones. Keep in mind that the list is both growing and shrinking. New exclusionary practices may be identified in future litigation. At the same time, however, practices once found to be exclusionary and anticompetitive have been subjected to later economic analysis and found to be competitive or harmless.

1) Predatory Pricing

Predatory pricing has been dealt with by most courts as an *attempt* to monopolize. For that reason it is discussed below at chapter III.C. As that discussion indicates, however, there are good reasons for considering predatory pricing to be part of the law of monopolization, rather than part of the law of attempt to monopolize. *Any practice that will support a charge of attempt to monopolize will also support a charge of illegal monopolization, provided that the defendant has monopoly power.*

2) Mergers to Monopoly

Courts have consistently held that a merger that creates a monopoly may be condemned as illegal monopolization. Such mergers are not really "exclusionary" practices. On the contrary, a prospective entrant's knowledge that it might be bought up would probably encourage it to enter the market. Nevertheless the case for condemnation is well established. Mergers that create monopolies can also be condemned as attempts to monopolize under § 2 of the Sherman Act, as combinations in restraint of trade under § 1 of the Sherman Act, and of course under § 7 of the Clayton Act.

3) Purchase and Shutdown of Rivals' Plants

Any purchase of a rival's plant would be treated as a merger today. *Historically, however, the purchase and shutdown of a rival's plant has been treated as illegal monopolization, particularly in the* Standard Oil *and* American Can *cases, both cited above.* The shutdown of the purchased plant effectively reduces market capacity. Once again, however, such a practice is literally not "exclusionary" but rather would seem calculated to invite new entrants to enter the market, unless the monopolist first engaged in predatory pricing and then purchased the victims' plants at very low prices.

4)   Expansion of Output or Capacity

In the Alcoa *case, cited above, Judge Hand held that Alcoa's expansion of capacity to meet anticipated increases in demand for aluminum was an "exclusionary" practice sufficient to warrant condemnation of a monopolist.* To be sure, increases in *output* are exclusionary: as the monopolist produces more, the market contains less room for the output of others. However, the monopolist does this only by giving up its monopoly profits. As it produces more, the market clearing price drops. Presumably the monopolist could exclude all rivals by charging a competitive price; but in the process it would give up its monopoly profits.

Expansion of capacity can be a different story. A monopolist in a market subject to economies of scale and having specialized plants can deter entry by building more capacity than it actually intends to use. The effect of the excess capacity is to deter rivals who know that the monopolist could respond to their entry attempts by immediately increasing output and dropping price. See Hovenkamp § 7.3.

5)   Price Discrimination

In U.S. v. United Shoe Machinery Co., 110 F.Supp. 295 (D.Mass.1953), affirmed per curiam, 347 U.S. 521, 74 S.Ct. 699 (1954) Judge Wyzanski identified price discrimination as an impermissible exclusionary practice. The defendant had charged a high lease rate for equipment in which it faced little competition, and a lower rate for equipment in which the competition was greater. Many monopolists operate in more than one market, and they may not have a monopoly in all of them. They naturally charge their profit-maximizing price for each individual product. Price discrimination may be exclusionary, but only if it results in increased total output by the monopolist. From a purely economic perspective it is difficult to justify condemning a monopolist merely for engaging in price discrimination. See Hovenkamp § 7.4.

6)   Vertical Integration

Ever since Eastman Kodak Co. of New York v. Southern Photo Materials Co., 273 U.S. 359, 47 S.Ct. 400 (1927), vertical integration has been held to be an impermissible exclusionary practice by the monopolist if it results in an extension of the scope or duration of the monopoly. However, recent courts have been skeptical about such claims, and several have permitted vertical integration by the monopolist. For example, Paschall v. Kansas City Star Co., 727 F.2d 692 (8th Cir.1984), en banc, cert. denied, 469 U.S. 872, 105

S.Ct. 222 (1984). The competitive consequences of vertical integration by the monopolist are discussed in chapter IV.A. below. *In most cases vertical integration is efficient, even if it is undertaken by the monopolist.*

7) Price and Supply "Squeezes"

Closely related to vertical integration is the price or supply "squeeze," by which the vertically integrated monopolist allegedly manipulates a market in order to injure vertically related firms.

> ***Example:*** In U.S. v. Aluminum Co. of America, 148 F.2d 416 (2d Cir.1945), Judge Hand found that Alcoa both fabricated its own raw aluminum (i.e., turned the raw aluminum into various products) and sold raw aluminum to independent fabricators. However, Alcoa allegedly sold the raw aluminum to the independent fabricators at a relatively high price, but priced fabricated aluminum products produced by its own internal fabricators at a low price. The first of these practices is known as the "supply" squeeze, and the second as the "price" squeeze. The result was to squeeze the independent firms between a high price for raw aluminum and a low market price. As a result, they earned a markup insufficient to give them reasonable profits.

Courts have usually condemned the price and supply squeezes by the monopolist when they have found them, most recently in Bonjorno v. Kaiser Alum. & Chem. Corp., 752 F.2d 802 (3d Cir.1984). Nevertheless, few explanations have been offered for what would motivate the monopolist to engage in such a practice or why it would be profitable. Presumably, if the monopolist wanted to drive the independent fabricators out of business, it could simply refuse to deal with them. Recently the First Circuit found a price squeeze unlikely in the electric power industry, given the presence of governmental regulation, and the likelihood that the alleged "squeeze" simply reflected the defendant's greater efficiency. Town of Concord v. Boston Edison Co., 915 F.2d 17 (1st Cir. 1990).

8) Tying Arrangements

Courts have frequently condemned tying arrangements by the monopolist, particularly when they have denied market access to competitors or vertically related firms. For example, if a monopoly manufacturer of photographic film ties processing by selling film and processing as a pre-priced package, film processors will have no business, for there is no independent supply of film. *Tying arrangements by the monopolist are usually condemned under the same test as that applied to tying arrangements in general.* See chapter V. below.

9) "Predatory" Research and Develpment; Failure to Predisclose

Many recent monopolization cases brought by private plaintiffs have contained allegations that the defendant engaged in "predatory" research and development (R & D), or used R & D in some other way to exclude competitors from the market.

As a basic premise, R & D is efficient and ought to be encouraged, even when it is accomplished by the monopolist. If R & D is ever "predatory" it would be only when the monopolist somehow innovated a product that was no better than earlier products, but which somehow undermined the market position of one or more competitors.

Example 1: This allegation was made in California Computer Products v. IBM Corp., 613 F.2d 727 (9th Cir.1979), where IBM was accused of replacing older computers which had externally attached memory devices with a new generation of computers containing internal memory devices. The result greatly injured independent manufacturers of memory devices, who formerly had been able to sell their own devices for attachment to IBM computers. At the same time, the trial court found that the new machines operated more quickly, took up less space, and were less expensive to manufacture than the older machines. *The court exonerated IBM, holding that any legal rule limiting the monopolist's right to engage in R & D and the introduction of new products would do great harm to technological progress.*

Example 2: C.R. Bard, Inc. v. M3 Sys., Inc., 157 F.3d 1340, 1371 (Fed. Cir. 1998), found a Sherman § 2 violation when a monopoly producer of a "gun" that took tissue samples for medical purposes re-designed it to that it would accept only its own disposable needles, and not the various unpatented needles of its rivals. The court stressed that the defendant's only purpose in redesigning their gun was to make competitors' needles incompatible. See Hovenkamp § 6.4b.

Competitors have also alleged that the monopolist's refusal to predisclose technology that was in the process of being developed and brought to market is an illegal exclusionary practice.

Example: In Berkey Photo, Inc. v. Eastman Kodak Co., 603 F.2d 263 (2d Cir.1979), cert. denied, 444 U.S. 1093, 100 S.Ct. 1061 (1980), the plaintiff alleged that Kodak violated the antitrust laws by secretly developing a new camera and a new film that worked only with each other, and then introducing them both on the market at the same time. The result was that it took the plaintiff many months to be prepared with either a camera or film that would compete with the new products. The plaintiff alleged that the monopolist, unlike the competitor, has a duty to tell competitors *in advance* what it is developing, and provide them with sufficient technical information so that they can bring competing products to market sooner. *The court dismissed this part of the complaint, holding that the monopolist just as much as anyone else is entitled to keep its R & D efforts secret.*

Both of the practices outlined above—the introduction of new products that destroy the business of a competitor, and the failure to predisclose new innovations, are literally "exclusionary"—that is, they make life more difficult for competitors and may even drive some competitors out of business. However, they are generally exclusionary because they are efficient. *Nothing injures a competitor more than an efficient practice which must be matched if the competitor is to survive. As a general rule, however, such practices should be legal.*

10) Patent "Abuse"

Courts have considered several types of charges that the monopolist has illegally used its position as a patent owner, or has acquired patents illegally. *First, the monopolist's tying of unpatented products to its patented product has frequently been condemned, both as illegal monopolization and under the law of tying arrangements.* Motion Picture Patents Co. v. Universal Film Manufacturing Co., 243 U.S. 502, 37 S.Ct. 416 (1917).

Enforcing a patent obtained by fraud has been held to violate § 2. Walker Process Equip., Inc. v. Food Machinery & Chemical Corp., 382 U.S. 172, 86 S.Ct. 347 (1965).

A monopolist's policy of accumulating all patents in its market area, thus making it much more difficult for other firms to compete, is generally held not to violate the antitrust laws. SCM Corp. v. Xerox Corp., 645 F.2d 1195 (2d Cir.1981), cert. denied, 455 U.S. 1016, 102 S.Ct. 1708 (1982); Automatic Radio Mfg. Co. v. Hazeltine Research, Inc., 339 U.S. 827, 70 S.Ct. 894 (1950): "The mere accumulation of patents, no matter how many, is not in and of itself illegal." *A few courts have condemned patent accumulation when the monopolist followed a policy of accumulating patents simply for the purpose of denying others access to the market, and did not make use of the patents itself. Even here, however, the basic rule is that mere nonuse of an acquired patent is not an antitrust violation.* Continental Paper Bag Co. v. Eastern Paper Bag Co., 210 U.S. 405, 28 S.Ct. 748 (1908).

Recently the Ninth Circuit held that a mere refusal to license a patent violated § 2 of the Sherman Act. Image Technical Services v. Eastman Kodak Co., 125 F.3d 1195 (9th Cir. 1997), cert. denied, ___ U.S. ___ 118

S.Ct. 1560, 140 L.Ed.2d 792 (1998). However, that decision is in apparent conflict with a provision of the Patent Act declaring that no patentee can be guilty of patent "misuse" because it sought to enforce those rights or refused to license. 35 U.S.C. § 271(d). Patent "misuse" is most often defined by antitrust principles, and something that is expressly permitted by the Patent Act is not an antitrust violation. Other courts have not followed the Ninth Circuit's *Kodak* decision.

Importantly, patent abuse is an *antitrust* violation only if reasonably calculated to create a monopoly, and the patent monopoly itself does not generally define a relevant antitrust market. Thus, for example, if someone is accused of acquiring or maintaining a patent monopoly of widgets by fraud, the accusation claims an antitrust violation only if widgets constitute a property defined relevant market. See, for example, Brunswick Corp. v. Riegel Textile Corp., 752 F.2d 261 (7th Cir. 1984), cert. denied, 472 U.S. 1018, 105 S.Ct. 3480 (1985).

11)   Raising Rivals' Costs

Sometimes a dominant rival may be able to create a "price umbrella" for itself by raising the costs of competitors. For example, if a dominant firm had a profit maximizing price of $5.00 per unit in the absence of competition, a rival that charged only $4.00 would limit the monopolist's price to $4.00 as well. The dominant firm might try to force the rival from the market, but it might also take some action calculated to raise the rival's costs so that its price went up and the monopolist could raise its own price accordingly. The court approved such a theory in Reazin v. Blue Cross and Blue Shield of Kansas, 899 F.2d 951 (10th Cir. 1990).

> ***Example:***   A dominant firm makes 100,000 widgets per year while its only rival makes 10,000 per year. The dominant firm engages in baseless patent litigation against the rival, and the litigation costs each firm $100,000 per year. For the dominant firm the cost of litigation is $1 per unit, but for the smaller rival the cost of the litigation is $10 per unit.

12)   Refusal to Deal With a Competitor

As a general rule no firm, not even a monopolist, has a duty to deal with a competitor—for example, by participating in a joint venture. *However, in Aspen Skiing Co. v. Aspen Highlands Skiing Corp., 472 U.S. 585, 105 S.Ct. 2847 (1985), the Supreme Court held that a monopolist's refusal to participate in a joint ticket-selling venture with a competitor could be considered by the jury as evidence of the monopolist's intent to exclude competition by improper means.* In this particular case the monopolist's refusal to participate in the sale of joint ski slope lift tickets with a competitor changed an existing distribution pattern to the detriment of the competitor. Furthermore, participation would have been profitable, in terms of increased consumer demand, to both the monopolist and the competitor. Refusal to participate was probably profitable to the monopolist only on the assumption that the refusal would cause the competitor to lose substantial market share to the monopolist, which was unable "to offer any efficiency justification whatever for its pattern of conduct." This, the Supreme Court held, justified the jury finding that the defendant was guilty of monopolization.

By the same token, the Supreme Court held in Eastman Kodak Co. v. Image Technical Services, 504 U.S. 451, 112 S.Ct. 2072 (1992), that Kodak's refusal to permit independent service companies to obtain replacement parts for its photocopiers (by tying its replacement parts to its own service contracts) could have been anticompetitive where Kodak's proferred business justifications seemed merely pretextual and the result of the tying requirement was a substantial increase in maintenance prices. The Court held that summary judgment for the defendant was improper, because Kodak may have been taking advantage of "captured" customers who had already purchased its photocopier machines, by forcing them to purchase high priced service from it as well.

13)   "Essential Facility" Doctrine

A dominant firm that controls a qualifying "essential facility" may have a duty to share the facility with a competitor. Exactly what constitutes an essential facility is unclear, but it is some productive asset that is essential to operation in some business and that cannot be duplicated. Further, refusal to share the facility must give the defendant a monopoly, which means that the facility must account for a dominant share of a properly defined relevant market. Alaska Airlines v. United Airlines, 948 F.2d 536 (9th Cir. 1991).

In Otter Tail Power Co. v. United States, 410 U.S. 366, 93 S.Ct. 1022, (1973) the Supreme Court applied the doctrine to hold that an electric utility must share its transmission facilities with smaller utilities. Fishman v. Estate of Wirtz, 807 F.2d 520 (7th Cir. 1986), held that a public sports stadium could be an essential facility. If the facility can be duplicated it is not essential. Further, most courts hold that the antitrust duty to share the facility extends to competitors, but not to vertically related firms. Finally, the dominant firm has no duty to share the facility if doing so will impair or undermine its own business.

Illinois, ex rel. Burris v. Panhandle Eastern Pipe Line Co., 935 F.2d 1469 (7th Cir. 1991).

Other illustrative exclusionary practices are discussed in Hovenkamp, § 7.1–7.13.

B.   ATTEMPT TO MONOPOLIZE

1.   THE COMMON LAW AND THE OFFENSE OF ATTEMPT TO MONOPOLIZE

Section 2 of the Sherman Act expressly condemns every "person who shall ... attempt to monopolize...." *As Justice Holmes developed the offense in Swift & Co. v. U.S., 196 U.S. 375, 25 S.Ct. 276 (1905), it includes three elements: 1) specific intent to control prices or eliminate competition in some market; 2) predatory or anticompetitive conduct directed at accomplishing this unlawful purpose; 3) a dangerous probability that the conduct, if permitted to run its course, would have created a monopoly.* The courts' statement of these three elements has not changed over the years. However, today individual circuit courts are in wide disagreement over how the elements should be interpreted. See Hovenkamp §§ 6.1–6.5.

2.   SPECIFIC INTENT

A business firm in competition naturally "intends" to injure its competitors. It would like nothing more than to do better than its rivals. Nevertheless, courts need evidence of intent in order to evaluate the purpose and likely effects of certain business conduct. *No one has ever developed a general rule for distinguishing legitimate from illegitimate intent to injure one's competitors.*

a.   The Problem of Identifying Illegitimate Intent

Much evidence of intent is consistent with both competition and attempted monopolization—for example, evidence that a firm lowered its price for a product, knowing that a rival firm would probably be driven from the market; or that a firm knew that its failure to predisclose a technical innovation it was developing would greatly injure a competitor.

The problem of identifying harmful intent is compounded by the fact that a business corporation has not one mind but several. Often middle ranking corporate officials produce memoranda which appear to reveal anticompetitive intent, but which may not represent the true policy of the corporation.

b.   Judicial Attempts to Define Illegitimate Intent

Courts that have tried to determine the kind of specific intent necessary for an illegal attempt to monopolize have generally defined it in two different ways:

(1)   Some say that the plaintiff must show the defendant's intent to achieve monopoly power, or to acquire sufficient power to control price.

(2)   Others say that the plaintiff must show the defendant's intent to exclude competition.

However, in U.S. v. Empire Gas Corp., 537 F.2d 296 (8th Cir.1976), cert. denied, 429 U.S. 1122, 97 S.Ct. 1158 (1977), the court concluded that the "mere intention ... to exclude competition ... is insufficient to establish specific intent to monopolize by some illegal means.... To conclude otherwise would contravene the very essence of a competitive marketplace, which is to prevail against all competitors."

The difficulty in distinguishing competitive from anticompetitive intent has operated to reduce the relative importance of the specific intent requirement in cases involving alleged attempts to monopolize. Many commentators have urged that the intent requirement be eliminated in attempt cases, particularly those involving predatory pricing. To date, however, no court has gone that far.

3. DANGEROUS PROBABILITY OF SUCCESS

A few courts once held that the dangerous probability requirement is unnecessary in attempt cases. However, in Spectrum Sports v. McQuillan, 506 U.S. 447, 113 S.Ct. 884, 122 L.Ed.2d 247 (1993), the Supreme Court affirmed the traditional view that (1) a dangerous probability of success must be established in any attempt to monopolize case; and (2) this requires a definition of a relevant product and geographic market in which the attempt is likely to succeed. In any event, the market share requirement is somewhat less than for monopolization. The purpose of the dangerous probability requirement is to help courts characterize ambiguous conduct that could be anticompetitive, but might also be quite competitive (such as aggressive innovation or pricing); such conduct cannot violate § 2 unless it is likely to create a monopoly in a well defined market. See Hovenkamp § 6.5.

a. The Purpose of the Dangerous Probability Requirement

The chief purpose of the "Dangerous Probability of Success" requirement in attempt cases is to help courts characterize ambiguous conduct that could be either competitive or anticompetitive. Ambiguous conduct is more likely to be condemned in markets that are conducive to monopolization, because in such markets the threat of monopoly is significantly greater than it is in competitive markets.

b. Dangerous Probability and Market Power

Today most courts hold that the dangerous probability requirement will not be met unless the defendant has a certain amount of market power. See, for example, Bright v. Moss Ambulance Service, Inc., 824 F.2d 819 (10th Cir. 1987). In any case, the market power requirement for the attempt offense is much less than it is for the offense of monopolization.

4. CONDUCT REQUIREMENTS

Generally, the offense of attempt to monopolize has narrower and more specific conduct requirements than the offense of monopolization. This is so because the defendant in the attempt case is generally not already a monopolist.

a. Basic Premises for Evaluating Conduct

When analyzing conduct in attempt litigation it is important to keep these three limitations in mind:

(1) The conduct, or planned or threatened conduct, must be capable of giving the defendant monopoly power.

(2) Conduct that is legal for someone who is already a monopolist is necessarily legal for someone who is not yet a monopolist.

(3) Sometimes efficient, socially beneficial conduct can create substantial market power.

b. Business Torts Distinguished

Many acts and practices, such as false advertising, misrepresentation, and various "dirty tricks" are illegal under state or federal law. *However, such actions, no matter how worthy of condemnation, are not attempts to monopolize unless they are capable of giving the defendant monopoly power.* The distinction is important because of the remedy structure in the antitrust laws. Most business torts yield the plaintiff single damages. An antitrust violation, however, yields treble damages plus attorneys fees.

C. PREDATORY PRICING AS AN ATTEMPT TO MONOPOLIZE

"Predatory Pricing" refers to a firm's attempt to drive a competitor out of business, or to discourage a potential competitor from entering the market, by selling its output at an "artificially" low price. Once the rival has been dispatched from the market, the predator will be able to reap monopoly profits which will more than pay for the losses incurred during the predatory period.

1. ANTITRUST POLICY AND THE PROBLEM OF PREDATORY PRICING

Low prices and high output are among the most important goals of the antitrust laws. In a predatory pricing case, however, a court must deal with the plaintiff's allegation that a price violates the antitrust laws because it is too low. *Often a price that is alleged to be "predatory" is a function of nothing more than the fact that the defendant is more efficient than its rivals.*

2. HOW OFTEN DOES PREDATORY PRICING OCCUR?

Courts once believed that predatory pricing was very common. As a result, they condemned it under tests that made it very easy to prove. For example, in such old monopolization cases as Standard Oil Co. of N.J. v. U.S., 221 U.S. 1, 31 S.Ct. 502 (1911), the Supreme Court required only the fact that the defendant "cut" prices in an area, with the intent to destroy its rivals. *Today, however, courts are inclined to believe that most price cutting is competitive rather than anticompetitive, and injuring one's rivals by selling at a low price is part of the competitive game.* Since 1975 only a few plaintiffs have won predatory pricing cases.

3. THE AREEDA–TURNER TEST FOR PREDATORY PRICING

In 1975 Areeda and Turner formulated an influential economic test for analyzing allegations of predatory pricing. *Since 1975 every circuit court that has addressed the issue has adopted some variation of the Areeda–Turner test, although many have changed important elements of the test. The Supreme Court has not as yet considered the Areeda–Turner test for predatory pricing.*

a. The Orthodox Formulation of the Areeda–Turner Test

Competition drives prices to marginal cost, although in many real world markets prices may stabilize at a point somewhat higher than marginal cost. (At this point, you might want to review the basic elements of price theory in chapter I.A. above.) If a firm has an opportunity to make an additional sale at a price lower than its marginal cost, it ordinarily will not do so, for it will lose money on the sale—i.e., the additional revenue produced by the sale will be less than the additional cost of producing and selling the additional unit. *For this reason, marginal cost pricing is absolutely consistent with competition. However, prices lower than marginal cost are not consistent with competition and must have some alternative explanation. A likely possibility is that the firm is charging a price lower than marginal cost today so that it can reap the benefits of monopoly pricing at some future time. As a basic premise, Areeda and Turner concluded that a price lower than marginal cost should be presumed to be predatory.*

1) The Average Variable Cost (AVC) Surrogate

Marginal cost is probably a good standard for determining whether a price is predatory. Unfortunately, courts are unable to measure marginal cost. For this reason Areeda & Turner argued that average variable cost should be used as a surrogate for marginal cost.

A firm's costs consist of two kinds, fixed and variable. Fixed costs are those costs such as amortization (e.g., mortgage payments) on the plant, investment in durable equipment, and other costs that do not change as the plant's output increases or decreases. Variable costs are costs such as utilities, wages, and raw materials that vary with output.

Example: When a wholesale bakery receives an order for an additional 1000 loaves of bread, it will incur additional costs in filling the order. It will have to purchase additional flour, yeast, salt and other ingredients. It may have to ask employees to work more hours, and pay them more wages. It will have higher utility bills, for it will run its ovens a longer time. All these are variable cost items. On the other hand, the bakery's invested cost in its plant, its property taxes, the salary of its president, and the cost of its durable equipment such as its ovens, probably will not change when it fills this additional order. These are fixed cost items.

Areeda and Turner proposed that AVC be used as a surrogate for marginal cost in predatory pricing, for these reasons:

(1)   In a competitive market in equilibrium marginal cost and average variable cost are often very close to one another, with marginal cost a little higher than AVC. See Hovenkamp § 8.2.

(2)   When a firm calculates its own "shutdown point"—i.e., the point at which it is no longer profitable to continue production—it uses AVC rather than marginal cost. See Hovenkamp § 8.2.

(3)   AVC is easier to measure than marginal cost. To measure AVC one merely sums the costs of all variable cost items and divides by the number of units produced.

2) The Basic Presumptions of the Areeda–Turner Test

Areeda and Turner conceded that there might be times when a price *higher* than AVC could be predatory—particularly if such a price was higher than AVC but lower than marginal cost. As a result, they concluded that a price higher than AVC should be *presumed* to be nonpredatory; however, in certain cases that presumption could be defeated. On the other hand, Areeda and Turner argued that any price above *average total cost* should be conclusively presumed to be legal. Average total cost is the sum of all costs, both variable and fixed, divided by output. Since a price higher than average total cost (sometimes called simply "average cost," or AC) covers *all* the firms cost, such a price is fully profitable. Areeda and Turner concluded that no fully profitable price should ever be condemned as predatory.

From this reasoning, Areeda and Turner drew the following conclusions:

(1)   A price above "full cost" (i.e., average total cost) is nonpredatory, and therefore legal.

(2)   A price at or above average variable cost is presumed to be nonpredatory, and therefore legal.

(3)   A price lower than average variable cost is *conclusively* presumed to be predatory, and therefore unlawful.

3) The Areeda–Turner Test and the Elements of the Attempt Offense

In dealing with the Areeda–Turner test as an attempt to monopolize, keep these things in mind:

(1) The average variable cost pricing test describes the *conduct* element of the attempt offense. The cost figures themselves say nothing about the "specific intent" or "dangerous probability of success" elements;

(2) Areeda and Turner virtually ignore *specific intent* as an element in predatory pricing. Their test looks only at market structure and at the relationship between the defendant's prices and its average variable costs.

(3) Areeda and Turner designed their test to apply to a "monopolist's ... pricing in the market in which he has monopoly power.... " That is, the Areeda–Turner test meets the "dangerous probability of success" requirement by requiring that the defendant *already* be a monopolist. The effect of this requirement is that the Areeda–Turner predatory pricing test might more appropriately be considered a text for the offense of substantive monopolization, rather than attempt to monopolize. However, many courts have ignored the requirement that the alleged predator must already be a monopolist (or at least a very dominant firm in the market) before the predatory period begins. Further, entry barriers into the market must be very substantial, or else the monopoly won by predation will last only a very short time, and predation will have been unprofitable.

b.   The Areeda–Turner Test in the Courts

Courts were initially enthusiastic about the Areeda–Turner predatory pricing test, and several circuit courts adopted it. E.g., Pacific Engineering & Prod. of Nevada v. Kerr–McGee Corp., 551 F.2d 790 (10th Cir.1977), cert. denied, 434 U.S. 879, 98 S.Ct. 234 (1977). In recent years, however, the test has become more controversial. *Nevertheless, all circuits have retained the basic Areeda–Turner AVC paradigm, although some have changed a few of the presumptions.*

Basically, the problems that courts have had with the Areeda–Turner test, and the solutions they have devised, are these:

1)   Computation of Average Variable Cost

In practice the AVC test has not been as easy to implement as Areeda and Turner originally implied, although nearly everyone agrees that AVC is still easier to determine than marginal cost is. One of the most serious problems facing courts is the difficulty of distinguishing between fixed and variable costs. Areeda and Turner initially attempted to solve this problem by proposing a categorical "laundry list" of costs that should be considered fixed, to be applied in all markets. Many courts have rejected this approach, however, and have decided that the decision whether a particular cost is fixed or variable must be made on a case-by-case basis. This approach was adopted by the Ninth Circuit in William Inglis & Sons Baking Co. v. ITT Continental Baking Co., Inc., 668 F.2d 1014 (9th Cir.1981), cert. denied, 459 U.S. 825, 103 S.Ct. 58 (1982).

2)   The Proper Role of Intent

Courts have expressed disagreement with Areeda's and Turner's attempt
to minimize or eliminate the specific intent requirement in predatory
pricing cases. Some, like the Ninth Circuit in the *Inglis* case, cited above,
have simply disagreed with Areeda and Turner and maintained a distinct
intent requirement. One of the results of this disagreement is that in the
Ninth Circuit all of Areeda's and Turner's presumptions are considered
rebuttable, with intent usually being the factor that can rebut them. Thus
in the Ninth Circuit a price lower than AVC is presumed to be predatory,
but the defendant can rebut the presumption by showing some
nonpredatory purpose for the low price.

3)   The Proper Response to "Limit" Pricing

Some courts have had difficulty with Areeda's and Turner's conclusion
that a price above average total cost is always nonpredatory. As they note,
a price might be higher than average total cost, but still could be much
lower than the monopolist's profit-maximizing price. (See the discussion of
the monopolist's profit-maximizing price at chapter I.A. above.) In such
cases the monopolist might be engaged in anticompetitive "limit"
pricing—i.e., charging a price that is fully profitable but that is
nevertheless low enough to discourage new entrants from competing. The
result might greatly extend the duration of the monopolist's monopoly.

The Ninth Circuit once responded to the possibility of "limit" pricing by
holding that a price above average total cost could be predatory.
Transamerica Computer Co. v. IBM Corp., 698 F.2d 1377 (9th Cir. 1983),
cert. denied, 464 U.S. 955, 104 S.Ct. 370 (1983). However, strongly
worded dicta in the Supreme Court's decision in Brooke Group Limited v.
Brown & Williamson Tobacco Co., 509 U.S. 209, 113 S.Ct. 2578 (1993),
indicate that predatory pricing can be established *only by proof of prices
below an appropriate measure of cost*. However, the Supreme Court did not
expressly embrace either the Areeda–Turner test or any other cost-based
test.

4.   "DANGEROUS PROBABILITY OF SUCCESS": WHEN IS PREDATORY PRICING PLAUSIBLE?

Predatory pricing is plausible only in markets that are conducive to the creation of
a monopoly by means of predatory pricing. Areeda and Turner were well aware of
this, and therefore made their test applicable only to a firm that is already a
monopolist. Some courts seem to be unaware of this fact. This is unfortunate,
because analysis of the plausibility of predatory pricing in a particular market is
often far simpler and more likely to be accurate than is analysis of the defendant's
prices and costs.

*Analysis of the following aspects of market structure is essential in predatory pricing
cases:*

a.   High Barriers to Entry

A barrier to entry is some factor in a market that makes it more expensive for new entrants to operate than for firms that are already established in the market. *Predatory pricing is not plausible in markets containing low entry barriers, because monopolization is not plausible in such markets. As soon as the predator drives out a rival and attempts to raise price to monopoly levels, the market will once again be flooded with new rivals who will add their output to that of the predator's and drive price back to the competitive level.* Some courts have held that predation simply cannot be proven unless entry barriers are high. American Academic Suppliers v. Beckley–Cardy, 922 F.2d 1317 (7th Cir. 1991).

b.   The Problem of Excess Capacity

Often in "declining industries" the demand for the product at a competitive price will be far less than the capacity of the industry to produce. When this happens, many firms in the market will be carrying excess capacity. Such a market will exhibit two important characteristics: 1) price will be driven down to unremunerative levels; 2) some firms may be driven from business. Such markets are often involved in predatory pricing litigation—bankrupt firms are quick to allege that they were driven from business by the predatory pricing of more successful rivals. The *Inglis* case, cited above, occurred in such a market.

Predatory pricing is implausible in such a market because the predator will not be able to reap monopoly profits. As soon as it attempts to raise price, rivals remaining in the market will increase their own output. Furthermore, when firms go out of business, more often than not their capacity is not retired from the market; it is merely transferred to another firm, perhaps in a bankruptcy sale. The predator cannot succeed in predatory pricing as long as remaining rivals hold substantial excess capacity.

c.   Predatory Pricing and the Nonmonopolist, Recoupment

As a general rule, only a firm with a very large market share can succeed in predatory pricing. This is so because the predator must pick up all the victim's lost sales, losing money on every one as long as the predation continues. For example, if a firm with a 30% market share attempted to drive its rivals out of business by predation, it would probably have to triple its own output (incurring losses on each sale) simply to reduce its victims' sales by half. By contrast, if a market contained two rivals, one with a 90% market share and another with a 10% share, the dominant firm could steal *all* the smaller firms sales by increasing its own output only by 10% or so. (For the arithmetic of these propositions, see Hovenkamp § 6.10.)

Predatory pricing is so expensive that it is implausible in a competitive market containing several, relatively small rivals, unless they are acting in concert. As a general rule predatory pricing is a realistic pricing strategy only for a firm that is already dominant in a market, and which has a very large market share, perhaps exceeding 70% or so. In Cargill v. Monfort of Colo., 479 U.S. 104, 119 n. 15, 107 S.Ct. 484, 494 n. 15 (1986) the Supreme Court suggested in dicta that a 21% market share was so low as to make predation unlikely.

In Brooke Group Limited v. Brown & Williamson Tobacco Co., 509 U.S. 209, 113 S.Ct. 2578 (1993), the Supreme Court held that the plaintiff seeking to show unlawful predatory pricing under either the Sherman Act or the Robinson–Patman Act must prove the reasonable likelihood of profitable "recoupment." This means that the plaintiff must show that the when it cut its price the defendant had a reasonable expectation that its below cost price cut would be followed by a lengthy period of monopoly or oligopoly prices which, after discounting for the time value of the monies spent on predation, would be large enough to make the entire predation scheme profitable. Successful recoupment cannot occur unless entry barriers are high, and the defendant succeeds in creating a durable monopoly or oligopoly. See Hovenkamp, § 8.4.

D. PREDATORY PRICING UNDER THE ROBINSON–PATMAN ACT

Predatory pricing can also violate § 2 of the Clayton Act, which was amended in 1936 and is today called the Robinson–Patman Act. The Act forbids sales of the same product at two different prices under certain conditions. Robinson–Patman Act lawsuits based on a predatory pricing theory are called "primary-line" Robinson–Patman cases. So-called "secondary-line" Robinson–Patman cases, which make up most of Robinson–Patman litigation, are discussed in chapter X. below.

1. THE RECOUPMENT THEORY OF PREDATORY PRICING

The framers of § 2 of the Clayton Act in 1914 adhered to the "recoupment" theory of predatory pricing. Under that theory a predator that sold its product in many geographic areas could *subsidize* predatory pricing by raising its price in some areas in order to finance below-cost sales in the target area. The theory is generally implausible. A monopolist will naturally charge its profit-maximizing price in each market in which it makes sales. The firm that raises price in one area in order to finance below-cost sales somewhere else, will generally make *less* money in the former area rather than more, for it will be charging more than its profit-maximizing price. (See the discussion of the monopolist's determination of its profit-maximizing price at chapter I.A. above.)

2. THE EFFECT OF THE ROBINSON–PATMAN ACT

The Robinson–Patman Act may prevent a firm from charging its profit-maximizing price in each market. The firm will have to charge the same price in all markets. In that case the Act might operate to make predatory pricing either far more expensive, or else far easier to detect. The dominant firm that operated in many markets but wanted to engage in predatory pricing in only one would have two choices.

(1)   It could cut its price to the same level in all markets (in many of which it already had a monopoly). This would keep the firm in compliance with the Robinson–Patman Act, but it would make predatory pricing far more expensive, for the firm would suffer losses in all markets, not just the one in which it was attempting to get rid of a rival.

(2)   The firm could cut its price in only the predatory market; however, then it would be violating the Robinson–Patman Act. Furthermore, different prices charged for the same product in two different areas would be far easier to detect than predatory pricing under a complex price-cost test such as the Areeda–Turner test.

Unfortunately, the Robinson–Patman Act makes *competition on the merits* more expensive in exactly the same way that it makes predation more expensive. For example, a firm that operates in several markets and earns comfortable monopoly profits in one of them, may suddenly be faced with new competition in that market. It will be able to compete with the new rivals, however, *only by cutting prices in other markets at the same time.* The Robinson–Patman Act contains no mechanism for distinguishing a *competitive* price cut by a firm operating in multiple markets from a *predatory* price cut by such a firm.

As a result of this problem the Robinson–Patman Act has probably been used to condemn healthy competition by multi-market sellers far more often than it has been used to condemn predation.

Example: In Utah Pie Co. v. Continental Baking Co., 386 U.S. 685, 87 S.Ct. 1326 (1967) the Supreme Court condemned the pricing activities of three wholesale pie baking companies, Pet, Carnation, and Continental, that operated in several geographic markets. The companies were not in collusion. Their "victim" was a small company that operated in the Salt Lake City area. During the period involved in the litigation there was an intense price war in this area, and the three defendants sold pies at lower prices than they sold the same pies in other cities. However, the plaintiff-victim made a profit the entire time, and always had a market share larger than any of three defendants. The Supreme Court cited a "declining price structure" as evidence of predation. More likely the three defendants were stripping the plaintiff of its monopoly position. The Supreme Court almost certainly condemned hard competition on the merits, rather than predation.

3.   THE BROOKE GROUP REVISION OF ROBINSON–PATMAN ACT PREDATORY PRICING LAW

In its important decision in Brooke Group Limited v. Brown & Williamson Tobacco Co., 509 U.S. 209, 113 S.Ct. 2578 (1993), the Supreme Court refused to overrule *Utah Pie*, but it significantly rewrote the law of predatory pricing under the Robinson–Patman Act. The Supreme court held:

a. The concerns of predatory pricing under the Robinson–Patman Act are identical with the concerns under the Sherman Act. The one significant difference is that predatory pricing under the Sherman Act is unlawful when it threatens to maintain or create a single-firm monopoly. Predatory pricing under the Robinson–Patman Act can also be unlawful when it threatens to create or shore up an oligopoly. This difference is dictated by the use of "substantially lessen competition" in the language of the Robinson–Patman Act, rather than the "monopolize" language that § 2 of the Sherman Act uses.

b. A price cannot violate the primary-line provisions of the Robinson–Patman Act unless it is below an appropriate measure of cost; this test applies in both Sherman Act and Robinson–Patman Act cases.

c. In both Sherman Act and Robinson–Patman Act cases the plaintiff must also show that the rationale for the below cost pricing was a significant likelihood of post-predation "recoupment"—that is, that the unprofitable predation period would be followed by a lengthy period of oligopoly profits sufficient to make the entire predatory enterprise profitable, even after taking the time value of money into account. This will not occur unless there is a well disciplined oligopoly protected by high entry barriers.

See Hovenkamp § 8.8.

E.   CONSPIRACY TO MONOPOLIZE

In addition to monopolization and attempt to monopolize, § 2 of the Sherman Act condemns every "person who shall ... combine or conspire with any other person or persons, to monopolize.... " There are few cases that analyze this provision separately, for all conspiracies to monopolize are also conspiracies in restraint of trade, and usually can be more easily condemned under § 1 of the Sherman Act.

In general, the elements of the conspiracy offense are

(1) the existence of a combination or conspiracy among two or more participants;

(2) specific intent to monopolize some part of trade or commerce;

(3) some overt act carried out in furtherance of the conspiracy;

(4) an effect on interstate commerce.

U.S. v. Yellow Cab Co., 332 U.S. 218, 67 S.Ct. 1560 (1947).

Proof of conspiracy to monopolize does not require the plaintiff or prosecutor to show a "dangerous probability of success." The violation is established merely by the proof of an agreement, plus an overt act carried out in furtherance of the scheme. American Tobacco Co. v. U.S., 328 U.S. 781, 66 S.Ct. 1125 (1946).

F. REVIEW QUESTIONS

1. **T or F**   Any bad conduct that will support the offense of monopolization will also support the offense of attempt to monopolize.

2. **T or F**   It is legal for a firm to be a monopolist, provided that the firm does not engage in an impermissible exclusionary practice.

3. **T or F**   It is impossible to compute a relevant market accurately without considering elasticity of supply.

4. Why is market share used as a surrogate for market power in monopolization cases?

5. X Company is a monopolist in the market for widgets, which has been determined to be a relevant market. Over the years several people have developed patented processes for making products similar to widgets. X Company has always purchased these patent rights. It has seldom or never used the patents, and it has consistently refused to license to others the right to manufacture under the patents. Is X Company guilty of monopolization?

6. A market contains eight competitors of roughly equal size. The market has been in decline, and most of the firms have operated their plants at about 30% of full capacity. Few of the companies have earned a profit during this period and one firm, A, has actually made several sales at a price less than the cost of the raw materials contained in the product. Firm B, which is finally driven into bankruptcy, sues Firm A, alleging predatory pricing. Who should win? Why?

*

Analysis

A. INTRODUCTION: THE NATURE OF VERTICAL INTEGRATION

A firm is "vertically integrated" whenever it performs for itself some function that could otherwise be purchased in the marketplace. This definition should suggest that a firm does not have to be large in order to be vertically integrated. In fact, every firm is vertically integrated to some degree. The owner of an ice cream parlor who sweeps his own floors is vertically integrated, because there is a market for janitorial services where floor sweeping could be purchased from another firm.

1. THREE METHODS OF VERTICAL INTEGRATION AND WHY FIRMS CHOOSE THEM

A firm can integrate vertically in three different ways: (1) It can enter a new market on its own; (2) It can merge with another firm that carries on the vertically related activity; (3) It can enter into a long-term contract with another firm, covering the provision of a certain good or service.

Which of these routes to vertical integration a firm chooses depends on several factors.

a. The Nature of the Service or Product

If a product or service is fungible and cheaper for a firm to produce itself than to procure from others, it will likely produce that product or perform that service itself from the beginning—i.e., it will integrate vertically by new entry. For example, an ice cream parlor seeking to have its floors swept would be unlikely to acquire a janitorial firm (a vertical merger). More likely it would integrate vertically by new entry—in this case, by purchasing a broom and ordering an employee to spend a few minutes each day sweeping the floor. On the other hand, if the service or product is "brand specific" (i.e., customers have built up a loyalty to a particular brand) then a firm might profit by integrating by merger with an established firm that has obtained such brand recognition. For example, a petroleum refinery seeking retail outlets for its gasoline might well look for a chain of gasoline stations with which it can merge.

b. The Size of the Firms

Often vertical integration is profitable only for larger firms. For example, a single-store grocery operation would be unlikely to acquire its own dairy or vegetable farm. However, a nationwide grocery chain that owns hundreds of stores might acquire a going dairy business in order to provide its stores with milk and other dairy products. This is so because the vertical integration process is often subject to economies of scale—i.e., often large firms can save proportionately more money from integrating vertically than small firms can.

c.   The Applicable Antitrust Laws

The antitrust laws may influence a firm's decision about how to integrate. For example, it has frequently been suggested that aggressive enforcement of the law against vertical mergers has forced firms to integrate by new entry—i.e., by building their own vertically related facilities rather than by acquiring facilities that already exist. This means that if antitrust policy is not designed with efficiency considerations in mind, a firm may be forced to integrate in a relatively costly way (or not integrate at all) in order to avoid antitrust prosecution if it should integrate in the most efficient way.

2.   TWO FORMS OF VERTICAL INTEGRATION

a.   Ownership

Vertical integration by new entry or by vertical merger are the "closest" forms of vertical integration. Under them the owners of one production level become the owners of the second production level as well.

b.   Contract

Looser forms of vertical integration by long-term contract are very common as well. Under such contracts, the firms are owned and controlled separately, but they enter into long-term commitments of their resources to a particular, vertically-related contract partner. Although such contracts are market exchanges, they eliminate many of the uncertainties that attend frequent uses of the market. Franchise contracts and exclusive dealing contracts, both of which fall into this category, are discussed below in chapter V. Seller-reseller contracts containing various vertical price or nonprice restraints are also contracts of this kind. They are discussed in chapter VI.

3.   ANTITRUST TREATMENT OF THE FORMS OF VERTICAL INTEGRATION

Antitrust treatment of vertical integration varies greatly with the form of integration. *Vertical integration by new entry is of least concern to the antitrust laws, and is illegal if at all only when the primary firm (i.e., the firm as it existed before the integration) is a monopolist.* Many refusals to deal by the monopolist are merely instances when a monopolist integrates vertically and then stops selling to or purchasing from independent firms in the market into which the vertical integration occurred. *Such vertical integration by the monopolist by means of new entry was condemned by the Supreme Court in Eastman Kodak Co. of New York v. Southern Photo Materials Co., 273 U.S. 359, 47 S.Ct. 400 (1927). However, the trend in recent lower court cases has been to permit vertical integration, even by the monopolist, unless there is clear evidence that the monopolist is attempting to use the integration to create a barrier to entry, or to increase the scope or duration of its monopoly in some other way.* For example, Paschall v. Kansas City Star Co., 727 F.2d 692 (8th Cir.1984), en banc, cert. denied, 469 U.S. 872, 105 S.Ct. 222 (1984).

Traditionally, vertical integration by merger has been much more closely scrutinized by antitrust policy makers. Such vertical mergers are analyzed under the antimerger provisions of § 7 of the Clayton Act, or occasionally under § 1 of the Sherman Act. Vertical mergers are discussed later in this chapter.

Vertical integration by contract receives varying antitrust treatment, depending on the nature of the contractual arrangement. For example, vertical integration by exclusive dealing or franchise agreements (many of which include tying arrangements) are analyzed under § 1 of the Sherman Act and § 3 of the Clayton Act. Vertical price maintenance and vertical nonprice restraints are analyzed under § 1 of the Sherman Act.

4. FORWARD AND BACKWARD VERTICAL INTEGRATION

If a firm integrates into a market from which it would otherwise obtain some needed input, such as a raw material or business service, the integration is said to be "backward." The ice cream parlor that begins sweeping its own floors has vertically integrated in this direction. If a firm integrates in the direction of the final consumer the integration is said to be "forward." The petroleum refinery that purchases its own gasoline stations is integrating in this direction.

B. VERTICAL INTEGRATION, EFFICIENCY AND ANTITRUST POLICY

The best way to construct an appropriate antitrust policy toward vertical integration is to determine why firms do it. In most cases simple analysis reveals that firms integrate vertically not in order to become monopolists and earn monopoly profits, but rather to reduce their costs. In competitive markets these reduced costs will be passed on to the consumer. *This analysis suggests that most instances of vertical integration should be legal under the antitrust laws.*

1. VERTICAL INTEGRATION AND EFFICIENCY

Vertical integration can enable firms to save money in a wide variety of ways.

a. Production Cost Savings From Vertical Integration

Some cost savings that result from vertical integration are a result of savings in production costs, usually because the vertically integrated firm is able to take advantage of technologies unavailable to the firm that is not vertically integrated.

Example: The manufacturing of steel parts for building materials involves two distinct operations, steel production and steel rolling. The steel production process turns iron ore (plus other ingredients) into construction quality raw steel. The steel rolling process forms the raw steel into various shapes that will be used for building materials. Each of these processes involves a tremendous outlay for plant and equipment and is capable of supporting a very large business. Nevertheless, most often steel production and steel rolling are carried on by the same firm. This is so because a number of cost savings accrue to the firm that performs both of these functions together. If the steel were produced by one firm and rolled by another firm, the unrolled steel would have to be inventoried, sold and transported. In the process it would cool down. The cost of transporting steel is substantial, as are the costs of storing it and reheating it. It is far cheaper for steel to be rolled while it is still hot, in the same plant in which it was produced.

As the example suggests, such economies in production generally cannot be achieved by vertical merger, for the integration results from the fact that steel production and steel rolling are conducted in the same plant. A merger would result merely in two separate plants coming under the control of the same owner. The creation of an integrated steel production and rolling plant would probably have to occur by new entry.

b.   Transaction Cost Savings From Vertical Integration

Transaction costs are the costs of relying on the marketplace. *The potential for vertical integration to reduce transaction costs is far greater than its potential to reduce production costs.*

Use of the market is expensive. Negotiating, drafting contracts, trusting another party, and planning for sufficient supplies in a market containing many self-interested actors can be much riskier and more expensive than arranging for things internally.

Example: A manufacturer of televisions has designed a new television model that will be lighter and more durable than existing television designs. However, the television requires the mass production of a television tube, and the production process has yet to be designed. Formerly, this television manufacturer purchased its television tubes "off the shelf" from manufacturers of standard television tubes. However, no tube like the one needed for the new television has yet been produced. The television manufacturer attempts to contract with a tube manufacturer to develop a process for producing the new tubes, and then to produce a certain quantity of them.

The negotiation of this contract raises a number of problems. First, neither firm knows what the costs of developing the tube production process will be. If the television manufacturer gives the tube manufacturer a "cost-plus" contract (under which the tube manufacturer will receive its costs of developing the tube production process plus a certain percentage markup as profit), the tube manufacturer will have no incentive to keep costs low. On the contrary, if the development costs of the process are high, the amount of profit will be high too.

Alternatively, the television manufacturer might insist on a fixed bid for the development of the process, but permit an application for cost "overruns"—i.e., costs larger than those anticipated in the original bidding process. However, this places the television manufacturer in the position of a regulatory agency, monitoring all of the tube manufacturer's costs. Furthermore, it invites bidding tube manufacturers to submit artificially low bids in order to win the contract, in the knowledge that they can easily add in overruns at a later time.

If the television manufacturer insists on an absolutely "firm" bid—i.e., a bid for a contract in which the tube manufacturer is asked to assume all risks of unanticipated costs in the development of the production process—then the tube manufacturer will insist on a large risk premium and the bids will likely be high.

Finally, even assuming a suitable contract could be drafted and agreed to, the television manufacturer would still have to *trust* the tube manufacturer to comply with its terms (sometimes contract breaches are cheaper than performance). Furthermore, there is no guarantee that the tube manufacturer will not go bankrupt.

After considering all these problems and the risks that go with them, the television manufacturer may decide that it is cheaper to design and produce its own television tubes. Whether the television manufacturer decides to do this, depends on a number of empirical factors, such as economies of scale in tube manufacturing, the amount of trust that the television manufacturer has in the tube manufacturer, the relative expertise of the two firms in designing such manufacturing processes. In some cases the contract might be the preferred solution, all the above risks notwithstanding. In other cases the television manufacturer would be better off to produce its own tubes.

c. The Problem of Market Power Held by Other Firms

Often a firm will integrate vertically in order to avoid dealing with a monopolist or perhaps a cartel at a different level of production. *The vertically integrated firm always obtains the integrated inputs at the marginal cost of producing them, just as it would in perfect competition.* For example, if the television manufacturer in the previous example receives an order for 1000 televisions, the cost to the manufacturer will be the cost of producing the additional tubes if it is producing the tubes itself. If it must buy the tubes on the market, however, the cost will be the cost of producing the tubes, *plus* any additional markup that the tube seller might take because of its monopoly position.

A firm that is forced to deal with a monopolist or cartel can frequently save money by integrating vertically into the market level in which the monopolist or cartel is located. This rule applies to both backward and forward vertical integration.

Example: A shoe manufacturer has average costs of $20.00 per pair for shoes, and sells them at that price to shoe stores. In a competitive retail market the shoe stores would take a 25% markup and retail the shoes for $25.00 per pair. However, the shoe stores in one particular city appear to be engaged in price fixing (although the shoe manufacturer does not know for sure) because all of them are taking a 50% markup for shoes and selling them at $30.00 per pair. The result of this high markup is that the shoe manufacturer sells fewer shoes in this city than it otherwise would, and earns fewer profits. (Remember, when price goes up, the quantity demanded goes down.) The manufacturer might be much better off simply to open one or more of its own shoe stores in this city. In that case the manufacturer could either sell the shoes at the competitive price, in which case the number of sales would increase. Alternatively, it could charge a price slightly under the price charged by other shoe stores. Then the manufacturer's output would not increase substantially; however, any monopoly profits would accrue to the manufacturer rather than to the independent shoe stores with whom it dealt previously.

For more on the use of vertical integration in order to avoid monopoly in vertically related markets, see Hovenkamp § 9.2.

d. Vertical Integration and Optimum Product Distribution

Firms often integrate vertically in order to distribute their product in a way that will maximize their sales or their profits. As the discussion below in chapter VI shows, firms frequently can market their products more efficiently if they control the location of resale outlets, the identity of the customers with whom a particular reseller deals, or perhaps even the price at which the product is resold. Often such restrictions force resellers to perform more efficiently. When it is legal and economically feasible, a firm might accomplish this kind of vertical integration by contract. For example, the contract might contain location clause restrictions under which a dealer agrees to resell the supplier's product only at a certain store. Vertical regulation of a reseller's *prices* is generally illegal *per se,* however. (See chapter VI.C. below.) As a result, a manufacturer that wants to regulate the prices at which its products are sold may have to acquire or build its own reseller outlets.

Example: Golden Arches, Inc., runs a nationwide chain of fast-food restaurants. These restaurants are recognized by travellers nationwide. As a result, people from faraway places often prefer to go to a Golden Arches restaurant, which they recognize, rather than an unknown local restaurant. This makes uniformity of product and service quality, and perhaps even of price, very important. Someone who goes to a Golden Arches restaurant in Phoenix, Arizona, expects it to be similar to the Golden Arches restaurant back home in Madison, Wisconsin. Golden Arches can achieve this uniformity by two different mechanisms of vertical integration. First, it could own all the restaurants itself. That way, the manager of each restaurant would be a Golden Arches employee, and the central office could make all decisions respecting food, service and price. Secondly, Golden Arches could enter into detailed franchise contracts with individual investors across the country. These contracts would essentially require, by means of elaborate specifications, that certain foods be on the menu, that they be prepared a certain way, and that the service be of a certain quality. *By using such a franchise agreement Golden Arches may be able to achieve its goal of substantial similarity of restaurants without having to make an enormous initial investment itself. Rather, the investment would be shared by many individual investors who want to become Golden Arches franchisees.*

2. PERCEIVED DANGERS TO COMPETITION FROM VERTICAL INTEGRATION

a. Increased Market Power

Increased market power is not a likely consequence of vertical integration, because the monopolist of any single distribution level can generally obtain all monopoly profits available in a given distribution chain. This is so because the profit-maximizing price of a product is generally determined by its final consumer demand.

> *Example:* Waffles, Inc., produces patented toasters at a cost of $15.00. The cost of retailing them is $5.00. In a competitive market the toasters would retail at a price of $20.00. Waffles has substantial market power in its particular toaster, however, and the profit-maximizing price for them is $28.00. If the retail market is competitive, Waffles will maximize its profits by wholesaling its toasters at a price of $23.00. The retailers will add a $5.00 markup, and the toasters will be sold at the profit-maximizing price of $28.00. *All* of the $8.00 in monopoly profits will go to Waffles. *Importantly, however, if Waffles would acquire its own retail outlets, the profit-maximizing price of its toasters would still be $28.00, and it would still earn $8.00 per toaster in monopoly profits.*

b. Barriers to Entry

Vertical integration can make it more difficult for new firms to enter a market. This will generally happen, however, only if the integrating firm has a very large share of the market. For example, if a monopolist aluminum manufacturer acquired all the independent aluminum fabricators, there would no longer be independent firms left at either production level. In that case any firm that wanted to enter either level would have to enter both levels simultaneously, or else it would have no one with which to deal.

Such integration creates a true barrier to entry, however, *only* if the need for two-level entry makes entry more expensive than it would be otherwise—perhaps by increasing the risk of entry. If new entry at both levels is just as inexpensive as independent entry by multiple firms, then the monopolist's high profits will continue to encourage new firms to enter the market.

c. **Price Discrimination**

Price discrimination occurs when a seller obtains two different rates of return on two different sales. Price discrimination can be very profitable, for it enables a firm to maximize its profits with respect to different groups of customers, rather than finding some "average" profit-maximizing price. Only a firm with a certain amount of market power can engage in price discrimination, for it will be earning monopoly profits from those groupings of sales in which its profits are highest. For more on price discrimination see chapter X below.

A firm can use vertical integration in order to facilitate price discrimination.

> ***Example:*** An aluminum monopolist knows that it faces two different demand curves in two different segments of the market for aluminum parts, automobile parts and aircraft parts. Automobile manufacturers like to use aluminum parts, but they can quite easily substitute parts made of steel or plastic. As a result they are quite sensitive to price increases in the aluminum market. However, airplane manufacturers absolutely need parts made of aluminum, because parts made of steel are too heavy, and parts made of plastic are not strong enough.

If the aluminum monopolist simply sold all its aluminum to independent, competitive fabricators (which make parts from raw aluminum), automobile parts and airplane parts would end up being sold for the same price per unit of aluminum they contained. Even though the airplane manufacturers value aluminum more highly than the automobile manufacturers do, competition among the fabricators would drive prices down to the price of aluminum plus the fabrication cost. Also the aluminum manufacturer would not be able to charge two different prices for the same raw aluminum—a lower price to automobile parts fabricators, and a higher price to airplane parts manufacturers. This plan would be frustrated by arbitrage: the automobile parts fabricators would resell their cheap aluminum to the airplane parts manufacturers. The aluminum monopolist would lose its monopoly profits.

The optimal solution in this case is for the aluminum monopolist to integrate vertically into the fabrication of *automobile* parts. It could then sell raw aluminum at the higher price to the fabricators of airplane parts. There would be no arbitrage, for the aluminum monopolist controls the automobile parts fabricators. It would make a high rate of return on the aluminum sold to airplane parts fabricators, and a lower but nevertheless profitable return on aluminum which it fabricated itself into automobile parts.

Whether vertical integration in order to price discriminate should be condemned under the antitrust laws is a difficult question. On the one hand, such price discrimination makes consumers as a group poorer and monopolists wealthier. On the other hand, price discrimination often increases the monopolist's output and may reduce the deadweight loss caused by monopoly. (See chapter X.A. below.) *As a general rule antitrust law today does not single out price discrimination as a particular reason for condemning vertical integration, except occasionally in the law of tying arrangements. (See chapter V. below.)*

d. Rate Regulation Avoidance

Price regulated firms can sometimes integrate vertically into unregulated markets in order to "cheat" on the regulatory scheme. For example, if an electric utility purchases a coal company and sells itself coal at an inflated price, it will make its monopoly profits in the coal, which is not price regulated, rather than in the delivery of the electric power. The higher price "paid" for the coal will show up in the utility's ledger as higher operating costs, and will be used to justify increased electric rates. For this reason it is important that utility regulators either prevent vertical integration into unregulated markets by price regulated firms, or else that regulators scrutinize carefully the internal transactions between a utility and its vertically related parent or subsidiary.

e. Vertical Integration by Cartels

As chapter II.A. above argues, sometimes cartel members will integrate vertically in order to discourage cheating on the cartel agreement. If the effect of vertical integration is that the cartel members' final output sales are small, and made at publicly announced and unnegotiated prices, then cheating on the cartel by a cartel member will be much more difficult.

C. VERTICAL MERGERS

The above discussion should suggest to you that vertical integration contains a much greater potential for efficiency and cost reductions than for monopolization. In fact, vertical integration is anticompetitive only when undertaken by a monopolist, or when it is used to facilitate rate regulation avoidance or cartelization.

Nevertheless, vertical integration has been treated harshly under the antitrust laws. The balance of this section deals with the law of vertical integration by merger. The subsequent two chapters discuss various forms of vertical integration by contract, including tying arrangements, exclusive dealing, and vertical price and nonprice restraints.

1. VERTICAL MERGERS IN THE CASE LAW

Before 1950 Vertical mergers were condemned only under § 1 of the Sherman Act. However, in 1950 § 7 of the Clayton Act was amended by the Celler–Kefauver Amendments to make clear that it covered vertical mergers as well as mergers of other kinds. *Today virtually all vertical mergers are analyzed under the provisions of § 7 of the Clayton Act, which condemns mergers whose effect "may be substantially to lessen competition, or to tend to create a monopoly."*

a. Subjective Intent and Pre–1950 Merger Law

Initially, the Supreme Court analyzed vertical mergers by looking at the "intent" of the acquiring party. If it found an intent to monopolize some part of trade or commerce, or to raise the price of a certain commodity or service, the merger was usually condemned. This was the rationale of U.S. v. Yellow Cab Co., 332 U.S. 218, 67 S.Ct. 1560 (1947), which eventually approved a taxicab manufacturer's acquisition of several taxicab operating companies, many of which were monopolists in their respective cities, because the defendant did not have the requisite anticompetitive intent.

> *Note:*   In the *Yellow Cab* case the defendant probably had one of two different motives for its acquisition of various taxicab operating companies. First, it might have been trying to acquire these monopoly companies in order to transfer their monopoly profits to itself. If the taxicab companies were monopolists (perhaps because they held municipal franchises that gave them legal protection from competition) but purchased taxicabs in a competitive manufacturing market, the taxicab manufacturers would earn only competitive profits. However, by acquiring the taxicab operating companies, a manufacturer could also acquire the taxicab operators' monopoly profits. A second possibility is that the taxicab companies were rate regulated and that the vertical acquisition was a rate regulation avoidance scheme. After the acquisition the manufacturer would transfer taxicabs to its operating company subsidiaries at an inflated price, which would then be used to justify higher taxicab fares.

b. The Law of Vertical Mergers Since 1950

1) The Foreclosure Theory

Since 1950 most judicial opinions condemning vertical mergers have relied on the "foreclosure" theory. Foreclosure occurs when vertical integration by one firm denies another firm access to a market. For example, if a monopoly manufacturer of widgets purchases sufficient retail outlets to sell its entire capacity, independent retail outlets will no longer be able to purchase widgets for resale.

True foreclosure really occurs only when one of the firms being integrated is a monopolist. For example, suppose that a market contains eight manufacturers and ten retailers. One manufacturer acquires two of the retailers. There will probably be some realignment of buyers and sellers in the market, but no foreclosure will occur. There are still seven independent manufacturers and eight independent retailers remaining.

Nevertheless, the Supreme Court has condemned vertical mergers on the basis of low foreclosure percentages, sometimes as low as one or two percent, on a "domino" theory. The theory is that if the court should permit a merger today that forecloses a relatively small percentage of the market, other similar mergers would occur until a large percentage of the firms in the market were vertically integrated. At that point some of the remaining independent firms might very well be foreclosed from the market. The basis for this domino theory is the "incipiency" test in § 7, which condemns mergers that "may" substantially lessen competition or "tend to" create a monopoly.

Example 1: This theory was applied by the Supreme Court in U.S. v. E.I. du Pont De Nemours & Co., 353 U.S. 586, 77 S.Ct. 872 (1957). The Court condemned du Pont's acquisition of 23% of the stock of General Motors Corp. du Pont produced fabrics and finishes, some of which were used for automobiles. General Motors produced automobiles. At the time General Motors produced about 50% of the nation's automobiles, and du Pont supplied about 67% of General Motors' requirements for automobile finishes. That suggested that about one-third (50% multiplied by 67%) of the market for automobile finishes was foreclosed.

(Note: The du Pont case had been brought in 1949, before § 7 of the Clayton Act had been amended to cover vertical mergers. Although the Supreme Court could not literally apply the amended statute, it applied the "policy" of the statute as amended. Today most people treat the case as a § 7 vertical merger case.)

Example 2: In Brown Shoe Co. v. U.S., 370 U.S. 294, 82 S.Ct. 1502 (1962), the Supreme Court went much further and condemned a merger between a shoe manufacturer and shoe retailer which foreclosed only 1% or 2% of the market. The Court relied heavily on the "incipiency" test and its "domino" theory of vertical mergers, holding that condemnation was warranted even on such low foreclosure percentages, because the market had exhibited a "trend" towards concentration and vertical integration.

In *Brown Shoe* the Court overlooked the fact that markets generally exhibit a trend toward vertical integration because vertical integration reduces the costs of operating in the market. As one firm integrates vertically and enjoys reduced costs, it will likely lower its prices and increase its market share. Other firms will be forced to follow suit or else face a loss of sales and profits. The market will then exhibit such a trend until it reaches a new equilibrium in which all firms are vertically integrated. The result of permitting such mergers to continue will be higher output and lower prices for consumers.

Recently, lower courts have been less likely to condemn mergers unless the foreclosure was sufficiently substantial to make it difficult for the remaining firms to find buyers or sellers. For example, Alberta Gas Chemicals v. E.I. du Pont De Nemours, 826 F.2d 1235 (3d Cir. 1987), cert. denied, 486 U.S. 1059, 108 S.Ct 2830 (1988).

2)   The Entry Barrier Theory

In Ford Motor Co. v. U.S., 405 U.S. 562, 92 S.Ct. 1142 (1972) the Supreme Court condemned an automobile manufacturer's acquisition of a spark plug manufacturer on the theory that the acquisition would raise a "barrier to entry" against new firms trying to enter spark plug manufacturing. After the acquisition such new entrants would not be able to compete for Ford's business, for Ford would be producing its own spark plugs.

Such an acquisition would generally raise a barrier to entry, however, *only* if integrated Ford could supply itself with spark plugs more cheaply than it could before the integration occurred. Otherwise, the existence of any unintegrated buyers looking for spark plugs should provide an incentive to new firms who want to fill that need.

Today vertical mergers are commonly analyzed under both the foreclosure and entry barrier theories. In both cases, today courts generally hold that the vertical acquisition is illegal if the transactions between the merging firms account for 15% or more of the market. High entry barriers in a particular market will generally warrant condemnation at somewhat lower percentages. Unfortunately, there is little consistency among the circuit courts, and they disagree widely over the relevant percentages. The Supreme Court has not decided a vertical merger case since the Ford Motor Co. decision cited above.

2.   VERTICAL MERGERS AND THE 1984 JUSTICE DEPARTMENT MERGER GUIDELINES

In 1984 the Department of Justice reissued Guidelines that discuss its merger enforcement policy. *The guidelines are not a restatement of the law, but merely reflect the Justice Department's enforcement position.* The Guidelines virtually abandon the foreclosure theory as a rationale for condemning vertical mergers. Furthermore, they give the impression that the Justice Department believes that most vertical acquisitions are efficient and should be legal. Indeed, since 1984, when the Guidelines were issued, the Department has not challenged a single vertical merger. Nevertheless, the Guidelines do cite three dangers to competition that might result from vertical acquisitions.

a. Increased Barriers to Entry

The 1984 Justice Department Guidelines cite increased barriers to entry as a competitive concern of vertical mergers. However, the theory is far more rigorous than the theory applied by the Supreme Court in the *Ford Motor Co.* case, discussed above. Before the Justice Department will challenge a vertical merger under an entry barrier theory the following must be true:

(1) Vertical integration in the market must already be so extensive that new entrants would have to enter two market levels simultaneously;

(2) There must be a showing that this need for two-level entry increases the risks, and therefore the costs, of new entry. If the costs of new entry are no higher than the cost of operation for incumbents, then the incumbents could not succeed in charging monopoly prices in the market. In that case the Justice Department will probably not challenge the merger.

Finally, the Justice Department notes that the existence of high entry barriers is not important in a market that is already competitive. If a market contains 99 vertically integrated firms, and the 100th firm becomes vertically integrated by merger, it does not matter whether the market has high entry barriers. The fact that the market contains 100 firms means that it will probably perform competitively. *The Justice Department will not challenge a vertical merger unless market concentration in one or more markets affected by the merger is very high, at least 1800 measured by the Herfindahl–Hirschman Index (HHI).*

> *Note:* The Herfindahl–Hirschman Index (HHI) is discussed below at chapter VIII.B. The HHI equals the sum of the squares of the market shares of all the firms in the market. A typical market with an HHI of 1800 might have firms with the following market shares: Firm A = 30%, Firm B = 20%, Firm C = 10%, Firm D = 10%, Firm E = 10%, Firm F = 10%, Firm G = 10%.

b. Vertical Mergers and Collusion

The Justice Department might also challenge a vertical merger if it is likely to facilitate collusion. Once again, however, this theory applies only in concentrated markets that are conducive to collusion. The Justice Department is not likely to challenge a merger on this theory unless concentration in the market in which the collusion might occur exceeds 1800 measured by the HHI.

c. Rate Regulation Avoidance

Finally, the Justice Department Merger Guidelines note that the Department may challenge a merger that will enable a price regulated firm to cheat on the rate regulation. However, even price regulated firms can achieve operating economies from vertical integration. Therefore the Department will challenge such mergers under this theory only if they provide "substantial opportunities for such abuses."

D. REVIEW QUESTIONS

1. **T or F**   Only large firms are vertically integrated.

2. How was the Supreme Court's decision respecting the vertical merger in *Brown Shoe* anticompetitive?

3. Why does vertical integration, particularly by merger, generally produce larger transaction cost savings than it does production cost savings?

4. Suppose you were a firm just beginning to manufacture bicycles. You need to decide whether to produce your own bicycle tires or buy them from a bicycle tire manufacturer. What factors would influence your decision?

V

TIE–INS, RECIPROCITY, EXCLUSIVE DEALING AND THE FRANCHISE CONTRACT

Analysis

A. INTRODUCTION

A tying arrangement, or tie-in, is a sale or lease of one product (the "tying" product) on the condition that the buyer or lessee take a second product (the "tied" product) as well. The law against tying arrangements covers any combination of sales or leases. Tying arrangements can be illegal either as contracts in restraint of trade under § 1 of the Sherman Act, or else under the more explicit provisions of § 3 of the Clayton Act, which prohibits the making of a lease, sale or contract for sale of goods or other commodities, whether patented or unpatented "on the condition, agreement or understanding that the lessee or purchaser thereof shall not use or deal in the goods ... of a competitor or competitors of the lessor or seller, where the effect ... may be to substantially lessen competition or tend to create a monopoly in any line of commerce." *The Clayton Act provision has been held not to apply to business "services," such as advertising, but only to commodities. As a result tying arrangements in service markets must generally be treated under § 1 of the Sherman Act.* See Times–Picayune Pub. Co. v. U.S., 345 U.S. 594, 73 S.Ct. 872 (1953).

B. JUDICIAL TESTS FOR THE ILLEGALITY OF TIE–INS

The United States Supreme Court has never articulated a complete test for tying arrangements. However, the various circuit courts have created their own tests. The verbal formulations of the tests differ from one circuit court to another. However, close inspection reveals that the tests are more-or-less similar. See Hovenkamp § 10.1. The most frequently cited test comes from the Ninth Circuit's decision in Siegel v. Chicken Delight, Inc., 448 F.2d 43 (9th Cir. 1971), cert. denied, 405 U.S. 955, 92 S.Ct. 1172 (1972):

First, ... the scheme in question involves two distinct items and provides that one (the tying product) may not be obtained unless the other (the tied product) is also purchased.

Second ... the tying product possesses sufficient economic power appreciably to restrain competition in the tied product market.

Third ... a "not insubstantial" amount of commerce is affected by the arrangement.

Some other circuits add the requirement of "anticompetitive effects in the tied product market." Others add an ambiguous "coercion" requirement, which is considered in section E.5 below.

C. THE AMBIGUOUS PROBLEM OF TIE–INS AND CONSUMER WELFARE

The law of tying arrangements is addressed to forced, combination or "package" sales. Congress obviously did not intend to condemn every forced combination sale. For example, sellers can still refuse to sell shoes unless the customer agrees to purchase a pair of them; they can still refuse to sell shirts without their buttons, bananas without their peels, belts without their buckles, and automobiles without their tires. Any law that required a seller to atomize each product to any degree demanded by every consumer would impose unimaginable costs on the market system.

The law of tying arrangements is concerned with the difficult problem of identifying "anticompetitive" forced package sales, while tolerating those that are not anticompetitive. In general, a practice is anticompetitive when it creates market power or facilitates the exercise of market power. Thus a properly defined law of tying arrangements should try to identify those instances when the tie-in results in reduced output, higher overall consumer prices, or both.

D.   TIE–INS, MARKET POWER, AND THE PER SE RULE

1.   THE DIFFERENCE BETWEEN THE SHERMAN ACT AND CLAYTON ACT TESTS

Because tying arrangements are analyzed under two different statutes (see section A above), they should perhaps be analyzed under two different legal standards. (However, for a contrary argument, see Hovenkamp § 10.3.) Justice Clark assumed as much in the *Times-Picayune* case, cited above. The Court held that a tying arrangement should be condemned under a *rule of reason* test under § 3 of the Clayton Act if it involved the forced combined sale of separate products, and the seller had *either* substantial market power in the tying product market *or* the tying arrangement affected a "not insubstantial" amount of commerce. (Note: sales of the tied product totaling $50,000 have been held by lower courts to satisfy this requirement; the Supreme Court has found sales totaling $60,800 to be sufficient. U.S. v. Loew's, Inc., 371 U.S. 38, 83 S.Ct. 97 (1962)).

However, the Court in *Times-Picayune* concluded that a tying arrangement could be condemned under the *per se* rule under § 1 of the Sherman Act if the plaintiff could show *both* market power in the tying product and a "not insubstantial" amount of commerce affected in the tied product market.

2.   THE CONSEQUENCES OF A TWO–FOLD TEST

The Court's analysis in the *Times-Picayune* case raised two unfortunate possibilities that have affected the legal analysis of tying arrangements ever since:

a.   Rule of Reason Ties in the Absence of Market Power

The Court's analysis suggested that a firm could be condemned of a rule of reason tying arrangement under the Clayton Act even though it had no market power in the market for the tying product. But how could a forced combination sale produce monopoly prices if the seller had no market power?

Suppose a perfect competitor in the shoe retailing market attempted to make more money by "tying" shoes and hose—each person who wishes to buy a pair of shoes must also take a package of three pair of hose. The seller intends to make monopoly profits from such a scheme by charging a higher-than-competitive price for the hose instead of the shoes. Clearly, the scheme will not work. Customers will treat the requirement that they buy the hose at a monopoly price as a price increase for the shoes themselves. Since the shoe seller is a competitor, they will go to a different shoe seller who does not force them to take the hose.

b. Per Se Illegal Tie-ins

The Court's analysis suggested that if a firm had sufficient market power in the tying product market and if the arrangement affected a "not insubstantial" amount of commerce in the market for the tied product, then the arrangement was *per se* illegal—that is, it would be condemned without further analysis, and without regard to any economic defenses that the defendant might raise. The Supreme Court justified such a rule in Northern Pacific Rwy. Co. v. U.S., 356 U.S. 1, 78 S.Ct. 514 (1958), holding that

> "tying agreements serve hardly any purpose beyond the suppression of competition.... " They deny competitors free access to the market for the tied product, not because the party imposing the tying requirements has a better product or a lower price but because of his power or leverage in another market. At the same time buyers are forced to forego their free choice between competing products.

However, such a rule overlooks the fact that even a monopolist might use tying arrangements for very efficient purposes. In fact, most tie-ins are efficient, whether or not the firm imposing them has market power in the market for the tying product. *In Jefferson Parish Hosp. Dist. No. 2 v. Hyde, 466 U.S. 2, 104 S.Ct. 1551 (1984), a bare majority of the Supreme Court (five justices) voted to preserve this "per se" rule for tying arrangements, while four concurring justices voted to abolish it.*

The Court appeared to adhere to the per se formulation in Eastman Kodak Co. v. Image Technical Services, 504 U.S. 451, 112 S.Ct. 2072 (1992). More controversially, the court held that sufficient market power could be inferred in the market for replacement parts for Kodak photocopiers, even though Kodak lacked market power in the market for the photocopiers themselves. The inference was warranted by evidence that Kodak was able to charge a higher price than competitors for the repair service and parts, was able to force some customers to switch to Kodak service even though they preferred not to, and because buyers of Kodak photocopiers were "locked in" to Kodak replacement parts. The Court refused to adopt for summary judgment purposes the proposition that competition in the market for the primary good (photocopiers) dictated that Kodak could not have sufficient market power in the market for replacement parts.

Most lower courts have read *Kodak* restrictively. For example, they hold that a buyer cannot be locked-in if he or she purchased the tying product and the tied product at the same time. In that case, one can see the high price of the tied product before the purchase of the tying product is made. Thus, for example, a computer purchaser cannot be said to be "locked-in" for *Kodak* purposes to the software that is pre-bundled on the new computer's hard drive. E.g., Digital Equip. Corp. v. Uniq Digital Tech., 73 F.3d 756 (7th Cir.1996). For this reason most courts hold that a franchise does not have market power in its tied products simply because the franchise contract permits the franchisor to charge any price it wishes: a reasonable franchisee would know what the contract permits at the time he or she entered the contract. See, e.g., Queen City Pizza v. Domino's Pizza, 124 F.3d 430 (3d Cir.), cert. denied, 118 S.Ct. 1385 (1998). Most courts also hold that there is no lock-in unless the seller changed its market policy after a large number of purchasers made the underlying investment. For example, a washing machine manufacturer might have a very large installed base of users and even be contemplating discontinuing that model. Then it triples its parts price, thereby taking advantage of those who cannot obtain parts from a different manufacturer. Finally, if the aftermarket parts are in fact made by multiple manufacturers, then there ordinarily can be no lock-in.

3. THE EMERGING UNITY OF THE SHERMAN ACT AND CLAYTON ACT TESTS

Although the two dimensional test created by Justice Clark in the *Times-Picayune* case has never been overruled by the Supreme Court, many lower courts virtually ignore it. *Today most lower courts apply a single test under both statutes that resembles Justice Clark's Sherman Act test and requires both market power and a significant amount of commerce in the tied product market.* Although some circuit courts have suggested that a tying arrangement can be established under the Clayton Act without a showing of the defendant's market power, no recent cases have condemned tie-ins when there was an express finding that the defendant had no market power in the tying product market. After the *Jefferson Parish* case, cited above, there are not likely to be any. See Hovenkamp, § 10.3.

> ***Note:*** The *per se* rule for tying arrangements is sometimes called a "soft core" per se rule, because tying arrangement litigation generally requires the plaintiff to define a relevant market and to demonstrate that the defendant has a certain amount of market power in that market. But courts have not assessed the same market power requirement in tying cases that they have in, say, monopolization cases. *In United States Steel Corp. v. Fortner Enterprises, Inc., 429 U.S. 610, 97 S.Ct. 861 (1977), the Supreme Court held that in Sherman Act tying cases the market power requirement must be taken seriously. Market power should not be inferred from the mere fact that the defendant's tying product (in this case, low cost financing, offered only to people who purchased its somewhat overpriced prefabricated homes) was "unique."*

In the Jefferson Parish *case, cited above, the Court went much further and held that a market share of 30% was insufficient to establish an illegal tying arrangement.*

4. MARKET POWER IN MARKETS FOR INTELLECTUAL PROPERTY

Courts generally presume market power in the market for the tying product when the product is patented or copyrighted. A few courts give the same presumption when the tying product is trademarked.

The result of these presumptions is that market power is often "found" where it probably does not exist, at least not in substantial amounts. In a world of diversified manufactured products (as opposed to fungible products like wheat and popcorn) many things are patented or copyrighted. Far from conferring market power on their owners, most patents do not even confer the power to produce the product and sell it at a profit. Likewise, any group of words or symbols can be copyrighted, provided that one is willing to file a copyright application and pay the fee. Automobiles, stereo equipment, home computers, watches, fast food franchises, clothing and canned food are all likely to be patented, trademarked or copyrighted. All are sold in at least moderately competitive markets. As a result, the economic case for this presumption is very weak, although some courts continue to recognize it. See, for example, Digidyne Corp. v. Data General Corp., 734 F.2d 1336 (9th Cir. 1984), cert. denied, 473 U.S. 908, 105 S.Ct. 3534 (1985) (recognizing the presumption for a copyright); Grappone v. Subaru of New England, 858 F.2d 792 (1st Cir. 1988) (refusing to recognize presumption).

E. WHY DO COURTS CONDEMN TIE–INS AND WHY DO FIRMS USE THEM?

The best way to determine the economic, or competitive, consequences of any practice is to analyze why firms engage in it. A firm generally employs a particular practice only if it predicts that the practice will be profitable. Profits can result from both increased efficiency and from increased market power. As a general rule, if a practice is profitable because it increases a firm's efficiency, the antitrust laws should not be concerned with it. However, if a practice is profitable because it increases a firm's market power, it presents an antitrust concern. Unfortunately, the courts have not done a particularly good job of analyzing why firms engage in the various types of tying arrangements.

1. THE LEVERAGE AND ENTRY BARRIER THEORIES

The leverage theory holds that tying arrangements are bad because monopolists use ties to "leverage" additional monopoly profits in a second market by means of forced combination sales. For example, in Carbice Corp. of Amer. v. American Patents Development Corp., 283 U.S. 27, 51 S.Ct. 334 (1931), the Supreme Court condemned a requirement assessed by the seller of patented ice boxes that purchasers take its dry ice as well. Justice Brandeis wrote for the majority that the practice was bad because it enabled the defendant to:

> derive its profit, not from the invention on which the law gives it a monopoly, but from the unpatented supplies with which it is used.... If a monopoly could be so expanded, the owner of a patent for a product might conceivably monopolize the commerce in a large part of the unpatented materials used in its manufacture. The owner of a patent for a machine might thereby secure a partial monopoly on the unpatented supplies consumed in its operation.

Under the leverage theory, the perceived evil of tying arrangements is twofold:

a.   Double Monopoly Profits

By creating two monopolies where there had been one, the seller can earn a double monopoly profit and force consumers to pay even more for products sold subject to a tie.

The theory is implausible. As the discussion of vertical integration in chapter IV. above shows, monopoly prices are determined at the final output level, and for each final product there is a single profit-maximizing price. *As a result, a monopolist who controls a single distributional level for a product can generally obtain all the monopoly profits available from that product. The same analysis applies to tying arrangements.*

Example: Suppose that bolts and nuts are used by consumers in pairs (one bolt and one nut). A bolt manufacturer has a monopoly in bolts, but nuts are sold in a competitive market. The cost (and competitive price) of bolts is 10 but they are sold for 16 which is the bolt manufacturer's profit-maximizing price. The cost of nuts is 7 which is also their price.

Suppose now that the monopoly bolt manufacturer attempts to make additional monopoly profits by tying bolts and nuts: anyone who purchases one of the monopolist's bolts must purchase one of its nuts as well. What will be the monopolist's profit-maximizing price for the nut-bolt package?

The answer, quite clearly, is 23¢ which is 16¢ for the bolt and 7¢ for the nut. This is so because the monopolist's calculation of its profit-maximizing price for bolts was *already based on the fact that consumers were buying nuts at 7¢.* Someone who buys both nuts and bolts together is generally indifferent as to how the price is divided between the two. She would attribute a 1increase in the price of the package to the bolt as well as the nut. As a result, *either* a bolt monopolist or a nut monopolist could extract all available monopoly profits from the sale of bolts and nuts.

A variation of the leverage theory might be plausible if the tied product market were cartelized. Suppose in the above example that the nut manufacturers are engaged in a cartel and are selling nuts at 11¢ instead of the competitive price of 7¢ In that case the bolt manufacturer is being injured, because the monopoly price for nuts lowers the profit-maximizing price for bolts. (Remember, the consumer is interested only in the price of the package.) The bolt monopolist in this case might be able to evade the cartel by selling its own bolts and nuts in a package, thus restoring all the available monopoly profits to itself.

In Eastman Kodak Co. v. Image Technical Services, 504 U.S. 451, 112 S.Ct. 2072 (1992), the Supreme Court gave some plausibility to one version of the leverage theory: that a firm could use a tying arrangement to take advantage of consumers that were "locked in" to its replacement parts by virtue of the fact that they had purchased the defendants durable equipment (in this case, photocopiers). The theory was apparently that, although the photocopier market was competitive, Kodak could earn monopoly profits by forcing buyers, once they were locked in, to purchase its service and replacement parts at supracompetitive prices.

b.   Barriers to Entry in the Tied Product Market

When the monopolist in one product ties a second product that is not monopolized, the monopolist effectively "monopolizes" the second product as well, and makes it very difficult for other sellers to sell the second product.

This is sometimes known as the "entry barrier" argument against tying arrangements. The theory is marginally more plausible than the double monopoly profit theory outlined above. *The theory holds that tying arrangements are bad because they may make it necessary for a prospective competitor in one of the products to enter the market for both products at the same time.* For example, if the monopoly bolt manufacturer described above forced all its customers to purchase its nuts as well, then anyone who wanted to enter the nut market would have to manufacture bolts too, or else purchasers of its nuts would not have a source for bolts.

The theory is subject to the criticism that the "barrier to entry" will not be created unless the tying arrangement itself reduces the firm's costs. If the integrated production and sale of nuts and bolts produces no cost savings, then two independent firms operating at each level would still be able to compete with the monopolist. However, if integrated production or sale is cheaper than separate production and sale, then the tying arrangement might create a "barrier to entry."

Example: Suppose it costs a distributor 10¢ to sell bolts and another distributor 7¢ to sell nuts, but because of efficiencies in marketing a single distributor can sell them in packages for 16¢. In that case the "tying arrangement" will create a barrier to entry. Anyone who wants to compete effectively with the combination distributor will have to sell the combination as well. As a general rule, however, barriers to entry are harmful to consumers only when they are inefficient.

The one place the entry barrier argument may work well is when the monopolist is protected by law from competition in its primary market. For example, for many years American Telephone & Telegraph Company forced lessees of its telephone lines to lease a telephone instrument from the company as well. Since A.T. & T. had a monopoly in the lines, the requirement effectively excluded everyone except Western Electric (A.T. & T.'s subsidiary for manufacturing telephones) from a very large market. See Hovenkamp, § 10.6b.

2. EVASION OF STATUTORY PRICE REGULATION

Price-regulated firms are required by law to sell their products at a price determined by a regulatory agency, often on the basis of cost information provided by the regulated firm itself. Local telephone companies, electric, gas and water utilities, some intrastate trucking and bus routes, certain cable television systems, taxicabs, and trash hauling by private firms are only a few of the many price regulated markets. The price regulator may be an agency of the federal, state or local governments.

Most (not all) price regulated firms are monopolists in their services areas. Furthermore, for most of them the unregulated profit-maximizing price is higher than the regulated price, i.e., the firm would likely charge more for its service if it were not price regulated. When that is not the case, then the rationale for price regulation may be hard to determine, since most price regulation is designed to prevent price "gouging" by natural monopolists.

A price regulated firm may be able to "cheat" on the statutory price regulation by tying an unregulated product to its regulated product or service.

> *Example:*   Suppose that a local telephone company, which is a monopolist in its service area, could maximize its profits by charging subscribers $15.00 per month for telephone service. However, its costs for that service are only $10.00, and the telephone regulatory agency holds the company to that rate. The company might be able to cheat on the price regulation by forcing all its customers to lease a telephone instrument from the company as well. The instrument has a fair market rental value of $2.00 per month; however, the telephone company charges the customer $7.00 per month. The result is that the telephone company picks up the $5.00 in monopoly profits it loses in the regulated market by means of an overcharge in a tied, unregulated market. Even though monopoly profits in the tied market are high, the telephone company need not worry about competitive entry, for it has a statutory monopoly.

For this reason it is important that regulatory agencies scrutinize carefully any unregulated markets in which price regulated firms do business. See Hovenkamp § 10.6c.

3.   TIE–INS AS PRICE DISCRIMINATION AND METERING DEVICES

Today it is well known that sellers use tying arrangements as price discrimination devices. Courts have now acknowledged this as well, although the discovery has not had much impact on the legal standard that judges apply in tie-in cases. In general, the competitive effects and the impact on consumers of price discrimination tying arrangements are ambiguous. However, there is some reason for thinking that price discrimination ties are efficient and should not be condemned under the antitrust laws.

a.   Price Discrimination

Price discrimination occurs when a seller makes different levels of profit from different buyers. (See chapter X. below). A monopolist can generally maximize its profit by charging each customer the most that particular customer is willing to pay for the product (i.e., the customer's reservation price). As a result, a monopolist capable of engaging in price discrimination can generally earn more than one who is not. However, there are both legal and practical barriers to price discrimination. The chief legal barrier is the Robinson–Patman Act, which prevents certain sales of the same product to different buyers at different prices, and thus reaches some kinds of price discrimination. The physical problems are that the seller must be able to *identify* different buyers who place different values on the product and then must prevent *arbitrage,* which occurs when buyers who obtain the product at a lower price resell it to other buyers at a slightly higher price.

Some sellers can solve both of these problems by means of variable proportion tying arrangements. A variable proportion tying arrangement is one in which different customers use the tied product in differing amounts. For example, some lessees of a photocopy machine may make 1000 copies per month, others may make 10,000 copies per month, and still others may make as many as 50,000 copies per month. It is generally a safe assumption that those who make the most copies place the highest value on the copy machine. In such a case the monopolist lessor of copy machines might be able to make more profits by tying copy paper to the lease of the copy machine, and charging a monopoly price for the paper.

Example: Zyrex Company builds and leases a patented copy machine which is efficient, reliable, and makes better copies than any other machine on the market. As a result, Zyrex has substantial market power in the copy machine market. In a competitive market the Zyrex machine would lease to customers for $100.00 a month. Zyrex's monopoly profit-maximizing price is $150.00 per month. Copy paper is unpatented and can be purchased in a competitive market for 2¢ per sheet.

Zyrex leases the machine for $100.00 per month, but requires all lessees to purchase their copy paper from Zyrex as well, at a price of 4¢ per sheet. As a result, Zyrex earns no monopoly profits on the machine, but it earns 2¢ in monopoly profits on each copy made by the machine. The small lessee who makes 1000 copies per month gives Zyrex $20.00 per month in monopoly profits. The medium-sized lessee who makes 10,000 copies per month gives Zyrex $200.00 in monopoly profits. The large lessee who makes 50,000 copies per month gives Zyrex $1000.00 per month in monopoly profits. Zyrex's net monopoly profits are far higher than they would be if it leased the machine to each user at its profit-maximizing price of $150.00 per month.

Is such price discrimination by means of a variable proportion tying arrangement bad? That question is difficult to answer. Unquestionably, the monopolist who uses such an arrangement can enlarge its profits; however, there is no policy in the antitrust laws opposed to high profits *per se*. It is also clear that *some* lessees of the copy machine end up paying more than they would have to pay if the lessor simply charged its profit-maximizing price for the machine. However, other lessees pay less, and some of these lessees would not have leased at all if the lessor had charged everyone its profit maximizing price. *In short, price discrimination tying arrangements can increase output. Whether they do so in any particular case is very difficult to say.* See Hovenkamp, § 10.6e.

Many well known Supreme Court cases almost certainly involved variable proportion tying arrangements used for price discrimination. One example is IBM Corp. v. U.S., 298 U.S. 131, 56 S.Ct. 701 (1936), in which the defendant tied paper computer cards to its leases of computing machines. Another example is Henry v. A.B. Dick Co., 224 U.S. 1, 32 S.Ct. 364 (1912). The defendant required purchasers of its mimeograph machines to purchase their supplies from the defendant as well.

Note: A tie-in case such as International Salt Co. v. U.S., 332 U.S. 392, 68 S.Ct. 12 (1947) would at first glance appear to be a case involving price discrimination. The defendant leased its salt injecting machines (for canned food) only to lessees who agreed to purchase the defendant's salt as well. However, the lessees were required to purchase the salt from the defendant only if the defendant was willing to match the prevailing market price. If a lessee was able to purchase salt cheaper elsewhere, he was free to do so. Since tying arrangements work as price discrimination devices *only* if the lessor can charge a monopoly price for the tied product, it is unlikely that the *International Salt* case involved price discrimination. In this case the tying arrangement was probably being used for the reason that the defendant argued; to make sure that only high quality salt, suitable for its machines, was used by the lessees.

b. Tie-ins as Metering Devices

Not all variable proportion tying arrangements are used for price discrimination. In some cases the lessor of a machine may have maintenance or use costs which vary with the intensity of the machine's use. The tying arrangement may be a good way of "metering" a machine's use, so that each lessee pays its own share of maintenance costs.

Example: Zyrex Company is in the business of leasing copying machines. Whether or not it is a monopolist, it has maintenance costs that vary with the intensity that the machine is used. The maintenance costs equal ½¢ per copy made on the machine. Zyrex rents the machines at a price that is not calculated to cover these variable maintenance costs. However, it requires each lessee to purchase all its copy paper from Zyrex at a price of 2½¢ which is ½¢ more than the competitive price. As a result, Zyrex earns the same rate of profit on each lessee, but each lessee is forced to pay the maintenance costs it actually imposes on the machine which it leases.

4. THE TWO–PRODUCT TEST

Most forced combination sales are the product of simple efficiency—that is, firms can reduce the costs of either manufacturing or distributing something by assembling it or selling it in combination with other things. This explains why most shoe stores refuse to sell shoes except in pairs. If they accommodated the occasional customer who wanted a solitary shoe—such as Captain Ahab—they would be stuck with the costs of ordering a new mate, returning the remaining shoe to the manufacturer, or holding it in inventory until Captain Ahab's mirror image came around to purchase it. Simple efficiency, and not the ability to earn monopoly profits, explains why automobiles are sold only with their tires, shirts only with their buttons, and bananas only with their peels.

a. A Shortcoming in the Judicial Test?

The judicial test for tying arrangements formulated in section A above rarely takes efficiency into account. This is unfortunate because it means that courts are never invited to consider the efficiency effects of a particular tying arrangement. The problem is exacerbated by the *per se* rule for tie-ins, which effectively tells the court that it may not consider efficiencies in its analysis. The result has been to mislead courts into condemning many tying arrangements that were in fact beneficial to consumers.

b. The "Separate Products" Requirement

A tying arrangement is not illegal unless it involves the forced combination sale of separate "tying" and "tied" products. The term "separate products" should be treated as a term of art for the purpose of tie-in analysis. Sometimes your common sense will tell you that two items (such as a right shoe and a left shoe, or a banana and its peel) should be considered a single product. But other times your common sense may not work so well.

One kind of analysis that makes good sense is to hold that two items are a single "product" for purposes of the law of tying arrangements when they are subject to certain economies of joint production or distribution that can be achieved only if all customers can be forced to take the entire package. The reason our "common sense" tells us that a right shoe and a left shoe constitute a single product (a pair of shoes) is that we are accustomed to buying shoes that way. The reason shoes are sold that way, however, is that it is much cheaper for shoes to be sold in pairs. First of all, almost everyone who buys shoes wants a pair. Secondly, pairs of shoes have to be matched with one another, and the costs of matching a solitary shoe could be high—a special order or a single return to the manufacturer might be necessary. *In this case, we would say that economies of distribution make it cheaper to serve shoes up in pairs; so a pair should be treated as a single product.*

The most frequently used test is that the tying item is a separate product if one observes it being sold separately under competitive market circumstances. For example, a new car and its tires are a single product, because one almost never sees new cars marketed without tires (Note: one looks at the tying item, not the tied item—tires are frequently sold without cars, but that is because tires have a shorter lifecycle).

Example: The Supreme Court implicitly recognized this efficiency element in the "separate product" requirement in Times–Picayune Pub. Co. v. U.S., 345 U.S. 594, 73 S.Ct. 872 (1953). The defendant newspaper publisher was accused of forcing buyers who wanted to advertise in one of its newspapers to advertise in the other one as well. One paper came out in the morning and the other in the evening. Justice Clark and the Court concluded that the relevant product in this case was "readership," and held that readership covered readers of both the morning and evening papers. However, Justice Clark was also impressed by the fact that when the sale of morning and evening advertising was combined into a single transaction many of the costs of advertising were reduced, including the costs of soliciting and billing and, most importantly, the costs of setting type. Under the joint advertising practice the morning and evening classified sections were identical and could be produced far more cheaply than if type for each were set separately. The result was that the *Times-Picayune could charge a much lower rate for advertising in the two papers together than the rate would have been for advertising in each paper separately.* See also Jack Walters & Sons Corp. v. Morton Bldg., Inc., 737 F.2d 698 (7th Cir. 1984) (identifying "economies of joint provision" as rationale for concluding that two things are a single "product.")

Note: Transaction-cost savings (i.e., a savings in the cost of using the market) is a likely explanation of the "block booking" arrangement condemned by the Supreme Court in U.S. v.

Loew's, Inc., 371 U.S. 38, 83 S.Ct. 97 (1962). The defendant was accused of licensing films to television stations only in blocks of multiple films, rather than separately. The rationale for "block booking," however, may be no more complicated than the reason a grocer might be unwilling to sell a single strawberry, but *will* sell them in quart boxes. The costs of negotiating contracts for the licensing of films may have been such that it was far more efficient to sell them in blocks.

Note:
Technological
ties:
Microsoft. Sometimes two items are tied together, not by a contract, but by technology. In United States v. Microsoft Corp., 147 F.3d 935 (D.C.Cir. 1998) the court concluded that Microsoft's Windows 95 operating system and its Internet Explorer browser were a single "product" for tying purposes because both functions and the computer code for the two was so interspersed that one would not work effectively without the other.

5. COERCION

"Coercion" is also a term of art in the law of tying arrangements. Today the word "coercion" is used in different ways at different times and by different circuit courts. The "coercion" issue may refer to the following:

(1) whether purchasers were actually forced to take the tied product as a condition of taking the tying product, or had the option of taking the tying product alone;

(2) whether the defendant-seller had market power in the market for the tying product;

(3) whether a particular purchaser would have taken the tied product anyway, and therefore was not injured by being "forced" to take it;

(4) whether the tie-in foreclosed other options that the customer would have exercised but for the tying arrangement.

a. Coercion as Conditioning

It seems clear that no tying arrangement should be illegal unless the seller actually *forces* the buyer to take an unwanted tied product as a condition of obtaining the tying product. As a general rule, that is true. However, establishing such "coercion" raises some evidentiary problems. For example, suppose a tying arrangement case is brought as a class action in which the class members are a large number of purchasers of the package alleged to be an illegal tie. Rule 23(b)(3) of the Federal Rules of Civil Procedure provides that a class action cannot be brought unless issues capable of being established by proof common to all class members "predominate" over issues that must be established separately. (See the discussion of class actions in chapter XI below.) In such cases, however, the defendant has generally dealt with each buyer individually and may have put different amounts of pressure on each to take the tied product. Some may simply have asked for the tied product at the same time they asked for the tying product; that is, the fact that they purchased the entire package is not good evidence that they were *forced* to purchase the package.

Some courts have held that such coercion will be inferred if there is a written contract that stipulates the purchase of both the tying and tied product. Does such a contract establish coercion, however? For example, does a contract to purchase "one thousand shadow boxes, with their mounting brackets" provide good evidence that the buyer was forced to take the mounting brackets as a condition of obtaining the shadow boxes? Probably not. It just as plausibly suggests that the buyer wanted both shadow boxes and mounting brackets. See Hovenkamp § 10.4.

> ***Note:*** The language of section 3 of the Clayton Act makes it clear that discounts or rebates given upon the condition that the buyer take the tied product are sufficient "coercion" to come under the statute. The same thing applies under the Sherman Act. If someone says "The price is $1.00 for each item if you buy them separately, but $1.50 for both if you take the two together," the requirement meets the basic "conditioning," or coercion, requirement for illegal tying arrangements.

b.   Other Meanings of "Coercion"

A few courts use the word "coercion" to refer to the fact that the defendant has market power in the market for the tying product. To be sure, a seller who had no market power in the tying product market could not "coerce" someone into taking an unwanted tied product. However, it is not necessarily true that a seller who *has* market power will coerce someone into taking something else. Market power establishes that the seller is *capable* of coercing the buyer into taking an unwanted tied product, but it does not establish that the defendant is actually engaging in illegal tying.

The third and fourth meanings of "coercion" cited above are closely related and look at the tying arrangement from the buyer's side rather than the seller's. Must the buyer show that it was forced to take something that it would not have taken anyway? Until the decision in Jefferson Parish Hosp. Dist. No. 2 v. Hyde, 466 U.S. 2, 104 S.Ct. 1551 (1984) the circuit courts were split on this requirement, with some explicitly assessing it and others explicitly rejecting it. In *Hyde*, however, the Court said that tying arrangements should be condemned when the defendant has sufficient market power "to force a purchaser to do something that he would not do in a competitive market." The statement is dicta; however, it is quite important in its context. In the case the

Court upheld an arrangement under which a hospital entered into an exclusive dealing contract with a particular anesthesiologist and required all users of its operation room facilities to use that anesthesiologist. The Court decided that the arrangement was not anticompetitive because there were several other hospitals in the market area. As a result, someone who wanted to use a different anesthesiologist than the one provided by the defendant could easily seek out an alternative hospital. *The Jefferson Parish case analysis appears to require "coercion" in this particular sense.*

c. Private Damages Actions and the "Coercion" Requirement

Today virtually all tying arrangement litigation is initiated by private plaintiffs, and in most cases they are seeking damages. If the plaintiff is a purchaser of the tied package, the damages will be equal to the "monopoly overcharge"—that is, the difference between the amount that the plaintiff was forced to pay for the tied package and the amount the plaintiff would have paid had the tying arrangement not been employed. In that case the plaintiff presumably would either not have purchased the tied product at all, or perhaps could have obtained it elsewhere at a lower price. Under the antitrust laws this difference will then be trebled. Whether or not a lower court assesses a "coercion" requirement, it seems clear that a plaintiff has not suffered monetary injury unless the tying arrangement has "coerced" it into doing something it would not have done anyway. If the evidence indicates that the plaintiff would have purchased the tied product from the defendant even if the defendant had not assessed the requirement that the plaintiff purchase it, then the plaintiff has not suffered monetary injury.

> ***Example:*** Aardvark Company sells trucks equipped with dealer installed radios. Shepherd Trucking purchases such trucks and never complains about the installed radios. Shepherd hears that Aardvark has been found guilty of engaging in illegal tying by forcing its truck customers to purchase radios with their trucks. Shepherd's attorney files an action against Aardvark, taking advantage of the principle of offensive collateral estoppel (see chapter XI.A. below) in order to collect damages. However, the jury finds that Shepherd has always purchased trucks with radios, even when a tying requirement was not assessed, and that it would have purchased the radios from Aardvark whether or not there was an illegal tying arrangement. Shepherd will not be able to collect damages from Aardvark.

F. TIE–INS AND THE FRANCHISE CONTRACT

A great deal of tie-in litigation, particularly during the last twenty years, has involved franchise contracts, particularly in the so-called "fast food" industry. In most such cases the plaintiff is a franchisee (or class of franchisees) and the defendant is the franchisor.

The gist of the complaint is generally that the franchisee was able to obtain a franchise (i.e., the right to do business under the name "Chicken Delight," or "McDonald's," or "Baskin–Robbins Ice Cream Co.") only on the condition that it purchase some additional item from the franchisor as well. This additional, tied item was usually essential food ingredients or the primary product sold by the franchise. Sometimes the tied item was a leasehold estate in the franchise store or restaurant. Initially plaintiffs won many of these cases, but in recent years they have tended to lose. See, for example, Principe v. McDonald's Corp., 631 F.2d 303 (4th Cir. 1980), cert. denied, 451 U.S. 970, 101 S.Ct. 2047 (1981). *The court held that it was not illegal for McDonald's Corp. to require all its franchisees to rent their McDonald's restaurant locations from the defendant at a rental rate based on gross sales volume.*

1. FRANCHISE TIES AND PRICE DISCRIMINATION

Most franchise tying arrangements are price discrimination devices which enable the franchisor to earn higher profits from successful, high volume franchisees than it does from relatively less successful franchisees. In almost all cases the tied product is something that varies with the number of sales that the franchisee makes. This is clearly true, for example, where the tied product is food or other things sold by the franchise outlet. It was also true in the *Principe* case cited above, where the rental rate for the "tied" leasehold was eight per cent of gross sales. Under such an arrangement the franchisor might charge only a nominal fee for the franchise itself (although sometimes the fee is quite large, particularly for very popular franchises). However, the tied product is sold at a high price. For example, in the *Principe* case it was conceded that the actual rent paid by highly successful McDonald's franchisees was generally far more than the fair market rental value of the locations that were being rented. The result was that the franchisor earned relatively low profits from relatively unsuccessful franchisees, and much higher profits from successful ones.

2. FRANCHISE TIES YIELD MORE FRANCHISE LOCATIONS

Most generally, the result of franchise tying arrangements is that more franchise outlets exist than if such arrangements or their equivalents were impossible. For example, if a highly successful franchisor, such as McDonald's or Baskin–Robbins (which "ties" its ice cream to the franchise contract) were required to charge all franchisees exactly the same fee, the profit-maximizing fee would likely be very large. In that case many "marginal" franchisees would not be able to obtain a franchise. However, even the marginal franchises are profitable to the franchisor. As a general rule, the costs to the franchisor of licensing one additional franchise are relatively small. Most of the initial investment is made by the franchisee. For this reason, virtually any franchise that is profitable to the operating franchisee will also be profitable to the franchisor. The tying arrangement price discrimination device enables the franchisor to set up all profitable franchises—not merely those that are so profitable that the franchisee would be able to afford a large, nondiscriminatory profit-maximizing franchise fee. See Hovenkamp § 10.6e.

3. FULL–LINE FORCING

Full-line forcing occurs when a franchisor or manufacturer requires the dealer to sell the full line of the former's products—for example, if an automobile manufacturer should require a car dealer to carry every model the manufacturer produces. Full-line forcing is generally analyzed under the rule of reason and is probably legal unless the supplier is found to have substantial market power. The trend is to treat full-line forcing under the law of nonprice restraints rather than the law of tying arrangements. See Southern Card & Novelty v. Lawson Mardon Label, 138 F.3d 869, (11th Cir. 1998) (lawful for maker of post cards to require stores to carry its full line).

G. RECIPROCITY

Reciprocity is closely related to tying. Economically, it is almost identical. *Reciprocity occurs when someone conditions the purchase of one product on the sale of another product, or vice versa. For example, "I will buy processed food from you only if you will buy food containers from me."* Like tying, reciprocity also applies to leases as well as sales.

Courts have generally analyzed reciprocity in the same way they have analyzed tying, and applied the same tests. In general, however, there is no operative "separate products" requirement for reciprocity as there is for tying arrangements. This is because there is no single tied "package," but only two different items moving in the market in opposite directions. The general test for illegal reciprocity is that the plaintiff must show that the defendant had market power in the market for one of the products, and refused to sell (buy) that product unless the other party agreed to sell (buy) something else in return. Some circuit courts hold that there are separate *per se* rules and rules of reason for reciprocity, just as there are for tying arrangements.

1. RECIPROCITY AND THE LEVERAGE THEORY

The leverage theory works no better for reciprocity than it does for tie-ins. Suppose that X has a market power in the market for a certain kind of processed food container. It also engages in a certain amount of food processing itself. The competitive price for its food containers is $1.00 each, but its profit-maximizing price is $1.40. Now X goes to Z, a food processor, and says "I will sell you my containers at $1.40 only if you sell me processed food at 20% less than the prevailing market price." Z will probably refuse the offer. Z will treat the low price sale of processed food to X as an increase in the price of containers. If Z's reservation price for the containers is $1.40, it will buy something else instead. X cannot "leverage" additional monopoly profits by means of reciprocity any more than he could by means of a tying arrangement.

2. RECIPROCITY AND PRICE DISCRIMINATION

In general, there is no business equivalent in reciprocity to the variable proportion, price discrimination tying arrangement described above. Nevertheless, reciprocity can facilitate certain kinds of price discrimination, particularly the kinds that might otherwise violate the Robinson–Patman Act.

Example: A seller has been selling cardboard packing boxes for $4.00 per dozen to a variety of customers. Suddenly she has a chance to make a very large sale to a large producer of cleaning solvent at a price of $3.50 per dozen. The sale is profitable and the seller would like to make it; however, the Robinson–Patman Act may prevent the sale at that price. (See the discussion of the Robinson–Patman Act in chapter X. below.) However, the seller also uses a great deal of cleaning solvent in her own business. She makes a deal with the cleaning solvent manufacturer. She will sell the boxes at the prevailing price of $4.00 per dozen; however, in return she will purchase a large quantity of cleaning solvent at a premium price, 10% above the prevailing market price. The net effect of the transaction is that the cleaning solvent manufacturer is in the same position it would have been in had it paid $3.50 for the boxes.

This particular instance of reciprocity is probably legal under the tests applied to tying arrangements and reciprocity, for the reciprocity is not "coercive" on the part of the seller of cardboard boxes. However, the reciprocity may be illegal *on the part of the cleaning solvent manufacturer,* if the manufacturer has sufficient market power and if the agreement can be construed as saying that the solvent manufacturer would purchase the boxes only if the box manufacturer would purchase the solvent in return.

3. RECIPROCITY AND CARTELS

Reciprocity can be used by a cartel member to "cheat" on the cartel. Because such a use of reciprocity tends to undermine the cartel, it is generally efficient.

Example: ABC Lumber Co. is engaged in a cartel of retail lumber products. However ABC can make additional profits if it can figure out ways to "cheat" on the cartel by making secret sales at a price lower than the cartel price. ABC Lumber Company also purchases a great deal of house paint, which it resells to customers. It strikes a deal with National Housing Products, Co., a large dealer in paint and lumber: ABC will sell National a large amount of lumber at the stipulated cartel price; however, in return ABC will purchase from National a large quantity of paint at a premium price. As a result of the transaction National effectively pays a lower price for the lumber than the price stipulated by the cartel.

H. EXCLUSIVE DEALING

An exclusive dealing arrangement is a contract under which a buyer promises to purchase all its requirements of a particular product from a particular seller. Exclusive dealing arrangements are analyzed under both § 1 of the Sherman Act and § 3 of the Clayton Act, as well as § 5 of the Federal Trade Commission Act.

The attitude of courts and the enforcement bureaus toward exclusive dealing has changed substantially over the years, and less of it is condemned today than used to be.

1. EXCLUSIVE DEALING AND THE FORECLOSURE AND ENTRY BARRIER THEORIES

Exclusive Dealing has traditionally been regarded as anticompetitive under the same "foreclosure" theory that the courts apply in cases involving vertical mergers. (See chapter IV. above.) The theory is that a long-term requirements, or exclusive dealing, contract "ties up" one or both levels of a market, so that remaining participants or potential entrants do not have adequate sources of supply or outlets. At the extreme, exclusive dealing might foreclose a market so much that one level of the market is made completely inaccessible to participants at the other level. This will generally occur only if one level of the market is controlled by a monopolist, or perhaps if it is controlled by a small number of firms and *all* of them engage in exclusive dealing.

Closely related to this foreclosure theory is an "entry barrier" theory—namely, that exclusive dealing makes it more difficult for new firms to enter a market, because all suitable trading partners have already committed their capacity to others.

Example: The retail market for garlic in a certain area is competitive. However, garlic is produced by three firms which pay close attention to each other's business. Each of the three firms signs an exclusive dealing contract with a particular retailer—producer A with retailer A, producer B with retailer B, and producer C with retailer C. The garlic retailers agree to purchase *all* their garlic needs from their respective suppliers. The result of the three contracts is that anyone who now wants to become a garlic producer may have a hard time finding outlets—the best retailers have already committed themselves to the established suppliers. On the other side, if the garlic suppliers have committed most of their capacity by means of exclusive dealing contracts, new entrants into the garlic retail business may have difficulty finding a source of supply. As a result, a firm that wants to enter the garlic market may have to enter both levels (garlic production and garlic retailing) simultaneously.

Some observations about this example are important to consider:

(a) If a market is competitive at both levels, then exclusive dealing cannot be anticompetitive. There will still be ample trading partners remaining at each market level. The only result of exclusive dealing contracts will be a certain amount of re-alignment of buyers and sellers in the market.

(b) Even if the market is monopolized at one level, it is not easy to see how the exclusive dealing arrangement will generate more monopoly pricing, or lower output, than would occur otherwise. First of all, a monopolist of any single distribution level is capable of earning all monopoly profits available from a particular distribution chain (disregarding the possibility for price discrimination, which is not easily achieved by exclusive dealing). As a result, it is difficult to see how additional monopoly profits might be earned, even assuming that the exclusive dealing forecloses some competitors or potential competitors.

(c) The exclusive dealing will likely act as a barrier to entry only if it reduces the costs of the firms engaged in exclusive dealing. If firms not engaged in exclusive dealing can operate just as efficiently, then individual entry at the two different market levels will still be quite possible.

(d) However, exclusive dealing in a situation in which one market level is monopolized (or subject to an oligopoly, as in the above situation) might injure consumers, not by increasing the monopoly price, but rather by delaying competitive entry. The result will be that the monopolist will be able to earn monopoly profits for a longer time. This is most likely to be the case if two-level market entry is riskier or more expensive than single level entry—for example if there are no firms that have experience at both levels. In that case providers of capital might ask for a risk premium that would make the cost of two level entry higher than the cost of entry at a single level. In any case, exclusive dealing will create a need for two level entry only if it is pervasive in a market—i.e., either one party to the exclusive dealing contract is a monopolist, or else virtually all firms in the market are using exclusive dealing contracts (perhaps because they are in a cartel and have used exclusive dealing in order to delay competitive entry).

2. EXCLUSIVE DEALING AND CARTELS

Exclusive Dealing can be used to facilitate collusion in certain markets. For example, collusion is often frustrated by well-informed, "disruptive" buyers who force cartel members to trade against one another for the buyer's business. The effect of exclusive dealing, however, will be to isolate buyers by assigning them to a single cartel member. The result is that each buyer will deal with only a single cartel member and the opportunity for such disruption will be considerably less. For this reason the participants in a cartel may be motivated to impose exclusive dealing contract on their buyers. Such a use of exclusive dealing is clearly inefficient.

3. EXCLUSIVE DEALING AND EFFICIENCY

A great deal of exclusive dealing is efficient—that is, it enables the participants in the exclusive dealing arrangement to lower certain costs of using the market. Since the result of such instances of exclusive dealing is lower prices for consumers, these uses of exclusive dealing should be legal. *Because exclusive dealing can be efficient it receives rule of reason treatment under the antitrust laws, and much of it is legal.*

a.   **Exclusive Dealing and the Costs of Using the Market**

Exclusive dealing arrangements can enable both buyers and suppliers to avoid many of the uncertainties that accompany use of the market. The result is a reduction in the risk that the buyer will not be able to find an adequate source of supply and that the seller will not be able to find suitable outlets. When risks are reduced costs are reduced, and eventually consumers will reap the benefits.

Example: A gasoline refiner believes it might be profitable to build a refinery in a certain area, but is not certain about what the market will be like. Perhaps other suppliers will build refineries; perhaps there will be long periods of slack demand in which gasoline dealers might be able to hold established refiners "captive"—i.e., take advantage of the fact that they have already built refineries which must be paid for, and must operate them in order to generate enough income to pay off the indebtedness. The refiner may decide that these risks are so great as to make the scheme unprofitable, unless the refiner is able to guarantee its market in advance. Therefore it goes into the market area and tries to obtain commitments from several gasoline dealers that they will purchase all their requirements of gasoline from the new refinery. On the dealer's side, this arrangement can also be beneficial: it gives the dealer a guaranteed source of supply in case there should be a shortage of gasoline in the area.

Note: In this situation the result of the exclusive dealing arrangements can be to *increase* output in the market. Because exclusive dealing is available, refiners will build refineries that they would not otherwise build. Alternatively, they might build larger refineries than they would otherwise build.

b.   **The Problem of "Interbrand Free Riding"**

The exclusive dealing arrangement can also solve the problem of "interbrand free riding," which occurs when a retailer is able to take advantage of amenities supplied by one manufacturer and give them to customers buying the goods of another manufacturer which the retailer also sells.

Example: A "split-pump" gasoline station sells the gasoline of two different refiners. One of them is a "full service" refiner such as Standard Oil Company. The other is a discounter who sells "generic" gasoline. Because of its relationship with Standard, the gasoline station operator receives many valuable amenities. Most importantly, he receives the right to display the "Standard" sign and insignia on his station, and thus takes advantage of the substantial brand name recognition and other goodwill that standard dealers enjoy. He may also receive from Standard such things as road maps, which he gives to customers, and, importantly, credit: customers who use a Standard Oil credit card essentially finance their purchase through money supplied by Standard Oil Company. However, suppose the retailer operates a set of pumps that sell "equally good" generic gasoline 4per gallon cheaper than the Standard brand. The customers will come in because they see the Standard sign and expect the Standard amenities. But they may buy the generic gasoline. In that case, Standard reaps no benefits from the expensive amenities which it provides. Standard will be highly motivated to solve this problem by entering into exclusive dealing contracts. It will contract with its authorized Standard dealers that in return for the right to display the Standard insignia and take advantage of the other amenities, they must sell Standard gasoline exclusively. Such a use of exclusive dealing is generally efficient. If such contracts were forbidden, the amenities would likely disappear.

4.   THE JUDICIAL TEST FOR EXCLUSIVE DEALING

The judicial test for exclusive dealing is predicated almost entirely on the foreclosure theory described above. In Standard Oil Co. v. U.S. (Standard Stations), 337 U.S. 293, 69 S.Ct. 1051 (1949) the Supreme Court adopted a rule that eventually became known as the "quantitative substantiality" test. As originally formulated, the test looked only at the percentage of the relevant market "foreclosed" by the exclusive dealing arrangement. In the *Standard Stations* case the Court condemned exclusive dealing contracts between Standard and its retail dealers covering gasoline and various accessories. The Court found that the Standard contracts foreclosed approximately 7% of the market; however, other major refiners also used the contracts, and collectively about 65% of the market was foreclosed by exclusive dealing. As a result, it would not be a fair statement of the *Standard Stations* case that 7% foreclosure by a *single* contract party is sufficient to warrant condemnation.

The court appeared to change its test to one of "qualitative substantiality" a decade later in Tampa Electric Co. v. Nashville Coal Co., 365 U.S. 320, 81 S.Ct. 623 (1961). First of all, the Court defined the market in such a way that the percentage foreclosed by an exclusive dealing contract covering coal to be supplied to an electric utility was less than 1%. However, rather than relying exclusively on that low percentage, the Court instructed that the general effect of the arrangement on competition must be considered as well. *Thus the Tampa case invited a more broadly based rule-of-reason analysis, which is generally what the lower courts do today.*

Today courts will look largely at the percentage of the market foreclosed by the arrangement. Generally, they will dismiss the complaint if that percentage is less than 15%. If it is greater than 15%, then the court will apply the Rule of Reason to look at other factors—the degree to which the contracts actually appear to be hindering new entry, the duration of the contracts (the longer, the more threatening to competition), and the number of other firms in the market who are also relying on exclusive dealing.

I. TIE–INS AND EXCLUSIVE DEALING UNDER THE JUSTICE DEPARTMENT VERTICAL RESTRAINTS GUIDELINES

In 1985 the Justice Department issued its Vertical Restraints Guidelines, declaring its enforcement policy with respect to vertical *non*-price restraints—including tying arrangements, exclusive dealing, and vertical territorial and customer division (which is discussed in the following chapter). These Guidelines have had little apparent influence on judicial decisions, although they may influence Justice Department decisions to prosecute. Further the Guidelines have been the subject of a great deal of criticism, much of it adverse. The criticism has focused on two issues: 1) the fact that the Guidelines appear to be a radical departure from existing case law; 2) the fact that over the last decade the Justice Department has not been a particularly active enforcer of the law governing vertical nonprice restraints.

The Vertical Restraints Guidelines begin with the premise that the vast majority of vertical restraints, including most tying arrangements and exclusive dealing contracts, are procompetitive. However, the Justice Department recognizes the following possible anticompetitive consequences:

(1)   Facilitation of Collusion;

(2)   Exclusion of Rivals from a Market;

(3) Rate Regulation Avoidance.

In any case, the Justice Department notes that the third of these applies only to price regulated industries. The first and second are likely to occur only in concentrated markets in which the restraints themselves cover a significant portion of sales in the market. The Guidelines then provide formulas for determining how market concentration and restraint coverage should be computed. These formulas, which apply equally to tying arrangements, exclusive dealing, and vertical nonprice restraints, are discussed in chapter VI.E. below.

J.   REVIEW QUESTIONS

1. **T or F**   Tying arrangements should all be condemned under the *per se* rule, because they have almost no redeeming value.

2. Explain the purpose of the market power requirement in tying arrangement cases.

3. **T or F**   The most socially harmful effect of tying arrangements is that they can enable a monopolist to earn additional monopoly profits in a second market, in which it does not really have a monopoly.

4. Baskin–Robbins Ice Cream Co. sells much of its ice cream through stores operated by independent store owners who are franchisees of Baskin–Robbins. Baskin–Robbins requires its stores to sell *only* ice cream that is provided by Baskin–Robbins. a) Is this requirement a tying arrangement or an exclusive dealing arrangement? b) Why might Baskin–Robbins want to use the arrangement? c) Does the arrangement make consumers better off or worse off? d) Should it be legal?

VI

RESALE PRICE MAINTENANCE AND VERTICAL NONPRICE RESTRAINTS

Analysis

A. INTRODUCTION

Resale price maintenance and vertical nonprice restraints are two kinds of contractual agreements between vertically related firms. The two kinds are sometimes collectively called "restrictions on distribution," because they both involve restrictions imposed by the upstream party (usually a manufacturer) on how the downstream party (usually a distributor or retailer) resells the merchandise covered by the agreement. Both kinds of restrictions are analyzed as contracts in restraint of trade under § 1 of the Sherman Act.

For the purposes of this chapter, the word "supplier" will refer to the upstream party. The words "dealer" or "retailer" will refer to the downstream party.

1. VERTICAL PRICE RESTRAINTS

Resale price maintenance (RPM) is supplier control of the price at which merchandise is resold by the dealer. Some RPM arrangements are much more explicit than others. At one extreme, RPM may involve a written contract including a term that the dealer, who is a party to the contract, must resell the supplier's merchandise at a price specified in the contract. At the other extreme, RPM may involve rather subtle coercion imposed by a supplier on its dealers or retailers. *In any case, since the Supreme Court decided Dr. Miles Medical Co. v. John D. Park & Sons Co., 220 U.S. 373, 31 S.Ct. 376 (1911) three-quarters of a century ago, resale price maintenance is per se illegal under the antitrust laws.* However, that rule is subject to numerous judicially created exceptions, which are discussed in section C below.

2. "FAIR TRADE"

During the period 1937–1975 Congressional enabling legislation authorized individual states to permit resale price maintenance within their borders. This practice, known as "fair trade," was adopted at one time or another by 46 different states. In 1975 Congress repealed the enabling legislation, finding that prices tended to be higher for fair traded merchandise in fair trade states than for the same merchandise in non fair trade states, where RPM was illegal *per se*. The result of the 1975 legislation (known as the Consumer Goods Pricing Act) was to restore the *per se* rule of *Dr. Miles* to resale price maintenance. *Today the fair trade era is largely of historical interest, except for one thing: the Consumer Goods Pricing Act which repealed fair trade has been interpreted as a mandate for the preservation of the per se rule for resale price maintenance.* In Continental T.V., Inc. v. GTE Sylvania, Inc., 433 U.S. 36, 97 S.Ct. 2549 (1977) the Supreme Court concluded that by repealing the fair trade enabling statute Congress "expressed its approval of a *per se* analysis of vertical price restrictions."

3. VERTICAL NONPRICE RESTRAINTS

The other kind of restriction on distribution is known as vertical *non*-price restraints. Such restraints involve supplier control of the location, sales territories or customers of its dealers. Vertical nonprice restraints can take a number of different forms.

a. Vertical Territorial Division

Vertical territorial division is supplier assignment of territories in which dealers are permitted to make sales. Vertical territorial division is frequently applied to wholesale distributors.

b. Location Clauses

Location clauses are supplier regulation of the locations of retailers' stores (although generally customers may come from anywhere).

c. Vertical Customer Division

Vertical customer division is supplier regulation of particular classes of customers to whom a particular dealer may sell. Like vertical territorial division, this kind of restriction is generally imposed on wholesalers.

d. "Air Tight" Restrictions

In some cases the restrictions described above are "air tight"—that is, the dealer is absolutely forbidden to make sales outside its assigned territory or with any customers not assigned to it.

e. Areas of Primary Responsibility

The alternative to "air tight" restrictions is "areas of primary responsibility," in which dealers are assigned a primary area for which they are chiefly responsible. However, in such cases dealers may be permitted to make sales in adjacent territories after they have done their best in their own assigned territories.

f. Exclusive and Nonexclusive Territories

Some territories are "exclusive," which means they are assigned to a single dealer; others may be shared by more than one dealer.

Vertical nonprice restraints come in an enormous variety. Different products are distributed in different ways, and sometimes even different manufacturers of the same product use different kinds of restrictions on distribution.

Since 1977, when the Sylvania *case was decided, vertical nonprice restraints cases have been decided under the rule of reason. Under that rule, only a tiny few have been found illegal.*

4. CONTROVERSY OVER ANTITRUST POLICY TOWARD VERTICAL RESTRICTIONS

Few areas of antitrust law have provoked more controversy than resale price maintenance and vertical nonprice restraints. In fact, in the last decade courts and commentators have made serious arguments for every possible liability rule for these two practices: *per se* illegality, rule of reason analysis, and *per se* legality. The reason for this great difference of opinion is twofold. First, historically neither Congress nor the courts has adequately explained exactly what is bad about these two practices—that is, whether they can result in monopoly pricing to consumers, or perhaps whether they should be condemned merely because they deprive dealers and retailers of the power to make individual decisions about how much to charge for a product and how and where to sell it. Secondly, economic analysis of vertical restrictions has been both fairly complex and fairly controversial. We still do not know all we should about the reasons that businesses engage in these two practices, and what their effects on competition might be.

5. TWO DIFFERENT RULES

Equally controversial today is the fact that the two practices are governed by two different legal rules—*per se* illegality for resale price maintenance and rule of reason analysis for vertical nonprice restraints. This situation is controversial for two reasons. 1) Most economists argue that the effects of the two practices are very similar, or perhaps even identical. This suggests that the two should be governed by the same liability standard. 2) In many complex real world distribution schemes it is not easy to determine whether a particular restraint is "price" or "nonprice." This fact injects a certain amount of arbitrariness into legal decisions.

Characterization of vertical restraints as "price" or "nonprice" has become particularly important because the effect of the rule of reason for nonprice restraints is that well over 90% of the litigated cases involving such restraints end up in judgments for the defendant. In short, once a particular restraint is characterized as "nonprice," that is often the end of the matter.

B. WHY DO SUPPLIERS USE RESTRICTIONS ON DISTRIBUTION?

In spite of the fact that different legal rules apply to resale price maintenance (RPM) and vertical nonprice restraints, the two kinds of restrictions are used for similar purposes and have similar effects in the marketplace. For that reason they are combined in most of this section on understanding the economics of restrictions on distribution. When you study this section make sure you understand that it is concerned with determining when vertical restrictions are harmful to competition. It is not concerned with determining when they are illegal under current antitrust law. As sections C & D below indicate, the law of vertical restrictions, particularly the law of resale price maintenance, frequently condemns restraints that have no adverse anticompetitive effects.

The best way to determine when vertical restrictions are anticompetitive and ought to be condemned under the antitrust laws is to figure out why suppliers use them. As a basic premise, a supplier will use such restrictions only if they are profitable—that is, if the supplier can earn more with the restrictions than without them. Restrictions could be profitable for one of two reasons:

(1) because they increase the efficiency of the distribution system and thus help the supplier lower its costs;

(2) because they increase the supplier's market power and enable it to earn monopoly profits.

An antitrust policy that attempts to maximize the welfare of consumers would try to approve restrictions that had the first effect, and condemn those that had the second effect.

1. VERTICAL RESTRICTIONS AND MARKET POWER

Unfortunately, it is not always easy to look at a particular vertical restriction and determine why a supplier uses it and what its effects might be. But there are a few factors that suggest anticompetitive potential. If none of these factors is present, we can assume that the restrictions are harmless.

The most important "danger signal" is the market power of the firm imposing the restrictions. A firm with market power has the ability to earn more money by reducing output and raising price. *Conversely, a firm without market power is unable to earn monopoly profits, and will not become able to do so by the simple device of imposing price or territorial restrictions on its dealers.*

Example: The market for potatoes is highly competitive, and they retail at a price of $1.50 per ten pound bag. If Farmer Brown attempts to charge $2.00 per bag through her own retail stand, she will lose all her potato customers. However, if Farmer Brown requires retail stores which she supplies to charge $2.00 per pound, *they* will lose all their sales and will find another potato supplier who does not impose the restriction. Likewise, if Farmer Brown imposes vertical territorial restrictions, by dealing with one store in each of three different towns, and permitting that store to sell potatoes only within that town, the stores will *still* not be able to charge more than $1.50 for Farmer Brown's potatoes. Although the stores are insulated from competition with *each other,* they are not insulated from competition with other sellers of potatoes in this highly competitive market. No matter what kind of restriction Farmer Brown imposes, the profit-maximizing price of potatoes will remain at $1.50.

2. VERTICAL RESTRICTIONS AND SUPPLIER COLLUSION

One important exception to the rule that vertical restrictions can be anticompetitive only when the firm imposing them has market power occurs when the restrictions are used to facilitate horizontal collusion. In this case, of course, there is market power, but it is being exercised by a group of firms rather than a single firm acting alone.

Vertical restrictions can often make a market more conducive to tacit or express collusion. For example, many cartels deal with large, well informed wholesale buyers and conduct secret, individualized transactions with prices and terms that vary from one sale to the next. Such a situation is highly conducive to cheating. For example, the OPEC oil cartel has had a difficult time maintaining its ability to fix prices. The cartel members could detect cheating much more effectively if their output prices were final, publicly announced, unnegotiated prices that could be easily verified. Resale price maintenance might enable a cartel to accomplish this goal. Once the cartel agreed to impose resale price maintenance at a stipulated price on all resellers, then the quantity to be sold by the cartel could be more easily fixed. No one could easily make money by making large secret sales at prices lower than those fixed by the cartel, because the goods would eventually have to be sold at the maintained price anyway, or else the sales would be detected. As a result, the incentives and opportunities for cheating by cartel members could be much less under such an RPM scheme.

Vertical territorial division can also facilitate collusion, particularly if the cartel is engaged in horizontal territorial division. In a territorial division scheme the participants agree not to make sales in one another's territories. However, retailers or distributors who purchase from the cartel members would still be able to sell anyplace they wanted, and this could frustrate the cartel's allocation of price and output. The cartel would operate much more efficiently if the resellers could be assigned to specific territories, all within the larger territory assigned by the cartel to that particular supplier.

> *Note:* Although both RPM and vertical nonprice restraints can be anticompetitive when they facilitate collusion, such a use leaves one obvious trail: all, or nearly all, of the suppliers in the market will be imposing similar restrictions. *That is, vertical restrictions are not likely being used as cartel facilitators unless all the firms in the cartel agree to use them.* Secondly, the cartel itself will not be successful unless it includes most of the firms in the cartelized market. In the great majority of litigated cases involving vertical restraints, the restraints were not widespread in the market. As a result, it seems that the restraints are not frequently used in order to facilitate supplier collusion.

3. VERTICAL RESTRICTIONS AND DEALER COLLUSION

Resale price maintenance might also be used to facilitate *dealer* collusion—that is, collusion among the retailers or distributors upon whom the vertical restrictions are imposed. For example, suppose that a group of retailers wanted to fix the price of widgets. One way they could enforce the cartel would be to involve the supplier, who would "impose" the cartel price upon them in a resale price maintenance agreement.

The supplier might be in a better position to enforce such an agreement than the retailers themselves. First of all, the supplier deals directly with each of the retailers, but they do not generally deal with each other, and it might be suspicious for them to do so. As a result, the supplier might be in a better position to determine whether cheating is occurring. Secondly, even though resale price maintenance is illegal *per se,* the rule has some exceptions. For example, if the supplier is able to avail itself of the *Colgate* exception (see section C. below), it will be able to impose RPM legally. The same rationale generally applies to vertical nonprice restraints. Although horizontal territorial division is illegal *per se,* vertical territorial division receives rule of reason treatment. Therefore the retailers would be better off if they could convince the supplier to "impose" vertical nonprice restraints on them.

This analysis is quite true as far as it goes, but it raises two significant problems:

a.   Market Power and "Intrabrand" Cartels

A retailer cartel such as that described above could take advantage of vertical restrictions imposed by a supplier only if: 1) all suppliers of the same product agreed to participate in the scheme; or 2) the supplier was a monopolist, or at least held a very large market share. Only in the latter case would an "intrabrand" cartel—i.e., a cartel composed only of retailers of a single brand—be effective.

> ***Example:***   Suppose that typewriters are manufactured and sold in a competitive market. All the retailers of Superior brand typewriters conspire to engage in price fixing, and they convince Superior, Inc., who manufactures the typewriters and wholesales them, to "impose" resale price maintenance on the retailers. The scheme will fail, because customers will respond to the cartel price increase by buying a different brand of typewriter. In order for the scheme to work the retailers will have to involve retailers of other typewriter brands in their cartel as well, and will have to convince the manufacturers of those brands to impose RPM on the retailers. Such an "interbrand" cartel—a cartel composed of sellers of all the brands of a particular product—could be facilitated by vertical restrictions only if all (or at least most) manufacturers as well as most retailers participated.

On the other hand, if Superior, Inc. were a monopolist, an intrabrand cartel could be quite successful.

In any case, vertical restrictions would be evidence of *retailer* collusion only if 1) the restrictions were in widespread use by all or nearly all manufacturers or suppliers in the market; or 2) the market was dominated by a single manufacturer.

b.   Why Would the Supplier Participate in a Dealer or Retailer Cartel?

The analysis above assumed that a supplier or manufacturer would be willing to participate in such a retailer cartel. In the vast majority of cases, however, it is very difficult to understand why the supplier would want to do so. The retailer's mark-up is a distribution cost to the manufacturer: the more profit the retailer makes from a particular product, the less profit will remain for the manufacturer. (Recall the discussion of the economics of vertical integration in chapter IV. above.) Any cartel in which the retailers participate would result in some profits being lost to the manufacturer: after all, the cartel profits themselves are going to the retailers, and the only thing accruing to the manufacturer is the reduced output that will result from the cartel.

Could the retailers bribe the manufacturer by offering to share some of their monopoly profits? Possibly, but not likely. Any monopoly profits capable of being earned by the cartel could also be earned by the manufacturer alone. As a result the manufacturer would not often have a motive for sharing them. *It seems unlikely that either RPM or vertical nonprice restraints are used very often in order to facilitate retailer cartels.* See Hovenkamp, § 11.2b.

4. CONTROL OF "FREE RIDER" PROBLEMS

Many vertical price and nonprice restraints are likely imposed in order to avoid "free rider" problems. *A free rider is a person who is able to take advantage of the services offered by someone else without paying for them.* Many services offered by retail stores cannot be sold by the piece, but rather are priced into the price of the product. As a result, the seller who provides these services is not paid for them unless the buyer buys the product from the seller. If another nearby seller offers the same product without the services, that seller will likely be able to offer a lower price as well.

Example: Personal computers are popular items for use in homes and small offices. However, they come in many varieties and are very complex. As a result, most customers need instruction about what to buy for their own particular needs before they make their purchase decisions. Servicestore is a "full service" computer outlet. It employs a large number of highly trained salespersons who know a great deal about computers. On the other hand, Bare Bones Computers, Inc., is a computer discounter. The store is a large old warehouse full of cardboxes containing computers just as they were shipped from the factory. At most times the store is staffed by a single salesperson, who knows nothing about computers except the names and numbers on the boxes.

You are in the market for a personal computer. You begin your search by going to Servicestore and you talk for two hours to a trained employee. The employee shows you a half dozen computers and printers, describes their capabilities and analyzes your needs. You and the salesperson finally decide which model is optimal for you, and you record the name and number on a piece of paper. The price for this package is $1995.00. Then you tell the salesperson at Servicestore you will go home and "think about it." You immediately drive to Bare Bones Computers, show the salesperson the scrap of paper, and she sells you the same package for $1650.00.

You have gotten a good deal, right? Perhaps. But in the process you have "stolen" something from Servicestore as well. Both you and Bare Bones took a "free ride" on the services provided by Servicestore, but for which Servicestore was not able to collect any fees. If free riding is substantial in an industry, the result may be to force the high service stores to cut services themselves or perhaps eliminate them altogether. This may be very bad from the manufacturer's point of view, because customers will be reluctant to purchase a complex product such as computers unless they can have a certain amount of education concerning what is best for their needs.

The manufacturer has some options available for controlling free riding.

a. Controlling Free Riding by Vertical Ownership

One way the manufacturer can control free riding is to eliminate independent stores and deal only through stores which it owns and controls itself. That way the stores will always deliver the optimal amount of customer services. However, this option is not available to all manufacturers. Many products sell best when they can be merchandised through stores that sell a number of brands, so that customers can compare them. Customers might be reluctant, for example, to go to a store that sells only a single brand of personal computers or stereo equipment when other stores offer a half dozen brands under the same roof.

b. Controlling Free Riding by Resale Price Maintenance or Vertical Nonprice Restraints

Another option is for the manufacturer to impose RPM or vertical territorial division on independent retailers.

Example: Suppose in the above example that the manufacturer of the computer you finally purchased negotiated new contracts with both Servicestore and Bare Bones. Under the contracts both were required to resell the package you purchased at a price of $1995.00. Now Bare Bones' (and your) incentive to take a free ride on the services offered by Servicestore has disappeared. Since you will pay the same price at both stores, you will be likely to buy where the service is best. The two stores will continue to "compete" with each other—however, they will engage in service competition rather than price competition.

The same result might be achieved by territorial division. For example, the computer manufacturer might decide to terminate its contract with Bare Bones, and sell exclusively to Servicestore. In that case Servicestore would be the only store in town selling that particular computer and would not have to worry about free riding.

In general, RPM is most efficient at controlling free riding problems in markets in which a large number of outlets is quite important. Most small appliances and low priced items probably fall into this category. On the other hand, vertical territorial division works best in markets for "big ticket" items such as automobiles and perhaps personal computers, where a large number of dealers in a community is less important, and where price may be negotiated between the store and individual customers, at least over a relatively narrow range.

5. USING VERTICAL RESTRICTIONS TO PURCHASE RETAIL SERVICES

The "free rider" explanation for vertical restrictions applies best to products for which a certain number of point-of-sale services are essential. Other products, such as clothing, need little or no point-of-sale services. Vertical restrictions covering such products must depend on some other explanation. One explanation is that in such cases the manufacturer may be "purchasing" high quality retail space from the retailer.

> ***Example:*** Le Grande Department Stores contain a great variety of retail display space. Its best space includes the show windows and the "high traffic" areas in the center of the first floor. The basement, remote corners, and the upper floors may be much less valuable. Le Grande's suppliers try hard to have their merchandise displayed in the most favorable space, for that will maximize their sales. Vertical restrictions, particularly RPM, can help a supplier obtain better space in Le Grande's stores for its product. Such restrictions operate as a guarantee to Le Grande that this particular product will not be sold by discounters at a lower price. As a result Le Grande does not need to worry about price competition and can concentrate on service competition. The incentive of high profits will cause it to assign the best space to the price-maintained product.

C. RESALE PRICE MAINTENANCE IN THE COURTS

The basic judicial rule concerning resale price maintenance is clear. It is illegal per se, whether or not the defendant had market power, and regardless of the defendant's motives, such as the need to combat free riding. The Supreme Court reaffirmed this rule as recently as 1984 in Monsanto Co. v. Spray–Rite Service Corp., 465 U.S. 752, 104 S.Ct. 1464 (1984).

However, the *per se* rule against RPM is subject to two important judicially-created exceptions.

1. THE COLGATE EXCEPTION FOR "UNILATERAL" RPM

In U.S. v. Colgate & Co., 250 U.S. 300, 39 S.Ct. 465 (1919) the Supreme Court held that a government indictment did not allege illegal resale price maintenance because it did not mention the existence of an "agreement" between the supplier at issue and the resellers. The indictment merely alleged that Colgate announced that it would not deal with stores that undercut Colgate's posted retail prices. When a store did undercut those prices, Colgate refused to make any more sales to that store.

Section one of the Sherman Act, you will recall, requires an agreement between two or more persons. *The Colgate exception to the RPM rule rests on the rationale that certain RPM does not fall within § 1 of the Sherman Act because there is no "agreement" between the market participants. If a seller merely announces that it will refuse to deal with price cutters, and then refuses to deal with a firm who cuts price, there is no Sherman Act violation.*

a.   The Continuing Vitality of *Colgate*

Both lower courts and commentators have regarded the *Colgate* exception with skepticism and sometimes even disbelief. It seems clear under ordinary common law contract principles of offer and assent that a retailer who complies with a supplier's declaration that it will terminate price cutters has entered into an "agreement." Nevertheless, the *Colgate* exception remains viable today, and has even increased in importance in the last decade. In Russell Stover Candies, Inc. v. FTC, 718 F.2d 256 (8th Cir. 1983), the Eighth Circuit court vacated a Federal Trade Commission attempt to emasculate the *Colgate* exception. Under the FTC's proposed rule, once a supplier had actually terminated a retailer, it would effectively have communicated a message to other retailers. Further compliance from that point must rest on an implied agreement.

Nevertheless, in order to avail itself of the *Colgate* exception the supplier must choose its words and acts very carefully. It may merely announce its intention not to deal with price cutters, and then refuse to fill an order for a price cutter when the occasion arises. It may not threaten, intimidate, warn or take any other action which a court might characterize as an attempt to induce an agreement from a noncomplying retailer. See U.S. v. Parke, Davis & Co., 362 U.S. 29, 80 S.Ct. 503 (1960).

b.   Variations on the *Colgate* Doctrine

In order to violate § 1 of the Sherman Act an RPM agreement need not be between the supplier and the particular dealer upon whom RPM is imposed. It could just as easily be an agreement between the supplier and one or more different dealers.

> ***Example:***   Suppose that a manufacturer supplies three different dealers, A, B, and C. A continually sells at a price lower than B and C sell for, perhaps by taking a free ride on point-of-sale services provided by B and C, but not by A. Finally, B and C complain to the manufacturer, and the manufacturer terminates A as a

dealer. A sues, claiming the existence of an illegal RPM agreement between the manufacturer on the one hand, and dealers B and C on the other.

In Monsanto Co. v. Spray–Rite Service Corp., 465 U.S. 752, 104 S.Ct. 1464 (1984), the Supreme Court held that such conduct *did* constitute illegal resale price maintenance, entitling the terminated dealer to damages. However, the Court warned that there must be evidence that the complaint concerned A's *pricing,* and not merely the violation of some restriction that does not pertain to price. (Nonprice restraints are treated under the rule of reason. See section D. below.) Secondly, the plaintiff must present evidence that the manufacturer and the complaining dealers acted *in agreement.* For example, mere evidence that the dealers complained, and that the supplier later terminated the plaintiff, would be insufficient. Rather there must be evidence of a scheme or plan among two or more persons to discipline the offending dealer. Notwithstanding *Monsanto,* a great many lower courts have refused to infer an agreement from a dealer's complaint about a second dealer and the supplier's subsequent termination of the latter. For example, H.L. Hayden Co. of N.Y. v. Siemens Medical Sys., 879 F.2d 1005 (2d Cir. 1989); Bailey's v. Windsor America, 948 F.2d 1018 (6th Cir. 1991).

2. CONSIGNMENT EXCEPTION

The second exception to the *per se* rule against resale price maintenance involves consignment sales. A consignment sale is one in which a product is not sold to a retailer and then resold. Rather, title with the product stays with the supplier. Under the consignment agreement the reseller agrees to try to sell the product for the supplier. When it is sold, the reseller will keep a certain percentage of the price as its commission or markup. If the product is not sold within a certain period of time, it is typically returned to the supplier and the reseller bears no loss except for the expense of sales efforts and the space occupied by the product during the consignment period. *Thus in a true consignment agreement the risk of nonsale remains with the supplier, rather than being transferred to the reseller.* Some products, such as works of art and second hand industrial equipment, are frequently sold under consignment agreements.

In U.S. v. General Electric Co., 272 U.S. 476, 47 S.Ct. 192 (1926) the Supreme Court held that the rule against RPM does not apply to consignment agreements, because there was no transfer of title from manufacturer to reseller. As long as the manufacturer retained title, it should have the power to control the resale price. The Court was also heavily persuaded, however, by the fact that the product in this case—electric lightbulbs—was patented.

The consignment exception to the *per se* rule against RPM raises one important problem: manufacturers who want to engage in legal resale price maintenance can quite easily restructure *any* resale contract to make it into a consignment agreement instead. The Supreme Court met this problem in Simpson v. Union Oil

Co., 377 U.S. 13, 84 S.Ct. 1051 (1964), when it disapproved a "consignment agreement" between a large gasoline refiner and many retail gasoline stations. Under the agreement the gasoline remained the property of the refiner while it was in the retailer's tanks; however, risk of nonsale passed to the retailers themselves. The court held that the arrangement did not qualify for the consignment exception because it covered "a vast gasoline distribution system, fixing prices through many retail outlets." In such cases, concluded the Court, the inference was strong that the "consignment agreement" was simply a disguise for resale price maintenance. The Court also observed that in *General Electric* the product was patented, while in *Simpson* it was not. In a dissent Justice Stewart wrote that Simpson effectively overruled *General Electric*.

However, most lower courts have tried to put some meaning into the distinction between General Electric *and* Simpson. *They generally hold that a good faith, bona fide consignment, in which the risk of loss remains with the seller, qualifies for the consignment exception. For example, Illinois Corporate Travel v. American Airlines, 889 F.2d 751 (7th Cir. 1989), cert. denied, 495 U.S. 919, 110 S.Ct. 1948 (1990), held that travel agents did not "resell" airline tickets offered by the major air carriers. The travel agents carried no inventory of individual seats; and all risk of nonsale was on the airline. As a result, the carriers were entitled to set the retail price of tickets.*

3.   MAXIMUM RESALE PRICE MAINTENANCE

The *per se* rule against RPM has been widely criticized. However, it has not been criticized nearly as much as the *per se* rule against *maximum* resale price maintenance, or supplier setting of the highest price that its dealer may charge. *In Albrecht v. Herald Co.*, 390 U.S. 145, 88 S.Ct. 869 (1968), the Supreme Court initially found it per se illegal for a supplier to establish the maximum price at which its product may be resold. In that particular case the product was newspapers, and the defendant was a newspaper publisher attempting to control the subscription rates charged by its independent carriers. One result of the *Albrecht* ruling was that many newspapers switched from independent carrier delivery systems to employee carrier systems.

Why would a firm want to control the maximum prices of its dealers? In general, because the dealers are in a position to charge monopoly prices. If they do so the dealers will earn the monopoly profits, and the supplier will experience only reduced output. Likewise, consumers of the product will be injured. In the *Albrecht* case the carriers had exclusive territories (because newspaper delivery routes are natural monopolies). This gave them an opportunity to set monopoly prices. The *Herald* was undoubtedly doing no more than trying to control such monopoly pricing. See Hovenkamp § 11.5C.

In any event, in its very important decision in State Oil Co. v. Khan, 522 U.S. 3, 118 S.Ct. 275 (1997), the Supreme Court overruled *Albrecht* and declared that maximum RPM agreements would thereafter be treated under the rule of reason. It is likely that few will be condemned; it is hard to come up with any rational explanation how a manufacturer can monopolize a market by limiting its dealers' markups. One possible exception is if the monopolization is in the distribution of the product rather than the product itself—for example a monopoly purchaser of distribution services (a "monopsonist") might use its power to reduce the price it pays for such distribution. By monopoly power in distribution services is not common.

D. VERTICAL NONPRICE RESTRAINTS AND THE RULE OF REASON

The history of Supreme Court analysis of vertical nonprice restraints is much less consistent than that of vertical price restraints (RPM). In White Motor Co. v. U.S., 372 U.S. 253, 83 S.Ct. 696 (1963), the Supreme Court held that it was too early to determine whether a *per se* rule was appropriate for vertical nonprice restraints. However, in U.S. v. Arnold, Schwinn & Co., 388 U.S. 365, 87 S.Ct. 1856 (1967), the Court decided that vertical nonprice restraints should be treated the same way as RPM. It applied the *per se* rule.

Finally, a decade later in Continental T.V., Inc. v. GTE Sylvania, Inc., 433 U.S. 36, 97 S.Ct. 2549 (1977), the Court changed its mind. It expressly overruled the Schwinn *case and created a rule reason for vertical nonprice restraints. This rule is the law today.*

1. "INTERBRAND" COMPETITION V. "INTRABRAND" COMPETITION

In the *Sylvania* case the Supreme Court distinguished two kinds of "competition" in which dealers might engage. "Interbrand" competition is competition among all dealers in all the brands of a particular product—say, all television dealers. "Intrabrand" competition, on the other hand, is the competition that might exist among dealers of the same brand of a product—for example, competition among different dealers of Sylvania televisions. In the *Sylvania* case the Court concluded that vertical territorial restrictions could injure intrabrand competition by reducing the number of dealers of a particular brand in a given territory. However, to the extent that the restrictions made the manufacturer a more effective competitor with manufacturers of different brands of the same product, they improved interbrand competition. *A rule of reason was appropriate, the court suggested, because a court needed to balance these two effects against each other in order to find out whether a particular set of vertical nonprice restraints is, on balance, competitive or anticompetitive.*

What did the Supreme Court mean when it said that territorial restrictions might injure intrabrand competition? Apparently, it meant reduction in the number of dealers serving a given area. In the *Sylvania* case it could not have meant that the restrictions enabled the Sylvania dealers to charge monopoly prices. At the time of the litigation Sylvania controlled about 5% of the market for televisions. If individual Sylvania dealers attempted to charge monopoly prices for Sylvania televisions they would have lost most of their sales to the televisions manufactured by competitors. The restrictions could facilitate monopoly pricing by the dealers only if Sylvania was a television monopolist; or, at least if it had a very large share of the television market.

2. VERTICAL NONPRICE RESTRAINTS SINCE THE SYLVANIA CASE

The trend in lower court cases since *Sylvania* was decided has been to hold that vertical nonprice restraints cannot facilitate monopoly pricing unless the supplier imposing the restrictions has market power in the market and area being restricted. There is no injury to intrabrand competition when the firm imposing the restraints is a competitor. However, such restrictions can still improve interbrand competition by eliminating free rider problems and providing sanctions against dealers who fail to promote the product aggressively enough. *The majority of lower courts now hold that vertical nonprice restraints are legal if the supplier imposing the restraints has no market power.*

Even the monopolist, however, might use vertical nonprice restrictions for procompetitive reasons, such as control of free rider problems. In that case, the restrictions should not be condemned. Under the rule of reason, once it has been determined that a supplier has market power, further analysis is still necessary to determine whether the restrictions are being used for a competitive or anticompetitive purpose. The discussion in section B. above suggested some possible anticompetitive reasons, such as facilitation of an intrabrand dealers' cartel. However, the discussion also suggested that such cartels are unlikely to occur very often. It seems clear that most vertical restrictions, even those imposed by the monopolist, are procompetitive.

3. VERTICAL NONPRICE RESTRAINTS AND PRICE DISCRIMINATION

Vertical restrictions may be price discrimination devices. A manufacturer with market power in one geographic territory but not in another might attempt to capitalize on its position by segregating the territory in which it has market power. Such segregation would discourage arbitrage, which occurs when customers who pay a low price resell a product to customers who pay a higher price. Vertical territorial restrictions, which minimize the buyer-seller contact that firms in different territories have with one another, may be an effective mechanism for facilitating price discrimination. See Hovenkamp § 11.2d.

4. THE PROBLEM OF DUAL DISTRIBUTION

"Dual distribution" refers to a scheme under which a manufacturer both distributes its product through independent dealers and engages in a certain amount of self-distribution. For a long time there was a tendency among courts to characterize terminations of independent dealers in dual distribution settings as "horizontal," on the theory that the independent dealers competed with the dealerships owned by the supplier itself. However, the trend is for courts to disregard the fact that the supplier is engaged in dual distribution. Once again, within a single brand, the dealers collectively have no more market power than the supplier has. It is hard to see how a dual distributor's termination of an independent dealer could facilitate monopoly pricing.

5. DISTINGUISHING BETWEEN PRICE AND NONPRICE RESTRAINTS; BUSINESS ELECTRONICS CASE

Increasingly courts have taken the position that any restraint that contains no *explicit* price element is a nonprice restraint. Many courts (including perhaps the Supreme Court in the *Monsanto* case, cited above) have erroneously identified as a price restraint something that in fact operated as a nonprice restraint. In the *Monsanto* case, for example, the dealers were assigned adjacent territories and given certain duties to inform customers about the chemicals that were being sold. Spray–Rite, the plaintiff, simultaneously made sales in the territories of other dealers *and* made those sales at a lower price. It probably did the latter, however, because it was taking a free ride on the service efforts of the dealers who were assigned to those territories. When the competing dealers complained to supplier Monsanto, they naturally complained about *both* the invasion of their territories and the price cutting. The Supreme Court concluded that this evidence established the existence of illegal resale price maintenance. However, it probably established only that Spray–Rite violated Monsanto's nonprice restraints.

In Business Electronics Corp. v. Sharp Electronics Corp., 485 U.S. 717, 108 S.Ct. 1515 (1988) the Supreme Court held that a complaint by one dealer about another dealer's price cutting, and the supplier's termination of the second dealer, did not involve a "price" agreement. The plaintiff must show that the complaining dealer and the supplier specifically agreed on a price (or minimum price) that other dealers must charge. Some courts have read *Business Electronics* very broadly. See, for example, Ben Elfman & Son v. Criterion Mills, 774 F.Supp. 683, 684–685 (D.Mass. 1991) (terminated dealer must allege that the complaining dealer and the supplier "agreed to set the prices at which [the terminated dealer] would sell.... ").

E. REVIEW QUESTIONS

1. Priestley Chemical Company sells Aardvon, a paint extender, through a group of distributors who are assigned areas of primary responsibility. Three dealers, A, B, and C, have been assigned adjacent territories in Kansas. A, however, continually makes sales of Aardvon in B's and C's territories, generally at a lower price than B and C charge there. At the same time, however, A refuses to provide any instruction in the use of Aardvon to customers in territories B and C. When customers ask for such instruction, A informs them that B and C will provide it. B and C complain to Priestley Chemical that A is 1) making sales in their territories; 2) charging a lower price in their territories than they charge; and 3) refusing to provide essential instruction to Aardvon customers. Priestley investigates the charges and then terminates A as an Aardvon distributor. A sues Priestley, alleging a violation of § 1 of the Sherman Act. How should the case be decided?

2. **T or F**   A seller can avoid the *per se* rule against Resale Price Maintenance (RPM) by making sure that its sale-resale contracts with dealers use the word "consignment" rather than the word "sale."

3. **T or F**   An "intrabrand" cartel will be able to charge monopoly prices only if the manufacturer that supplies the cartelized product has market power.

4. Mountain High Beverages, Inc., is attempting to impose "unilateral" RPM on its 200 distributors nationwide. Mountain High has always followed a policy of announcing that it will deal only with distributors that charge $1.90 per six-pack for its beverages. When a distributor attempted to sell Mountain High at $1.75 per six-pack, Mountain High called the distributor and said that the distributor would be terminated immediately unless it returned to a policy of charging $1.90 per six-pack. The distributor initially raised its price, but later dropped it again. This time Mountain High terminated its relationship with the distributor. The distributor sued. Discuss the case.

VII

REFUSALS TO DEAL

A.   ANTITRUST POLICY AND REFUSALS TO DEAL

1.   THE BASIC RULE AND TWO EXCEPTIONS

In U.S. v. Colgate & Co., 250 U.S. 300, 39 S.Ct. 465 (1919), the Supreme Court stated the basic common law rule respecting refusals to deal: *"[i]n the absence of any purpose to create or maintain a monopoly" a private firm may freely "exercise his own independent discretion as to parties with whom he will deal." This rule remains the law today.*

Importantly, however, the common law rule concerning refusals to deal comes with two qualifications, both of which raise antitrust concerns:

a.   Concerted Refusals

Under the *Colgate* formulation, the decision not to deal with someone must be "independent," or unilateral. "Concerted" refusals to deal—agreements between two or more persons not to deal with someone else—raise many antitrust issues, and some are even characterized as illegal *per se*. Not all concerted refusals to deal are illegal, but many are.

b.   Refusals to Deal as Monopolization or Attempt to Monopolize

Secondly, even the unilateral refusal to deal is clearly lawful only if it is taken "in the absence of any purpose to create or maintain a monopoly." That is, a refusal to deal by a firm with market power may constitute illegal monopolization or attempt to monopolize.

2.   THE FUNCTION OF THE REFUSAL TO DEAL IN ANTITRUST LITIGATION

There is some reason for wondering whether the refusal to deal should really be described as a distinct antitrust offense. *In most antitrust litigation involving refusals to deal the refusal itself is not the alleged violation of the antitrust laws.* Many complaints alleging such refusals really allege that the defendants were involved in illegal monopolization, tying, price fixing, resale price maintenance or vertical nonprice restraints, or sometimes even in an illegal merger.

For example, most of the litigation concerning vertical price and nonprice restraints is brought by terminated dealers. They allege that the defendant supplier refused to deal with them in order to enforce or carry out an illegal RPM or territorial division scheme. In other cases, the antitrust complaint alleging a refusal to deal does not explicitly allege a "supporting" antitrust violation; however, the theory of the complaint makes sense only on the premise that some secondary violation was involved. If no such supporting violation is apparent, then it is often difficult to explain how the refusal to deal could have been anticompetitive. Given the basic rule stated above, of course, the proper action in such cases is to dismiss the complaint.

Nevertheless, the refusal to deal performs two important functions in antitrust litigation:

a. Identification of Highly Motivated Plaintiffs

First, the refusal to deal supplies an injury and a cause of action to a group of plaintiffs who have good knowledge about a market and are highly motivated to bring their cases. Few people are more likely to file an antitrust lawsuit than small businesses who lose their most important product or their right to do business under a certain name as a result of what they perceive to be an antitrust violation.

b. Aid in Characterizing Ambiguous Conduct

Second, the presence or absence of a refusal to deal can aid a court in determining whether certain activities, particularly joint ventures, are competitive or anticompetitive. As the discussion in chapter II. above indicated, many joint ventures are efficient, because they enable firms acting together to accomplish things more cheaply than firms acting alone. At the same time, however, joint ventures have the potential to be anticompetitive, particularly if they are joint ventures of competitors.

Unfortunately, no court has the economic tools to balance the efficiency potential and the anticompetitive potential of joint ventures, except in a few easy cases. *In ambiguous cases the presence or absence of a refusal to deal can give a court considerable guidance in determining whether a particular venture is, on balance, competitive or anticompetitive.* In fact, often an efficient joint venture will be accompanied by an inefficient, anticompetitive refusal to deal. In most such cases the court will be able to enjoin the refusal to deal while leaving other parts of the joint venture intact.

> ***Example 1:*** Appalachian Coals, Inc. v. U.S., 288 U.S. 344, 53 S.Ct. 471 (1933) involved an exclusive joint selling agency created by several competing producers of coal. (The case is discussed in chapter II. above.) The selling agency was instructed to sell all of the members' coal it could, at the highest price it was able to obtain. Since coal is fungible (i.e., customers generally cannot distinguish one producer's coal of a certain grade from another person's coal of the same grade), the agent had to charge the same price for each producer's coal. This naturally raised the possibility that the producers were engaged in price fixing. The court upheld the arrangement, holding that the depressed market conditions justified the joint sales activities, and that there seemed to be little likelihood that the defendants were reducing output and obtaining higher prices.

There is every reason to believe that the joint selling agency in this case was efficient—i.e., it reduced the participants' marketing costs and made them more efficient sellers than they otherwise would have been. Nevertheless, the exclusivity requirement is suspicious. Why did the members need a rule that participants could sell their coal *only* through a joint agency? If the agency were more efficient than individual sales by each member, an exclusivity requirement would not be necessary to protect the markets of other members. At the same time, the exclusivity requirement could facilitate cartelization by forbidding the members from making sales outside the cartel arrangement. In such a case the court would do well to uphold the general joint selling scheme, but enjoin the exclusivity requirement (which is an agreement to refuse to deal except through the joint selling agency) as too conducive to collusion.

Example 2: By contrast, Broadcast Music, Inc. v. CBS, 441 U.S. 1, 99 S.Ct. 1551 (1979), involved a nonexclusive joint sales agency engaged in the blanket licensing of the right to perform musical works. (This case is also discussed in chapter II. above.) Once again, the court upheld the arrangement. The nonexclusive nature of the arrangement made it clear that no price fixing was involved. The individual participants, which numbered in the thousands, were free to sell their performance rights outside the blanket licensing agreement on any terms they desired. No cartel could survive by permitting its members to make unlimited numbers of noncartel sales.

For the purpose of antitrust analysis, refusals to deal are divided into two kinds, concerted and unilateral. The former are generally dealt with as combinations in restraint of trade under § 1 of the Sherman Act. The latter are generally dealt with as monopolization or attempts to monopolize under § 2 of the Sherman Act.

B. CONCERTED REFUSALS TO DEAL

Concerted refusals to deal involve an agreement between two or more persons and firms that they will not deal with someone else. Those participating in the agreement are often competitors, but occasionally they are not. Likewise, sometimes the target of the refusal to deal is a competitor, and sometimes it is not. *Many courts have characterized concerted refusals to deal as per se violations of § 1 of the Sherman Act. However, that rule has become so riddled with exceptions that today it applies far less than half the time. Today most concerted refusals to deal are analyzed under the rule of reason.*

In Northwest Wholesale Stationers, Inc. v. Pacific Stationery & Printing Co., 472 U.S. 284, 105 S.Ct. 2613 (1985), the Supreme Court held that a concerted refusal to deal involving discipline and expulsion of a member of a buying cooperative should be analyzed under the rule of reason because the cooperative had no market power. Any such market power requirement in concerted refusal cases would come with its own exceptions, however. For example, a refusal to deal that resulted from enforcement of an illegal resale price maintenance scheme would still receive *per se* treatment, because RPM is illegal *per se*.

Likewise, a concerted refusal to deal used to enforce a naked price fixing agreement would be characterized as illegal per se. The Supreme Court so held in FTC v. Superior Court Trial Lawyers Association, 493 U.S. 411, 110 S.Ct. 768 (1990). The lawyers collectively refused to accept clients through Washington D.C.'s indigent criminal defense program unless the city agreed to increase its hourly rate for such representation. The Supreme Court condemned this agreement as a "classic restraint of trade," which should be condemned without any inquiry into the defendant's market power.

Note in the above cases that *Stationers* involved a restraint that was ancillary to the operation of a joint venture, a buying cooperative, while *Trial Lawyers* involved a boycott designed to facilitate naked price fixing. Ambiguously between the two is the Supreme Court's decision in FTC v. Indiana Federation of Dentists, 476 U.S. 447, 106 S.Ct. 2009 (1986), which condemned an agreement among dentists not to provide X-rays to a health insurer so that the insurer could verify claims submitted by the dentist. The Court stated that it was applying the rule of reason, noting that "the *per se* approach has generally been limited to cases in which firms with market power boycott suppliers or customers in order to discourage them from doing business with a competitor—a situation obviously not present here." Nonetheless, much of the Court's analysis—including an exceedingly truncated inquiry into market power—seemed more consistent with the *per se* rule.

1.   CONCERTED REFUSALS AND CARTELS

One of the most consistently anticompetitive uses of the concerted refusal to deal is as a device for facilitating the cartelization of a market.

Price fixers may use the concerted refusal to deal as a device for disciplining members of the cartel, or else for "sending a message" to nonmembers of a cartel whose activities are interfering with the cartel's operations. At the extreme, the members of a cartel may find it necessary to drive a nonmember out of business.

Example: In Eastern States Retail Lumber Dealers' Association v. U.S., 234 U.S. 600, 34 S.Ct. 951 (1914) the Supreme Court condemned an agreement among lumber retailers to identify and refuse to deal with lumber wholesalers who dealt directly with customers as well. The lumber retailers might have two different but closely related motives for engaging in such a concerted refusal:

(a) First, perhaps the lumber retailers were fixing prices. In that case vertically related firms such as lumber wholesalers would be injured. They would suffer reduced sales as a result of the cartel price increase; however, all the cartel's monopoly profits would accrue to the retailers. Lumber wholesalers in such a situation would be strongly motivated to avoid the cartel, perhaps by finding other retailers who are not part of the cartel, or perhaps—as in this case—by integrating vertically into retailing themselves. The concerted refusal in the *Eastern States* case may have been an effort by a cartel to prevent erosion of its dominant position in the market.

(b) Secondly, perhaps the lumber retailers discovered that they were more efficient retailers than the independent retailers themselves were. For example, by opening their own retail outlets at their mills they could save the additional transportation costs of shipping to a separate retailer. They could also eliminate one costly market transaction. The concerted refusal by the independent lumber retailers may have been an effort to protect their members from the entry of more efficient, vertically integrated firms.

In such cases, where there is no plausible argument that a concerted refusal produces economies, and where the only apparent purpose is facilitation of cartelization or protection from new entry, application of the per se rule is appropriate. Even in such a case, however, a market power requirement might aid the court in characterizing the defendant's conduct.

2. CONCERTED REFUSALS AND CARTELS: SOME VARIATIONS

Today, most concerted refusals to deal are somewhat more ambiguous than the one at issue in the *Eastern States Lumber* case. The *Trial Lawyers* case, supra, is a notable exception. As the cases become more ambiguous, application of the *per se* rule becomes more questionable.

a. Concerted Refusals and Free Rider Problems

The concerted refusal to deal may be a device by which a group of firms protects itself from free riding by others. Many such concerted refusals are suspect, however, because the concerted refusals often threaten to facilitate price fixing as well.

One of the most common instances of such a concerted refusal is the dealer complaint to a supplier that another dealer has been violating a vertical price or nonprice restriction. (See the discussion of vertical restraints in chapter VI. above.)

> ***Example:***   Suppose that a supplier has imposed vertical territorial restraints on dealers A, B, and C. C continually cheats on the restraints, however, by making unauthorized sales in the territories assigned to A and B. A and B jointly complain to the supplier, and the supplier agrees to terminate its relationship with C. The decisions in Monsanto Co. v. Spray–Rite Service Corp., 465 U.S. 752, 104 S.Ct. 1464 (1984), and Business Electronics Corp. v. Sharp Electronics Corp., 485 U.S. 717, 108 S.Ct. 1515 (1988) (discussed in chapter VI. C. & D. above) appear to make clear that such a concerted refusal would be analyzed under the rule of reason *provided that the complaint concerned a nonprice restraint.*

Note 1:   The *Monsanto* and *Business Electronics* cases considerably
narrow the Supreme Court's earlier concerted refusal decision in
Klor's, Inc. v. Broadway–Hale Stores, Inc., 359 U.S. 207, 79 S.Ct.
705 (1959). There the plaintiff, which owned a small appliance
store located very close to the defendant's larger appliance store,
alleged that the defendant used its "monopolistic buying power"
to force major appliance manufacturers to refuse to deal with
the plaintiff, or else to deal with it only on very discriminatory
terms. The court held that this allegation stated a cause of
action under the *per se* rule.

The *Klor's* case was not tried, and there is good reason to doubt that the
plaintiff could have proved its claim. First of all, why would giant appliance
manufacturers such as Maytag or General Electric bow to the pressure of a
medium sized department store not to deal with a pesky smaller competitor? If
Klor's were underselling Broadway–Hale, so much the better for the major
manufacturers; their sales volume would go up.

However, there is more plausible explanation than the one stated in the
plaintiff's complaint: Klor's, the plaintiff, was probably engaging in free riding.
It was underselling Broadway–Hale by taking advantage of the point-of-sale
services given there. Once a customer had received an education at Broadway–
Hale's expense about what to buy, then he or she could go to Klor's and receive
the same product, without the education, at a lower price. (See the discussion
of free riding at chapter VI.B. above.) In that case, if the major manufacturers
wanted each of their dealers to demonstrate their products and provide
adequate point-of-sale services, they might have disciplined Klor's for free
riding. But such decisions would ordinarily be unilateral, in that they would
benefit each manufacturer whether or not other manufacturers did the same
thing.

Note 2:   The *Monsanto* decision appears, at least ambiguously, to leave
intact the Supreme Court's earlier decision in U.S. v. General
Motors Corp., 384 U.S. 127, 86 S.Ct. 1321 (1966). In that case
several General Motors automobile dealers in the Los Angeles
area complained to General Motors that other General Motors
dealers were reselling cars to "discounters," or no frills
automobile sellers that substantially undercut the prices
charged by the full service dealers. General Motors responded by
pressuring all of its dealers into promising that they would not
resell automobiles to discounters. Thereafter these agreements
were policed by both General Motors and an association of
dealers. The Supreme Court held that this conduct was a *per se*
violation of the antitrust laws. Importantly, however, the
agreement among the association of dealers was horizontal
rather than vertical.

The interesting part of the *General Motors* case is this: each of the dealers
involved had a franchise agreement which contained a location clause.

Furthermore, the dealers who sold to discounters were in violation of their location clauses, because those automobiles were ultimately sold at a location not authorized in the franchise agreement. Under *Monsanto,* and *Business Electronics,* if General Motors disciplined the dealers in response to other dealers' complaints that the disciplined dealers were violating the location restrictions, its conduct would be subject to the rule of reason. (Note, however, that *General Motors* was decided long before the Supreme Court had adopted a rule of reason for vertical nonprice restraints.) By contrast, if General Motors disciplined the offending dealers in response to complaints that they were reselling to discounters *and* the agreement could be construed as setting a minimum price that the offending dealers or the discounters must charge, then the conduct would be a *per se* illegal price restraint.

b. Concerted Refusals and "Free Riding" in Intellectual Property: The *FOGA* Case

In Fashion Originators' Guild of America (FOGA) v. FTC, 312 U.S. 457, 61 S.Ct. 703 (1941), the Supreme Court condemned an arrangement under which the creators of original clothing designs (FOGA) collectively refused to sell their products to stores which also purchased clothing from design "pirates"— i.e., firms who copied the designs of the original creators and manufactured similar clothing. *The Supreme Court upheld the FTC's refusal to listen to FOGA's free rider defense, thus effectively applying the per se rule.*

Unquestionably, the design pirates in the FOGA case were engaged in free riding. They waited until a piece of designer clothing was available on the market, "reverse engineered" it (in this case by pulling the stitches and tracing a new pattern), and then manufactured copies. Unfortunately, however, lower courts at the time had already held that clothing designs could not be protected under either the patent or the copyright laws. Thus the members of FOGA were attempting to discipline the pirates even though the law refused to recognize that the pirates were guilty of any offense. The court did well to refuse to listen to the defense, particularly since the arrangement in FOGA contained a large potential to facilitate price fixing.

c. Concerted Refusals by Noncompetitors

The *Klor's* decision, discussed supra, involved allegations of a conspiracy between two or more appliance manufacturers to deny business to the plaintiff; that is, there was a horizontal agreement as well as a vertical one with Klor's competitor Broadway–Hale Stores. Some lower courts concluded that under *Klor's* an agreement between a single downstream firm (such as Broadway–Hale) and a single upstream firm (such as Frigidaire) could be illegal per se as well. However, in NYNEX v. Discon, 196 U.S. 128, 119 S.Ct. 493 (1998), the Supreme Court distinguished *Klor's* and held that a purely vertical agreement not to deal with a third party must be addressed under the rule of reason. This was so even though, on the facts of this particular case, the refusal to deal was part of an attempt to defraud consumers. See Hovenkamp § 5.4d.

Example: In Berkey Photo, Inc. v. Eastman Kodak Co., 603 F.2d 263 (2d Cir.1979), cert. denied, 444 U.S. 1093, 100 S.Ct. 1061 (1980) the court condemned under the rule of reason an arrangement under which noncompetitors Kodak and General Electric agreed to develop a camera and flash attachment, but also agreed that they would not predisclose their research to anyone else. The result of this concerted refusal to predisclose technical data was that plaintiff Berkey Photo was not able quickly to enter the market for either the camera or the flash attachment. However, in condemning the concerted refusal, the court noted that Kodak was already a monopolist in the market for cameras. As a result, the court regarded the arrangement as part of a monopolist's scheme to maintain its monopoly position. *In this case, the refusal to deal should probably be treated as illegal monopolization or attempt to monopolize under § 2 of the Sherman Act, rather than a concerted refusal to deal under § 1.* Research joint ventures by noncompetitors are not likely to be anticompetitive unless one of the firms involved is a monopolist, or there is a dangerous probability that the venture will create a monopoly.

3. NONCOMMERCIAL BOYCOTTS

A noncommercial boycott, established in furtherance of some political goal, is generally exempt *from antitrust liability, whether or not the boycott is anticompetitive.* This is so for two different reasons.

(1) The boycotters may be protected by Constitutional provisions, such as the First Amendment, that take precedence over a federal statute such as the Sherman Act. See NAACP v. Claiborne Hardware Co., 458 U.S. 886, 102 S.Ct. 3409 (1982). However, in FTC v. Superior Court Trial Lawyers Association, 493 U.S. 411, 110 S.Ct. 768 (1990), discussed supra, the Supreme Court held that a boycott furthering naked price fixing was illegal per se even though it had an "expressive component," and its target was the government, thus making it a kind of "petition" to the government. In this case, lawyers collectively refused to represent indigent criminal defendants until the City of Washington, D.C., agreed to raise its rate of payment for such services.

(2) One lower court has held that Congress never intended for the Sherman Act to be used to reach *noncommercial* activities. In that case, the boycott will be exempt from the Sherman Act, whether or not it is protected by the first amendment. See Missouri v. National Organization for Women, Inc., 620 F.2d 1301 (8th Cir.1980), cert. denied, 449 U.S. 842, 101 S.Ct. 122 (1980), which held that a boycott by members of the National Organization for Women directed against convention facilities located in states that had failed to ratify the Equal Rights Amendment was not within the jurisdiction of the Sherman Act.

4. CONCERTED REFUSALS AND EFFICIENCY

Many activities that involve refusals to deal are themselves efficient. This is particularly true of certain joint ventures. In that case the court will probably not want to destroy the efficiency-creating aspects of the joint venture. *However, it may be appropriate to consider whether the refusal to deal is really an inherent part of the joint venture. If it is not, then perhaps the joint venture can be restructured in a less anticompetitive way.*

Importantly, a refusal to deal by a joint venture will likely injure competition only if the venturers collectively wield a certain amount of market power in their market. If they do not, then someone excluded by the venturers might be individually injured, but the exclusion will not likely result in reduced market output and lower prices. As a general rule, such exclusions by joint ventures without market power should not be a concern of the antitrust laws.

a. Efficient Joint Ventures With Efficient Refusals to Deal

In some cases a joint venture will be efficient *and* its members' refusal to deal with outsiders is justified.

Example: Firms A, B, C, D and several others produce computers, a market characterized by a high degree of expensive technological innovation. A, B and C decide to pool their resources and jointly develop a new memory device that will greatly enhance the capabilities of computers. However, the technology in which the research will be done is merely promising; it is far from a sure thing. Furthermore, the research will be very expensive. By engaging in the joint venture, however, the firms will each have to bear only one third of the developmental costs, and will suffer only one third of the losses should the project fail. The firms invite D to participate in the joint venture as well, but D refuses. Two years later the joint venture has proved successful and yields a patented, low cost memory device much better than anything on the market. Now D asks to "buy in," and obtain a license to manufacture the device for itself. A, B, and C refuse.

In such a case it should be clear that the antitrust laws were not designed to give D the right to join the venture *after* it has proved successful. Such a rule would create enormous free rider problems. No one would enter the venture early and share the risk if others were legally entitled to wait until the venture had become a success before they make up their minds. Sharing in the rewards of such a joint venture means participating in the risks as well.

b. Efficient Joint Ventures With Inefficient Refusals to Deal

Other joint ventures are clearly efficient; however, the refusals to deal created by the venturers are anticompetitive. In such a case the optimal form of relief is an injunction that permits the joint venture to continue, but forces the members to deal with outsiders.

Example 1: U.S. v. Terminal R.R. Ass'n of St. Louis, 224 U.S. 383, 32 S.Ct. 507 (1912) involved an association of several railroad companies, bridge operators and freight transfer companies into a great railroad transfer and terminal system in St. Louis, Missouri, at the union of the Mississippi River and several railroad lines. The joint venture itself was a natural monopoly, and anyone with access to it could process freight through St. Louis at a lower cost than an outsider could. However, the venture had by-laws which permitted it to exclude nonmembers. Any railroad who wanted to join the venture needed the unanimous vote of all members. A nonmember also needed the unanimous consent of members in order to use the facilities of the terminal and transfer association.

The Supreme Court applied a rule that it frequently applied to natural monopoly utilities in the nineteenth century: it permitted the Terminal Railroad Association to operate as a monopoly, but it threw the association open to all potential customers willing to pay their fair share of the costs. The result was a good one, because it forced increased competition *within* the joint venture. The result could give shippers the advantage of the economies produced by the venture *and* the advantages of any competition that might be available in the hauling of freight.

Example 2: Associated Press (AP) v. U.S., 326 U.S. 1, 65 S.Ct. 1416 (1945), involved a joint venture of about 1200 newspapers. AP gathered news in behalf of its members, wrote stories, and then transmitted the stories by means of wire services to the member papers. Part of this news gathering was done by AP's own employees, but much of it was done by employees of the member newspapers, who gathered the news in their regions and disseminated it to other members. The United States did not challenge the joint venture itself, which was conceded to be very efficient. Rather, it challenged AP's regulations concerning the admission of new members. If a newspaper from a city not already serviced by an AP newspaper wanted to join AP, entry was generally easy. However, if a newspaper from a city already serviced by another AP newspaper wanted to join, the competing newspaper had the right to object. If the competing member objected to the entry, then the newspaper desiring entry had to pay a large fee and receive a majority vote of existing AP members. *The Supreme Court held that these regulations violated § 1 of the Sherman Act.*

AP's regulations are relatively easy to understand. Assume that the news stories describing a single event are all more-or-less alike. The costs to a newspaper of producing a particular news story are largely the costs of sending a reporter to the scene to gather the information and write the story. Once the story is finished, however, it can be transmitted to one newspaper or

1200 newspapers at very low cost. AP saved its members enormous news gathering costs by creating a scheme under which one reporter could gather a story that would be sent to hundreds of newspapers.

Assume that the world contains ten cities, each with one or two newspapers. One reporter is sufficient to cover one city's news, and the costs of maintaining a single reporter are $100 per week. Without news sharing each newspaper which wanted to cover the world's news would incur costs of $1000—$100 for maintaining a reporter in each of the ten cities. Suppose, however, that eight of the newspapers now create AP. They agree that each of them will maintain a reporter in its home city, who will write that city's news and transmit it to all eight papers. In that case each newspaper's costs (ignoring the cost of the wire service, which is assumed to be negligible) have been reduced from $1000 to $300—$100 for maintaining a reporter in the newspaper's home city, and $100 for remaining a reporter in each of the two cities that do not have AP members.

Now suppose that a newspaper in city #9 wants to join the news-sharing venture. All members will likely agree, for their news gathering costs will drop by another $100. However, what will happen if a *second* newspaper in, say, city #3 wants to join? The member newspaper from city #3 is almost sure to object, for it would then have a much more efficient competitor than it had before. At the same time, the second newspaper in city #3 can contribute little to the joint venture, because city #3 is already being served by an AP newspaper.

In short, the exclusionary rules employed by AP effectively enabled the members to obtain all the efficiencies that were made available by the joint venture without forcing them to compete. Competition would force many of the benefits of those efficiencies to be transferred to consumers. The decision in the *Associated Press* case was a good one.

5. STANDARD SETTING AND RULE MAKING

A significant part of the American economy is subject to self-regulation. This means that the persons and firms providing goods and services in those markets make and enforce rules governing product and service quality. In many professions, such as medicine, the quality of medical services is regulated by "peer review boards"— groups of doctors, often specialists, who evaluate the work of others in the same specialty. Likewise, in manufacturing industries the testing of products for performance and safety is often undertaken in laboratories controlled by associations of the manufacturers themselves. *Much of this self-regulation is put into place entirely at the initiative of the providers in the market. When this is so, the self-regulatory activities are fully within the reach of the antitrust laws.*

In other cases, however, a federal statute may give firms a limited right to engage in self-regulation. For example, the Securities Exchange Act of 1934 authorizes brokers on the stock exchanges to regulate their own activities to a certain degree. The result of such grants of regulatory authority is that there is relatively less room for the federal antitrust laws. Such problems of the scope of antitrust liability in regulated industries is taken up in chapter XII. below.

Even in markets where self-regulation is authorized by federal statute, the antitrust laws may have a role to play, however:

Example: In Silver v. New York Stock Exchange, 373 U.S. 341, 83 S.Ct. 1246 (1963) the Supreme Court used the *per se* rule to condemn the Exchange's exclusion of a broker from telephone access to the Exchange, the effect of which was to make it impossible for the broker to conduct transactions. The Court granted that the Exchange (which is composed of member brokers) had the statutory authority to regulate the activities of brokers. However, in this particular case they had cut Silver off without even telling him the reason why. The Court concluded that the antitrust laws should be used to perform the essentially "Due Process" function of ensuring that self-regulation is conducted in a forthright manner, and is not being used for anticompetitive purposes.

Note: In Northwest Wholesale Stationers, Inc. v. Pacific Stationery & Printing Co., 472 U.S. 284, 105 S.Ct. 2613 (1985), the Supreme Court narrowed the *Silver* case by holding that even an unexplained expulsion of a member would qualify for rule of reason treatment if the defendant association guilty of the expulsion had no market power. The New York Stock Exchange in *Silver* almost certainly had substantial market power. In the *Stationers* case the Supreme Court cited the Exchange's "dominant position in the securities trading markets" as a justification for application of the *per se* rule there. The Supreme Court also cited the Exchange's statutory power of self-regulation as creating a special obligation upon it to give disciplined brokers notice and an opportunity to be heard.

Almost invariably, the result of standard setting is that a certain percentage of firms will not meet the standard. In that case, the regulatory authority must impose some kind of sanction, the most common of which is removal of the offending product or service from the market until it is corrected. This poses an antitrust problem when those making and enforcing the standards are competitors of the person who is being excluded by them.

At the same time, the providers of a certain product or service are generally far better equipped than others to judge the quality or effectiveness of a certain product or service. For example, the best judges of a surgeon's expertise are likely other surgeons who specialize in the same area. Likewise, the best assessors of the efficiency or safety of a gas furnace are probably other people engaged in the same business. On the one hand, self-regulation can be a very efficient way to assess product or service quality. On the other, it can often facilitate collusion. For example, the group of surgeons evaluating a new surgeon's work in order to determine whether she should be given staff privileges in a hospital may decide that the hospital already has "too many" surgeons in the applicant's area. Rather than lowering their prices in order to draw in more business from elsewhere, the doctors would prefer to keep the supply of surgeons low. Such a motive is not standard-setting at all, but collusion.

Standard setting by associations of competitors is generally analyzed under the rule of reason, and the court will have to determine whether the activity was competitive or anticompetitive. If possible the court will try to make that determination by analyzing the rules themselves for reasonableness, or by inquiring whether the rules have been enforced in an arbitrary, inconsistent way. If this kind of external evidence is ambiguous, the court may face the far more difficult task of determining the intent of those engaged in the standard setting. This is particularly true in cases involving professional peer review.

In some instances, however, the Court may apply the *per se* rule, even to standard setting, if the standard setting involves unwarranted pressure to exclude the product from the market.

> ***Example:*** Radiant Burners, Inc. v. People's Gas Light & Coke Co., 364 U.S. 656, 81 S.Ct. 365 (1961) involved an association of gas heater manufacturers and natural gas utilities which evaluated products that burned natural gas. The association placed its "seal of approval" on products which it judged to be safe. The plaintiff, a manufacturer of a gas heater, was denied approval. It sued, claiming that 1) the standards applied by the association were arbitrary; and 2) the effect of nonapproval was that the member gas utilities refused to supply gas to facilities that used the heater. The Court held that the allegation of *both* of these factors—the arbitrary decision making and the forced removal of the product from the market—was sufficient to state a cause of action for a *per se* violation of the antitrust laws.

However, where the standard setting is conducted in a nonarbitrary way, courts have generally approved it, particularly if the only consequence of rejection is a denial of a seal or certificate of approval, without any attempt to force the product off the market. For example, this was the result in Eliason Corp. v. National Sanitation Foundation, 614 F.2d 126 (6th Cir.1980), cert. denied, 449 U.S. 826, 101 S.Ct. 89 (1980). Once again, the *Northwest Wholesale Stationers* decision, cited above, appears to require a rule of reason approach in all such cases, unless the defendant association has market power.

However, in Allied Tube & Conduit Corp. v. Indian Head, Inc., 486 U.S. 492, 108 S.Ct. 1931 (1988) the Court suggested that such a concerted refusal could be illegal under the rule of reason, especially if the standard setting organization had been captured by a group intent on keeping a competitor's superior product off the market. In this case, however, as in *Radiant Burner*, the effect of disapproval was that government regulators would not allow the plaintiff's product to be installed; as a result, the standard setting association's rejection was tantamount to a forced removal of the product from the market.

6. PROOF OF AGREEMENT IN CONCERTED REFUSAL CASES

In cases involving concerted refusals to deal it is essential that the plaintiff prove the existence of an "agreement" among the defendants, just as much as in a price fixing case. For example, Cement Manufacturer's Protective Ass'n v. U.S., 268 U.S. 588, 45 S.Ct. 586 (1926) involved an agreement among cement suppliers to exchange the names of contractors who ordered cement from several suppliers and then at the last minute cancelled all orders but one. *However, there was no evidence that the cement suppliers agreed to refuse to deal with such contractors. The Supreme Court held that there was no violation, as long as each cement supplier's decision either to deal or not to deal with the named contractors was unilateral.*

C. UNILATERAL REFUSALS TO DEAL

Unilateral refusals to deal are illegal, if at all, when they constitute monopolization or an attempt to monopolize a market. As a result, the tests for those offenses applies. The plaintiff must show that the defendant is a monopolist and that the refusal to deal is an anticompetitive exclusionary practice. Failing that, the plaintiff can make out an attempt claim if it can show: a) the defendant's specific intent to acquire a monopoly; b) that the refusal to deal is an anticompetitive act designed to carry out the scheme; and c) a dangerous probability that the scheme would have created a monopoly if it had been allowed to run its course. See the discussions of monopolization and attempt in chapter III. above.

Example: In Lorain Journal Co. v. U.S., 342 U.S. 143, 72 S.Ct. 181 (1951), the Supreme Court condemned a newspaper's policy of refusing to sell advertising to any customer who also purchased advertising on a nearby radio station. Lorain Journal's obvious intent was to preserve an advertising monopoly to itself. Such a scheme would succeed only if Lorain Journal *already* had a dominant position in the market. For example, if it were merely one of a half dozen newspapers, advertisers who wished to advertise on both the radio station and a newspaper would have selected another newspaper. Therefore the Court had no problem in finding the necessary elements for the attempt offense.

Be warned, however, that even the monopolist may refuse to deal, provided that the refusal is not anticompetitive—i.e., that the refusal does not unreasonably enlarge its monopoly power or extend its duration without achieving compensating efficiencies. For example, even a monopolist can achieve cost savings through vertical integration, and one frequent consequence of vertical integration is that a firm discontinues dealing with independent vertically related firms. For example, in Paschall v. Kansas City Star Co.,

727 F.2d 692 (8th Cir.1984 *en banc*), cert. denied, 469 U.S. 872, 105 S.Ct. 222 (1985) the court held that it was not an antitrust violation for a monopolist newspaper to began self-delivery of its newspapers, and therefore to cut off all its independent carriers.

But in Aspen Skiing Co. v. Aspen Highlands Skiing Corp., 472 U.S. 585, 105 S.Ct. 2847 (1985), the Supreme Court reaffirmed the Lorain Journal rule and held that a refusal to deal by a monopolist, together with a showing of anticompetitive motive or intent, violated § 2 of the Sherman Act. In this case there was evidence that a joint venture between the plaintiff and the defendant ski resort operators was profitable to *both parties. However, the defendant's refusal to participate injured the plaintiff's business far more than it injured the defendant's business. The effect was to strengthen the defendant's near monopoly command of the Aspen skiing market. This evidence was sufficient, the Supreme Court held, to support the jury verdict for the plaintiff.*

Finally, the **Essential Facility** doctrine holds that it is illegal for the controller of a properly defined essential facility to deny access to a competitor. That doctrine is discussed in chapter II.A.

D. REVIEW QUESTIONS

1. **T or F** Both at common law and under the antitrust laws a firm generally has the right to deal or to refuse to deal with whomever it pleases.

2. **T or F** Concerted refusals to deal are always *per se* illegal under the Sherman Act.

3. California contains thirty-five growers of Kiwi Berries. They face intense competition from New Zealand Kiwi Berry growers, who have lower costs than they do. Twenty-five of the California growers decide that they could market their Kiwi Berries much more effectively if they appointed a joint sales agent to represent all of them in seller negotiations. Soon after they appoint such an agent, Sam Spade, who owns Spade's Grocery Store, approaches one of the Kiwi Berry growers and asks to purchase some Kiwi Berries. The grower replies that he is no longer selling Kiwi Berries except through the joint sales agent. Does Spade have a cause of action under the antitrust laws?

4. **T or F** Concerted refusals to deal are legal if they are undertaken in order to prevent free riding.

5. **T or F** Refusals to deal by the monopolist are generally illegal under § 2 of the Sherman Act.

VIII

HORIZONTAL MERGERS

Analysis

A. HORIZONTAL MERGERS AND COMPETITION

For antitrust purposes, a merger occurs whenever two firms that had been separate come under common ownership or control. Mergers may come about in a number of ways:

(a) One corporation may acquire all or part of the shares of another corporation; this is known as a stock acquisition.

(b) One firm may acquire all or part of the assets of another firm; this is known as an asset acquisition.

(c) Two corporations may dissolve and combine their assets into a new corporation; this is known as a consolidation.

1. MERGERS AND § 7 OF THE CLAYTON ACT

a. Mergers and Original § 7

Mergers are generally analyzed under § 7 of the Clayton Act, which condemns them if their effect "may be substantially to lessen competition, or to tend to create a monopoly." In the past some mergers were evaluated as combinations in restraint of trade under § 1 of the Sherman Act. This was so because as originally passed in 1914 § 7 contained several jurisdictional "loopholes." First of all, as originally drafted the statute applied only to mergers that eliminated competition "between" the merging firms. Since vertical mergers are not concerned with competition between the merging firms, but rather with competition between the post-merger firm and other firms in the market, the original Clayton Act did not apply to them. Second, as it was originally drafted § 7 applied to stock acquisitions but not to asset acquisitions. As a result many mergers avoided scrutiny under § 7 by structuring their union as an asset acquisition which often left only the empty shell of the acquired firm.

b. The Celler–Kefauver and Subsequent Amendments to § 7

Both of these problems were corrected in 1950, when § 7 was amended by the Celler–Kefauver Act, so as to apply to both vertical and horizontal mergers, and to asset acquisitions as well as stock acquisitions.

More recently the statute has been amended two more times. It now reaches all mergers "in or affecting" interstate commerce, rather than merely those mergers that are in the flow of commerce. The statute now goes to the full limit of Congress's ability to regulate interstate commerce under the federal constitution. Finally, the statute was amended to refer to "persons" instead of "corporations." Now it is clear that the statute applies to both incorporated and unincorporated firms. *The result of all these jurisdiction broadening amendments is that today § 1 of the Sherman Act has become nearly superfluous in merger enforcement.*

2. IDENTIFYING HORIZONTAL MERGERS

A merger is "horizontal" when it involves the union of two firms that had been selling the same product in the same geographic market. That is to say, the two firms were competitors before the merger occurred. If only one of these two things is true—that is, if the merger involves two firms that manufacture the same product but sell it in different areas, or two firms that sell somewhat different products in the same area—then the competition between the two firms will be characterized as "potential" rather than "actual." Such unions are generally called conglomerate mergers. They are treated in chapter IX. below.

Because the horizontal merger involves two firms in the same market, it produces two important consequences that do not flow from other kinds of mergers:

(a)   after the merger the relevant market contains one firm less than it did before;

(b)   the post-merger firm has a larger market share than either of the merging partners had before the merger occurred.

3. THE DANGERS OF HORIZONTAL MERGERS: COLLUSION AND UNILATERAL PRICE INCREASES

Since horizontal mergers simultaneously reduce the number of firms in a market and increase the size of one firm in the market, they can make the post-merger market more conducive to collusion or monopolization. In extreme cases a merger could yield a single firm with a market share of 100%. Early in the history of federal antitrust enforcement, such "mergers to monopoly" were not uncommon, but they presumably are rare today.

The more realistic danger is that a merger will increase the likelihood of express collusion or else make tacit collusion (oligopoly price leadership) more possible than it was before the merger occurred. The effect of either of these is reduced output and higher consumer prices. Several lower courts have recognized the importance of tacit (oligopoly) collusion in merger law. See, for example, Hospital Corp. of America v. F.T.C., 807 F.2d 1381 (7th Cir. 1986), cert. denied, 481 U.S. 1038, 107 S.Ct. 1975 (1987) (policy concern is that merger "may enable the acquiring firm to cooperate (or cooperate better) with other leading competitors on reducing or limiting output.... ").

4. THE RULE OF REASON AND THE EFFICIENCIES PRODUCED BY MERGERS

If monopolization or the increased likelihood of collusion were the *only* results of mergers, then we would be well off to condemn them under a *per se* rule that made all mergers automatically illegal. However, the problem is not so simple. Many mergers create substantial economies in production or distribution that enable the post-merger firm to operate at lower cost than either of the pre-merger partners. These economies come in various kinds:

a. Economies of Plant Size

Economies of plant size result from the fact that a larger plant may cost less to operate per unit of output than a smaller plant costs. (See the discussion of economies of scale in chapter I above.) Since mergers do not usually generate larger plants, but only the union of different plants under common control, economies of plant size do not frequently result from mergers. However, there are some exceptions to this rule:

Example: Before a merger firm A manufactured metal parts of both type 1 and type 2 in its only plant. Firm B did the same thing. After the merger, however, firm AB shifts all the production of part type 1 to one plant, and all the production of part type 2 to the other plant. The result is longer production runs, more specialization, and lower operating expenses.

b. Multi-plant Economies

Multi-plant economies are economies that arise from the fact that it may be cheaper to operate several plants than it is to operate one or a few. For example, the firm that controls several plants can shift production back and forth to meet geographic changes in demand. The firm that has high output in many plants can also purchase inputs in large amounts. Generally, the larger the quantity of raw material that it purchases, the lower the price. Finally, things like research and development and advertising are cheaper for the large firm than they are for the smaller one, for the large firm can spread the costs over a larger amount of output.

c. Economies of Distribution

Economies of distribution result when a firm is able to find cheaper ways of getting its product to the final consumer. The achievement of economies of distribution is one of the most important results of vertical mergers. (See chapter IV above.) However, horizontal mergers can produce such economies as well, particularly in situations where large horizontal size is necessary to make certain economies of distribution possible.

Example: Before the merger Jack's small grocery chain and Jill's small grocery chain were each too small to support a company-owned dairy and chicken farm. However, after the merger Jack'n'Jill's Grocery Chain is large enough to support such a farm. The result is that the new chain is able to obtain these farm products more reliably and generally at a lower price, since market transactions between the farm and the grocer have been eliminated. In a competitive market the consumer will receive most of the benefit of these costs savings.

Today the law of horizontal mergers has the difficult job of balancing the potential for these efficiencies against the dangers of collusion.

5.   EFFICIENCY AND MERGER POLICY

At one time or another courts and the antitrust enforcement agencies have considered three different positions concerning the relationship between efficiencies and merger enforcement policy:

(1)   Mergers should be evaluated for their effect on market power or likelihood of collusion, and efficiency considerations should be ignored;

(2)   Mergers that create substantial efficiencies should be legal, or there should be at least a limited "efficiency defense" in merger cases;

(3)   Mergers should be condemned *because* they create efficiencies, in order to protect competitors of the post-merger firm.

a.   Efficiency and Merger Policy During the Warren Era

In the 1960's the Warren Supreme Court adopted the third of these policies. Well known cases such as Brown Shoe Co. v. U.S., 370 U.S. 294, 82 S.Ct. 1502 (1962), and U.S. v. Von's Grocery Co., 384 U.S. 270, 86 S.Ct. 1478 (1966) condemned these mergers *because* the merger made the merging firms more efficient than they had been before. Although efficiency benefits consumers by producing lower prices, it injures competitors, who have a more difficult time competing with the new, more efficient rival. *Thus the Warren Court adopted a policy that the purpose of antimerger law was to protect competitors rather than consumers.*

Although the Court defined the promotion of "competition" as the underlying goal of merger policy, "competition" did not refer to a state of affairs in which price is reduced to marginal cost and marginal costs are minimized. (See chapter I.A.) Rather, "competition" referred to the rivalry of a large number of small firms. Under this definition horizontal mergers decreased the amount of "competition" in the market even if output was higher and price lower than it had been before the merger.

b.   Efficiency and the Legislative History of § 7

The *Brown Shoe* case relied heavily on the legislative history of the 1950 Celler–Kefauver Amendments to § 7 of the Clayton Act. In fact, the *Brown Shoe* and *Von's Grocery* opinions were generally consistent with that legislative history, which makes clear that in 1950 Congress was more concerned with the welfare of small businesses and with the "rising tide of concentration" in many American markets than they were with low consumer prices. The legislative history reveals a strong concern that too many small businesses were being "gobbled up" by larger firms.

c.   Efficiency and Mergers: The Emerging Policy

Congress has not amended the substantive provisions of § 7 since 1950. Nor has the Supreme Court ever overruled its *Brown Shoe* and *Von's Grocery* decisions. Nevertheless, current merger policy with respect to efficiency has drifted far away from the concerns expressed in the legislative history of the Celler–Kefauver Amendments, and even further away from the early Supreme Court decisions interpreting those amendments, particularly the *Brown Shoe* decision. Congress (together with the President) has the power to make its policy clear, should either the courts or the antitrust enforcement agencies (the Justice Department and the FTC) adopt a policy which is too much in conflict with Congress's current wishes. However, it has not done so. Thus it appears that the political branches are at least tacitly in agreement with the economic revolution in merger policy.

Today mergers are no longer condemned because they are efficient. Rather, the object of merger policy is to reach those mergers likely to facilitate tacit or express collusion, or in some cases, monopolization.

d. An "Efficiency Defense" in Merger Cases?

Generally courts focus heavily on the possibility that a merger will increase the likelihood of collusion or monopolization, without explicitly considering efficiencies. Many people have argued that the courts should recognize an explicit "efficiency defense" in merger cases. The 1992 Horizontal Merger Guidelines issued by the Department of Justice and Federal Trade Commission (see section B. below) have adopted at least a limited efficiency defense. However, those Guidelines represent the enforcement position of these two agencies. They are not legislation and they are not binding on the courts.

Under an "efficiency defense," a merger which would otherwise be condemned would nevertheless be approved because it yielded compensating efficiencies.

The argument for an "efficiency defense" in merger cases is illustrated by Figure One. The graph shows the consequences of a merger that gives the post-merger firm more market power than it had before the merger (either because the merger creates a monopoly or facilitates collusion). As a result of this increased market power the post-merger firm reduces output from Q_1 to Q_2 on the graph, and increases price from P_1 to P_2. Triangle A_1 represents the monopoly "deadweight loss" created by this increase in market power (see the discussion of the social cost of monopoly in chapter I above.)

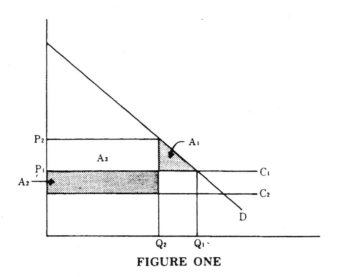

FIGURE ONE

The merger also produces measurable economies, however, which reduce the firm's costs from C_1 before the merger to C_2 after the merger. Rectangle A_2 represents efficiency gains that will result from these economies.

If A_2 is larger than A_1 the merger produces a *net* efficiency gain, even though the merger increases the post-merger firm's market power and enables it to raise its price above marginal cost. In fact, the merger is "efficient" even if it results in higher consumer prices, provided that the cost-savings which accrue to the merging firm exceed the increased costs imposed on consumers.

The analysis illustrates some of the great problems with an "efficiency defense" in merger cases:

1) Political Problems

   A purely economic approach to an efficiency defense in merger cases (that is, an approach that looked only at welfare gains and losses and ignored the way in which wealth is distributed) would end up approving some mergers even if they resulted in higher prices and lower output. This would happen when the losses suffered by consumers as a result of the post-merger firm's increased ability to charge monopoly prices are less than the efficiency gains, even though the gains show up as profits to the post-merger firm.

   Such an "efficiency defense" would almost certainly be politically unacceptable, regardless of its economic soundness. More plausibly, someone raising an efficiency defense in a merger case would have to show that, because of economies achieved by the merger, the resulting output will increase and price will decrease, even though the merger is beyond the threshold that would indicate it is a threat to competition.

2) Problems of Measurement

The problems of quantifying the efficiency gains and losses resulting from mergers are substantial, and clearly beyond the competence of courts in all but the clearest situations. As the figure above illustrates, a merger is efficient if the savings produced by the cost reductions exceeds the deadweight loss produced by the increase in market power. However, the measurement of both cost reductions and deadweight loss requires knowledge about the firm's marginal cost curve. The measurement of the deadweight loss requires additional information about the shape of the demand curve, or the elasticity of demand which the firm faces. No court today is capable of quantifying these things, certainly not with enough precision to engage in "balancing" one against the other.

e. The Efficiency Defense in the 1992 Horizontal Merger Guidelines

The 1992 Horizontal Merger Guidelines decline to recognize a *general* efficiency defense in merger cases. However, the government will consider efficiencies relating to "achieving economies of scale, better integration of production facilities, plant specialization, lower transportation costs, and similar efficiencies relating to specific manufacturing, servicing, or distribution operations of the merging firms." It may also consider efficiencies relating to savings in marketing and distribution. In all events, it "will reject claims of efficiencies if equivalent or comparable savings can reasonably be achieved by the parties through other means." Further, "the expected net efficiencies must be greater the more significant are the competitive risks.... "

B. THE BASIC TESTS FOR LEGALITY IN HORIZONTAL MERGER CASES

Every market is different. Furthermore, the likelihood of monopoly pricing or collusion in a market is a function of many different variables, such as:

(1) the homogeneity of the product;

(2) the way the product is sold;

(3) the number of buyers and their level of sophistication;

(4) the sensitivity of the product to changes in price;

(5) the existence of barriers to entry;

For this reason it is not possible to come up with a single rule that will apply to all markets and tells us reliably whether a particular merger is anticompetitive. Neither could courts or even the Federal Trade Commission administer a host of "rules" specifically tailored for each market in which a horizontal merger might occur. *Rather, some compromises must be made and a more-or-less unitary test adopted. Then certain individual factors about specific markets can be taken into account and perhaps used to vary the results.*

1. MARKET STRUCTURE, POST–MERGER MARKET SHARE, AND PRIMA FACIE ILLEGALITY

A positive correlation probably exists between the concentration level of a market—that is, the number and size of the firms in the market—and the likelihood of collusion or monopolization. Furthermore, the greater the size of the merging firms, the greater impact the merger will have on resulting market concentration.

These facts suggest it is possible to formulate a rule that ties the legality of particular mergers to the concentration level in a market and the size of the merging parties. The courts have attempted to do exactly that. Unfortunately, the problem is not quite as simple as first appearance suggests. Different markets become anticompetitive at different concentration levels. Economists themselves differ greatly over the relevant numbers. For example, many liberal economists, particularly during the New Deal, believed markets ceased to perform competitively at rather moderate concentration levels. By contrast, economists from the "Chicago School" believe that even very concentrated markets can perform competitively.

Nevertheless, in U.S. v. Philadelphia National Bank, 374 U.S. 321, 83 S.Ct. 1715 (1963), the Supreme Court approved the general approach of using data concerning market concentration and firm size to establish the prima facie illegality of a merger, and then using non-market share considerations as mitigating or aggravating factors on a case-by-case basis. At least one recent decision, however, has called *Philadelphia Bank* into question, and suggested that a merger achieving a stated concentration level should be condemned only if there is independent evidence of noncompetitive performance. U.S. v. Baker Hughes Inc., 908 F.2d 981 (D.C.Cir. 1990).

The 1992 Merger Guidelines seem to reflect the doubts about *Philadelphia Bank* expressed in recent decisions. They contain a long discussion of factors relating to the competitive significance of concentration data (including entry barriers, buyer sophistication, conditions and terms of sale, product differentiation, and the like). But the Guidelines are silent about who has the burden of proof on these issues. Since the basic rule is that the plaintiff must prove its case, the Guidelines seem implicitly to suggest that the government, rather than defendant, has the burden.

a. Measuring Market Concentration—The Four–Firm Concentration Ratio

The measurement of market concentration traditionally most used by courts is the four-firm concentration ratio (CR4), which consists of the sum of the market shares, expressed as a percentage, of the four largest firms in the market.

> **Example:** A market contains six firms, with market shares as follows: Firm A = 25%, Firm B = 20%, Firm C = 20%, Firm D = 15%, Firm E = 10%, and Firm F = 10%. The CR4 in this market is 80 (25 + 20 + 20 + 15)

> **Note:** Some economists also use the CR8, which is simply the sum of the market shares of the eight largest firms in the market.

As noted above, economists differ widely as to how concentrated a market must be before the possibility of collusion becomes significant. *However, over the years antitrust enforcement agencies and the courts have developed a broad consensus that markets in which the CR4 exceeds 75 or 80 are conducive to collusion and any merger in such markets should be scrutinized carefully. By contrast, markets in which the CR4 is less than 40 are generally safe.* In such a market the average size of even the four largest firms is 10% market share or less.

b. Measuring Market Concentration—The Herfindahl–Hirschman Index (HHI)

Today both the Justice Department and the Federal Trade Commission have generally replaced the CR4 measure of market concentration with the Herfindahl–Hirschman Index (HHI). The HHI is also widely used by the lower courts.

The HHI of any market is computed by summing the squares of the market shares of every firm in the relevant market.

Example: Consider the same market as illustrated above, containing six firms with market shares as follows: Firm A = 25%, Firm B = 20%, Firm C = 20%, Firm D = 15%, Firm E = 10%, and Firm F = 10%. In this case the HHI in the market equals $25^2 + 20^2 + 20^2 + 15^2 + 10^2 + 10^2$, or 1850.

1) Some Advantages of the HHI

Most economists believe that the HHI is capable of giving a more accurate picture than the CR4 of the dangers to competition in a particular market. This is so for a number of reasons:

(a) The HHI accounts for the market shares of every firm in the market while the CR4 considers only the market shares of the four largest firms.

(b) The HHI accounts for the size *distribution* of the largest firms in the market, while the CR4 does not. For example, a market in which the four largest firms each have a 20% market share has a CR4 of 80. So does a market in which the largest firm has a 77% market share and the next three firms have 1% each. However, there is widespread agreement today that the second market is far more conducive to oligopoly price leadership than the first market is. In fact, a market dominated by four equal sized firms could operate quite competitively. The HHI accounts for the differences in these two markets quite dramatically. In the first market the HHI is around 1700, depending on the size distribution of the smaller firms in the market. In the second market the HHI is around 6000, depending on the size distribution of the smaller firms in the market.

(c)   The HHI does a more reliable job than the CR4 of predicting the *impact* of a particular merger on the concentration index. For example, under the CR4 a merger of two firms who were not among the top four might not affect the CR4 at all, unless the resulting firm became one of the top four in size. Under the HHI every merger has a predictable effect on the increase in market concentration: the HHI will increase by two times the product of the market shares of the two merging firms.

Note: This is so because before the merger the two firms were calculated into the HHI as $A^2 + B^2$. However, after the merger the two firms have become one, with a market share equal to the sum of the market shares of the two premerger firms. Thus the new firm will be calculated into the HHI as $(A + B)^2$. The square of a binomial such as this one equals $A^2 + 2AB + B^2$. The 2AB thus represents the *difference* between the premerger and postmerger HHI.

(d)   The HHI does a better job than the CR4 of accounting for size disparities between the merging firms. For example if two firms with 20% market shares merge, the resulting firm will have a 40% share. The same thing will be true of a merger between a 38% firm and a 2% firm. Nevertheless, most economists agree that the first merger has a much more serious impact on competition than the second. The first merger may double the size of the dominant firm or create a new dominant firm. The second merger merely makes a very large firm marginally larger. The CR4 accounts for this difference in result only haphazardly, depending on whether one or both of the merging firms are among the four largest in the market. The HHI accounts for the difference rather precisely: the first merger increases the HHI by 800 points; the second merger increases the HHI by only 152 points.

2)   Some Disadvantages of the HHI

Use of the HHI produces some difficulties as well, however:

(a)   The HHI is more accurate because it accounts for the size of every firm in the market. For the same reason, however, measurement is more difficult. The statistician must estimate the size of *all* firms, rather than merely the size of the top four firms. As a practical matter, fringe firms do not all need to be measured when the HHI is used. For example, a firm with a 2% market share contributes only 4 HHI points, and a firm with a .5% market share contributes only .25 HHI points. Since the relevant thresholds for considering mergers are 1200 and 1800, a rough estimate of the HHI contributed by the smallest firms is often good enough.

(b)   Under the HHI great care must be taken when the largest firms are measured, because the market shares are squared. The result is that an error in the calculation of the market share of the largest firm in the market can greatly exaggerate or understate the market's true HHI.

Example: Assume that a market contains four firms with market shares of 35%, 15%, 10% and 10%. The CR4 is 70, and the HHI in the market is around 1700, depending on the size of the other firms. If the largest firm is erroneously measured as 40%, the CR4 will jump to 75—not a dramatic difference. However, the HHI will jump to around 2100. In this case a 5% error in the measurement of the largest firm alone has about the same impact on the HHI as a 5% error in each of the other three firms in the CR4.

2.   MARKET DEFINITION UNDER THE 1992 HORIZONTAL MERGER GUIDELINES

Horizontal Merger Guidelines issued by the Justice Department and Federal Trade Commission in 1992 replace older Guidelines issued in 1968 and again in 1982/1984. The 1992 Guidelines apply only to horizontal mergers, leaving vertical and potential competition mergers to be covered under Guidelines issued in 1984. The 1992 Guidelines contain a detailed description of how the government agencies will define relevant markets in horizontal merger cases. The Guidelines generally reflect more economic sophistication in market definition than has been shown by the courts.

a.   The Relevant Product Market Under the Guidelines

The Guidelines define a relevant product market as "a product or group of products and a geographic area in which it is produced or sold such that a hypothetical profit-maximizing firm, not subject to price regulation, that was the only present and future producer or seller of those products in that area likely would impose at least a 'small but significant and nontransitory' increase in price, assuming the terms of sale of all other products are held constant." The "small but significant" price increase is generally presumed to be five percent.

1)   The Demand Side

In trying to define a relevant product market on the demand side the government will begin with the product of the defendant. Next the government will hypothesize a "small but significant and nontransitory" price increase, and estimate how many buyers would shift to substitutes. If a large number would substitute away, the market is too small. The government will then redraw the market to include the "next best substitute" and repeat the process. *When the government has identified a grouping of products such that large numbers of customers could not substitute away in response to the small but significant price increase, it has defined a relevant product market on the demand side.*

2)   The Supply Side

The Guidelines note that "if a firm has existing assets that likely would be shifted or extended into production and sale of the relevant product within one year, and without incurring significant sunk costs of entry and exit, in response to a "small but significant and nontransitory" increase in price for only the relevant product, the Agency will treat that firm as a market participant. The Guidelines generally follow the same procedure as on the demand side of the market: they hypothesizes a 5% price increase and considers how many firms could easily switch production into the defendant's product. Those firms will be included in the relevant market. It will repeat this process until it reaches a product definition for which the elasticity of supply is low.

b.   The Geographic Market

The Guidelines' definition process for geographic markets is identical in principle to its process of product market definition. On the demand side, the government will begin with the sales area covered by the defendant and its immediate competitors and hypothesize a "small but significant and nontransitory" price increase. Then it will consider how many consumers would substitute away by making their purchases outside this geographic area. If the number of consumers who look elsewhere is substantial, the larger area into which they look for alternatives will be drawn into the market.

On the supply side the government agency will hypothesize a "small but significant and nontransitory" price increase and ask how many suppliers outside the area could ship into the defendant's area in response to that increase. If that number is large, it will draw a larger market.

In making assessments of the geographic market, the government will give heavy consideration to:

"(1) evidence that buyers have shifted or have considered shifting purchases between different geographic locations in response to relative changes in price or other competitive variables;

"(2) evidence that sellers base business decisions on the prospect of buyer substitution between geographic locations in response to relative changes in price or other competitive variables;

"(3) the influence of downstream competition faced by buyers in their output markets; and

"(4) the timing and costs of switching suppliers."

c. The "Cellophane Fallacy" in the Guidelines

By using current prices as a starting position, the Guidelines may ignore the fact that the market is already collusive, and the firms in it are already charging their profit-maximizing price. As a result, a further price increase would be unprofitable. In monopolization cases this is called the "Cellophane fallacy," named after the Supreme Court's decision in U.S. v. E.I. du Pont De Nemours & Co., 351 U.S. 377, 76 S.Ct. 994 (1956). The fallacy is described further in chapter III.A.

Those defending the Guidelines' approach note that Clayton § 7 appears to condemn only those mergers that "lessen" competition; if a market is already noncompetitive, then competition cannot be "lessened" any further. Critics generally respond that mergers in oligopolistic or cartelized markets only serve to make things worse, by reducing the number of effective rivals or permitting the oligopolists to eliminate a disruptive firm.

3. MERGER STANDARDS UNDER THE 1992 MERGER GUIDELINES—MARKET SHARE THRESHOLDS

a. Mergers that Threaten to Facilitate Collusion

The 1992 Guidelines establish relatively clear standards for assessing the anticompetitive consequences of mergers, as follows:

(1) A market in which the *post*-merger HHI is less than 1000 is a "safe harbor," in which the government agency is "unlikely" to challenge a merger.

(2) If the *post*-merger HHI falls between 1000 and 1800, the government will probably not challenge a merger that produces an HHI *increase* of less than 100 points. However, if the increase is greater than 100 points, the government will be more likely to challenge the merger, depending on its assessment of non-market share factors discussed later in this chapter.

(3) The government will challenge most mergers where the *post*-merger HHI exceeds 1800 and the merger adds more than 100 points to the HHI. The only likely exception to this rule is where entry barriers in a market are so low that no firm could profitably charge monopoly prices. If the post-merger HHI exceeds 1800 and the mergers adds between 50 and 100 points to the HHI, the government may challenge the merger depending on the post-merger concentration in the market and the presence or absence of the non-market share factors. If the merger increases the HHI by less than 50 points it will probably not be challenged.

b. Unilateral Anticompetitive Effects

The Government Agencies also recognize that some mergers are anticompetitive, not because they threaten to collusion, but because they might enable a firm in a product differentiated market to raise its price unilaterally. This is more likely to occur as (a) market differentiation is more substantial; (b) the output of the two merging firms is more similar to one another; and (c) the collective output of the two merging firms is more distinctive from that of other firms in the market.

Example: The market for automobiles has 15 manufacturers, but it is divided into "luxury" cars and "standard" cars. There are only three manufacturers of "luxury" cars: Mercedes, BMW, and Lexus. Customers regard these cars as close substitutes for one another, but most of these customers would regard one of the "standard" cars (Chevrolet, Ford, Chrysler, Toyota, etc) as a much poorer substitute. In this case a merger between Mercedes and BMW is much more likely to be anticompetitive than a merger between, say, Mercedes and Chrysler. The closer the customers regard Mercedes and BMW as substitutes for each other, and the more they regard a standard car as a poor substitute, the greater the anticompetitive potential of this merger.

See 1992 Horizontal Merger Guidelines § 2.21; and Hovenkamp § 12.3.

4.   NON–MARKET SHARE FACTORS UNDER EXISTING LAW AND THE 1992 HORIZONTAL MERGER GUIDELINES

In considering the legality of a merger, both the courts and the enforcement agencies generally look at the relevant market concentration-market share thresholds in order to establish prima facie legality. If the market is unconcentrated, they need look no further. However, if the merger falls within one of the "danger zones" described above, it is prima facie illegal. Then one must consider several non-market share factors in order to assess the overall impact of the merger on competition. As noted previously, the Guidelines are generally unclear about who has the burden of proof with respect to these factors.

Note: The discussion here implies that a court or enforcement agency will look at market concentration and shares *first* in assessing the competitive consequences of a merger. However, this is not always the case. Calculating the HHI is complex and expensive. Sometimes it is more efficient to look at non-market share factors first in order to determine whether further consideration of a merger is necessary. For example, if barriers to entry in a market are obviously so low that no firm could profitably increase its price to monopoly levels, then there is no point in computing the HHI. The merger is legal.

Example: In U.S. v. Waste Management, Inc., 743 F.2d 976 (2d Cir.1984) the court refused to condemn a merger between two solid waste disposal companies, in spite of the fact that the post-merger market share of the firm was about 49% and the post-merger HHI in excess of 2700 or 2800. The merger was legal, the court held, because entry barriers were so low that people had frequently gone into the business by working out of their homes. Once that fact was established, computation of the market concentration and post-merger market share was irrelevant. Accord U.S. v. Baker Hughes Inc., 908 F.2d 981 (D.C.Cir. 1990); U.S. v. Country Lake Foods, 754 F.Supp. 669 (D. Minn. 1990).

The courts and the Merger Guidelines have considered the following non-market share factors to be relevant in merger analysis:

a. Barriers to Entry

A barrier to entry is something that makes the cost of doing business higher for a new entrant than it is for existing firms. The existence of barriers to entry creates a "spread" between the competitive price in a market and the price that the firms already in the market can charge without encouraging new firms to come in. For example, if it costs existing firms $1.00 per unit to produce a product, but it would cost someone yet to come into the market $1.20 to produce the same product, then the firms already in the market can profitably charge $1.19 without encouraging new firms to come in.

The converse of the above argument is that if costs are identical for incumbents and new entrants, then *any* monopoly returns being produced by the incumbents will invite outsiders to invest their money in this market. In that case even an incumbent firm with 100% of the market could not charge a monopoly price for very long. The market would become flooded with other people trying to earn the monopoly returns as well, and soon price would be driven back to the competitive level.

Historically courts have ignored low entry barriers or found them readily. *Certain Supreme Court decisions, such as U.S. v. Von's Grocery Co., 384 U.S. 270, 86 S.Ct. 1478 (1966), have been criticized for condemning a merger of two grocery store chains even though entry barriers in the grocery market are usually considered to be very low.* The 1992 Merger Guidelines recognize the importance of entry barriers and state that the government will not prosecute an action if it finds entry barriers to be very low. Several more recent courts have followed this suggestion, even when the plaintiff was the government itself, and refused to condemn mergers in the absence of significant entry barriers. See, for example, the *Waste Management, Country Lake* and *Baker Hughes* cases cited above. In Cargill v. Monfort of Colo., 479 U.S. 104, 107 S.Ct. 484 (1986), the Supreme Court suggested in dicta that a *competitor* could not challenge a merger on the ground that the merger would facilitate predatory pricing if entry barriers into the market were low.

Entry barriers are most readily found in markets requiring a large initial investment the is "committed," or "sunk." This means that this part of the investment cannot be recovered in the event of failure. For example, the fact that entry into a market requires a $10,000,000 truck fleet does not suggest high entry barriers if (a) the trucks can practicably be leased for short terms; or (b) if the firm fails the trucks can readily be converted to other uses and there is a good market for them. By contrast, if entry requires a $10,000,000 investment in a specialized chemical plant that cannot be converted to other uses and will have only salvage value if the firm fails, entry barriers should be reckoned as high. See, for example, FTC v. Elders Grain, 868 F.2d 901 (7th Cir. 1989) (entry barriers high when industry had expensive, specialized plants with "little salvage value" in the event of withdrawal from the market).

The 1992 Horizontal Merger Guidelines identify entry barriers as low where "entry would be timely, likely, and sufficient in its magnitude, character and scope to deter or counteract the competitive effects of concern." In markets where the prospects for entry passes these three tests—timeliness, likelihood, and sufficiency—the merger will ordinarily not be challenged. Entry is "timely" only if it can proceed "within two years from initial planning to significant market impact." Entry is "likely" if (a) it would be profitable at pre-merger prices and (b) the entrant would be likely to obtain those prices. Entry is "sufficient" only if its magnitude will effectively prices back down to premerger levels.

In FTC v. Staples, 970 F.Supp. 1066, 1087 (D.D.C. 1997) the court found high entry barriers into the market for office supply superstores, notwithstanding that the stores themselves seemed to be quite generic in design and that the firms purchased virtually all of their inventory from other manufacturers. The real barrier was in the need to have a large number of stores in order to attain various economies. The FTC found that as the number of competing office supply superstores within a single community increased, their prices decreased. See Hovenkamp § 12.6.

b. Adequacy of Irreplaceable Raw Materials

Sometimes the current output of a firm overstates its position in a market. This is particularly true in markets for scarce natural resources that cannot be replaced. For example, a firm currently producing 10% of the nation's oil, but whose reserves are about to dry up, is not likely to be producing 10% of the nation's oil in the future unless it can acquire some new reserves. In this case it is appropriate to "adjust" the firm's market share downward.

Example: In U.S. v. General Dynamics Corp., 415 U.S. 486, 94 S.Ct. 1186 (1974), the Supreme Court refused to condemn a merger of two coal producers. The acquiring firm had 6.5% of current output in one of the relevant markets, and the acquired firm had 4.4%. However, the acquired firm owned only 1% of the reserves in that market, and all other known reserves were claimed by others. As a result, the current market share severely overstated the firm's future production potential.

c. Excess Capacity

Excess capacity is the difference between the total efficient capacity of the plants in the market and the amount that the market is currently producing and selling. A market containing widely distributed excess capacity is less conducive to monopolization or collusion than a market without excess capacity, particularly if the excess capacity is held by fringe firms. The fringe firms will be in a position to respond to a monopoly price increase by increasing their own output out of existing capacity. Excess capacity has sometimes been treated as a non-market share factor to be applied in merger cases.

d. Degree of Product Homogeneity

The real world contains few perfectly fungible products—i.e., products that are so similar to one another that customers are indifferent as to their source. Some agricultural products and minerals, and a few standard manufactured items may fall into this category, but most "brand-specific" products— automobiles, clothing, stereo and television equipment, computers, cameras, processed foods, furniture, and a host of other things—are differentiated, and consumers may strongly prefer one brand over another.

The more product differentiation a market contains, the more difficult collusion becomes. This is particularly true of tacit collusion, where the firms cannot meet together in order to work out a detailed schedule that accounts for differences in brand quality and perception. As a general rule a market with a certain concentration level and a homogeneous product is more conducive to collusion than a market with the same concentration level and a heterogeneous product.

Judicial analysis of product differentiation in merger cases has not been particularly sophisticated. In general, courts have looked at product differentiation only in order to determine whether the two merging firms were really "competitors"—i.e., whether the products they produced were sufficiently similar to warrant grouping the two firms in the same market. The 1992 Horizontal Merger Guidelines list product differentiation as a mitigating factor in most merger cases.

Importantly, the 1992 Merger Guidelines also note instances where product differentiation will *increase* the competitive threat of a merger. This occurs, not because the merger facilitates collusion, but because a product differentiated firm may be able to increase its price unilaterally, provided that its own product offering is significantly different from the offerings of others. Further, the merger will tend to increase price most if the products of the merging firms are close substitutes. The Guidelines suggest that these concerns become substantial when overall market concentration takes the merger out of the "safe harbor" provisions noted earlier—i.e., concentration must exceed 1000—and the post-merger market share of the merging firms exceeds 35%. As yet, no court has interpreted this theory.

e.   Marketing and Sales Methods

Some methods of distribution and sale of a product are more conducive to collusion than others. For example, the amount of competition in a market varies with the ease with which customers can obtain information about price. A physician who performs emergency surgery may have a fair amount of market power even though her share of a relevant market is very small. People who are not in need of emergency surgery are not strongly motivated to learn about its costs; by contrast, people who need emergency surgery are not in a very good position to engage in comparison shopping. At the other extreme, the opportunity for monopoly pricing may be very small in a market such as the Chicago Board of Trade, where commodities prices are posted and everyone has instant, inexpensive access to information about market conditions. If the going price of potatoes in such a market is $8.00 per hundredweight, a seller who attempts to charge $8.25 will make few sales.

Likewise, the size of sales in a market and the way in which price is negotiated can have an impact on the likelihood of collusion. Collusion is easiest, and therefore most likely to occur, in markets in which sales are small, prices are nonnegotiable and publicly announced, and most sales are made to buyers who have little knowledge about market conditions. Collusion is much more difficult if a market is characterized by a small number of large sales to well-informed buyers, and the terms each sale are established in negotiations that are not open to the public.

Courts have generally ignored questions about marketing and sales methods in evaluating the consequences of mergers. The 1992 Horizontal Merger Guidelines are more sophisticated; they observe that "If orders for the relevant product are frequent, regular and small relative to the total output of a firm in a market, it may be difficult for the firm to deviate in a substantial way without the knowledge of rivals and without the opportunity for rivals to react. If demand or cost fluctuations are relatively infrequent and small, deviations may be relatively easy to deter." In such cases the merger poses a greater competitive threat.

f.   The Significance of a "Trend" Towards Concentration

Earlier Supreme Court merger decisions such as *Brown Shoe* and *Von's Grocery,* both cited above, expressed a great concern for a "trend toward concentration" which those markets exhibited. Each year firms were becoming larger, often by merger, and the result was a smaller number of firms in the market. The Supreme Court responded by developing a "domino theory" respecting mergers in such markets: if the court permitted relatively innocuous mergers now, there was no telling how many mergers would occur in the future. Therefore, the best rule was to reach the trend toward concentration in its "incipiency," before the likelihood of collusion in a market was significant, or before large numbers of small businesses lost their identities.

One of the ironies of the Warren Court's decision to condemn mergers in markets exhibiting a trend toward concentration, was that the rule made life even more difficult for small businesses than simple approval of the mergers would have. Firms that cannot achieve available economies of scale by merger are likely to do so by new entry. When that happens they will be able to undersell the smaller firms. The smaller firms will be in trouble but will have no one to whom they can sell their stores. As a result they will be forced merely to close their doors.

The 1992 Guidelines ignore the issue of "trends" toward concentration, and with good reason. Most often a market contains such a trend because it has become subject to economies of scale—that is, larger firms are able to do business more cheaply than smaller firms. As one or two firms become larger and enjoy reduced costs, they will respond by earning above average profits and by increasing their output. Other firms will then want to grow larger as well, both to enjoy higher profits and to prevent their own market shares from being taken away by the firms that have already claimed these efficiencies. The market will exhibit a "trend" toward concentration until most firms in the market have become large enough to take advantage of these scale economies.

5. THE PROBLEM OF CHARACTERIZATION IN MERGER LAW: WHEN IS A MERGER "HORIZONTAL"?

A merger is truly "horizontal" only if it involves two firms that 1) produce exactly the same product; and 2) sell the product in exactly the same geographic area. The real world probably contains no "perfectly horizontal" mergers. There are always differences, ever so slight, between the products offered by two firms or the geographic areas in which they sell.

The Supreme Court has frequently characterized a merger as "horizontal" even though the firms involved were not in perfect competition with each other. For example:

(1) In the *Von's Grocery* case, cited above, it described the merger as horizontal even though all of one firm's stores were in northeast Los Angeles and all the other firm's stores in southwest Los Angeles.

(2) In the *General Dynamics* case, cited above, it described the merger as horizontal even though one of the firms engaged in deep mining of coal while the other strip mined coal.

(3) In the *Brown Shoe* case, cited above, it described the merger as horizontal even though one of the firms manufactured relatively high quality, expensive shoes and the other manufactured lower quality, cheaper shoes.

(4) In U.S. v. Continental Can Co., 378 U.S. 441, 84 S.Ct. 1738 (1964) it described as horizontal a merger between a firm that manufactured metal cans and a firm that manufactured glass bottles.

a. When Is a Merger Horizontal? Factors to Consider

In each of the cases described above there was a certain amount of competition between the merger partners. In some cases there was far more competition than in others. Generalizing is quite difficult. Nevertheless, the consequences of characterizing a merger as "horizontal" are significant. If these firms had not been characterized as competitors, then the mergers would have been evaluated under the far more lenient "potential competition" standard that is applied to conglomerate mergers; mergers are rarely condemned today under that standard. (See chapter IX below).

In determining whether to characterize a merger as "horizontal" the court will look at a variety of factors, including:

1) The Degree to Which the Firms Bid for the Same Sales

In the *Continental Can* case the lower court had found that there was very intense competition between can manufacturers and bottle manufacturers for certain markets, such as baby food and beer. It characterized the merger as horizontal. By contrast, in U.S. v. Columbia Steel Co., 334 U.S. 495, 68 S.Ct. 1107 (1948) the Supreme Court noted that the two merging firms (one a manufacturer of heavy grade steel, and the other of light grade steel) had submitted about 9000 bids between them for various projects. However, they had bid for the same jobs only 166 times. The court found no "substantial" competition between the firms and dismissed the complaint.

2) Elasticity of Supply

Even though two firms manufacture slightly different products, one may be able to switch into the other's product area very easily. For example, U.S. v. Aluminum Co. of America (Rome Cable), 377 U.S. 271, 84 S.Ct. 1283 (1964), involved the merger of a company that made aluminum and copper conductor and a larger firm that made only aluminum conductor. The lower court grouped aluminum and copper conductor into the same market, finding that there was "complete manufacturing interchangeability" between them. The Supreme Court reversed and found the aluminum to be a relevant market by itself. In this case the Supreme Court was probably wrong and the lower court correct, provided that the lower court's fact finding was correct.

3) Responsiveness of One Product's Price to Demand and Price Changes in the Other Product

If prices of the products produced by two firms rise and fall together, that is evidence that there is substantial competition between the two, even though they may look different from one another.

b. Litigation Strategies

Strategy becomes very important for the defendant arguing a merger case on the basis of market definition. In a monopolization case the defendant frequently argues that the relevant market should be larger than the plaintiff alleges. The result will be to make the defendant's market share smaller. The strategy in a merger case is more complex. The defendant will want to argue for a large market if the result will be to make the market appear less concentrated and the post-merger firm's market share smaller. For example, if a manufacturer of men's shoes acquired a manufacturer of women's shoes, the defendant might argue that the relevant market is "footwear." If "footwear" includes more than shoes—perhaps boots, rubbers, and mocassins—the result might be to place more manufacturers in the relevant market and perhaps make it appear less concentrated, and also to lower the relative market shares of the two merging firms.

However, the defendant should also try to look at the market from a different perspective and argue that it is actually *smaller* than the plaintiff alleges. For example, in this case the defendant might argue that there are really two relevant markets, "men's footwear" and "women's footwear." If the defendant succeeds, then the court will conclude that this merger is not horizontal and apply the much more lenient potential competition standard.

c. The "Fix It First" Rule

Frequently a merger will involve two firms that operate in substantially different markets; however the two markets overlap in some way. In such cases the Justice Department or FTC may approve the merger (i.e., agree not to challenge it), *provided* that the firm divests certain assets in the overlapping segment of the market.

Example: Plateau Petroleum Company owns several hundred gasoline stations west of the Mississippi River. Grande Petroleum Co. owns several gasoline stations east of the Mississippi River. However, both companies own stations throughout Missouri and in part of Illinois. Plateau acquires Grande. The Justice Department approves the acquisition, provided that Plateau sells all of Grande's stations in those two states to a third party. Once that happens the merger eliminates almost no actual competition.

6. THE "FAILING COMPANY" DEFENSE

The failing company defense can make it legal for a firm to acquire qualifying "failing companies" even though market structure and other indicators suggest that the merger is illegal. The failing company defense is not explicit in the language of § 7; however, when Congress passed the Celler–Kefauver Amendments to § 7 in 1950, it made clear that it wanted to permit acquisitions of failing firms that would otherwise go out of business. However, Congress did not say how a "failing company" should be identified, or what the elements of the defense should be.

a.   The Economics of the "Failing Company" Defense

The failing company defense was probably designed to protect small firms that might otherwise go out of business and not be able to find a legal buyer. However, the defense is not well designed to further this objective. To be sure, it may protect a particular small, failing business which is acquired by a larger firm. In the process, however, the acquisition may injure other smaller firms that compete with the acquired firm.

The failing company defense can also operate to condone quite anticompetitive mergers. For example, suppose a market contains four firms of roughly equal size, one of which is failing. If the failing company were left to close its doors, its sales would probably be divided among the other firms in proportion to their market share. That would leave three firms of roughly equal size. However, if the failing company defense permitted one of the firms to acquire the failing competitor, the result would be one firm with a 50% market share, and two with 25% market shares. This market is much more conducive to monopolization or oligopoly price leadership.

b.   The "Failing Company" Defense in the Case Law

The "failing company" defense is well established in the case law, but qualifying failing companies are seldom found. In Citizen Pub. Co. v. U.S., 394 U.S. 131, 89 S.Ct. 927 (1969), the Supreme Court held that before the defense can be used the defendant must show:

(1)   that the acquired firm was almost certain to go bankrupt and could not be reorganized successfully—that is, it would have to shut down;

(2)   that no less anticompetitive acquisition (i.e., by a smaller competitor or else by a noncompetitor) was available.

The 1992 Horizontal Merger Guidelines assess similar requirements. They note that a merger is not likely to create or enhance market power if

"1) the allegedly failing firm would be unable to meet its financial obligations in the near future;

"2) it would not be able to reorganize successfully under Chapter 11 of the Bankruptcy Act;

"3) it has made unsuccessful good-faith efforts to elicit reasonable alternative offers of acquisition of the assets of the failing firm that would both keep its tangible and intangible assets in the relevant market and pose a less severe danger to competition than does the proposed merger; and

"4) absent the acquisition, the assets of the failing firm would exit the relevant market."

The Guidelines also acknowledge a "failing division" defense, which might permit a firm to acquire the unprofitable division of another firm upon a showing that the division would have been liquidated had the acquisition not occurred. The "failing division" defense appears to have no precedent in either the legislative history of the antitrust laws or in the case law.

Closely related to the failing company defense is the **Newspaper Preservation Act**, which permits joint ventures between competing newspapers if the Attorney General finds one to be "in probable danger of financial failure." 15 U.S.C.A. § 1802. The statute was construed in Michigan Citizens for an Independent Press v. Thornburgh, 868 F.2d 1285 (D.C. Cir.1989), affirmed by an equally divided Court, 493 U.S. 38, 110 S.Ct. 398 (1989).

7. PARTIAL ACQUISITIONS AND ACQUISITIONS "SOLELY FOR INVESTMENT"

Section 7 condemns the acquisition of the "whole or any part" of the stock or assets of another firm, if the acquisition is anticompetitive. When does a partial acquisition violate § 7?

a. Partial v. Total Acquisitions

As a basic premise, no partial acquisition violates § 7 unless a total acquisition involving the same two firms would violate § 7.

b. Partial Acquisitions and Corporate "Control"

The acquisition of corporate "control" is not necessarily the dividing line between legal and illegal partial acquisitions. First of all, the meaning of "control" is ambiguous. Under state corporation law a single holder might need 50+% of a corporation's shares in order to have legal control. However, someone who owns, say, 25% of the shares of a large publicly-owned corporation has a great deal of influence on corporate decision making, and may have "control" for most practical purposes. For example, in U.S. v. E.I. du Pont De Nemours & Co., 353 U.S. 586, 77 S.Ct. 872 (1957) the Supreme Court condemned a vertical merger even though du Pont owned only 23% of General Motors' shares. "Control" was largely assumed. (The case is discussed in chapter IV above on vertical mergers.)

Second, the explicit mandate of § 7 is not to pursue mergers that yield "control," but rather mergers that are anticompetitive. The two can be very different.

Example: Firm A, Firm B and Firm C are intense competitors in a market. Then Firm A purchases 15% of the shares of Firm B. Suddenly, the competitive game has taken a new turn. Before, A would like nothing better than for B to fall on bad times, reduce its market share, or even go out of business. Now A, whose 15% interest gives it absolutely no "control" over B, nevertheless has a strong, affirmative interest in B's survival and prosperity. A court would probably condemn the acquisition as anticompetitive, in spite of the small size of A's purchase.

c.   Partial Asset Acquisitions

The problem of partial asset acquisitions is somewhat different than the problem of partial stock acquisitions. For example, suppose that Firm A has three plants and Firm B has two plants. Firm B purchases one of A's plants. The effect of this acquisition is that now A has two plants and B three. Quite possibly the merger has little or no effect on competition. This would certainly not be the case, however, if Firm B had purchased one third of A's shares. *In dealing with partial asset acquisitions, the courts generally look to increased concentration in productive capacity in the relevant market. A mere transfer of productive capacity will not necessarily increase concentration at all.*

By contrast, the effect of a *total* asset acquisition is generally the same as the effect of a total stock acquisition.

d.   Acquisitions for Investment Purposes Only

Section 7 does "not apply to persons purchasing ... stock solely for investment.... " But how does one tell whether a purchase is "solely for investment?" The Supreme Court has never interpreted this part of the statute. The lower courts have tended toward this rule: *if an acquisition has any measurable, adverse affect on competition, then it cannot be considered "solely for investment. "As a result the statutory language does not exempt many defendants. If a merger has no adverse effect on competition it is legal. If it has an adverse effect on competition, the "exception" does not apply.*

8.   JOINT VENTURES UNDER § 7 OF THE CLAYTON ACT

Most joint ventures between competitors are analyzed under § 1 of the Sherman Act. They are discussed in chapter II above. When the joint venture is itself a new corporation, then the parties to the venture have acquired the stock or assets of another firm (namely, the incorporated joint venture) and § 7 applies. In U.S. v. Penn–Olin Chem. Co., 378 U.S. 158, 84 S.Ct. 1710 (1964), the Supreme Court condemned a joint venture under the potential competition doctrine, which is discussed below in chapter IX. Since most joint ventures involve the development of some new product, they are treated more often under the potential competition doctrine than as horizontal mergers.

In general, the same standards apply in a joint venture case as in a merger case, except that the courts generally look only at the market involved in the joint venture. For example, if two chemical companies who already make chemical XYZ create a joint venture to manufacture it, the effects will be analogized to a merger of the XYZ production capacity of the two firms. Furthermore, there is some precedent for the view that joint ventures of explicitly shorter duration will be treated more leniently than joint ventures that appear to be permanent.

C.   PRE–MERGER NOTIFICATION

The Hart–Scott–Rodino Antitrust Improvements Act of 1976 established premerger notification requirements, including a prescribed "waiting period," for larger mergers.

The purpose of the statute is to permit the FTC and DOJ to analyze a large merger's impact on competition before it occurs. The statute applies when:

(1) One of the merging firms has annual net sales or total assets of $100 million or more, and the other firm has annual net sales or total assets of $10 million or more, if that firm is engaged in manufacturing. If the smaller firm is not engaged in manufacturing, then the statute applies only if it has total assets of $10 million or more.

(2) In addition to (a), the premerger notification statute applies only when the acquiring firm acquires an interest with a value exceeding $15 million in the acquired firm, or acquires 15% or more of the stock or assets of that firm.

If an acquisition is subject to the statute, the parties must ordinarily wait thirty days after notification before the merger can be consummated. However, if the acquisition is by tender offer, the waiting period is only fifteen days.

D. INTERLOCKING DIRECTORATES OR OFFICERS UNDER § 8 OF THE CLAYTON ACT

Section 8 of the Clayton Act prohibits the same person from serving as a director or administrative officer on two or more corporations, if:

(1) each of the two corporations has "capital, surplus, and undivided profits of more than $10,000,000.

and

(2) the corporations are competitors, *and none* of the following apply: (1) the competitive sales of either are less than one million dollars annually; (2) the competitive sales of either are less than two percent of that corporation's total sales; or (3) the competitive sales of each corporation are less than four percent that corporation's sales.

The "competitor" requirement has generally been interpreted to mean that the companies must be horizontally related. So-called "vertical interlocks" are not covered by the statute, even though vertical agreements may be illegal under the antitrust laws. Such agreements do not eliminate competition "between" the vertically related firms. In applying § 8 courts generally use a Sherman Act standard: if two companies compete, § 8 comes into play. It is not necessary to consider market concentration, the market shares of the firms, etc. That is to say, interlocking directorates are analogized more to price-fixing agreements than to mergers.

Section 8 explicitly exempts "banks, banking associations, trust companies [or] common carriers." In 1983 the Supreme Court decided that the exemption applies if *either* of two firms served by the same director is a bank. Thus the statute did not apply to an interlock between an insurance company and a bank. Bankamerica Corp. v. U.S., 462 U.S. 122, 103 S.Ct. 2266 (1983).

E.   REVIEW QUESTIONS

1. **T or F**   Before any merger can be consummated, the parties must notify the government.

2. **T or F**   Asset acquisitions are not covered by § 7 of the Clayton Act.

3. **T or F**   A horizontal merger involves two firms that either manufacture the same product, or which sell their products in the same geographic area.

4. A market contains seven firms with the following market shares. Firm A = 25%, Firm B = 25%, Firm C = 15%, Firm D = 15%, Firm E = 10%, Firm F = 5%, and Firm G = 5%. What is the market's CR4? Its CR8? What is its HHI? How would a merger between Firm C and Firm F fare under the 1984 Merger Guidelines? How about a merger between Firm E and Firm G?

5. Baby Bottoms, Inc., a company which manufactures disposable paper diapers, has proposed to acquire Diaper–B–Gone Corp., which operates a nationwide diaper service chain that delivers clean cloth diapers to homes and takes away dirty diapers. Is the merger horizontal? What are the important factors to consider in answering that question?

IX

CONGLOMERATE AND POTENTIAL COMPETITION MERGERS

Analysis

A. ANTITRUST POLICY AND THE CONGLOMERATE MERGER

Strictly speaking, a "conglomerate" is a company that has diversified into a number of product areas. A pure conglomerate merger is a merger of two companies that produce completely unrelated products. The antitrust laws have not often been concerned with pure conglomerate mergers. Rather, antitrust scrutiny has focused largely on two classes of mergers of firms that are not thought to be "actual" competitors, but which nevertheless stand in a close relationship with one another. These are:

(a) "Market extension" mergers, which are mergers between two firms that sell the same product in different geographic markets;

(b) "Product extension" mergers, which are mergers between two firms that sell different, but closely related, products.

1. CONGLOMERATE MERGERS AND § 7 OF THE CLAYTON ACT

The framers of § 7 of the Clayton Act were not particularly concerned about conglomerate mergers, and there is little evidence in the legislative history that they even intended for § 7 to apply to conglomerate mergers. There is some indication, however, that the framers of the 1950 Celler–Kefauver Amendments to § 7 were concerned about large firm size, and a conglomerate merger makes a firm larger, just as much as a vertical or horizontal merger does. See Hovenkamp § 13.1.

Regardless of Congress's intent, however, today it is clear that conglomerate mergers come within the technical reach of § 7; however, they are only rarely illegal.

2. CONGLOMERATE MERGERS AND EFFICIENCY

If conglomerate mergers produced no efficiency gains whatsoever—that is, if their only economic effects were anticompetitive or neutral—then it might be appropriate to have a *per se* rule against such mergers. However, conglomerate mergers can produce significant economies.

The economies produced by conglomerate mergers are generally not as substantial as some of the economies produced by vertical and horizontal mergers. First of all, in a conglomerate merger the firms do not stand in a buyer-seller relationship, so such mergers do not yield the kinds of transactional or distributional economies that vertical mergers yield (see chapter 4 above). Secondly, the firms are not actual competitors, so there may not be as much opportunity for the economies of scale or multi-plant economies that can be achieved by horizontal mergers.

The economies that might be obtained from conglomerate mergers include these:

(a) *If two merging firms produce complimentary products, they might obtain substantial efficiencies in distribution and marketing.* Products are compliments if they are frequently purchased or used together by the consumer—for example, laundry soap and bleach, stereo receivers and stereo speakers, or staplers and staples. The available efficiencies also include advertising: sometimes complimentary products can be advertised together at a much lower cost per product than separate advertising would cost.

(b) *If two merging firms produce products that employ similar technologies in their production processes the post-merger firm may benefit from traditional economies of scale in manufacturing. Likewise, often technologically dissimilar products can be distributed together.* For example, the merger of a motorcycle manufacturer and a bicycle manufacturer might permit the two products to be sold by the same distributors at lower costs than if each were sold by separate distributors.

(c) *Acquisition of a small company by a large firm may provide instant name or brand recognition for the small company's product.* As a result less money must be spent on advertising in order for the product to obtain the same market share.

(d) *If a company that is poorly managed is taken over by a firm that is efficiently managed, the company will enjoy any efficiencies that can be achieved by more efficient management.* Poorly managed companies frequently perform poorly in relation to the value of their assets or the amount of their sales. The result is depressed stock prices. A well managed company can buy such companies at a relatively low price and obtain a higher return from the same assets than the target company was obtaining from them.

(e) *A merger of firms that manufacture the same product in two different geographic areas may enable the post-merger firm to cut costs* by coordinating buying of materials, transportation, production, and distribution, particularly if demand periodically shifts from one market area to the other.

(f) *Research and development is often more cost-effective for the multi-product firm than it is for the single-product firm.* This is so because research and development frequently has "spillover" effects that can benefit other products as well.

(g) *The conglomerate can often raise capital internally, particularly if it has some stable markets producing substantial revenue and some growth markets requiring the infusion of capital.* In such a situation the small growth firm would have to borrow money from outside and incur all the costs imposed by the capital market. The large conglomerate, by contrast, can make the transfer of capital internally, often at much lower cost.

(h) *Sometimes size itself can create efficiencies, no matter what markets the firm operates in.* For example, a larger firm is more likely to be able to hire its own "in house" lawyers and accountants, rather than relying on the more expensive services of professional law firms and accounting firms.

3. INEFFICIENCIES FROM CONGLOMERATE MERGERS?

There is some evidence that firms can become too diversified and that their management then becomes less effective at watching over every aspect of the conglomerate's business. Some evidence also suggests that the conglomerate is inclined to pump money into a losing business too long, after an independent business would have shut its doors, simply because the conglomerate has the money available from other divisions and its management would be embarrassed to admit a failure to the stockholders.

Assuming that such inefficiencies exist, should the antitrust laws be used to condemn conglomerate mergers for these reasons? Probably not, for several reasons:

(a) Although the evidence suggests *that* conglomerate mergers can result in such inefficiencies, there is no way of predicting exactly when such inefficiencies will occur. As a result, a rule that condemned conglomerate mergers because of the possibility of such inefficiencies would probably end up condemning far too many such mergers.

(b) No court is capable of balancing the efficiencies that might be produced from a conglomerate merger against the possible inefficiencies.

(c) *Internal inefficiency is self-deterring.* The firm that raises its own costs as a result of inefficient behavior will lose profits and market share. In extreme cases it may go out of business. Since such internal inefficiencies are unprofitable, the firm has every incentive to avoid them.

4. EFFICIENCY AND ANTITRUST POLICY TOWARD CONGLOMERATE MERGERS

There is no general "efficiency defense" in conglomerate merger cases, just as there is not in horizontal merger cases. Rather, courts try to establish a threshold of legality that will permit mergers that are not harmful to competition to proceed, so that any efficiencies available from them will be realized. By contrast, mergers that threaten competition are forbidden, in spite of the fact that they may create substantial economies. The economies and the dangers to competition simply cannot be measured and balanced against each other.

B. COMPETITION AND CONGLOMERATE MERGER POLICY

Conglomerate mergers have been perceived to injure competition in a variety of ways. Although all of these ways have been used upon occasion as reasons for condemning conglomerate mergers, *only the potential competition doctrines have any vitality today and even these have seen little use in the last decade.*

1. RECIPROCITY

Reciprocity, or reciprocal dealing, occurs when two firms both buy from each other. Most reciprocity is fortuitous and of no concern to the antitrust laws. For example, a firm may consider it to be good business to purchase from a firm to whom it also sells a great deal. *Reciprocity becomes an antitrust problem when a firm attempts to force others to engage in it—for example, Firm A agrees to purchase widgets from Firm B only if Firm B agrees to purchase gidgets from Firm A.* When such reciprocity occurs it is usually analogized to tying arrangements and treated under the same legal standard. See chapter V above.)

Example: In FTC v. Consolidated Foods Corp., 380 U.S. 592, 85 S.Ct. 1220 (1965), the Supreme Court condemned a food wholesaler's acquisition of a manufacturer of dehydrated onion and garlic because after the acquisition the food wholesaler frequently urged the food processors which supplied it to purchase their dehydrated onion and garlic from its new subsidiary. The Supreme Court held that *if a firm commands a substantial share of the market, a finding that such coercive reciprocity is probable should warrant condemnation of the merger.*

The rule in *Consolidated Foods* condemns mergers that *might* facilitate reciprocity, before the reciprocity occurs, and importantly, before it is known whether the reciprocity will be efficient if it does occur. Today the enforcement agencies have virtually abandoned reciprocity as a rationale for condemning conglomerate mergers, and there have been few such cases in recent years. See Hovenkamp § 13.3a.

2. LEVERAGE AND TIE–INS

Conglomerate mergers can also facilitate tying arrangements. For example, if a manufacturer of photocopy machines acquires a company that manufacturers office supplies, the new firm may require all lessees of its machines to purchase its requirements of photocopy paper from the firm as well.

But why should § 7 be used to reach such tying arrangements? They are already covered by § 3 of the Clayton Act. A rule that condemns a merger that *might* facilitate tying deprives the economy of any potential for efficiencies before any determination can be made whether the tying will occur, and, if it occurs, whether it will be efficient or inefficient.

3. PREDATORY PRICING

Conglomerate mergers have been condemned under the theory that they might facilitate predatory pricing. Two rationales have been presented for this:

a. The Deep Pocket Theory

Courts once opined that conglomerate mergers might facilitate predatory pricing simply by creating a firm which has a "deeper pocket," and thus can afford long periods of loss selling. See U.S. v. Alum. Co. (Cupples), 233 F.Supp. 718, 727 (E.D.Mo.1964), affirmed mem., 382 U.S. 12, 86 S.Ct. 24 (1965). As the discussion of predatory pricing in chapter II. suggests, however, the plausibility of predatory pricing generally does not increase simply because the predator is well financed. Furthermore, a predator who operates in several markets cannot "finance" predatory pricing in one market by raising prices in a different market.

b. Signaling

However, a firm that operates in many markets may use well-publicized predation in one market to "send a message" to competitors in a number of markets. The ability to do this might make predatory pricing more profitable, and thus increase its plausibility.

As with reciprocity and tying arrangements, it is once again important to ask whether § 7 should be used to condemn a merger that probably creates substantial efficiencies on the theory that it *might* facilitate predatory pricing. Would it not be far better to wait until predatory pricing actually occurs, and then prosecute it as an attempt to monopolize under § 2 of the Sherman Act?

4. THE POTENTIAL COMPETITION DOCTRINES

All the rationales described above for condemning conglomerate mergers are more-or-less in disrepute today. However, two theories under which certain conglomerate mergers can be anticompetitive are still considered viable. These are the two forms of the potential competition theory:

(1) the perceived potential entrant doctrine; and

(2) the actual potential entrant doctrine.

a. "Potential Competition"

"Potential Competition" is really a misnomer. The term usually refers to actual competition viewed from the supply side rather than the demand side. A firm's market power is limited by the response of consumers to a price increase *and* by the entry responses of other firms looking for higher profits.

> ***Example:*** Firm A and Firm B currently make somewhat different products, but Firm A knows that Firm B would respond to Firm A's price increase to a supracompetitive level by instantly switching into A's product and flooding the market with it. As a result, Firm A has no market power, even though Firm A is currently the only firm manufacturing its product. Firm A and Firm B are in competition just as "actual" as if the two firms currently manufactured the same product.

The potential competition merger is really a variation of the horizontal merger. That is, the merger is analyzed for the likelihood that it will diminish competition *between* the merging firms and result in higher *effective* market concentration in some particular market. Vertical mergers and most of the other conglomerate mergers described above do not eliminate competition between the merger partners. Rather, they allegedly injure competition between the post-merger firm and firms in other markets.

b. The Line Between Actual Competition and Potential Competition

The ambiguity between "actual" and "potential" competition has often appeared in the case law.

1) Franchise Bidding Situations

In a franchise bidding situation a particular market contains room for only one supplier at a given time; however, any number might bid for the right to be the supplier.

> ***Example:*** In U.S. v. El Paso Natural Gas Co., 376 U.S. 651, 84 S.Ct. 1044 (1964), the first case in which the Supreme Court used the term "potential competition," the Court condemned a merger of two gas suppliers. El Paso, the acquiring firm, was the only out-of-state supplier of natural gas into California, and sold more than half of the gas consumed there. It acquired stock in Pacific Northwest, a gas company that had frequently made bids for sales into the California market, but had never actually made sales there. The two firms had often competed for contracts, but El Paso had always won the bids. There was evidence, however, that El Paso had periodically revised a bid downward in order to prevent Pacific Northwest from winning the sale. In condemning the merger, the Court concluded that "unsuccessful bidders are no less competitors than the successful one...."

Did the El Paso case involve "actual" competition or "potential" competition? It seems clear from the bidding behavior that the competition between the two firms was "actual," even though only El Paso had been successful in making sales into California.

2) The Firm on the "Edge" of the Market

The most common kind of potential competition merger involves a firm that may never have made a bid to come into the "target" market (i.e., the market in which the harmful effect on competition is alleged to occur). However, the firm is positioned very close to the market, either by geography or product identity, and could easily come into the market if the market became profitable enough.

> ***Example:*** In FTC v. Procter & Gamble Co. (P & G), 386 U.S. 568, 87 S.Ct. 1224 (1967) the Supreme Court condemned the

merger between P & G, a manufacturer of household products such as laundry detergent, but not including household bleach; and Clorox Co., a manufacturer of household bleach. The Supreme Court found that:

(1) the bleach market was highly concentrated, and conducive to oligopoly pricing—in fact, Clorox itself controlled 50% of the market;

(2) although P & G had not contemplated entering the bleach market *de novo* (i.e., by building its own plants rather than acquiring another firm), P & G was the most likely entrant into the bleach market;

(3) P & G's acquisition of Clorox eliminated the possibility that P & G would enter the market *de novo,* and thus undermined any chance that the market might become more competitive.

As it stands, the *Procter & Gamble* case represents an incomplete theory of potential competition. More recently courts have developed the two refinements that are discussed in the following sections.

c.   The Perceived Potential Entrant Theory

The perceived potential entrant theory suggests that a merger can be anticompetitive when it eliminates a firm whose perceived presence on the edge of a concentrated market tended to restrain monopoly pricing.

Example: In U.S. v. Falstaff Brewing Corp., 410 U.S. 526, 93 S.Ct. 1096 (1973) the Supreme Court condemned a merger between Falstaff, a large brewer which made no sales in New England, and a regional brewer located in New England which had a 20% share of the New England market. Entry *de novo* by Falstaff would have increased competition in the market. The Supreme Court condemned the merger, not because Falstaff could have entered *de novo* and made the market more competitive, but because as long as Falstaff was on the "edge" of the New England market the firms actually selling in that market would be likely to restrain their urge to charge too high a price, for fear that Falstaff would enter. Once Falstaff acquired a large firm in the market, however, it was no longer on the edge of the market, *and* the market was no more competitive by virtue of the entry than it had been before.

Is the perceived potential entrant theory plausible? Perhaps, but only in the most carefully defined circumstances:

(1) The "target" market (the New England market for beer in the *Falstaff* case, and the bleach market in the *Procter & Gamble* case) must be highly concentrated, and conducive to oligopolistic behavior. If a market is already operating competitively, then the perceived potential entrant theory is superfluous.

(2) Barriers to entry in the target market must be substantial.

(3) At the same time, there must be some plausible explanation why these high entry barriers do not exclude the perceived potential entrant from coming in.

> *Example:*   In Tenneco, Inc. v. FTC, 689 F.2d 346 (2d Cir.1982) the court refused to condemn a merger under the perceived potential entrant theory. The target market contained high barriers to entry; however, the barriers were so high that they prevented even the acquiring firm from being perceived as a potential entrant.

(4) There must be only a small number of perceived potential entrants— perhaps two or three. If the market contains dozens of perceived potential entrants, then the elimination of one of them by merger will not have any measurable effect on competition. There will still be plenty of perceived potential entrants remaining.

(5) The merger itself must not increase competition in the target market, or else the doctrine would be counterproductive.

See Hovenkamp, § 13.4.

d. The Actual Potential Entrant Theory

The actual potential entrant theory is even more speculative than the perceived potential entrant theory. Furthermore, the actual potential entrant theory is arguably inconsistent with the language of § 7 of the Clayton Act. Under the theory a potential competition merger is "anticompetitive" because the acquiring firm *could* have entered the market *de novo* and made the market more competitive, but entered by merger instead. *Thus under the actual potential entrant theory a merger is illegal even though it leaves the current status of competition in the market unaffected. The merger simply reduces the possibility that the market might become more competitive at some future time.*

Generally all the requirements of the perceived potential entrant doctrine apply equally to the actual potential entrant theory. *In addition, however, it must be shown that the acquiring firm would have entered the market de novo if it had no opportunity to enter by merger.*

> *Example:*   In U.S. v. Marine Bancorporation, Inc., 418 U.S. 602, 94 S.Ct. 2856 (1974) the Supreme Court refused to condemn a market extension merger between two banks on actual potential entrant grounds. The acquiring bank would not have been likely to enter *de novo* as an alternative to merger, because de novo entry was heavily restricted by state banking laws.

The trend in recent cases has been towards requiring convincing evidence that the acquiring firm would have entered de novo were it not permitted to enter by merger, and that such de novo entry would have occurred in the immediate future. Very few mergers have been condemned under the actual potential entrant doctrine. *The Supreme Court has never condemned a merger under the actual potential entrant theory. However, neither has it disapproved the theory.*

e. Potential Competition Mergers Under the 1984 DOJ Merger Guidelines

The 1984 Justice Department Merger Guidelines state that the Justice Department will challenge mergers under both the perceived potential entrant and the actual potential entrant theories in appropriate cases. In practice, however, the DOJ has virtually ignored the potential entrant theories, as well as all other theories of conglomerate mergers.

The Guidelines' description of the circumstances under which it will challenge potential competition mergers are the same as those outlined in subsections (c) and (d) immediately above. The Department attempts to quantify the degree of concentration that must exist in the target market by suggesting that the HHI should exceed 1800. The Department is unlikely to challenge a merger if barriers to entry into the target market are low, or if there are more than three potential entrants. See Hovenkamp § 13.5.

C. REVIEW QUESTIONS

1. T or F   Today the majority of conglomerate mergers are analyzed under one of the potential competition theories.

2. T or F   Conglomerate mergers generally contain a greater potential to create efficiencies than do either horizontal or vertical mergers.

3. T or F   Predatory pricing is a threat in many conglomerate merger cases.

4.   What role do entry barriers play in the analysis of potential competition mergers?

5. T or F   Two bidders for the same natural monopoly franchise (such as the right to operate a city's only cable television system) are "actual" competitors.

6. T or F   The "actual potential entrant" theory is not entirely consistent with the language of § 7 of the Clayton Act.

7. T or F   A merger involving a market which has six perceived potential entrants is more likely to be condemned than a merger in a market which has only one or two perceived potential entrants.

*

X

PRICE DISCRIMINATION AND DIFFERENTIAL PRICING UNDER THE ROBINSON–PATMAN ACT

Analysis

A. THE ECONOMICS OF PRICE DISCRIMINATION

Price discrimination has appeared in this discussion of the antitrust laws several times—for example, in the treatment of attempt to monopolize, vertical integration, and tying arrangements. Here a more formal and comprehensive analysis of price discrimination is presented.

1. DIFFERENTIAL PRICING AND PRICE DISCRIMINATION

Differential pricing and price discrimination are two very different phenomena:

(a) *Differential Pricing* occurs whenever the same product is sold to two different buyers at two different prices. Costs are irrelevant. If A sells widgets to B for $5.00 and C for $4.50, differential pricing has occurred.

(b) *Price Discrimination,* by contrast, occurs when a seller *obtains two different rates of return from two different sales.* An economist is more likely to say that price discrimination occurs whenever two different sales produce two different ratios of price to marginal cost.

Example 1:   A manufacturer of widgets has marginal costs of $4.50 and sells them in two different markets. One market is perfectly competitive; in the other the manufacturer has a moderate amount of market power. In the first market the manufacturer sells the widgets for the competitive price, $4.50. In the second market it sells them for $5.00. There is price discrimination between the two markets.

Example 2:   A producer of concrete for construction projects serves both large contractors who need a truckload of concrete at a time, and small contractors who need only a few hundred pounds. The small loads cost much more per pound to deliver to the job site than the large loads do, because at least one whole truck is needed for each delivery, even though it might be only 10% filled. For a small job the producer's costs of purchasing cement (the raw material of concrete), and mixing and delivering the concrete is $3.00 per hundredweight. For a large job the producer's costs are $2.00 per hundredweight. The producer charges $6.00 per hundredweight for the large jobs and $4.00 for the small jobs.

There is no price discrimination in Example 2. Although the price is different for the two classes of buyers, the price difference is in direct proportion to the difference in the costs of serving them. But there *is* differential pricing, for the seller is charging two different prices.

Note: In the above example, if the concrete producer charges the two buyers the same price, it *will* be engaging in price discrimination.

Sometimes a seller can avoid price discrimination only by engaging in differential pricing, or can avoid differential pricing only by engaging in price discrimination.

Example 3: A wholesaler of plywood includes the delivery charge in its per unit price. The delivery charge is the same whether the buyer is 10 miles from the wholesaler or 50 miles from the wholesaler. However, the cost of delivering the plywood varies with the distance, and is greater for the 50 mile delivery than the 5 mile delivery. The seller is engaging in price discrimination because it charges the two buyers the same price, even though it incurs lower costs with respect to the closer buyer.

Price discrimination and differential pricing have a vocabulary all their own. These are the most important terms:

(a) The *Favored Purchaser* is the purchaser who pays the lower price, or from whom the seller makes the smaller amount of profit (or incurs the larger loss). In the above example concerning delivered pricing, the favored purchaser is the purchaser who is furthest away from the seller.

(b) The *Disfavored Purchaser* is the purchaser who pays the higher price, or from whom the seller makes the larger profit (or incurs the smaller loss).

(c) *Arbitrage* occurs when a buyer who pays a low price resells the product to a buyer who is asked by the seller to pay a higher price. For example, suppose a wholesaler of lumber attempts to price discriminate between professional builders and do-it-yourself builders. The lumber seller charges licensed contractors $4.00 per unit for a certain kind of lumber, but it charges anyone without a license $7.00 per unit. An enterprising licensed contractor might make some additional money by purchasing lumber at $4.00 from the wholesaler and reselling it to the do-it-yourselfers at $6.00 per unit.

Note: Arbitrage will generally work only when price discrimination is also differential pricing. It will not work, for example, in the case of the plywood seller who charges the same delivered price to nearby and remote buyers. By the time the plywood reaches the remote buyers (the favored purchasers), the cost differential has already been eaten up in the additional transportation costs.

Furthermore, arbitrage will work only if the transaction costs of the arbitrage are less than the amount of price discrimination. For example, price discrimination will work for the lumber wholesaler described above only if the costs of arbitrage itself are less than $3.00 per unit.

2. PRICE DISCRIMINATION IN COMPETITIVE MARKETS

a. Price Discrimination in the Perfect Competition Model

Price discrimination could not exist in a perfectly competitive market in equilibrium. In such a market all sales would be made at marginal cost, and any seller who attempted to charge more than the market price would not make any sales. See the discussion of perfect competition in chapter I above.

b. Price Discrimination in Moderately Competitive Real World Markets

In imperfectly competitive markets *sporadic* price discrimination is a daily occurrence. Sporadic price discrimination should be distinguished from *persistent* price discrimination: Price discrimination is *sporadic* when it is more-or-less random as to individual buyers. Price discrimination is *persistent,* or systematic, when a seller establishes a general policy of discriminating in price between identifiable groups of buyers who are capable of being segregated.

Competitive markets in the real world undergo daily, even hourly, changes that have little to do with the marginal costs of individual sellers in the market. For example, even in a highly competitive market such as the Chicago Board of Trade we expect the price of a commodity to rise and fall constantly in response to certain kinds of information. Furthermore, in real world markets not all buyers and sellers have equal information about market conditions. Some transactions will occur at relatively high prices and some at relatively low prices. As a result *sporadic price discrimination is absolutely consistent with healthy competition. In fact, the absence of any price discrimination in a market that contains several sellers may be a sign that the market is cartelized.* When firms engage in price fixing they must establish more-or-less rigid pricing formulas and force members of the cartel to adhere to them.

Sporadic price discrimination is an essential mechanism for balancing supply and demand in competitive markets. When the market price for apples is high, growers respond by growing more apples. When it is low they respond by growing less. Likewise, if Houston, Texas, goes through a building boom that greatly increases the demand for bricks, the shortage there will drive the price up. When that happens brick suppliers in other cities will begin diverting more bricks into the Houston market in order to take advantage of the larger profits available there. As a result the balance between supply and demand will gradually be restored. *A law that prohibited price discrimination in such a situation would likely create surpluses and shortages.*

3. PERSISTENT PRICE DISCRIMINATION BY THE FIRM WITH MARKET POWER

Persistent, or systematic, price discrimination is possible only if a firm has a certain amount of market power in the markets containing the disfavored buyers. The monopolist then tries to segregate groups of people based on the amount of market power it has over each group. In more technical language, the monopolist tries to segregate buyers who have different elasticities of demand for the monopolist's product.

Note: This discussion of price discrimination uses the word "monopolist" to describe the firm with market power. However, a firm need not be a true monopolist in order to be able to engage in persistent price discrimination. Any firm with a modest amount of market power in certain markets can do it. In fact, even the relatively small amount of market power created by product differentiation, such as brand differences in many manufactured products, can facilitate price discrimination.

a. Perfect Price Discrimination

Perfect price discrimination occurs when a monopolist charges every buyer its *reservation price* for a product. A reservation price, you may recall from chap. 1 above, is the highest price that a buyer is willing to pay for a certain product. The most profitable situation possible for any monopolist would be to charge every buyer the highest amount that that buyer was willing to pay.

Figure One illustrates the price and output consequences of perfect competition, nondiscriminatory monopoly pricing, and perfect price discrimination. The figure shows the demand curve, marginal cost and marginal revenue curves of a seller with market power. In a perfectly competitive market (in which the demand curve would be the *market* demand curve; the individual firm in perfect competition would face a horizontal demand curve) a seller would produce Q(c) output and sell at price P(c), both of which are determined by the intersection of the marginal cost and market demand curves. In a perfectly competitive market triangle 1–3–6 is consumers' surplus: that is, the excess value that accrues to consumers because in a competitive market most are able to purchase the product at *less* than their reservation prices. (At this time you might find it helpful to review the discussion of price theory in chapter I above.)

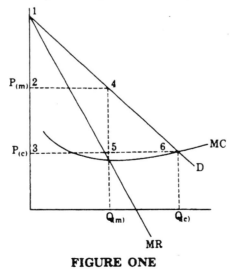

FIGURE ONE

The monopolist will reduce its output to the profit-maximizing rate, Q(m) where its marginal cost and marginal revenue curves intersect, and raise the price to P(m). We call this the monopolist's "nondiscriminatory profit-maximizing price," for it is the price that will maximize the monopolist's profits *assuming that the monopolist is unable to engage in any price discrimination.* As soon as the possibility of price discrimination exists, determination of the monopolist's ideal pricing structure becomes far more complex.

The monopolist's charging of its nondiscriminatory profit-maximizing price reduces the size of the consumers' surplus to triangle 1–2–4 in Figure One. It also produces triangle 4–5–6, which is the traditional "deadweight loss triangle" caused by monopoly. (See chapter I above). Rectangle 2–3–5–4 is generally thought of as monopoly profits.

The monopolist engaged in perfect price discrimination will make every sale to every customer at that customer's reservation price, provided that the sale is profitable. In short, customers who are willing to pay only the marginal cost price, will buy the product at that price. Customers located at point 4 in Figure One will pay the nondiscriminatory profit-maximizing price. Customers located on the demand curve at point 1 have a very high reservation price, and they will end up paying much more than the nondiscriminatory profit-maximizing price. By contrast, customers whose reservation price is less than marginal cost (located below point 6 on the demand curve) will not buy the product, just as they would not buy it in a competitive market. Sales to them at their reservation prices would be unprofitable.

Note the consequences of perfect price discrimination:

(1) All the consumers' surplus that would exist in a competitive market (triangle 1–3–6) has now become producers' surplus—that is, it shows up as increased profits to the producer, rather than as increased value to the consumer.

(2) The deadweight loss triangle has been eliminated, because every customer willing to pay the marginal cost of the product will be able to purchase it.

(3) *Output has been restored to the competitive level.* That is, under both perfect competition and perfect price discrimination, sales will be made to all customers willing to pay marginal cost or higher, and to no customers unwilling to pay marginal cost.

b. Imperfect Price Discrimination

Perfect price discrimination never exists in the real world, just as perfect competition never exists in the real world. The primary value of the model of perfect price discrimination is conceptual, to enable us to understand some of the consequences of real world price discrimination. Price discrimination in the real world has the following attributes:

(1) In the real world the monopolist will never be able to identify each buyer's reservation price, but only groups of buyers who have different reservation prices.

Note: One exception is the variable proportion tying arrangement, discussed above in chapter V. In a variable proportion tie-in the amount of price discrimination varies continuously with the amount of use of the tied product.

(2) As a result of (1), output is never as high under imperfect price discrimination as it would be under perfect price discrimination. In fact, sometimes output under imperfect price discrimination is even less than it would be under nondiscriminatory monopoly pricing.

(3) Real world price discrimination is limited not only by the seller's ability to segregate customers with different reservation prices, but also by the seller's ability to prevent arbitrage. If arbitrage is exceptionally easy an absolute monopolist, with customers that have widely varying reservation prices, will have no power to price discriminate.

c. The Social Cost of Price Discrimination

Price discrimination is generally profitable to the seller engaged in it, but it can be costly to society as a whole. First of all, remember that the person engaged in price discrimination is already a monopolist, and monopoly produces its own social costs (see the discussion of the social cost of monopoly in chapter I above). Here we are interested in the *additional* social costs of price discrimination. Measuring this social cost is very difficult, because two effects of price discrimination pull in opposite directions:

(1) On the one hand, *if* the price discrimination results in larger output than nondiscriminatory monopoly pricing would, the effect will be to *reduce* somewhat the deadweight loss of the monopoly—i.e., some customers will be able to purchase the product who would not have purchased it under nondiscriminatory monopoly pricing.

(2) On the other hand, the cost of identifying customers with different reservation prices, segregating them in order to prevent arbitrage, etc., is very high. The entire cost of such schemes is a pure social loss. In most real world price discrimination schemes these costs probably outweigh the savings from (1) above. See Hovenkamp § 14.5.

B. THE ROBINSON–PATMAN ACT

The Robinson–Patman Act is § 2 of the Clayton Act. In 1936 § 2 was amended by the Robinson–Patman Amendments to create the statute we have today. The statute makes it illegal for a seller "to discriminate in price between different purchasers of commodities of like grade and quality ... where the effect of such discrimination may be substantially to lessen competition or tend to create a monopoly.... "

1. THE LEGISLATIVE HISTORY OF THE ROBINSON–PATMAN ACT

The framers of the Robinson–Patman Act in 1936 were not interested in the social cost of price discrimination. They were far more concerned about what the Great

Depression and particularly the "chain-store revolution" was doing to small business. *The Robinson–Patman Act was designed to protect small businesses from the more efficient buying and selling practices of larger, more integrated businesses.*

2. THE MEANING OF "PRICE DISCRIMINATION" UNDER THE ROBINSON–PATMAN ACT

"Price discrimination" under the Robinson–Patman Act means a price difference, and has nothing to do with true economic price discrimination. FTC v. Anheuser–Busch, Inc., 363 U.S. 536, 80 S.Ct. 1267 (1960). In short, the statute is designed to condemn differential pricing rather than true price discrimination. It reaches some price discrimination which is also differential pricing; however, it can also condemn differential pricing which is nondiscriminatory because the ratio of price to marginal cost was the same even though price was different.

3. PRIMARY–LINE AND SECONDARY–LINE VIOLATIONS

The Robinson–Patman Act recognizes two offenses so different from one another it is difficult to imagine that both can be covered by the same statutory language.

a. Primary–Line Violations

A primary-line violation of the Robinson–Patman Act is really a form of predatory pricing, in which the victim of the violation is the defendant's competitor. The theory is that the defendant engages in predatory pricing in the victim's geographic area while charging a higher price in other markets, in order to finance the predation. Primary-line violations of the Robinson–Patman Act are discussed above in chapter 3.D on predatory pricing.

b. Secondary–Line Violations

Secondary-line violations are directed against the violator's disfavored customers. The violation occurs when the defendant-seller sells the product to two buyer-resellers at two different prices, *and* the two buyers compete with each other. As a result the buyer who is forced to pay the higher price is placed at a competitive disadvantage against the buyer who pays the lower price.

4. THE COVERAGE OF THE ROBINSON–PATMAN ACT

The Robinson–Patman Act is a morass of technical requirements that make the statute very difficult to use and often undermine its basic purpose. The following summarizes the most important of these:

a. Commerce Requirement

Unlike the Sherman Act, which applies to all transactions "affecting" commerce, the Robinson–Patman Act requires the seller to be "engaged in" interstate commerce. *This generally means that at least one of the sales at issue must be made across a state line.*

b.   The "Sales of Commodities" Requirement

The Robinson–Patman Act applies only to sales, not to leases or offers to sell. Furthermore, the statute applies only to the sales of commodities, not of services. This second requirement is unfortunate, because price discrimination with respect to services is generally easier to accomplish than price discrimination with respect to commodities. For example, arbitrage of most services is impossible. (If the dentist fills your tooth for $100, you cannot transfer the service to someone else at a price of $125.)

c.   The "Like Grade and Quality" Requirement

In order to come under the statute the different sales at different prices must be of products of "like grade and quality." In most cases the high priced product and the low priced product are identical and this requirement is met. If there are physical differences between the products involved in the two different sales, then the requirement is generally not met. *The Supreme Court has held, however, that mere differences in the way products are advertised or named will not take them out of the "like grade and quality" requirement.*

> *Example:*   A milk producer sells evaporated milk to a large chain store under a "house brand" label which is not nationally advertised. The producer also sells the same milk under its own, nationally advertised brand label to smaller stores at a higher price. The two sales constitute products of "like grade and quality," and the Act could be violated. FTC v. Borden Co., 383 U.S. 637, 86 S.Ct. 1092 (1966).

d.   The "Competitive Injury" Requirement

The theory of a secondary-line Robinson–Patman Act injury is that the disadvantaged purchaser (the purchaser forced to pay the higher price) was injured because it could not afford to compete effectively with the favored purchaser. *This means that in order for a private plaintiff-disfavored purchaser to collect damages the plaintiff must show that it competed with the favored purchaser.* See National Distillers & Chem. Corp. v. Brad's Machine Prods., Inc., 666 F.2d 492 (11th Cir. 1982).

However, most courts also hold that a plaintiff in a secondary-line case need not prove injury to competition, which is ordinarily measured by higher prices or lower output in a properly defined market. Rather, they say, the Act requires only injury to a particular competitor. As a result, plaintiffs can recover for secondary-line violations even in robustly competitive markets. See Chroma Lighting v. GTE Products Corp., 111 F.3d 653, 655 (9th Cir.), cert. denied, ___ U.S. ___, 118 S.Ct. 357 (1997); George Haug Co. v. Rolls Royce Motor Cars, 148 F.3d 136 (2d Cir. 1998).

e.   "Direct" and "Indirect" Discrimination

"Direct" price discrimination under the act involves the sale of goods of like grade and quality at two different prices. "Indirect" discrimination, which is also condemned by the statute, involves the discriminatory provision of services to different customers—for example, if the seller provides better delivery, stocking, credit terms, etc., to one buyer than to another. Such "discrimination" is legal, however, if it is "functionally available" to all buyers, even if not all buyers take advantage of it. "Functionally available" generally means that the offer must be made realistically available to all buyers regardless of their size. For example, if a seller provides free delivery for sugar if the order is for 5,000 cartons or more, but only 10% of all wholesale sugar buyers are large enough to take a 5,000 carton lot, then the requirement is not "functionally available" to all buyers, even though it is formally offered to all buyers.

In Texaco, Inc. v. Hasbrouck, 496 U.S. 543, 110 S.Ct. 2535 (1990), the Supreme Court rejected the defendant's argument that discriminatory "functional" discounts are permissible if market conditions in the locations of the buyers receiving the discounts and those not receiving it differ. Rather, the Court adhered to the traditional view that functional discounts can be given only to buyers who actually perform some function normally provided by the seller, and then only to the extent of the buyer's costs of performing this function.

f. Allowances for Brokerage and Services

Section 2(c) of the Robinson–Patman Act prohibits sellers from giving buyers allowances in lieu of brokerage or commission fees, unless the services for which the fees would ordinarily be due were actually performed. However, the Supreme Court once found it to be illegal for a real live broker to reduce his commission in order to complete a sale, if the result was that the customer who benefitted from the reduction received a lower price than other customers did. FTC v. Henry Broch & Co., 363 U.S. 166, 80 S.Ct. 1158 (1960).

Section 2(d) of the statute permits a seller to give "allowances" to buyers who perform certain services themselves, such as promotion, handling or hauling. However, the allowances must be made available to all customers "on proportionally equal terms." Likewise, § 2(e) prohibits a seller from itself furnishing such facilities to a buyer for processing, handling or resale of a commodity unless it makes the same facilities available to all buyers on proportionally equal terms.

g. Violations by Buyers

Section 2(f) of the statute makes it illegal for a buyer "knowingly to induce or receive a discrimination in price which is prohibited" by the Act. In fact, the legislative history of the statute makes clear that it was directed as much against large, "high pressure" buyers as against sellers. But the Supreme Court has weakened this provision by holding that a buyer cannot be in violation unless its seller is also in violation.

Example: A solicits a bid from Seller for a wholesale quantity of milk. When Seller makes a $3.00 per unit bid, A *untruthfully* says

"You're not even in the ballpark; I can get the same milk somewhere else for $2.50." Seller makes the sale at $2.50, even though Seller is making other sales elsewhere at $3.00.

In this case A has *not* violated the statute because Seller had a good faith belief that it was meeting competition from another offeror. Since Seller is able to claim the "good faith meeting competition" defense (see subsection h(2). below), A has not obtained a price discrimination "which is prohibited by this Act." *In short, a buyer cannot violate the statute unless the seller would be violating it too. This is true even though the seller was not actually meeting competition, but was deceived by a lying buyer.* Great Atlantic & Pacific Tea Co. v. FTC, 440 U.S. 69, 99 S.Ct. 925 (1979).

h. Affirmative Defenses

The Robinson–Patman Act contains two affirmative defenses. *The defenses apply only after the plaintiff has made out a prima facie case, and the burden of proof is on the defendant.*

1) The Cost Justification Defense

Section 2(a) of the statute provides "that nothing herein contained shall prevent [price] differentials which make only due allowance for differences in the cost of manufacture, sale, or delivery.... " Theoretically, a seller who makes small deliveries of its product to small stores and large deliveries to large stores could justify higher prices to the smaller stores, if it can show that the smaller deliveries are more expensive on a per unit basis. *In fact, however, the Supreme Court has required highly detailed cost studies that are not practicable for many sellers.* U.S. v. Borden Co., 370 U.S. 460, 82 S.Ct. 1309 (1962). As a result, many sellers engage in *true* price discrimination by charging the same price to different classes of customers, even though the costs of serving them differ.

2) The "Good Faith Meeting Competition" Defense

A seller who has made the requisite sales at two different prices may avoid liability by showing that the low price sale was a good faith effort to meet a competitor's bid with respect to that sale. Historically, this requirement meant that the seller had to have actual, verifiable knowledge that a competitor had offered a low bid. At least, this was the general interpretation of the Supreme Court's decision in FTC v. A. E. Staley Mfg. Co., 324 U.S. 746, 65 S.Ct. 971 (1945). Statements from buyers to the effect "I can get this cheaper somewhere else," were not sufficient. This suggested to some sellers that they actually had to telephone the competing offeror to find our whether a low price bid had been given.

Such a phone call, however, was at least potentially a price information exchange among competitors in violation of § 1 of the Sherman Act. This fact generally supported the argument that the Robinson–Patman Act and the Sherman Act were so inimical that frequently one could comply with one statute only by violating the other. *However, in U.S. v. United States Gypsum Co., 438 U.S. 422, 98 S.Ct. 2864 (1978), the Supreme Court held that the "good faith meeting competition" defense could be raised if the seller merely had a good faith belief that it was meeting competition.* Reliance on a statement from a buyer that the buyer could obtain the product at a lower price somewhere else was sufficient to activate the defense, provided that the buyer's statement was believable.

The "good faith meeting competition" defense once applied only when a seller attempted to meet a particular bid from a competitor for a particular sale. *However, in Falls City Industries, Inc. v. Vanco Beverage, Inc., 460 U.S. 428, 103 S.Ct. 1282 (1983), the Supreme Court held that a seller could "meet competition" by meeting the generally lower price structure in a different geographic area, rather than a particular competing bid.*

i. Damages for Secondary–Line Injuries

Successful plaintiffs in Secondary–Line Robinson–Patman Case frequently collected "automatic damages" equal to the amount of the price difference that the plaintiff had to pay, multiplied by the number of units the plaintiff purchased, and then trebled, as most antitrust damages are. *In J. Truett Payne Co. v. Chrysler Motors Corp., 451 U.S. 557, 101 S.Ct. 1923 (1981), the Supreme Court rejected the automatic damages rule and held that the secondary-line plaintiff was entitled only to damages that reflected the injury caused by decreased competition in the marketplace. No further guidance has been provided as to how such damages should be computed.*

C. REVIEW QUESTIONS

1. **T or F**   Price discrimination and differential pricing are the same thing.

2. **T or F**   True price discrimination is never condemned by the Robinson–Patman Act.

3. **T or F**   Price discrimination does not occur in competitive markets in the real world.

4. **T or F**   The complete absence of price discrimination in the real world is a sign of a healthy market.

5. Ryder's, Inc., sells toy trucks to toy stores across the country. One day Kiddie Toys, a toy store in Pontiac, Michigan, discovers that Ryder's wholesales a certain truck to a toy store in Houston for $4.50, but charges Kiddie Toys $5.10. Kiddie Toys files a secondary-line Robinson–Patman action against Ryder's. Who will win? Why?

*

XI

JURISDICTIONAL, PUBLIC POLICY AND REGULATORY LIMITATIONS ON THE DOMAIN OF ANTITRUST

Analysis

A. THE JURISDICTIONAL REACH OF THE ANTITRUST LAWS

The federal antitrust laws were passed on the authority of Congress to regulate interstate commerce, as well as commerce with foreign nations. *The jurisdictional reach of most of the federal antitrust laws extends to the full limit of Congress' power to regulate commerce, and that power is substantial.*

1. DOMESTIC (INTERSTATE) COMMERCE

Today most of the federal antitrust laws will apply to any activity that is either in the flow of interstate commerce, or else which "affects" interstate commerce. The only exceptions to this rule are the Robinson–Patman Act, which requires that an offending sale actually be in the stream of commerce (i.e., that it involve the interstate movement of goods, or a transaction between persons located in different states); and perhaps § 3 of the Clayton Act, covering tying arrangements and exclusive dealing, which appears to contain the same limitation.

The scope of Congress's powers over activities "affecting" commerce is very broad. For example in Burke v. Ford, 389 U.S. 320, 88 S.Ct. 443 (1967), the Supreme Court held that an intrastate market division scheme affected interstate commerce because it resulted in fewer sales within the state, and thus fewer purchases from out of state suppliers. Likewise, in McLain v. Real Estate Board of New Orleans, Inc., 444 U.S. 232, 100 S.Ct. 502 (1980), the Supreme Court held that a citywide price fixing scheme among real estate brokers could be reached by the Sherman Act, because the scheme affected the ability of sellers moving outside the state to sell homes, of buyers coming from outside the state to purchase homes, and because much of the financing for the homes affected by the cartel, as well as the provision of title insurance, came from outside the state.

Finally, in Summit Health v. Pinhas, 500 U.S. 322, 111 S.Ct. 1842 (1991) the Court held that a boycott designed to deny hospital staff privileges to a surgeon was reachable under the Sherman Act because the hospital itself was within the reach of Congressional regulation and both the hospital and the plaintiff regularly served out-of-state patients. Today only a few highly localized activities, such as intracity trash collection, are even arguably out of reach of the antitrust laws.

The lower courts remain divided on the question whether the defendants activities generally can be used to satisfy the commerce requirement, or if only the activities challenged as unlawful can be used; the *Summit* case, supra, only ambiguously suggests the former.

2. FOREIGN COMMERCE

The import and export of goods to and from the United States is clearly "foreign commerce" within the jurisdictional reach of the antitrust laws. However, the federal antitrust laws have also been held to reach activities abroad that do not involve imports to or exports from the United States, but which have an adverse affect on American foreign commerce.

Indeed, United States courts even have the power to apply the criminal provisions of the antitrust laws to activities that occurred abroad. United States v. Nippon Paper Indus. Co., 109 F.3d 1 (1st Cir. 1997) (approving Sherman Act criminal indictment that applied entirely to price fixing in Japan, where the price-fixed goods were to be shipped into the United States).

The reach of the federal antitrust laws to activities affecting foreign commerce has been shortened a bit, however, by several doctrines of international law that might force an American court not to apply American law even though it may have the constitutional power to do so.

a. Comity and Act of State

It is not the purpose of the American antitrust laws to supervise or interfere with the policy making of foreign sovereigns. The principle of comity and the Act of State doctrine hold that when adjudication of an antitrust complaint would require an American court to pass judgment on or become entangled in the public policy of another state, the court should not proceed. However, the Act of State doctrine does not require a United States federal court to dismiss a complaint merely because the litigation might embarrass the foreign sovereign; it applies only when the court is required to pass on the legality of a foreign sovereign act. The Supreme Court so held in W.S. Kirkpatrick & Co. v. Environmental Tectonics Corp., 493 U.S. 400, 110 S.Ct. 701 (1990). And in Hartford Fire Insurance v. California, 509 U.S. 764, 113 S.Ct. 2891 (1993), the Supreme Court held that anticompetitive activity abroad could be challenged even if it was lawful in the country where it was performed, as long as it was not compelled. In this case, Lloyds of London was a consortium of insurers permitted (but not required) by British law to enter cartel-like arrangements refusing certain types of insurance coverage. Because Lloyds' members had discretion about whether to enter such agreements respecting insurance sold to United States buyers, comity did not compel that the case be dismissed.

b. Foreign Sovereign Compulsion

As a general rule, no one will be held liable under the American antitrust laws if the activity alleged to constitute a violation was compelled by a foreign sovereign. The defense generally applies only if the foreign power had the authority to compel the activity—for example, when the activity was carried on within the territory of the foreign sovereign. Furthermore, the activity must actually be *compelled* by the foreign sovereign, not merely approved or tolerated.

c. Foreign Sovereign Immunity

The Act of State doctrine and the doctrine of foreign sovereign compulsion apply to *private* defendants who can show that activities alleged to violate the antitrust laws were bound up in some way with the policy making of a foreign nation. The doctrine of foreign sovereign immunity, by contrast, applies to a foreign sovereign which is itself an antitrust defendant. Today the liability of foreign sovereigns and their agents or instrumentalities under the federal antitrust laws is governed by the Foreign Sovereign Immunities Act of 1976, which generally recognizes foreign sovereign immunity only for noncommercial activities. As a general rule, if a foreign sovereign makes a profit from an activity alleged to violate the antitrust laws, the American court will find the activity to be commercial, and refuse to grant immunity.

Note: In all antitrust cases, both domestic and foreign, the court must be able to obtain personal jurisdiction over the defendant. The inability of an American court to obtain such jurisdiction frequently defeats attempted antitrust actions against foreign defendants who are not directly importing into or exporting from the United States. In any event, the Clayton Act is one of those federal statutes that contains its own "long arm." As a result, personal jurisdiction may be based on the defendant's contacts with the nation, and need not be based on contacts with the particular state in which the antitrust action is filed. Go–Video v. Akai Electric Co., 885 F.2d 1406 (9th Cir. 1989).

B. LEGISLATIVE AND CONSTITUTIONAL LIMITATIONS ON ANTITRUST ENFORCEMENT

1. STATUTORY AND JUDICIALLY CREATED EXEMPTIONS

a. Labor

Section 6 of the Clayton Act generally permits labor unions to organize and bargain without violating the antitrust laws. Section 20 of the Clayton Act provides that strikes, as well as some other labor activities, are not "violations of any law of the United States." However, the scope of the "labor exemption" has been quite controversial. In U.S. v. Hutcheson, 312 U.S. 219, 61 S.Ct. 463 (1941) the Supreme Court held that the exemption applied "so long as a union acts in its self-interest and does not combine with non-labor groups.... "

A union can lose this exemption when it combines with a nonlabor group and when it fails to act in its self-interest. However, in Connell Construction Co. v. Plumbers Local, 421 U.S. 616, 95 S.Ct. 1830 (1975), the Supreme Court held that a collective bargaining agreement with an employer (clearly a member of a "nonlabor" group) nevertheless qualified for at least a limited exemption from the antitrust laws.

The problem of when a labor union acts in its "self-interest" is a complex one with no easy solution. However, courts generally define self-interest broadly, even when the effect of a union agreement is to reduce output in a particular market. For example, in Amalgamated Meat Cutters Local No. 189 v. Jewel Tea Co., 381 U.S. 676, 85 S.Ct. 1596 (1965) the Supreme Court, in a plurality opinion, permitted a union to agree with grocery stores to fix the hours during which meat could be sold in the stores. The Supreme Court made clear, however, that a union would not be permitted to agree as to the prices to be charged for a certain commodity. (Why not? Aren't unions better off when employers are making a good profit?). In Brown v. Pro Football, 518 U.S. 231, 116 S.Ct. 2116 (1996), the Supreme Court held that the labor immunity even applied to a group of *employers* (football team owners) who fixed the maximum salaries of certain employees (low seniority players). Essential to that ruling, however, were the facts that the agreement simply kept in effect a provision that had been in a collective bargaining agreement that had expired, and the agreement itself was part of the collective bargaining process.

b.   Insurance

The McCarran–Ferguson Act permits states to regulate the business of insurance, and exempts the insurance business from the antitrust laws insofar as such state regulation exists. What constitutes the "business of insurance" is controversial, but at the least the essence of insurance is the "spreading and underwriting of a policyholder's risk." *Thus in Group Life & Health Ins. Co. v. Royal Drug Co., 440 U.S. 205, 99 S.Ct. 1067 (1979) the Supreme Court held that a health insurer's agreements under which it stipulated a maximum price that it would pay for drugs was not exempt, largely because the stipulation attempted to regulate the relationship between the insurer and someone who was not its insured, namely the providers of drugs.*

In Union Labor Life Ins. Co. v. Pireno, 458 U.S. 119, 102 S.Ct. 3002 (1982), *the Supreme Court identified three criteria for recognizing the "business of insurance" that would qualify for the antitrust exemption:*

> first, whether the practice has the effect of transferring or spreading a policyholder's risk; second, whether the practice is an integral part of the policy relationship between the insurer and the insured; and third, whether the practice is limited to entities within the insurance industry. None of these criteria is necessarily determinative in itself....

The McCarran–Ferguson Act provides that the insurance exemption from the antitrust laws does *not* cover boycotts, coercion, or intimidation on the part of insurance companies. In St. Paul Fire & Marine Ins. Co. v. Barry, 438 U.S. 531, 98 S.Ct. 2923 (1978) the Court held that "boycott" under McCarran–Ferguson generally has the same meaning as "boycott" under the Sherman Act. Thus, for example, In re Workers' Compensation Insurance, 867 F.2d 1552 (8th Cir.1989), cert. denied, 492 U.S. 920, 109 S.Ct. 3247 (1989), found a "boycott" in insurers' exclusionary practices against competing insurers who charged lower rates.

Congress has looked very critically at the McCarran–Ferguson Act, and someday it may be substantially narrowed or even repealed. Repeal would probably mean that state insurance regulation would be exempt from the federal antitrust laws only if it qualified under the "state action" exemption, discussed below.

c. Agricultural Associations and Fisheries

Section 6 of the Clayton Act, together with the Capper–Volstead Act, give an exemption from the antitrust laws for agricultural cooperatives. The Acts were designed to permit persons such as farmers to create cooperatives for the purpose of marketing their agricultural products. Under the exemption the members of a cooperative may combine and set the price that they want for a particular product; however, if a cooperative engages in exclusionary practices or restraints of trade directed at competitors, the exemption does not apply. Likewise, the exemption does not apply to a cooperative's coercion of nonmembers to join.

The Fisheries Cooperative Marketing Act of 1976 exempts persons in the fishing industry who are engaged in "collectively catching, producing, preparing for market, processing, handling, and marketing" their products. The exemption is similar in scope to the agricultural exemption; that is, it permits internal price setting, but does not exempt exclusionary practices directed at competitors.

d. Export Associations

The Webb–Pomerene Act permits American firms to join together into export associations in order to compete with similar foreign associations, without incurring antitrust liability for joint activity among competitors. However, the export association may not engage in any activities that restrain trade within the United States or which injure other American exporters, and it may not engage in "unfair methods of competition" as defined by the Federal Trade Commission Act. Furthermore, the association may lose its exemption if it participates in a foreign cartel.

In 1982 Congress passed the Export Trading Company Act, which broadens the Webb–Pomerene Act by permitting the Department of Justice to certify properly qualified export trading companies. Once a company obtains a certificate from the Department, its activities properly within the scope described by the certificate are exempt from public prosecution under the antitrust laws. With respect to private actions, there is a presumption of legality for activities within the scope of the certificate, and if a plaintiff loses, it must pay the defendant's costs and attorney's fees.

e. Baseball and Other Professional Sports

In Federal Base Ball Club of Baltimore, Inc. v. National League of Professional Baseball Clubs, 259 U.S. 200, 42 S.Ct. 465 (1922) the Supreme Court held that professional baseball was not within the reach of the federal antitrust laws because it was not "interstate commerce." Even though the basis for that decision is clearly wrong under modern interpretations of the commerce clause, professional baseball retains its antitrust exemption. However, the exemption applies only to baseball and not to other sports.

2. FIRST AMENDMENT AND RELATED DEFENSES

a. The *Noerr-Pennington* Doctrine

In Eastern R.R. Presidents Conference v. Noerr Motor Freight, Inc., 365 U.S. 127, 81 S.Ct. 523 (1961) the Supreme Court held that the antitrust laws do not prohibit people from associating together ("conspiring") in order to convince the legislature or executive branch of the government to take some action, whether or not the action sought would be anticompetitive. The Court concluded that the Sherman Act would not reach an alleged conspiracy among railroad companies to campaign to the legislature to place anticompetitive restrictions on trucking companies, the result of which would be to put the railroads in a more favorable market position.

The basis for the decision was not the First Amendment, but rather the Court's construction of the antitrust laws themselves. The Court held that the drafters of the antitrust laws never intended them to be used to prohibit people from exercising their constitutional rights to petition the government.

The Court reiterated its view in United Mine Workers of America v. Pennington, 381 U.S. 657, 85 S.Ct. 1585 (1965). Today the doctrine is known as the "*Noerr-Pennington* Doctrine."

In City of Columbia, Columbia Outdoor Advertising v. Omni Outdoor Advertising, 499 U.S. 365, 111 S.Ct. 1344 (1991), the Supreme Court held that *Noerr-Pennington* protects private petitioning to the government even if there is an allegation that the private party somehow "conspired" with the governmental entity in order to obtain passage of the statute or ordinance that injured the plaintiff. The court noted that the plaintiff's injury resulted from the passage of the ordinance (that approved the defendant's advertising signs but not the plaintiff's), and that it was generally inappropriate to characterize a private persons request to the government for a statute, and the government's favorable response, as a "conspiracy."

But in FTC v. Superior Court Trial Lawyers Assn., 493 U.S. 411, 110 S.Ct. 768 (1990) the Supreme Court held that *Noerr-Pennington* did not protect a lawyers' collective boycott against the government for higher fees because (a) the lawyers stood in a buyer-seller relationship with the government, and a contrary rule would protect all cartels in which the government is a buyer; and (b) the anticompetitive injury resulted not from the government's acquiescence in the lawyers' demands, but rather from the boycott itself. As the court noted, every boycott has an "expressive component" in that it is designed to communicate a measure to its targets, but the First Amendment was not designed to protect such boycotts simply because the target is the government itself.

b. The Sham Exception to *Noerr-Pennington*

In California Motor Transport Co. v. Trucking Unlimited, 404 U.S. 508, 92 S.Ct. 609 (1972) the Supreme Court held that if a firm or group of firms petitions the government, but the petition is only a sham, really designed to hinder the activities of some competitor, then the *Noerr-Pennington* doctrine will not apply. Then, in Professional Real Estate Investors v. Columbia Pictures Industries, 508 U.S. 49, 113 S.Ct. 1920 (1993), the Supreme Court held that a lawsuit with an objectively valid basis cannot be a "sham." Thus, for example, a patent infringement suit cannot be an antitrust violation unless the infringement plaintiff obtained the patent by fraud, or knew or should have known that the patent was unenforceable under the circumstances. See Hovenkamp §§ 7.11, 18.3.

In *California Motor Transport* case the Court also made clear that the entire *Noerr-Pennington* defense is grounded in the First Amendment.

In Allied Tube & Conduit Corp. v. Indian Head, Inc., 486 U.S. 492, 108 S.Ct. 1931 (1988) the Supreme Court agreed in principle that *Noerr-Pennington* might even extend to petitions to private standard-setting bodies, if the bodies were in a position to dictate government policy. In this case, the National Fire Protection Association, a private organization, promulgated building safety standards that were adopted virtually automatically into state and local government building codes. However, the Court then held that the exemption did not apply where the defendant abused the private decision making policy by packing it with its own members, organizing a cartel of voters, and the like.

c. Some Noncommercial Boycotts Entitled to First Amendment Protection

Sometimes a boycott designed to further a political goal is protected activity under the First Amendment of the Constitution. In that case, the Sherman Act cannot be applied to the activity. The subject of noncommercial boycotts is discussed further in chapter VII.

C. ANTITRUST IN FEDERALLY REGULATED INDUSTRIES AND THE DOCTRINE OF PRIMARY JURISDICTION

Many American markets are not subject to free and open price competition, but rather are regulated as to price, output and other aspects of performance. In these regulated markets the antitrust laws generally occupy a somewhat smaller place than they do in unregulated markets. *Nevertheless, an industry is not exempt from the antitrust laws merely because it is regulated, and there is still substantial room for antitrust enforcement in the regulated industries.*

The extent to which the federal antitrust laws apply in regulated markets varies with the comprehensiveness of the regulatory scheme in that market. In some cases the regulatory agency in charge of overseeing a certain market has the exclusive right to protect competition in that market. In other cases the agency shares that power with the antitrust laws.

1. EXCLUSIVE AGENCY JURISDICTION

A few markets exist in which the authority of a regulatory agency to protect competition is exclusive and the antitrust laws have virtually no place. *In general, these markets are identified either 1) by a federal statute that expressly exempts a certain industry from the antitrust laws (for example the McCarran–Ferguson Act exempting the business of insurance, discussed above); or 2) by a regulatory scheme that is so pervasive that it appears to the court that there is no room for application of the antitrust laws, or that the antitrust laws would be inimical to the regulatory scheme.* For example, in Pan American World Airways, Inc. v. U.S., 371 U.S. 296, 83 S.Ct. 476 (1963) the Court held that a territorial division scheme in the airline industry could not be condemned under the antitrust laws, for it was under the exclusive jurisdiction of the Civil Aeronautics Board.

> The Supreme Court construes exemptions from the antitrust laws narrowly, however, and creates exemptions only when Congressional intent is clear. The Court has noted that "repeals of the antitrust laws by implication from a regulatory statute are strongly disfavored, and have only been found in cases of plain repugnancy between the antitrust laws and regulatory provisions....

Note: An important effect of the deregulation movement of the 1970's and 1980's has been to reduce the amount of agency regulation in many markets. The result has been an increased amount of room for antitrust enforcement. For example, today the Civil Aeronautics Board has been abolished and the market for commercial air transportation is completely within the jurisdiction of the federal antitrust laws.

2. "PRIMARY" JURISDICTION

In other markets a regulatory agency has the "primary" obligation to protect competition, but there is a certain amount of room for the antitrust laws. This generally means that before a court will consider an antitrust case in such a market, the relevant regulatory agency must first have a chance to pass on the matter at issue. *If the agency carefully scrutinizes the firms in the market and approves an activity only after evaluation of its competitive impact, then the courts will generally defer to the agency decision. However, if the agency's decision was merely pro forma, with little consideration of competitive consequences, then there will be room for antitrust enforcement.*

Example: In MCI Communications Corp. v. American Tel. & Tel. Co., 708 F.2d 1081 (7th Cir. 1983) the court observed that a price regulated firm's request for a rate or service change is commonly approved by a regulatory agency with very little consideration of the competitive consequences that might follow. As a result, a court should be free to consider in subsequent litigation a charge that the rate change constituted monopolization or predatory pricing.

Finally, in Square D Co. v. Niagara Frontier Tariff Bureau, 476 U.S. 409, 106 S.Ct. 1922 (1986), the Supreme Court affirmed the "filed rate" doctrine first recognized in Keogh v. Chicago & N.W. Ry., 260 U.S. 156 (1922). Under that doctrine, once a rate has been filed with a regulatory agency it cannot be challenged by consumers claiming an overcharge on the theory that the approved rate is monopolistic or the product of a cartel.

D.   FEDERALISM AND THE PROBLEM OF MUNICIPAL ANTITRUST LIABILITY

In Parker v. Brown, 317 U.S. 341, 63 S.Ct. 307 (1943) the Supreme Court decided that the framers of the antitrust laws did not intend to interfere too substantially in the ability of the individual states to displace competition in certain markets by creating regulatory regimes of various kinds.

Today this doctrine is variously called the "Parker" doctrine, or the "State Action" doctrine. In the *Parker* case the court held that a state-mandated "allocation" scheme that reduced the supply of raisins grown in the state could not be condemned by the antitrust laws. Clearly, if the scheme had been carried out entirely by private parties it would have been a cartel subject to condemnation under § 1 of the Sherman Act.

1.   THE "STATE ACTION" DOCTRINE AND STATE–IMPOSED REGULATION

a.   The Compulsion Requirement

Historically, the state action doctrine applied only to conduct *mandated* by the state. For example, in Goldfarb v. Virginia State Bar, 421 U.S. 773, 95 S.Ct. 2004 (1975) the Court held that a lawyer's fee schedule which was approved but not mandated by the state supreme court failed to qualify for the "state action" exemption. More recently, however, in Southern Motor Carriers Rate Conference v. U.S., 471 U.S. 48, 105 S.Ct. 1721 (1985), the Court decided that the activities of a legislatively authorized "rate bureau" (a legalized cartel in which price-regulated common carriers jointly propose rates to a regulatory agency) qualified for the "state action" exemption, even though the state legislation merely authorized, and did not compel, the activities. The Court made clear, however, that its holding was not a blanket rule that state compulsion is unnecessary in state action cases involving private defendants. Rather it looked closely at the joint rate-making activities in question and found that in this particular case mere authorization, rather than compulsion, would produce a more competitive result. The Court observed:

Most common carriers probably will engage in collective ratemaking, as that will allow them to share the cost of preparing rate proposals. If the joint rates are viewed as too high, however, carriers individually may submit lower proposed rates to the commission in order to obtain a larger share of the market. Thus, through the self-interested actions of private common carriers, the States may achieve the desired balance between the efficiency of collective ratemaking and the competition fostered by individual submissions.

b. The *Midcal* Test

In California Retail Liquor Dealers Ass'n v. Midcal Aluminum Co., 445 U.S. 97, 100 S.Ct. 937 (1980) the Supreme Court held that a state legislative scheme which permitted wine producers and wholesalers to set the retail prices of their products did not qualify for the state action exemption because the scheme was not actively supervised by the state itself. *In reaching that conclusion, the Court formulated a two-prong test for the state action exemption:*

(1) The challenged restraint must be "one [that is] clearly articulated and affirmatively expressed as state policy ..."; and

(2) The policy must be "actively supervised" by the state itself.

> *Note:*   In Hoover v. Ronwin, 466 U.S. 558, 104 S.Ct. 1989 (1984) the Supreme Court held that the method by which the Arizona Supreme Court administered the state's bar examination qualified for the "state action" exemption. However, the Court departed from the *Midcal* test by holding that "Where the conduct at issue is in fact that of the state legislature or supreme court [rather than private parties being supervised by a state agency], we need not address the issues of 'clear articulation' and 'active supervision.'" In this particular case the administration and grading of the bar exam were governed by the state supreme court acting in its sovereign capacity as an arm of the state.

In Patrick v. Burget, 486 U.S. 94, 108 S.Ct. 1658 (1988), the Supreme Court held that the "active supervision" requirement was not met with respect to a physician peer review process that was authorized by state law, but with no provision for a state agency or court to review the merits of the private peer review decision. "The active supervision prong [of *Midcal*] requires that state officials have and exercise power to review particular anticompetitive acts of private parties and disapprove those that fail to accord with state policy."

After *Patrick* one or two circuit courts held that if a regulatory agency has the *authority* to disapprove rates, the active supervision requirement is met, even though the agency may be delinquent in exercising its authority—i.e., it may rubberstamp most rate increase requests without ascertaining whether they are cost justified. However, in FTC v. Ticor Title Insurance Co., 504 U.S. 621,

112 S.Ct. 2169 (1992), the Supreme Court held that a regulatory agency may not merely rubber stamp a rate proposal jointly made by a group of price-regulated firms. Rather, it must review the proposal on the merits. "[S]tate officials [must] undertake[] the necessary steps to determine the specifics of the price-fixing or rate setting scheme. The mere potential for state supervision is not an adequate substitute for a decision by the State." The Court then held that a scheme under which proposed rates automatically went into effect after a defined period, generally without more than a cursory check of arithmetic by state regulators, did not meet the "active supervision" requirement.

2. THE "STATE ACTION" DOCTRINE AND MUNICIPAL ANTITRUST LIABILITY

The "state action" exemption from the antitrust laws is based on the fact that under the United States Constitution the individual states are at least qualified sovereigns. However, the Constitution does not recognize the sovereignty of municipalities or other governmental subdivisions such as counties and townships. As a result, these subdivisions have only as much regulatory power as the state in which they are located sees fit to grant them. *Thus the Supreme Court concluded in Lafayette v. Louisiana Power & Light Co., 435 U.S. 389, 98 S.Ct. 1123 (1978) that the "state action" doctrine "exempts only anticompetitive conduct engaged in as an act of government by the State as sovereign, or by its subdivisions, pursuant to state policy to displace competition with regulation or monopoly.... "*

a. The Consequences of Failing to Qualify for the "State Action" Exemption

In the *Lafayette* case, cited above, the Court held that a tying arrangement imposed by a municipally-owned electric utility did not qualify for the "state action" exemption, because it was not compelled by the State acting as a sovereign.

The consequence of that holding was not that the city policy was simply declared invalid because it conflicted with federal law. Rather, the consequence was a finding that the city could actually *violate* the antitrust laws and even be subject to treble damages. This decision raised the ominous spectre of treble damages being levied against cities. At least one municipality was ordered to pay a large treble damages award.

In 1984 Congress responded by passing the Local Government Antitrust Act, which provides that municipalities and private persons directed by them should not pay damages if they are found to be in violation of the antitrust laws. Rather the remedy will be limited to injunctive relief.

However, the Local Government Antitrust Act says nothing about the standard to be used for determining whether a municipal law or regulation violates the federal antitrust laws.

Note: It is important to keep in mind that a judicial finding that a municipality does not qualify for the "state action" exemption is only a finding that the municipality may be sued under the antitrust laws. It is *not* a finding that the municipality has violated the antitrust laws. A city or other governmental subdivision is still entitled to litigate the antitrust claim fully on the merits.

b. The "State Action" Exemption as Applied to Municipalities

Under the holdings in both *Midcal Aluminum,* cited above, and *Lafayette,* cited above, a municipality's regulatory activities *may* qualify for the "state action" exemption—but only if the following requirements are met:

1) *State* Authorization to Regulate in a *Particular* Market

Before a municipality can avail itself of the "state action" exemption, it must have express authority from the state to displace competition with regulation in a particular market area.

> **Example:**   In Community Communications Co. v. City of Boulder, 455 U.S. 40, 102 S.Ct. 835 (1982) the Supreme Court held that a "home rule" municipality which had the authority to regulate cable television under its home rule powers, nevertheless did not qualify for the "state action" exemption. The home rule provision, which is a state grant to a municipality of a *general* regulatory power, did not specifically authorize Boulder to displace competition with regulation in the market for cable television. The Supreme Court therefore characterized the home rule provision as being merely "neutral" on the question of whether the city of Boulder could regulate cable TV.

The clear implication of the Boulder decision is that if a city's regulation of, say, taxicab fares, is to qualify for the "state action" exemption, the state must pass a statute specifically authorizing the municipality to displace competition with regulation in the taxicab market.

However, in subsequent decisions the Court has appeared to narrow both *Lafayette* and *Boulder.* In Town of Hallie v. City of Eau Claire, 471 U.S. 34, 105 S.Ct. 1713 (1985), the Court held that the state authorizing statute need not compel the municipality to regulate; it is sufficient if the statute merely authorizes the municipality to regulate the specified market. *The Court also held that the authorizing statute need not expressly give the municipality the power to displace competition. It is enough if the state statute authorizes the municipality to regulate a specific market, and displacement of competition is a foreseeable result of that regulation.*

Finally in City of Columbia, Columbia Outdoor Advertising v. Omni Outdoor Advertising, 499 U.S. 365, 111 S.Ct. 1344 (1991), the Court held that once a city has been authorized by the state to regulate in a certain area, the motives of its decision makers (such as the city council) or the fact that their regulation was anticompetitive were generally irrelevant. The court refused to adopt any notion that a private person and the municipality might "conspire" to do something anticompetitive, and thus remove the state action exemption. The Court even suggested in dicta that bribery of a state official, and a resulting anticompetitive decision by the official, would not remove the exemption.

The conspiracy discussion in *Columbia* is consistent with the Supreme Court's earlier decision in Fisher v. City of Berkeley, 475 U.S. 260, 106 S.Ct. 1045 (1986) that a rate regulation statute should not be construed as an "agreement" between the government and the rate regulated firm for purposes of § 1 of the Sherman Act.

2) *Someone* Must Actively Supervise the Regulatory Scheme

Before a municipal regulatory statute qualifies for the state action exemption, the state must authorize the city to regulate in a specific market. However, until 1985 the "active state supervision" requirement was ambiguous when the defendant was a municipality. For some time it was unclear whether that supervision had to come from the State, or whether the city could supervise its own regulatory scheme. As a practical matter, however, the sovereign that creates a regulatory scheme is generally also responsible for supervising it. Thus it would be anomalous for a state agency to be in the business of supervising a municipally-created taxicab regulation or sewage disposal regulation scheme.

In Town of Hallie v. City of Eau Claire, 471 U.S. 34, 105 S.Ct. 1713 (1985), the Supreme Court decided that once a municipal regulatory scheme had been expressly and particularly authorized by the State, the "active state supervision" requirement did not apply to the municipality.

E.   REVIEW QUESTIONS

1. **T or F**   All of the antitrust laws extend to the full reach of Congress's power to control interstate commerce.

2. **T or F**   Under the "primary jurisdiction" rule the antitrust laws are never applied in certain regulated industries.

3. **T or F**   The Local Government Antitrust Act exempted municipalities from the federal antitrust laws.

4. Three members of a five member city council are shareholders in Westside Shopping Mall. Waldo proposes to build Westdale Shopping Mall, which would be across the street from Westside Mall. Before Westdale Mall can be built, however, Waldo needs a zoning amendment. Waldo applies to the city council for a zoning

amendment; Archie, who is the fourth shareholder in Westside Mall appears at the public hearing and speaks in opposition to the rezoning, urging the City Council not to buy it. After the meeting Archie and the three shareholder members go out for drinks together. A day later the city council members announce their vote, which is 3–2 against rezoning, with all three negative votes coming from the three Westside shareholders. Waldo sues (a) the city and (b) Archie, alleging an antitrust violation. Who wins? Why?

XII

ENFORCEMENT, PROCEDURE AND RELATED MATTERS

Analysis

A. PUBLIC ENFORCEMENT

The antitrust laws are enforced by two federally-created enforcement entities, the Department of Justice and the Federal Trade Commission, as well as by private parties who have been injured by an antitrust violation.

1. ENFORCEMENT BY THE DEPARTMENT OF JUSTICE

a. Criminal Enforcement

The United States Department of Justice, together with the United States Attorneys, has authority to enforce the criminal provisions of the antitrust laws contained in sections 1 and 2 of the Sherman Act, section 3 of the Robinson–Patman Act, and section 14 of the Clayton Act. Of these, only the criminal provisions of sections 1 (and occasionally 2) of the Sherman Act are enforced with any frequency. Criminal indictments for price fixing are issued regularly. Only the Department of Justice has authority to enforce the criminal provisions of the antitrust laws.

A corporation convicted under one of the criminal provisions of the Sherman Act may be fined up to $1,000,000. A natural person convicted of a criminal violation of the Sherman Act may be fined up to $100,000 and imprisoned up to three years. Prison sentences for criminal antitrust violations are not frequent, but several individuals have been sent to prison, mostly for short terms.

In U.S. v. United States Gypsum Co., 438 U.S. 422, 98 S.Ct. 2864 (1978), the Supreme Court held that criminal intent is a separate element that must be established in a criminal antitrust case. Thus the liability standard is stricter today in a criminal case than it is in a civil case.

b. Civil Enforcement

The Justice Department has broad power to investigate businesses for antitrust violations. In carrying out such an investigation the Department may issue a Civil Investigate Demand (CID) before filing a formal complaint. The CID entitles the Department to examine documents in the control of suspected antitrust violators, and sometimes even of third parties who are not suspected antitrust violators. Once the Department obtains sufficient evidence, it may file a civil action in the federal district court where the defendant is found or transacts its business. Once this action is filed, the Justice Department, just as any other party, is bound by the Federal Rules of Civil Procedure, the Federal Rules of Evidence, and other relevant procedural rules.

2. ENFORCEMENT BY THE FEDERAL TRADE COMMISSION (FTC)

The FTC has the exclusive power to enforce § 5 of the Federal Trade Commission Act, which condemns unfair methods of competition. It also has express authority to enforce the Clayton Act. Today, however, it is clear that "unfair methods of competition" includes any antitrust violation, so the Commission effectively has the power to enforce all the antitrust laws.

The commission is a regulatory agency, composed of five Commissioners appointed by the president. Its initial complaint process results in an adversary proceeding within the FTC itself, before an administrative law judge (ALJ). Within ninety days after this hearing the ALJ must file an "initial decision." The respondent (i.e., the firm against which the complaint was lodged) may appeal this initial decision to the five commissioners. If the entire Commission decides that the conduct was illegal, the respondent may appeal once again to one of the United States Courts of Appeals (circuit courts). When the circuit court reviews the FTC's decision, it considers only whether that decision was supported by substantial evidence in the record.

The FTC cannot assess prison terms or damages. Rather, the relief it gives is a type of injunction known as a "cease and desist" order. However, the FTC does have authority to bring an action in court to seek a fine of up to $10,000 for violation of an existing cease and desist order, or for "knowing violations" of the FTC Act and antitrust laws. In general, a knowing violation is a practice previously found by the Commission to be illegal.

B.   PRIVATE ENFORCEMENT

Today the great majority of antitrust enforcement comes from private plaintiffs in lawsuits, most of which are filed initially in the federal district courts.

Section 4 of the Clayton Act provides for treble damages and attorneys fees to someone who can prove that he has been injured in his business or property by an antitrust violation.

1.   STANDING TO SUE

a.   Injury to "Business or Property"

Before a private plaintiff has standing to sue for antitrust damages, it must show that it has been injured in its "business or property" as the result of an antitrust violation. It was once thought that these words really meant that a firm had to be injured in its "business property" or at least its "business" before it could sue for damages. *However, in Reiter v. Sonotone Corp., 442 U.S. 330, 99 S.Ct. 2326 (1979), the Supreme Court held that a retail consumer had standing to sue for damages in a price fixing case.*

b.   Only a Few of the Injured Have Standing

Many people who have no market relationship with an antitrust violator can be injured by an antitrust violation. For example, if one firm drives another firm out of business by predatory pricing, the immediate victim is not the only person injured in its business or property. The victim's landlord, creditors, perhaps customers, the public entities to which it pays taxes, other firms with whom it had ongoing contractual relationships, terminated employees, its shareholders if it is a corporation—all of these entities could suffer injury as a result of the predatory pricing. *Most likely, however, none of these would have standing to sue in this particular case. Only the immediate victim of the predatory pricing could bring an action, as well as consumers who were later forced to pay monopoly prices.* Courts have consistently held that landlords, creditors, and shareholders of an antitrust victim do not have standing to sue for their losses, even if the losses are substantial. Likewise, courts have held that an employee of the victim who lost her job as a result of the victim's exit from the market has no standing.

Currently, however, the circuit courts are divided on the issue whether an employee of an antitrust law *violator* has standing to sue his former employer because he was fired for refusing to participate in an antitrust violation.

c. Attempts at Generalized Standing Tests

Over the years courts have formulated their tests for standing in a variety of ways:

1) The "Direct Injury" Test

The "direct injury" test originated in Loeb v. Eastman Kodak Co., 183 Fed. 704 (3d Cir.1910), where the court denied standing to a stockholder in a corporation that allegedly was victimized by an antitrust violation. The court held that in order to have standing a plaintiff must show that its injury was "direct," rather than "indirect." However, the court did not clearly identify what constituted a direct injury, except to note that in this particular case the "direct" victim was the corporation itself. Presumably, anyone injured because of his relationship with the corporation suffered only an indirect injury. For more on the "direct injury" test, see Hovenkamp § 14.3.

2) The "Target Area" Test

The "target area" test, which was formulated in Conference of Studio Unions v. Loew's, Inc., 193 F.2d 51 (9th Cir.1951), cert. denied, 342 U.S. 919, 72 S.Ct. 367 (1952), requires a plaintiff to show "that he is within that area of the economy which is endangered by a breakdown of competitive conditions in a particular industry." The court concluded that a labor union and its members could not sue for antitrust injuries suffered by the firms that employed the labor union's members.

d. The Inconclusiveness of the Generalized Standing Tests

Both of the above tests are extremely ambiguous in application. As a result there is little consistency of result, even in cases decided by the Supreme Court. In general, courts have recognized two favored classes of plaintiffs, purchasers from and competitors of the violator. Although there are exceptions, most customers and competitors of the violator are granted standing; most people who are not customers or competitors of the violator are denied standing.

e. Recent Developments in Standing

One of the significant exceptions to the rule that disfavors those who are not customers or competitors of the violator is Blue Shield of Virginia v. McCready, 457 U.S. 465, 102 S.Ct. 2540 (1982). The Court granted standing to a user of psychologists' services who claimed she was victimized by a conspiracy between psychiatrists and a health insuror (Blue Shield) to deny health care coverage on its insurance policy for treatment by psychologists. Unquestionably, the intended victim of this alleged antitrust violation was the psychologists. However, an insured patient whose policy excluded psychologists' services was undeniably injured as well. *In granting standing, the Supreme Court appeared to require that:*

(1) *the plaintiff's injury be a "foreseeable" consequence of an antitrust violation; and*

(2) *that the plaintiff's injury be "inextricably intertwined with the injury the conspirators sought to inflict on psychologists...." (the intended victims of the violation); and*

(3) *the plaintiff was a victim of "antitrust injury," or of those things that made the alleged illegal act anticompetitive. On antitrust injury, see B.3., infra.*

In Associated General Contractors of California, Inc. v. California State Council of Carpenters, 459 U.S. 519, 103 S.Ct. 897 (1983), however, the Supreme Court appeared to revert to a more traditional "target area" test in denying standing to a labor union which alleged that the defendant non-union employers had coerced various developers into employing non-union rather than union contractors, thus restraining "the business activities of the unions." In this case the alleged boycott was aimed at union contractors who employed people who were members of the union—thus the union itself was two times removed from the target of the alleged conspiracy.

f. Standing in Parens Patriae Actions

A parens patriae action is an action brought by a sovereign in behalf of its citizens. Thus the parens patriae action contains some elements of both private enforcement and public enforcement. Because the federal government through the Department of Justice and Federal Trade Commission already have authority to enforce the antitrust laws in behalf of the public, the concept of parens patriae is relevant largely with respect to *state* enforcement of the federal antitrust laws for the benefit of the citizens of that state.

In Hawaii v. Standard Oil Co. of Cal., 405 U.S. 251, 92 S.Ct. 885 (1972) the Supreme Court held that a state did *not* have the authority to sue for treble damages for an antitrust violation which injured its citizens or the general economy of the state. *In 1976, however, Congress passed the Hart–Scott–Rodino Antitrust Improvements Act, which permits states, acting through their attorneys general, to sue as parens patriae for treble damages for any Sherman Act violation.* The state may collect treble damages; however, under the statute the damages must be reduced by any damages paid for the same injury in actions brought by the injured persons themselves. Furthermore, the statute permits the state to sue only in behalf of injured consumers, not in behalf of injured businesses.

For more on standing, see Hovenkamp § 16.4-16.5.

2. THE INDIRECT PURCHASER RULE

In Hanover Shoe, Inc. v. United Shoe Machinery Corp., 392 U.S. 481, 88 S.Ct. 2224 (1968), the Supreme Court decided that a plaintiff in a monopolization case could claim the entire monopoly overcharge (i.e., the difference between the competitive price and the illegal price) as damages, even though the plaintiff "passed on" part of its losses by charging its customers a higher price.

In Illinois Brick Co. v. Illinois, 431 U.S. 720, 97 S.Ct. 2061 (1977), the Supreme Court decided a very important corollary of the above rule: namely, an "indirect purchaser" from an antitrust defendant (i.e., someone who did not purchase directly from the defendant, but who purchased from someone who purchased from the defendant) may not bring an action for damages.

Lower courts have held that the *Illinois Brick* rule also applies to indirect sellers (i.e., those who dealt indirectly with a monopsonist or buyer's cartel).

a. Basis of the *Illinois Brick* Rule

There are two rationales for the indirect purchaser rule, although the first is stronger than the second.

1) Difficulty of Computing Damages

When the price of a product rises, demand for it goes down. When the direct purchaser from a cartel or monopolist pays a monopoly overcharge, it will naturally try to "pass on" the monopoly overcharge to its own customers. However, it generally will not succeed in passing on the entire monopoly overcharge, for in the process of raising the price it will lose some sales.

Example: Buildex Corp. is a building contractor which produces brick buildings. It purchases its brick from a group of suppliers who are engaged in price fixing. When the price of bricks rose from 30each (the competitive price) to 45each (the cartel price) Buildex submitted higher bids for the

construction of brick buildings. Even though other builders
of brick buildings submitted higher bids as well, Buildex
Corp. won fewer bids after the cartel came into existence
than it had before. Some customers responded to the high
price of brick buildings by opting to build wood or steel
buildings; others decided to make their old buildings last a
few years longer.

As a result, part of the monopoly (cartel) overcharge paid by Buildex was
"passed on" to those people who built brick buildings during the cartel
period and paid higher prices for them. However, part of the loss was
absorbed by Buildex in the form of lost sales.

In the vast majority of markets, no court would be capable of computing
the amount of the monopoly overcharge absorbed by Buildex and the
amount passed on to its customers. *The* Illinois Brick *decision responds by
giving the entire monopoly overcharge to Buildex Corp. Those people who
purchased brick buildings from Buildex have no damages action against the
cartel, even though they clearly were injured by it.*

2)   Deterrence

There is another argument justifying the indirect purchaser rule,
although there is little empirical evidence to support it. In many cases the
amount of damages suffered by each individual purchaser from a cartel or
monopolist is very small. If each such party were forced to bring its own
lawsuit, none might be brought. The *Illinois Brick* rule responds by giving
the entire damages action to a relatively small number of people—namely,
those who dealt directly with the defendant.

b.   **Exceptions to the *Illinois Brick* Rule**

The lower courts have created the following exceptions to the indirect
purchaser rule. None has yet been approved by the Supreme Court.

1)   Pre-existing, Fixed–Cost, Fixed–Quantity Contract

If a certain grouping of sales to a particular buyer was negotiated by
contract before a cartel came into existence, and the contract provided
that the supplier (also the direct purchaser) would take a specified
markup, then we can be confident that the entire monopoly overcharge
was passed on to the indirect purchaser. However, *both* the markup and
the quantity must be specified in the contract. If the quantity is not
specified, the indirect purchaser will respond to the cartel price increase
by purchasing less, and part of the monopoly overcharge will still be
borne by the direct purchaser.

Note: Some courts have mistakenly held that there should be an
                 exception for the "functional equivalent" of a pre-existing,

> fixed cost, fixed markup contract—namely, where the indirect purchaser can show that the direct purchaser always follows a pre-established formula in computing its markup. However, in such cases only the markup is fixed, not the quantity, and the indirect purchaser rule should apply.

See Hovenkamp § 16.6.

2) Co–Conspirator in the Middle

If the "direct purchaser" is not a victim of an antitrust violation at all, but rather a co-conspirator with the cartel or monopolist from whom it purchases, then the purchasers from the co-conspirator will still have a cause of action against the monopolist or cartel, as well as against the co-conspirator.

The same exception generally applies when the direct purchaser is in fact a subsidiary, or is wholly controlled, by the monopolist or a cartel member.

3) Actions for an Injunction

The problem addressed by the *Illinois Brick* rule is one of computing damages. Such problems do not arise in an action only for an injunction. Lower courts have held that even an indirect purchaser may maintain an action for an injunction.

Note 1: In Kansas & Missouri v. Utilicorp United, Inc., 497 U.S. 199, 110 S.Ct. 2807 (1990), the Supreme Court reaffirmed the *Illinois Brick* rule and applied it where the direct purchaser was a price-regulated public utility. The indirect purchasers (the utility's customers) unsuccessfully argued that a price regulated utility, unlike the ordinary competitive firm, will be able to pass on the entire monopoly overcharge.

Note 2: Several states have amended their own antitrust statutes to permit indirect purchaser lawsuits. In California v. ARC America Corp., 490 U.S. 93, 109 S.Ct. 1661 (1989), the Supreme Court held that such statutes were not preempted by federal law, citing a long history of federal tolerance and even encouragement of state antitrust enforcement.

Under existing law, then, a federal plaintiff is entitled to the *entire* monopoly overcharge, even if most was passed on, unreduced by any damages suffered by indirect purchasers. Theoretically, the indirect purchasers could recover treble the damages passed on to them under state law. Thus an antitrust defendant may be liable for damages far greater than three times the monopoly overcharge.

3. ANTITRUST INJURY

Not all forms of injury caused by antitrust violations are compensable. *The plaintiff must show that it was injured by the anticompetitive consequences of the antitrust violation.*

Example: Brunswick Corp. v. Pueblo Bowl–O–Mat, Inc., 429 U.S. 477, 97 S.Ct. 690 (1977) was a merger action brought by a competitor of the acquired firm. Before the merger the plaintiff and the acquired firm had been struggling small bowling alleys in a medium-sized community. However, the acquired firm was in poor financial condition and likely to go out of business. The plaintiff alleged that as a result of the acquisition of its competitor by a large operator of bowling alleys, the firm remained in competition with the plaintiff. In short, the plaintiff would have been a monopolist, or at least had a far larger market share, had the merger not occurred. It sought damages for this loss of additional business.

The Supreme Court observed that the plaintiff was actually complaining that the market was *more* competitive as a result of the merger, rather than less competitive. It then dismissed the complaint because the plaintiff had not suffered "antitrust injury," even though it clearly had suffered some kind of injury as a result of the merger.

Likewise, in Cargill, Inc. v. Monfort of Colo., Inc., 479 U.S. 104, 107 S.Ct. 484 (1986), the Supreme Court held that a competitor did not suffer antitrust injury from a merger of rivals, under the theory that the post-merger firm would charge lower, but nonpredatory prices. The Court left open the possibility that a competitor might challenge a merger on the theory that the merger would lead to predatory pricing; but it remains unclear what such a plaintiff would have to show—i.e., whether it must show that predatory pricing is merely possible after the merger, or that the post-merger firm would actually engage in predation.

Today it is well established that the antitrust injury doctrine applies not only to merger cases under § 7 of the Clayton Act, but also to other antitrust violations. In J. Truett Payne Co. v. Chrysler Motors Corp., 451 U.S. 557, 101 S.Ct. 1923 (1981), the Supreme Court applied the doctrine in a Robinson–Patman Act case. Lower courts have applied it in other areas. See Hovenkamp § 16.3.

In Atlantic Richfield Co. v. USA Petroleum, 495 U.S. 328, 110 S.Ct. 1884 (1990), the Supreme Court held that a competitor lacked antitrust injury to complain of *maximum* resale price maintenance imposed on its rival, even though maximum resale price maintenance is illegal *per se*. The Court noted that in this case the plaintiff was complaining about its competitor's low price, that there was no evidence that the low price was predatory, and as a result granting the plaintiff's relief would result in a less competitive rather than a more competitive market. The decision also appears to resolve a controversy about whether the "antitrust injury" doctrine should even apply to *per se* violations; it does.

Today the lower courts are divided on the question whether the target of a hostile takeover is a victim of antitrust injury. Suppose A Corp. tries to acquire B Corp., and B Corp.'s directors complain and allege that the resulting merger is illegal. If it is illegal it is because post-merger firm AB will be able to charge *higher* prices. As a result, to the extent the merger is anticompetitive B Corp.'s stockholders will be beneficiaries rather than victims of the unlawful acquisition.

4. CONTRIBUTION AMONG JOINT VIOLATORS

Contribution occurs when one co-conspirator or joint tortfeasor who has been ordered by a court to pay damages has a right to force fellow conspirators or tortfeasors to pay a share, since all were guilty together even though the plaintiff obtained a judgment against only one. In Texas Industries, Inc. v. Radcliff Materials, Inc., 451 U.S. 630, 101 S.Ct. 2061 (1981), the Supreme Court held that there is no right of contribution in antitrust cases involving joint violators (most notably, price-fixing).

5. DAMAGES AND ATTORNEYS' FEES

The prevailing private plaintiff in an antitrust case is entitled to *treble* damages plus attorney fees. The jury is not instructed that damages are to be trebled, and the judge simply multiplies the jury's award by three. Then the judge asks the plaintiffs' attorneys to submit time sheets and itemized expenses, and attorneys' fees are awarded on the basis of formulas that vary considerably from one federal circuit to another.

Damages in antitrust cases are calculated in two different ways, depending on the relationship between the plaintiff and the defendant:

a. Overcharge Injuries

If the plaintiff is a purchaser from a defendant found guilty of an "overcharge" violation, such as price fixing, monopolization, or perhaps some tying arrangements, the plaintiff's basic damages before trebling generally are the difference between the price that would have prevailed in a competitive market and the price that the plaintiff was forced to pay as a result of the antitrust violation.

> **Example:** Widgets sell at $2.50 in a competitive market, but at $4.00 in a market subject to price fixing. A direct purchaser from the cartel who successfully sued would be entitled to the $1.50 difference between the cartel price and the competitive price, multiplied by the number of units the plaintiff purchased at the cartel price. This number is then trebled.

The overcharge rule also applies to plaintiff *sellers* who dealt with a monopsonist or a buyers' cartel. In that case the overcharge is really an "undercharge"—that is, the monopsonist or buyers' cartel will drive their purchase price to a lower level than would prevail in a competitive market. The plaintiff is entitled to the difference between the price that would have obtained in competition and the price it received for its sales, multiplied by the number of sales, and then trebled.

b.   Lost Profits

Plaintiffs who are competitors of the defendant, such as the victims of predatory pricing or other exclusionary practices, terminated dealers, competitors in the tying or tied product markets in tying arrangement cases, and any other classes of business plaintiffs for whom the overcharge method of computing damages does not apply, are entitled to damages based on lost profits. Such damages are equal to the difference between the amount of money the plaintiff actually earned, and the amount it would have earned had no antitrust violation occurred.

c.   Methods of Damages Computation

Estimating damages, whether for overcharge injuries or for lost profits, is very difficult and often cannot be accomplished with any precision. *The Supreme Court has held that the fact of a violation and of the plaintiff's injury must be established with a fair amount of precision; however, the amount of damages can then be approximated on the basis of credible evidence.* See Hovenkamp § 17.5.

Both forms of damages described above are calculated in two different ways:

1)   Before-and-After Method

The before-and-after method of approximating damages looks at the market before the violation occurred, or after it ended, and tries to compare prices or profits at these times with prices or profits during the violation period. The method applies to both overcharge injuries and lost profits injuries.

2)   Yardstick Method

The yardstick method seeks to measure damages by finding another market similar to the market at issue in the litigation, but in which there was no antitrust violation. For example, in a lost profits case, the court will look for a firm similar to the plaintiff, but which was not victimized by the antitrust violation. The court will then compare the amount earned by this "yardstick" firm with the amount earned by the plaintiff.

The same methodology is applied for overcharge injuries. For example, in price fixing cases, the court will look for some market in which the same product is sold, and which is subject to more-or-less the same costs, but in which there was no price fixing. This will provide an estimate of the competitive price of the product.

6. OTHER PRIVATE REMEDIES—INJUNCTION AND DIVESTITURE

A private plaintiff is also entitled to obtain an injunction against the continuation of an antitrust violation, or against an antitrust violation which is threatened to occur in the future. Under § 16 of the Clayton Act a plaintiff who successfully obtains an injunction is entitled to collect attorney's fees from the defendant.

In California v. American Stores Co., 495 U.S. 271, 110 S.Ct. 1853 (1990) the Supreme Court held that a private party (in this case a state) could also obtain *divestiture*, or the forced separation of two firms that had illegally merged. The decision resolved a dispute among circuit courts concerning whether divestiture is authorized by § 16 of the Clayton Act, which authorizes "injunctive relief" but does not define what such relief might include.

7. CLASS ACTIONS

Not all antitrust violations are suitable for treatment as class actions. For example, the number of victims in a predatory pricing case is usually too small to warrant such treatment. By contrast, purchaser class actions in price fixing cases are relatively common. Such cases are generally brought under Federal Rule of Civil Procedure 23(b)(3), which permits certification of a class action if "the court finds that the questions of law or fact common to the members of the class predominate over any questions affecting only individual members, and that a class action is superior to other available methods for the fair and efficient adjudication of the controversy."

Courts have generally held that the antitrust violation and the fact of injury must be established by proof that is common to all class members. However, then each individual member of the class may show the amount of its damages. Such a mechanism works very well in price fixing cases involving large numbers of direct purchasers. In the typical price fixing class action the fact of the cartel and the amount of the overcharge per unit purchased is established with respect to the entire class of direct purchasers. Then each class member gives evidence of the particular amount that it purchased.

8. IN PARI DELICTO AND "UNCLEAN HANDS"

The common law defense of *in pari delicto* bars a plaintiff from recovering damages as a result of unlawful activities in which the plaintiff also participated. If the defense applied in antitrust cases, it could greatly reduce the number of successful damages suits. For example, many tying arrangement and exclusive dealing cases, and many cases brought by terminated dealers, involve alleged antitrust violations contained in contracts to which the plaintiff itself was a party. *However, in Perma Life Mufflers, Inc. v. International Parts Corp., 392 U.S. 134, 88 S.Ct. 1981 (1968), the Supreme Court held that the defense was not generally available in private antitrust litigation.* Today the lower courts are divided on the issue whether *in pari delicto* is *ever* available. Some have said it is never available; others have said it might be available if the plaintiff had actually been an active co-conspirator. For example, the Sixth Circuit has said that a plaintiff may not recover if it was "a co-initiator of the conspiracy and equally responsible therefor.... "

The defense of "unclean hands" applies when the defendant alleges that the plaintiff committed a *different* antitrust violation than the one that the defendant is accused of committing, and that this should bar the plaintiff's action. *In Kiefer–Stewart Co. v. Joseph E. Seagram & Sons, Inc., 340 U.S. 211, 71 S.Ct. 259 (1951) the Supreme Court held that the defense of unclean hands was not available in an antitrust case.*

9. SUMMARY JUDGMENT

The traditional rule in antitrust cases was that trials should be encouraged, and as a result summary judgment must be used sparingly. But in Matsushita Electric Industrial Co. v. Zenith Radio Corp., 475 U.S. 574, 106 S.Ct. 1348 (1986) the Supreme Court changed that position dramatically, and held that summary judgment is appropriate if pleadings, discovery, affidavits and other documents in the record at that time indicate that the party opposing summary judgment has failed "to make a showing sufficient to establish the existence of an element essential to that party's case." For example, if the plaintiff is alleging a conspiracy, its evidence must "tend to exclude the possibility" that the defendants in fact acted unilaterally. The Court also stated that the plaintiff's factual evidence must be particularly strong in order to avoid summary judgment if the plaintiff's *economic* theory was far-fetched, or "makes no sense."

The result of *Matsushita* has been a far-reaching shift in the way antitrust cases proceed, and two day a likely majority are dismissed on summary judgment before going to trial.

In Eastman Kodak Co. v. Image Technical Services, 504 U.S. 451, 112 S.Ct. 2072 (1992), the Supreme Court seemed to step back from the broadest implications of *Matsushita*. It held that summary judgment would not be issued against a plaintiff merely because prevailing economic theory suggested that injury to competition was impossible (in this case, that a seller without market power in a primary market could create an anticompetitive tying arrangement in markets for replacement parts and service), when there was independent evidence of higher prices, lost competitor opportunities, and other indicia of injury to competition. The Court concluded that *Matsushita* "did not hold that if the moving party enunciates any economic theory supporting its behavior, regardless of its accuracy in reflecting the actual market, it is entitled to summary judgment. *Matsushita* demands only that the nonmoving party's inferences be reasonable in order to reach the jury.... " In short, if the theory suggests that the plaintiff's claim is implausible but there is credible evidence suggesting to the contrary, summary judgment will be inappropriate.

10. STATUTE OF LIMITATION

Section 4B of the Clayton Act creates a four-year statute of limitation for private antitrust damages actions. The limitation period begins to run when the cause of action "accrues," which generally does not happen until damages are ascertainable. If the violation has already occurred, but the existence of injury and damages is unknown, or the damages are only speculative, then the statute will not run. For example, if a secret cartel is formed in 1978 but is not discovered and broken up until 1983, the statute of limitation will not begin to run until 1983.

11. THE "PRIMA FACIE EVIDENCE" RULE AND OFFENSIVE COLLATERAL ESTOPPEL

a. Section 5(a) of the Clayton Act

Section 5(a) of the Clayton Act provides that a final judgment obtained in a civil or criminal proceeding brought by the United States will be "prima facie evidence against such defendant in any action ... brought by any other party against such defendant under said laws as to all matters respecting which such judgment or decree would be an estoppel as between the parties thereto.... " However, the rule does not apply to consent judgments, or judgments entered before any testimony is taken. *The effect of the rule is that once the government has brought an antitrust case and won, private parties injured by the same violations may file suit against the same parties and have the benefit of a rebuttable presumption that the defendant has violated the antitrust laws.* Of course, the private plaintiff will still have to establish the fact and amount of its own injury. The provision applies to actions originally brought by the Federal Trade Commission as well as to those brought by the Justice Department, *provided* that the FTC action was one to enforce the "antitrust laws." Some courts have held that an action to enforce § 5 of the FTC Act, which prohibits unfair methods of competition, is not an action to enforce one of the antitrust laws.

b. Offensive Collateral Estoppel

Today the usefulness of the "prima facie evidence" provision has been eclipsed somewhat by the expanding doctrine of offensive collateral estoppel, which makes matters *actually and necessarily decided* in a former judicial proceeding *preclusive* in a later proceeding. When it applies, the preclusive effect of offensive collateral estoppel is absolute; that is, the defendant is simply prohibited from relitigating the issue which is barred. In Parklane Hosiery Co. v. Shore, 439 U.S. 322, 99 S.Ct. 645 (1979) the Supreme Court held that a plaintiff who was not a party in the first action could use offensive collateral estoppel to bar the defendant from relitigating issues that had been decided against it in the first suit. However, the Court held, offensive collateral could not be used if:

(1) the plaintiff could easily have joined in the first suit (this barrier will not apply if the first suit was brought by the Justice Department or FTC; they do not ordinarily permit private co-plaintiffs);

(2) the defendant in the first action was sued for "small or nominal damages," and therefore did not have an adequate incentive to litigate;

(3) the judgment relied upon for its collateral estoppel effects "is itself inconsistent with one or more previous judgments in favor of the defendant;" or

(4) "the second action affords the defendant procedural opportunities unavailable in the first action that could readily cause a different result."

C. REVIEW QUESTIONS

1. You are an associate working for a law firm in Maricopa County, Arizona. Shortly after the doctors' maximum price fixing scheme was declared illegal *per se* by the Supreme Court in the *Maricopa County* case (see chapter II. above) a physician comes to your firm. She says that she was not a member of the maximum price fixing scheme in that case. Furthermore, she lost several patients who had decided to obtain medical services from one of the participating doctors in order to save money. She wants to file an antitrust claim for profits that she lost as a result of the price fixing scheme. Your boss asks you to draft a short memorandum on the question whether the physician has a good damages action under the antitrust laws.

2. **T or F**   Most antitrust enforcement is done by private parties.

3. Arie, who is an estimator for a company that installs electric wiring in new buildings, was asked by his employer to "rig" a bid in collusion with other electric contractors. Arie refused and his boss fired him. Arie sues his boss under the antitrust laws. Will he win?

4. **T or F**   Under the indirect purchaser rule, someone who dealt only indirectly with a monopolist or cartel member never has a cause of action under the federal antitrust laws.

ANSWERS TO REVIEW QUESTIONS

I. ANTITRUST ECONOMICS

1. Economies of scale exist when the cost of some input declines as output increases. Economies of scale are relevant to antitrust policy because low consumer prices are an important goal of the antitrust laws. At the same time, in industries subject to substantial economies of scale, only large firms with large market shares will be able to attain all the economies. If antitrust policy is too aggressive against such practices as monopolization and mergers, it will prevent industries from attaining technologically available scale economies, and consumer prices will rise. On the other hand, if antitrust policy is not aggressive enough, firms will engage in inefficient, monopolistic practices, and prices will also rise.

2. *False.* A "reservation price" is the most someone will pay for a product. *No one* has the power to force someone to pay more than her reservation price.

3. *True.* The supply curve represents the sum of the costs of all the firms in a market at a particular level of output.

4. *False.* Under monopoly consumers' surplus is reduced, but it is almost never reduced to zero. There will still be some consumers whose reservation prices are higher than the monopolist's profit-maximizing price. Only perfect price discrimination reduces consumers' surplus to zero. (See chapter 10.)

5. **True.**   When a firm faces a low elasticity of demand, it will lose relatively few sales in response to a price increase. Thus the lower the elasticity of demand a firm faces, the more profitable a price increase will be.

6. **False.**   A wealth transfer makes the transferees wealthier by exactly the same amount as it makes the transferors poorer. Total social wealth is unaffected. A social cost makes society as a whole worse off, because the transferees receive less than the transferors give up.

7. **True.**   The more competitive the market, the closer prices will be to the marginal costs of the firms in the market. Thus a goal of encouraging marginal cost pricing is synonymous with a goal of encouraging competition.

II. CARTELS, TACIT COLLUSION, JOINT VENTURES AND OTHER COMBINATIONS OF COMPETITORS

1. The arrangement should be analyzed under the rule of reason, and it should probably be approved. The arrangement cannot be a scheme to suppress demand for either steel or aluminum, because collectively the bolt manufacturers consume very small percentages of these products. Although they control a high percentage of the market for bolts, it is difficult to see how an agreement to fix the content of bolts could be anticompetitive. The agreement might be designed to facilitate price fixing or oligopoly in bolts, but it probably should not be condemned on this ground unless there is other evidence of collusion.

2. **False.**   Price fixing is illegal *per se*, regardless of the absence of high market concentration or barriers to entry.

3. It appears that the electric radio market is not very conducive to collusion; so the Justice Department should not spend much of its efforts there. In most cases collusion will not work effectively in a market containing thirty manufacturers. The fact that the radios produced by each manufacturer vary widely in quality, size and individual capabilities, makes collusion even more difficult. The cartel members would find it hard to agree on a cartel price. Finally, cheating by cartel members is almost impossible to detect in a market in which sales are large (i.e., to wholesale buyers) and prices and terms are individually negotiated.

4. **True.**   Although tacit collusion is anticompetitive, the antitrust laws have yet not been able to deal with it effectively because § 1 of the Sherman Act requires an "agreement."

5. **False.**   Basing point pricing is generally evidence that a market is not performing competitively; however, if there is collusion, it could be tacit just as easily as express. For this reason, courts have not generally condemned basing point pricing in the absence of evidence that the sellers in a market agreed with each other to engage in the practice.

6. ***False.***   Most joint ventures are legal. A joint venture is illegal only when it is found to be engaged in some antitrust violation, such as price fixing, exchanges of price information, concerted refusals to deal, territorial division, or occasionally an illegal merger (see chapter VIII below).

7. The conduct should be governed by the rule of reason, and it should be legal. Even though General Motors Corp. is a very large company, the conduct described here is entirely intrafirm conduct. There are no conspiring entities for the purpose of § 1 of the Sherman Act.

III.   MONOPOLIZATION, ATTEMPT TO MONOPOLIZE AND PREDATORY PRICING

1. ***False.***   The attempt offense contains more specific conduct requirements. The reverse is generally true: any bad conduct that will support the offense of attempt, will also support the offense of monopolization.

2. ***True.***   Today there is no law of so-called "no fault" monopolization.

3. ***True.***   Regardless of the elasticity of demand in a market, a firm has no market power if competitors or potential competitors can respond to a price increase by instantly flooding the market with the same product or with very good substitutes.

4. Market share is used as a surrogate for market power in monopolization cases because market power, which is a relationship between a firm's marginal cost and its profit-maximizing price, cannot be computed directly, particularly not in the courtroom.

5. Perhaps. However, the trend in cases is to hold that even the purchase and *non*use of patents is legal. Furthermore, no firm, not even the monopolist, has a duty to license its patents to others.

6. The defendant, Firm A, should win this predatory pricing case. Even though Firm A has sold its products at a price lower than AVC, this market is simply not conducive to predatory pricing. There are too many firms. A's market share (about 12.5%) is much too small for it to be a predator. Further, the large amount of excess capacity would frustrate any attempt at predatory pricing. As soon as the predator attempted to raise its price other firms would increase their output and the price would drop back to the competitive level.

IV.   VERTICAL INTEGRATION AND VERTICAL MERGERS

1. ***False.***   All firms are vertically integrated to some degree.

2. The *Brown Shoe* decision was anticompetitive because it cited the defendant's ability to use vertical integration to reduce its costs as a reason for condemning the

merger. That is, under the *Brown Shoe* version of the foreclosure theory, a vertical merger is bad when it reduces a firm's costs and therefore makes it more difficult for other firms that are not vertically integrated to compete.

3. Vertical integration, particularly by merger, produces larger transaction cost savings than production cost savings because the latter are most often realized only within a single plant. Most instances of vertical integration by established firms do not result in the creation of larger, more integrated plants. However, all forms of vertical integration can reduce the transaction costs of using the market.

4. Several factors might influence a bicycle manufacturer's decision whether to manufacture its own bicycle tires or to purchase them from someone else:

   1) Economies of scale in tire manufacturing. If these economies are substantial, the tire manufacturer may be able to produce tires more cheaply, and the bicycle manufacturer will be better off to buy them.

   2) The amount of competition in the market for bicycle tires. If the market is competitive, then the bicycle manufacturer may be able to buy them at a price close to their cost of production. However, if the market is monopolized, it may have to pay a monopoly price. In the latter case, it might do better to manufacture the tires itself.

   3) Whether the tires are customized or "off the shelf." As a general rule, it is riskier to trust another firm to develop a customized product, particularly if the costs of development are uncertain when the contract is negotiated. In that case, the bicycle manufacturer might be better off to produce its own tires.

V. TIE–INS, RECIPROCITY, EXCLUSIVE DEALING AND THE FRANCHISE CONTRACT

1. *False.* Although the Supreme Court once took the position that tying arrangements have almost no socially redeeming value, today we believe that many such arrangements are efficient. As a result, a *per se* approach seems unwarranted. Nevertheless, many tying arrangements continue to be governed by the *per se* rule. In the *Jefferson Parish Hospital* case a bare five-justice majority of the Supreme Court advocated preserving the *per se* rule for tie-ins.

2. The market power requirement in tying arrangement cases distinguishes tying arrangement that *can* be anticompetitive from those that cannot be. That is, a *tying arrangement* imposed by a competitor could not be anticompetitive: someone who did not want the competitor's tied product would purchase the tying product elsewhere. However, even the firm with market power might use a tie-in for an efficient, competitive purpose. As a result, the market power requirement should be only the first step in the inquiry.

3. ***False.*** This theory of tying arrangements, known as the "leverage" theory, is rarely plausible. A firm with a monopoly in one product can earn all available monopoly profits from the sale of that product alone (assuming that it cannot price discriminate). Buyers will treat the forced sale of a second product at a monopoly price as a price increase in the price of the first product.

4. The arrangement could be either tying or exclusive dealing, depending on how the parties or the court choose to characterize it. It is tying because Baskin–Robbins requires the franchisees to take its ice cream (the tied product) as a condition of obtaining the franchise (the tying product). It is exclusive dealing because Baskin–Robbins requires the franchisees to deal in its ice cream exclusively. The question illustrates that it is not always easy to distinguish tying from exclusive dealing.

   Baskin–Robbins might want to use the arrangement because it enters into franchise agreements for the purpose of selling its own ice cream, and because it is concerned about interbrand free riding (i.e., the franchisee will take advantage of Baskin–Robbins' name recognition in order to sell a different product in which the profit to the franchisee may be higher). Baskin–Robbins might also charge a supracompetitive price for its ice cream, and use the requirement as a price discrimination device.

   The arrangement probably makes consumers better off. First of all, customers entering Baskin–Robbins stores expect to obtain Baskin–Robbins ice cream, so the arrangement is probably efficient. Second, if the requirement is a price discrimination device, it probably increases the number of Baskin–Robbins outlets.

   If the arrangement makes consumers better off, it should be legal under the antitrust laws.

VI. RESALE PRICE MAINTENANCE AND VERTICAL NONPRICE RESTRAINTS

1. Under the Supreme Court's *Monsanto* and *Sharp* decisions, there is probably no agreement. The mere complaint by a dealer to a supplier, and the supplier's subsequent discipline or termination of another dealer about whom the complaint was made, does not constitute an agreement. But in this case, even if there is an agreement it is likely not a qualifying agreement about "price." If not, the termination should be analyzed under the rule of reason. In order to establish an agreement Dealer A would have to show that the complaints plus termination revealed a common commitment among Priestley and the remaining dealers to terminate A. But then A would have to show that it was terminated as a result of an agreement between B or C and Priestley to regulate the minimum price that A would charge. This appears not to be the case. Even though the set of restrictions that Priestley employs are clearly *nonprice* restrictions, a firm that violates the restrictions generally does so by cutting price. Nonetheless, being terminated on account of one's prices is not sufficient to establish a qualifying "price agreement."

2. *False.*   Under the *Simpson* holding, the mere fact that a contract uses the word "consignment" is not sufficient. The arrangement must be a *bona fide* consignment contract, in which risk of loss remains with the seller.

3. *True.*   An "intrabrand" cartel is a cartel of dealers of the same brand of a product. If the brand itself commands no market power, then even a cartel including 100% of the dealers of that brand would be unable to charge a monopoly price for it. Customers would simply switch to a different brand.

4. Mountain High has probably fallen out of the *Colgate* exception, because it called the distributor and issued a warning before terminating it. Under *Parke, Davis,* such a warning will be interpreted by a court as a solicitation of an agreement. Mountain High has probably committed a *per se* violation of § 1.

VII.   REFUSALS TO DEAL

1. *True.*   A refusal to deal was generally legal at common law, except in the case of public utilities. Under the antitrust laws a refusal to deal is legal unless it is *concerted* (i.e., involves an agreement of two or more actors) or involves *monopolization or an attempt to monopolize.*

2. *False.*   Although the statement that concerted refusals are illegal *per se* is widely made, the majority of refusals to deal are analyzed under a rule of reason.

3. Perhaps. The refusal to deal in this case is suspicious because it is unnecessary to the joint selling agency. As a result, the joint selling agency could be engaged in price fixing. On the other hand, the kiwi berry growers appear to have no market power because of the foreign competition.

4. *False.*   Analysis of free riding is rarely explicit in antitrust opinions. Some concerted refusals designed to combat free riding are *per se* illegal—for example, if they involve resale price maintenance. Others, such as those involving nonprice restraints, are analyzed under a rule of reason.

5. *False.*   Even the monopolist may refuse to deal with other firms. Its refusal to deal is illegal only if it is part of a scheme to enlarge its monopoly or extend its duration, or if it involves denial of access to a qualifying essential facility.

VIII.   HORIZONTAL MERGERS

1. *False.*   The parties must notify the government only if the merger meets the premerger notification requirements of the Hart–Scott–Rodino Antitrust Improvements Act.

2. **False.**   Since 1950 § 7 expressly covers asset acquisitions.

3. **False.**   A horizontal merger involves two firms that *both* manufacture the same product and sell it in the same geographic area.

4. The CR4 is 80. The CR8 is 100 (any market with fewer than eight firms has a CR8 of 100). The HHI is 1850. The market is highly concentrated. A merger between Firm C and Firm F would increase the HHI by 150 points, and would be challenged. A merger between Firm E and Firm G would increase the HHI by 100 points and would probably also be challenged.

5. The merger is probably horizontal if the firms 1) frequently bid against one another for the same customers; or 2) if the price of one product rises and falls in response to price changes in the other product; or 3) if each firm can very quickly enter into the market currently occupied by the other.

IX. CONGLOMERATE MERGERS

1. **True.**   The theories of reciprocity, predatory pricing, and tying are used only infrequently to condemn conglomerate mergers.

2. **False.**   Although conglomerate mergers can create efficiencies, their potential to do so is less than that of horizontal or vertical mergers. This is so because firms involved in conglomerate mergers do not operate in the same market, so many transactional and production economies are not available. Furthermore, such firms do not stand in a buyer-seller relationship before the merger; so they cannot use the merger to eliminate the transaction costs of using the market.

3. **False.**   Predatory pricing is no more likely after a conglomerate merger than it is in any other circumstance. Nevertheless, conglomerate mergers have been condemned under this theory.

4. Both potential competition theories rely on the fact that entry barriers are high in the target market (i.e., the market in which the effect on competition is being analyzed). If they were not high, that market would not be conducive to collusion and the merger would be legal. At the same time, however, the entry barriers must not be so high as to prevent the acquiring firm from coming into the target market *de novo*, or from being perceived as able to come in.

5. **True.**   If the firms *actually* bid for sales in the same market, then they are actual competitors with respect to that market, even though only one has been successful in making sales there.

6. **True.**   § 7 condemns mergers that may "lessen" competition. However, the actual potential entrant theory condemns a merger that leaves competition currently unaffected, but reduces the possibility of future increases in competition.

7. *False.*   The lower the number of perceived potential entrants, the more anticompetitive the acquisition will be. If a market has six perceived potential entrants, then an acquisition by one of them will have little or no effect on pricing. There will still be five perceived potential entrants left to restrain pricing in the target market.

X.   PRICE DISCRIMINATION AND DIFFERENTIAL PRICING UNDER THE ROBINSON–PATMAN ACT

1. *False.*   Price discrimination occurs when a seller obtains different rates of return from different buyers. Differential pricing occurs whenever a seller charges two buyers two different prices. Sometimes price discrimination is also differential pricing, but often it is not.

2. *False.*   The Robinson–Act reaches price discrimination when it is also differential pricing. As a result, it reaches true price discrimination only sporadically.

3. *False.*   In real world markets *sporadic* price discrimination occurs all the time, as the market constantly goes through changes in supply and demand.

4. *False.*   The complete absence of price discrimination in a market suggests that the price structure is too rigid, probably because the market is subject to express or tacit collusion.

5. Ryder's, the defendant, will probably win, because the favored purchaser and the disfavored purchaser are not in competition with one another—i.e., a retail toy store in Michigan does not compete with a retail toy store in Texas.

XI.   JURISDICTIONAL, PUBLIC POLICY AND REGULATORY LIMITATIONS ON THE DOMAIN OF ANTITRUST

1. *False.*   Most of the antitrust laws extend this far. However, the Robinson–Patman Act and probably § 3 of the Clayton Act extend only to activities in the stream of commerce.

2. *False.*   Under the "primary jurisdiction" rule there is room for application of the antitrust laws, if the regulatory agency has not carefully scrutinized the effects on competition of a particular activity.

3. *False.*   The Local Government Antitrust Act exempted municipalities from *treble damages judgments*; however, municipalities can still be found in violation of the antitrust laws and may subjected to an injunction.

4. Waldo will probably lose against both defendants. As to the City: assuming its zone regulation has been adequately authorized by state law, its action will qualify for

the "state action" exemption, even if it is anticompetitively motivated and, indeed, even if the product of bribery or corruption. As to Archie: Archie is protected by *Noerr-Pennington*, because he petitioned the City Council for a particular result and the injury challenged under the antitrust laws is the result of that petition.

XII. ENFORCEMENT, PROCEDURE AND RELATED MATTERS

1. The physician's claim will be aided by the fact that the maximum price fixing scheme has already been condemned under the antitrust laws. The "prima facie" evidence rule of section 5(a) of the Clayton Act will not apply, because the first action was not brought by the Justice Department or the Federal Trade Commission. However, chances are good that our client will be able to claim the benefits of offensive collateral estoppel, provided that she can show that she could not easily have joined in the earlier litigation, that the defendants had every incentive to defend the earlier litigation, and that the earlier judgment is not inconsistent with one or more other judgments in the defendants' favor. She will also have to show that there are no procedural remedies available to the defendants this time that were not available in the earlier litigation, and that might affect the outcome.

One difficulty is that the physician may not be the victim of "antitrust injury," as defined in the *Brunswick* case. In this case, the physician is complaining that the defendants, her competitors, charged lower prices than she did. A few courts have held that antitrust injury will be presumed in the case of *per se* violations, and this was such a violation. However, the Supreme Court's *USA Petroleum* decision seems to make clear that the antitrust injury doctrine applies even to *per se* violations.

2. ***True.*** About 90% of antitrust actions are filed by private plaintiffs.

3. The circuit courts are currently divided on this issue, and the Supreme Court has not resolved the division.

4. ***False.*** An indirect purchaser usually has no cause of action *for damages*. However, he may pursue an action for an injunction. Furthermore, he may fall within one of the exceptions to the indirect purchaser rule.

*

PRACTICE EXAM

(Total Time: 4 Hours)

QUESTION ONE

(90 Minutes)

ARGYLCRU is a large manufacturer of men's hosiery. Although it manufactures all kinds of men's hosiery, its leading product is a distinctive man's argyle crew sock that is in particularly high demand among East Coast preppies. In the flourishing preppie market in New England, where ARGYLCRU concentrates its energies, ARGYLCRU supplies about 88% of the market for argyle crew sox. In other parts of the United States its market share is around 75%. However, argyle crew sox are not the only kind of argyle men's sox. There are also argyle knee sox. Last year approximately 6 million pair of argyle crew sox were sold in interstate commerce in the United States, while 16 million pair of argyle knee sox were sold. Furthermore, there are still many men in the United States who do not buy argyle sox but who prefer solid colors. The total market for men's crew sox last year was 160 million pair. This crew sox market makes up about one-fifth of the entire market for men's hosiery; and about one-tenth of the market for men's, women's and children's hosiery. ARGYLCRU manufactures and sells in all these markets, but in none of them does it have the dominance that it has acquired in argyle crew sox.

All of ARGYLCRU's growth has been internal. It has never merged with or acquired the assets of any other company. Its success in the argyle crew sox market came about largely through its development of the Argylcrewer, a patented device that efficiently makes argyle crew sox. Although ARGYLCRU's original patent on the Argylcrewer expired six years ago, ARGYLCRU has been able constantly to make small, patented improvements in its Argylcrewer that have enabled it always to perform more efficiently than the machinery operated by its competitors. ARGYLCRU's closest competitor, TINKLE TOES, Inc., uses an Argylcrewer whose technology is about three years behind that of ARGYLCRU. Other competitors use less sophisticated machinery. The result is that ARGYLCRU can produce a pair of argyle crew sox at a cost of $2 per pair. It costs TINKLE TOES $3 to make a pair of argyle crew sox, and it costs all other competitors $4 to make a pair.

ARGYLCRU distributes its argyle crew sox across the nation. In the New England area, where argyle crew sox buyers are most sophisticated, it distributes them without restriction. However, west of the Mississippi it has imposed territorial divisions which permit only one retailer in each major city. The ARGYLCRU argyle crew sox retailer in San Francisco is WRAP TEN!.

In the New England area, where ARGYLCRU's position is strongest, it sells its sox wholesale at $5.10 per pair, and they are normally retailed for $5.95 per pair. In the West, however, ARGYLCRU wholesales its sox for $4.10 per pair, and they normally retail at $4.95. If western stores attempt to sell ARGYLCRU argyle sox at less than $4.95, ARGYLCRU stops doing business with them.

Although ARGYLCRU's profits in the argyle crew sox market have been very high over the past ten years, its profits in other areas of sock manufacturing have been very poor—largely as a result of intense competition and overproduction in the men's hosiery market, as well as of substantial imports of cheap, low-quality men's sox. Overall, ARGYLCRU shows an average net return on capital of only 5%. ARGYLCRU has tried to correct this by shifting its production as much as possible into argyle crew sox, where profits are the highest. Three years ago, when its analysis predicted a 20% increase in demand for argyle crew sox (as a result of opinion polls given to students at sixty American Law Schools), ARGYLCRU responded by expanding its argyle crew sox manufacturing capacity by 20%. Thus it has been able easily to keep up with increased demand of its most profitable product.

Argyle crew sox have not caught on extremely well in San Francisco. They face substantial competition from men's plain knee stockings. WRAP TEN! (Argylcru's San Francisco retailer) sells about 60,000 pair of Argylcru's argyle crew sox per year. WRAP TEN! faces one serious difficulty: San Franciscans prefer blue to brown argyle crew sox by a 10-to-1 margin, and ARGYLCRU's west coast warehouses are becoming laden with brown argyle crew sox. ARGYLCRU has informed WRAP TEN! that unless it corrects the situation and sells more brown argyle crew sox, ARGYLCRU is going to license another authorized retailer in San Francisco. WRAP TEN! has responded by prepackaging all its argyle crew sox: two brown pair and one blue pair per package. The only way it will sell ARGYLCRU argyle crew sox is by the package at a price of 3 X $4.95 (or $14.85).

1. The U.S. DEPT. OF JUSTICE brings an antitrust action against ARGYLCRU—what are its theories of action? its arguments? ARGYLCRU's defenses? who will likely prevail on each theory?

2. Joe Treatise is a misplaced preppie at Black Letter Law College in San Francisco who wears nothing but blue argyle crew sox. He buys them from WRAP TEN! He is outraged because he must buy a package of three pair at a time, two pair of which (the brown ones) he throws away. Joe brings an antitrust action against WRAP TEN!. What are his theories? problems? outcome?

QUESTION TWO

(60 Minutes)

The taxicab industry in Chicago is pervasively regulated by the CHICAGO TAXI COMMISSION (CTC), which is a government agency of the City of Chicago. All rates are proposed to the CTC by the Association of Cabbies (AC) and approved or adjusted by the CTC. Thus, although cab drivers (cabbies) compete intensively for riders, there is no price competition among them. A one-way taxi fare to O'Hare International Airport from downtown is regulated by the CTC at $15.00.

The problem for the cabbies is that the trip from downtown to O'Hare is generally a "deadhead"—that is, most taxis return from the airport empty, because far fewer people take taxis from the airport back to downtown than take taxis from downtown to the airport. This is so because people going to the airport are generally in a hurry and need cabs; people coming home have plenty of time. People going from the airport to downtown generally take the AIRPORTER BUS, which is slower but costs only $6 per passenger.

The AC has requested the CTC to give them relief against the problem of deadheading. They claim the trip to the airport is unprofitable if they must return to downtown empty. The AC has proposed the following SHARE–A–CAB program, and the CTC has approved: under the program an area at the airport is designated SHARE–A–CAB. Cabs loading at that area 1) go only to downtown; 2) load up with three passengers each and charge each one $6. In this way each cabby who returns to Chicago under the SHARE–A–CAB program collects an additional fare of $18. Of this $18 the cabby keeps $15 and pays $3 to the CTC, which uses it to finance the SHARE–A–CAB program and puts the surplus into the municipal treasury.

The SHARE–A–CAB program has been enormously successful. Airline passengers returning to downtown love it, and it has substantially solved the problem of deadheading. However, it has greatly injured the trade of the AIRPORTER BUS COMPANY, which is now suffering substantial losses as a result. The AIRPORTER BUS COMPANY brings a lawsuit seeking damages and an injunction against the SHARE–A–CAB program as a conspiracy in restraint of trade, in violation of § 1 of the Sherman Act. Discuss the antitrust issues that will probably be litigated and predict an outcome.

QUESTION THREE

(90 Minutes)

Croton's Law Books, Inc., of New York City sells law books—mostly text books, casebooks and course outlines for law students. It is located one block away from

Columbia University Law School. Most law books are ordered wholesale by Croton's and come with a "suggested" retail price. It has been Croton's practice always to charge law students this suggested price. The average price of a Croton's law book is $20.00. In a normal transaction Croton's can expect to make a profit of $2.00 on the sale of a lawbook. The other $18.00 covers costs, as follows: variable costs $16.00 (this includes the wholesale price of the book, the costs of stocking it, labor, etc.); fixed costs, $2.00 (this includes rental for the store building and other miscellaneous expenses that do not vary with the number of books that Croton's sells).

Croton's is not the only law book store in New York City. There are five others. The largest are Blackstone's Lawbooks, Inc., which is part of a nationwide chain of stores. The New York City Blackstone's sells 30% of the law books sold in New York City. Equally large is Marshall's books, a general purpose bookstore that also carries student law books, and which also makes about 30% of New York City student law book sales. The third largest is Croton's, with about 20%. The fourth largest is O'Connor's books, which has about 10%. The fifth and sixth stores, Wrights's and Miller's have about 5% apiece. All the stores except for Blackstone's are single-store operations, owned by New Yorkers who operate the stores themselves. Outside New York City there are no law book stores for a fifty mile radius.

Over the past years law students have been buying fewer books, and many of the law book stores have been in financial trouble. O'Connor's in particular has had four consecutive years of losses, and O'Connor (its owner) has been looking for someone to buy the business. In 1983 Blackstone's Inc., made an offer for a 25% interest in the O'Connor business, and O'Connor accepted. The transaction was completed. Blackstone's, Inc. continued to operate its original Blackstone's book store.

Shortly after the Blackstone acquisition the general manager of Blackstone's sent the following memorandum to the general manager of O'Connor's. "I believe that because of our joint purchasing power we may be able to obtain some law books from some publishers at a quantity discount. If so, we could lower the retail price of student law books. As a result we would be able to obtain a much larger share of the New York City law book market."

Soon after Blackstone's book store and O'Connor's book store jointly placed a full page advertisement in the *New York Times*, announcing that they were reducing the price of all their student law books by 25%. As an example, an average student law book which formerly retailed for $20.00 would now retail for $15.00 at the two bookstores.

FOLLOWING IS A LIST OF STATEMENTS AND QUESTIONS CONCERNING ACTIONS TAKEN BY VARIOUS PEOPLE WHO HAD AN INTEREST IN THE EVENTS DESCRIBED ABOVE. AFTER EACH STATEMENT WRITE A BRIEF COMMENT OR EVALUATION. IF THE STATEMENT DESCRIBES A LEGAL ACTION OR A DEFENSE, YOU SHOULD EVALUATE THE CLAIM *AND PREDICT AN OUTCOME.* UNLESS ONE PART EXPLICITLY REFERS TO ANOTHER PART, ASSUME THAT ALL PARTS ARE ENTIRELY SEPARATE AND INDEPENDENT OF ONE ANOTHER.

PART 1

The Department of Justice must decide whether to challenge Blackstone's purchase of the 25% interest in O'Connor's under section 7 of the Clayton Act.

PART 2

The Justice Department files the action contemplated above, and Blackstone's raises the "failing company" defense.

PART 3

Wright's book store, which is right across the street from Blackstone's, suffered tremendous losses as a result of the joint advertisement and price reduction initiated by post-merger Blackstone–O'Connor's. Wright's also filed a private merger action under section 7, alleging that because of the unlawful merger the two stores had lowered their prices, with the result that Wright's lost $100,000 in profits. Wright's asked for that amount, trebled, plus attorney's fees.

PART 4

How might Wright's be benefited in its above action if the Department of Justice had already prevailed in its earlier merger action? What if the Department of Justice obtained a consent decree?

PART 5

Croton's law books brought an action against Blackstone's and O'Connor's, charging that the sales at a 25% discount were predatory pricing.

PART 6

Although the Blackstone's and O'Connor's stores in New York City were selling law books at a 25% discount, it turned out that the other Blackstone's stores—in San Diego, California, Salt Lake City, Utah, and Ithaca, New York, were continuing to charge the manufacturer's suggested retail price. Croton's charged Blackstone's with unlawful price discrimination, a violation of the Robinson–Patman Act.

PART 7

Brenda Bracton is a second year law student at Columbia, and purchases all her law books at Croton's. She suspects that the law book *publishers* have been engaged in a conspiracy to fix prices. She brings a damages action against the publishers, charging them with a *per se* violation of § 1 of the Sherman Act.

END OF EXAM

MODEL ANSWERS TO PRACTICE EXAM

ANSWER TO QUESTION ONE

The primary offenses with which Argylcru could be charged in the action brought by the United States Department of Justice are monopolization, resale price maintenance, and perhaps illegal vertical nonprice restraints. The Justice Department might also consider an action under the Robinson–Patman Act; however, at the present time the Department is not actively enforcing that statute. Nevertheless, it has the clear authority to do so.

Since Argylcru operates across the nation, and the alleged antitrust violations are multistate, the activities clearly fall within the jurisdiction of the federal antitrust laws under the Commerce Clause of the United States Constitution.

Monopolization

In order to prove that Argylcru is guilty of illegal monopolization under § 2 of the Sherman Act the Justice Department must show that Argylcru has 1) monopoly power in a relevant market; and 2) that it has engaged in one or more impermissible exclusionary practices.

The question of monopoly power is a very difficult one. First of all, in order to determine a relevant market the court must identify some grouping of sales such that if a single firm controlled those sales it would have the power to make money by reducing output and charging a monopoly price. Both a relevant product market and a relevant geographic market must be determined. In order to determine these markets the court will have to examine both the elasticity of demand and the elasticity of supply of any markets proposed by the parties.

In order to prevail in its monopolization case, the Justice Department must convince the court that the relevant market is "men's argyle crew sox," for only in that market does Argylcru have a sufficiently high market share (88% of New England sales and 75% of sales in the rest of the United States) to warrant a finding that Argylcru has monopoly power. As a general rule, before a defendant can be found guilty of monopolization, it must have at least 70% or so of a relevant market. On the other hand, Argylcru will try to convince the court that the relevant market is broader than "men's argyle crew sox." It may propose 1) all hosiery; 2) all men's hosiery; 3) all argyle hosiery; 4) all men's argyle hosiery. If the court finds that any one of these is the relevant product market, it will probably conclude that Argylcru's market share is too small to warrant a finding that it is a monopolist. For example, the next larger market, *all* men's argyle sox, is more than three times as large as the market for men's argyle crew sox.

On the demand side, we can probably assume that men's, women's and children's hosiery are sufficiently different from one another that the cross elasticity of demand among them is not very high. The court will probably conclude that men's hosiery in general lies in a different market than women's and children's hosiery. Likewise, it appears that there is a distinct group of customers—preppies—for whom the elasticity of demand for argyle crew sox is very low. This group of customers is reluctant to purchase nonargyle sox, and is also reluctant to purchase sox that are higher than crew sox. This tends to support the Justice Department claim that "men's argyle crew sox" is a relevant market, at least with respect to the demand side.

On the supply side the relevant question is whether a manufacturer of something *other* than men's argyle crew sox could easily enter the market in response to Argylcru's price increase; or whether other manufacturers of men's argyle crew sox could expand their own output sufficiently to frustrate any attempt by Argylcru to charge monpoly prices. Here the answer is pretty well settled by the fact that Argylcru has access to low cost technology that appears to be unavailable to its competitors. Although competitors or potential competitors may be able to enter Argylcru's market, all of them, even Tinkle Toes, which is its strongest competitor, faces higher costs than Argylcru. In fact Tinkle Toes' costs are 50% higher than those of Argylcru. As a result, Argylcru can charge a high price for its men's crew sox without occasioning substantial increases of output on the part of competitors.

The Justice Department will probably succeed in convincing the court that the relevant product market is "men's argyle crew sox."

The geographic market in this case appears to be the United States. The relevant question is whether shippers from outside the United States could flood the market with competing sox in response to Argylcru's monopoly price increase. Although there is foreign competition in the hosiery market, it is characterized as being "cheap" and of "low quality." There is no evidence in the question that foreign producers are capable of flooding the market with sox of Argylcru's quality. If foreign firms attempted to do so, they would presumably be limited by the same technological constraints (the lack of an argylcrewer) that hinders the domestic competitors.

The Justice Department will succeed in establishing that Argylcru has monpoly power in the market for men's argyle crew sox sold in the United States.

Next, however, the Department must show that Argylcru engaged in one or more illegal exclusionary practices. According to the facts, Argylcru's growth has been internal; so there are no illegal mergers.

Argylcru *has* manipulated the patent market somewhat, by consistently making small, patented improvements in the Argylcrewer. However, Argylcru is actually using the Argylcrewer, together with all its improvements. The prevailing law today is that the acquisition and actual use of patents is *not* illegal, even for the monopolist. Likewise, the monopolist is under no duty to license it patented technology to competitors. It appears that Argylcru's use of patents is legal.

Argylcru engages in price discrimination; that is, it charges higher prices (and presumably makes higher profits) in some parts of the United States than it does in others. Likewise, it makes a higher rate of return on its argyle crew sox than it does on its other products. In the *United Shoe Machinery* case Judge Wyzanski identified such price discrimination as an illegal exclusionary practice. Although it makes little economic sense to regard such a practice as exclusionary, *United Shoe Machinery* has never been overruled on this issue. On the other hand, recent courts have not regarded price discrimination in and of itself to be sufficient to support the conclusion that the defendant has engaged in illegal monopolization. The Justice Department will probably not succeed in establishing that Argylcru's discriminatory pricing is illegal.

Likewise, Argylcru has expanded its capacity in anticipation of increased demand for Argyle crew sox. Although Judge Hand regarded increases in capacity by the monopolist as illegal, no court would be likely to do so today. The Justice Department will probably lose here as well.

The Justice Department's monopolization case against Argylcru is not particularly promising.

Resale Price Maintenance

Argylcru has a policy of refusing to deal with retail stores that charge less than its "suggested" retail price of $4.95. By themselves, these facts suggest that Argylcru *is* engaged in resale price maintenance, which is *per se* illegal under § 1 of the Sherman Act. However, the facts also suggest that Argylcru is availing itself of the *Colgate* exception, which makes "unilateral" resale price maintenance legal. In order to prevail on its resale price maintenance claim, the Justice Department will have to show "an agreement" between Argylcru and at least one other party. Argylcru's unilateral decision to terminate its business relationship with a price cutter is not sufficient. However, if Argylcru has threatened, warned or coerced retailers who have deviated from Argylcru's posted prices, then Argylcru will fall outside the *Colgate* exception. The facts of the question do not suggest that this has happened. Argylcru will probably claim the *Colgate* exception successfully, and the Justice Department will lose its resale price maintenance case as well.

Vertical Nonprice Restraints

The basis for the Justice Department's vertical nonprice restraints case against Argylcru is the fact that west of the Mississippi River Argylcru has given individual retailers exclusive cities in which to sell Argylcru's argyle crew sox. Most circuit courts assess a market power requirement in vertical nonprice restraints cases (the Supreme Court has not passed on the issue). The Justice Department's own Vertical Restraints Guidelines suggest that it will not pursue vertical nonprice restraints litigation unless the defendant has at least some market power and the market in which the restraints are occurring is relatively concentrated. Although Argylcru has less market power in this part of the country than it does in New England, it still has a 75% market share, which is very substantial. This fact also tells us that the HHI in the western market is *at least* 6000 or so (i.e., Argylcru contributes 5625 to the HHI, not including other firms in the market). Thus it would appear from the market share/market concentration evidence that Argylcru's assignment of exclusive retail territories *could* be illegal.

However, the facts of the question give no clue as to how such restraints could be used *anticompetitively* by Argylcru. As a general rule, even the monopolist employs vertical nonprice restraints because they are efficient—i.e., they lower its distribution costs and increase its output. Here there is no evidence that Argylcru is engaged in collusion with its competitors. On the contrary, it appears to be competing with them quite intensely. The vertical nonprice restraints are probably legal, because there is no evidence that they are being used anticompetitively.

Robinson-Patman Act Violations

The Robinson–Patman case against Argylcru is not promising. Argylcru does wholesale sox at one price in New England and at a different price elsewhere. However, the theory of a secondary-line Robinson–Patman violation is that the disfavored purchasers (those charged the higher price) are placed at a competitive disadvantage vis-a-vis the favored purchasers. This requires that the favored purchasers and disfavored purchasers compete with each other. In this case, however, the favored purchasers and the disfavored purchasers are retailers in different parts of the United States. They likely do not compete with each other.

A primary-line Robinson–Patman action does not seem warranted by the facts of the case. Today primary-line Robinson–Patman violations are treated as a form of predatory pricing, and this generally requires that sales in the low price area be made at a price lower than the defendant's average variable cost. Even in the *Utah Pie* case the Supreme Court made a great deal of the fact that the defendant's low price sales were at prices lower than their costs. However, in this case Argylcru appears to be making profits on sales of argyle crew sox in all markets.

The Justice Department will also lose its Robinson–Patman action against Argylcru.

Joe Treatise's Action

The basis for Joe's antitrust complaint is that he must purchase a package containing two pair of brown argyle crew sox and one pair of blue argyle crew sox when he wants only the blue sox. He will allege that the package sale is a tying arrangement in which the blue sox are the tying product and the brown sox are the tied product.

Joe's case against Wrap Ten! is only slightly stronger than the Justice Department's case against Argylcru. Joe must show that there are two distinct products, that the defendant conditioned the purchase of one product on the purchase of the other, and that the defendant has sufficient market power in the market for the tying product to restrain competition in the market for the tied product. Finally, Joe must show that a "not insubstantial" amount of commerce has been restrained in the market for the tied product.

The question of "separate products" is tricky. Both products are argyle crew sox, and the only difference between them is color. Nevertheless, it appears that there is a very distinct demand for blue argyle crew sox in San Francisco. Furthermore, it appears that there is no efficiency reason why the products are being grouped together and sold in a single package. The evidence does not suggest that Wrap Ten! is taking advantage of any production or distributional efficiencies in combining three pair of sox into a single package. It is simply attempting to unload some unwanted inventory (brown sox) by forcing customers to purchase it. Although such a scheme is unlikely to succeed as a matter of economic theory (customers like Joe will treat the requirement that they purchase unwanted brown sox as an increase in the price of blue sox), it is nevertheless sufficient to support a finding that the defendant is selling separate products.

The question of "conditioning" is clear. Wrap Ten! absolutely requires all customers who want a pair of blue argyle crew sox to purchase two brown pair as well. Joe will prevail on this issue.

The market power question is the most difficult one for Joe. Importantly, the fact that Argylcru has market power in its national market does not dictate the conclusion that Wrap Ten! has market power in its local market. The facts state that Argyle crew sox have not caught on very well in San Francisco. Under the Supreme Court's decision in Jefferson Parish Hosp. Dist. No. 2 v. Hyde, Joe will have to show that Wrap Ten! accounts for at least 30% of the sales in a relevant market. First of all, we do not know what Wrap Ten!'s percentage of blue argyle crew sock sales in San Francisco is. Secondly, we do not know whether blue argyle crew sox is a relevant market, because these sox face substantial competition in San Francisco from other kinds of men's hosiery. We cannot be sure whether the market power requirement will be met. However, the facts do not look promising for Joe.

Joe will probably be able to show that Wrap Ten!'s sales restrain a "not insubstantial" amount of commerce in the market for the tied product. Wrap Ten! sells 60,000 pair of argyle crew sox per year, and under the tying arrangement two-thirds of these are brown sox (the tied product). Since the retail price is $4.95 per pair, its sales of the tied product amount to 40,000 times $4.95, or slightly less than $200,000. This is sufficient to meet the "not insubstantial" requirement.

On balance, Joe will probably lose his tying arrangement case, unless he can show that Wrap Ten! has market power in the market for blue argyle crew sox.

ANSWER TO QUESTION TWO

Question Two raises two important issues: 1) whether the activities of the Chicago Taxi Commission qualify for the "state action" exemption from the federal antitrust laws; 2) if the activities do not qualify for the exemption, whether they violate the antitrust laws. Since the entire restraint takes place in the Chicago area, the question conceivably raises an issue concerning the jurisdiction of the antitrust laws under the Commerce Clause. However, the Sherman Act (which is the relevant statute here) applies to all activities "affecting commerce." Since O'Hare airport is an international airport the taxicab drivers undoubtedly aid in transporting a great many passengers into and out of the state of Illinois. This certainly affects commerce sufficiently to support jurisdiction under the antitrust laws.

State Action Exemption

The "state action" exemption from the federal antitrust laws is based on the premise that Congress did not intend for the antitrust laws to be used to interfere too deeply into the official regulatory decisions of the individual states. When an activity qualifies for the "state action" exemption from the antitrust laws, the antitrust laws simply do not apply to that activity. In the *Midcal* case the Supreme Court held that a state law or policy will qualify for the "state action" exemption if it represents 1) a clearly articulated and affirmatively expressed state policy to displace competition with some form of regulation; and 2) the program thus created is "actively supervised" by the state.

The "state action" exemption formally applies only to states themselves. Nevertheless, a state can "transfer" the state-action exemption to a governmental subdivision, such as a municipality, if it follows the rules laid down by the United States Supreme Court. In this particular case the Chicago Taxi Commission (CTC) is an agency, not of the state, but rather of the City of Chicago. The facts state that the taxicab industry is "pervasively regulated" by the CTC. This would indicate that the "active supervision" requirement of the *Midcal* test has been met. In Hallie v. Eau Claire the Supreme Court held that the state itself need not be the sovereign that supervises a regulatory activity. It if sufficient if an agency of the municipality does the supervising.

The question whether the CTC regulates pursuant to a clearly articulated and affirmatively expressed *state* policy is more difficult, for we do not know the basis of the regulatory authority of the CTC and the City of Chicago. In Community Communications v. City of Boulder the Supreme Court held that it was not sufficient for a municipality to regulate under a home rule provision, because such a provision is "neutral" on the question whether the municipality has the express authority from the state to regulate in a *particular* market. Rather, it must be shown that the CTC and the City of Chicago are operating under a state statute that specifically authorizes them to displace competition with regulation in the taxicab market. The facts of the case do not indicate whether such a statute exists. If it does not, however, then the CTC probably does not qualify for the "state action" exemption. Under the *Hallie* decision, however, if there is state authorizing legislation and the Share-a-Cab program is a "foreseeable" consequence of that legislation, then the authorization requirement has been met.

Any conspiracy that Airporter alleges will have to be among the cab drivers. Under the Supreme Court's *Columbia* decision, the relationship between the Chicago Taxi Commission and the Association of Cabbies, cannot be considered a "conspiracy."

If a court finds that a municipality's or other governmental subdivision's regulation meet the requirements for the "state action" exemption from the federal antitrust laws, then no further inquiry into whether an antitrust violation occurred is necessary. In this case, however, we do not know if the requirements for the "state action" exemption have been met, because we do not know the statutory basis for the municipality's regulation of taxicab fares. Assuming that they have not been met, the plaintiff must still prove that a violation of the federal antitrust laws has occurred.

Violation of the Sherman Act

Assuming there is no "state action" exemption, the Airporter Bus Company must prove that there has been an antitrust violation and that it has suffered "antitrust injury" as a result. Since the defendant is an agency of a municipality, Airporter cannot obtain treble damages. The 1984 Local Government Antitrust Act limits recovery against municipalities and their agencies to injunctive relief. However, if a violation of the antitrust laws is found, Airporter will be able to obtain an injunction against the Share-a-Cab program.

If a violation exists, it is a combination in restraint of trade under § 1 of the Sherman Act, or else perhaps an attempt to monopolize under § 2 of the Sherman Act.

The basis for the § 1 violation is an agreement between the CTC and the Association of Cabbies (AC), or perhaps the cabbies themselves, to set the maximum price that will be charged for a ride to downtown from the airport. Clearly, maximum price fixing can be a *per se* violation of § 1 of the Sherman Act. The Supreme Court recently so held in the *Maricopa* case. Even if such a violation has occurred, however, Airporter will have a difficult time proving "antitrust injury." In this particular case Airporter is a competitor complaining about *lower* prices, and there is no evidence that the lower prices are predatory. It appears that Airporter is complaining that as a result of the Share-a-Cab program there is now *more* competition, rather than less, in the market for transportation from the airport to downtown. The "antitrust injury" doctrine applies even to *per se* violations.

Another problem Airporter will face is that the cabbies' request to the CTC for the Share-a-Cab arrangement, and the CTC's favorable response, probably does not qualify as an "agreement" under the Supreme Court's holding in Fisher v. Berkeley that one generally cannot infer a qualifying antitrust agreement from a private request to the government for a particular rule and the government's favorable response. Of course, there could still be a qualifying agreement among the cabbies themselves.

Airporter might also show that the Share-a-Cab program is really a conspiracy or attempt to drive the Airporter out of business so that the taxicabs can obtain a monopoly of airport-downtown public transportation. In order to show a conspiracy to monopolize, Airporter will have to show an agreement between two or more persons to restrain trade by the creation of a monopoly, as well as some act in furtherance of the conspiracy. Unfortunately for Airporter, nothing in the question suggests that the taxicab operators or the CTC had any desire to drive the Airporter out of business. They simply wanted to improve their own position in the market by returning from the airport with full taxicabs rather than empty ones.

In order to show an attempt to monopolize Airporter must show the defendants' 1) specific intent to monopolize some market; 2) some anticompetitive or exclusionary act designed to achieve this result; and 3) a dangerous probability that the attempt, if permitted to run its course, would have succeeded in creating a monopoly. Once again, there is no evidence that the CTC or the AC had any specific intent to drive Airporter from the market. Furthermore, all the evidence indicates that the Share-a-Cab program was both efficient and that it was profitable to the taxicab drivers.

Although Airporter may succeed in showing that the CTC, the AC and the City of Chicago do not qualify for the "state action" exemption, it will have a difficult time showing that the defendants have violated the antitrust laws, and that it has suffered antitrust injury as a result. Airporter may win on the § 1 count, provided that the court presumes antitrust injury in cases involving *per se* violations. Airporter will almost certainly lose on the § 2 count.

ANSWER TO QUESTION THREE

Part 1

The merger of Blackstone and O'Connor's is a partial acqusition. However, the two firms are competitors. As a result, the fact that Blackstone's purchased only a 25% interest of O'Connor's is not particularly important. Such a partial acquisition clearly has the potential to injure competition, because its gives each company an interest in the well being of its competitor.

In evaluating the merger, the Justice Department will rely on the 1992 horizontal Merger Guidelines. It would appear that "law books" is a relevant product market for the purpose of analyzing this merger. On the demand side, there are no good substitutes. The question provides very little information about elasticity of supply—that is, whether other book stores could easily enter the law book market in response to an attempt by one of the firms there to charge monpoly prices. If such entry is particularly easy, the merger would be legal under the Guidelines no matter how concentrated the market. Assuming such entry is not easy, however, the Justice Department will analyze market concentration next. Since there are no law book stores outside New York City for fifty miles, we assume that New York City is a relevant geographic market.

In this particular case, the HHI in the New York City market is 2350, obtained by taking the market shares of the New York City law book stores, squaring them, and then adding them together. This is a highly concentrated market, and in this particular case the merger adds 600 HHI points (obtained by doubling the product of the market shares of the merging firms). The Justice Department will likely challenge this merger, assuming it finds entry barriers to be sufficiently high.

Part 2

In order to raise the "failing company" defense successfully, Blackstone must show that O'Connor's is a qualifying failing company. The mere fact that O'Connor's has been losing money is not sufficient. It must be shown that O'Connor's is likely to go into bankruptcy and probably could not successfully be reorganized, *and* that there are no less anticompetitive alternatives to the acquisition by Blackstone. The evidence in the question does not indicate that these facts can be shown.

Part 3

In order to prevail in a private action for damages, Wright's book store must show not only that the merger between Blackstone's and O'Connor's is illegal, but also that it has suffered "antitrust injury" as a result. The facts of the case suggest two possibilities: 1) that after the merger the Blackstone's and O'Connor's stores were better competitors rather than worse ones, because the post-merger firm faced lower costs; 2) that the post-merger firm is engaging in predatory pricing. If a merger appears to a court to facilitate actual predatory pricing, it might be condemned on that ground. However, if Wright's is merely complaining about the post-merger firm's increased efficiency, then it is not a victim of antitrust injury as defined by the Supreme Court in the *Brunswick* and *Cargill* decisions. In any case, if Wright succeeds in this claim, lost profits is the correct measure of damages. The amount of lost profits will be trebled. In addition, as a prevailing plaintiff Wright will be permitted to collect attorney's fees.

Part 4

Under the "prima facie" evidence rule of § 5(a) of the Clayton Act, condemnation of the Blackstone merger in a successful action brought by the Department of Justice would become "prima facie" evidence that the defendant had violated the antitrust laws. However, the rule does not apply to consent decrees or decrees obtained before any testimony has been taken. Likewise, if the Justice Department had prevailed in a litigated action against the Blackstone merger, the doctrine of offensive collateral estoppel could be used by Wright to create a conclusive presumption that § 7 of the Clayton Act was violated. In order to take advantage of offensive collateral estoppel, Wright would have to show 1) that it could not have joined in the earlier action (it can make this showing easily, for the Justice Department does not usually permit private co-plaintiffs); 2) that the defendant had every incentive to litigate the first action vigorously; 3) that the judgment obtained against the defendant in the first action is not inconsistent with one or more other judgments on the same facts; 4) that the current action does not afford procedural opportunities unavailable in the first action, and which might affect the outcome.

Part 5

Croton's predatory pricing action against Blackstone's and O'Connor's will be analyzed by the court under the Areeda–Turner test. The evidence suggests that the prices charged for books by Blackstone's and O'Connor's were lower than the average variable costs of a *different* book store in the same area—namely, Croton's. Blackstone's and O'Connor's price was $15.00; however Croton's AVC was $16.00. If Blackstone's and O'Connor's have the same costs as Croton's, then the cost element of the Areeda–Turner test—a price lower than average variable cost—will be satisfied. Thus inquiry must be made into the costs of post-merger Blackstone–O'Connor's. The evidence in the memorandum from Blackstone's to O'Connor's indicates that the two firms have purchasing power that gives them *lower* costs than their competitors. This suggests that the firms are *not* engaged in predatory pricing, but are merely taking advantage of economies of scale.

In addition to looking at the relationship between the defendant's prices and its costs, the court should (but frequently will not) inquire into whether the *market* has a structure that makes predatory pricing likely. In this particular case, the market, although concentrated, is not particularly conducive to predatory pricing. Post-merger Blackstone–O'Connor's has a market share of 40%, which is generally not enough to engage in predatory pricing.

In sum, the facts do not strongly suggest that Blackstone–O'Connor's is engaging in predatory pricing.

Part 6

Because Blackstone's is selling the same books at different prices in different cities, it may be committing a primary-line violation of the Robinson–Patman Act. However, today the trend among courts is to apply the Areeda–Turner average variable cost test to primary-line Robinson–Patman violations just as to predatory pricing cases. As in part 5 above, the plaintiff's successs will depend on whether the defendant's prices in New York City were lower than its average variable costs.

Part 7

Brenda is an indirect purchaser from the law book publishers. Under the Supreme Court's rule in Illinois Brick Co. v. Illinois she will not be able to bring an action for damages against the law book publishers. However, she would be entitled to obtain an injunction.

*

APPENDIX C

TEXT CORRELATION CHART

Black Letter Antitrust	Areeda & Kaplow, Antitrust Analysis (1997)	Fox & Sullivan (1989)	Handler, Pitofsky, Goldschmid & Wood, Trade Regulation (1997)	Goetz & McChesney, Antitrust Law (1998)	Posner & Easterbrook, Antitrust (1981)	Schwartz, Flynn & First, Free Enterprise & Economic Organization: Antitrust (1983)	Sullivan & Hovenkamp, Antitrust Law, Policy & Procedure (1999)
Chap. I Antitrust Economics: Price Theory and Industrial Organization	1-38	3-10	152-221	1-12	1055-1070	33-45	47-68
Chap. II Cartels, Tacit Collusion, Joint Ventures, and other Combinations of Competitors	165-443	37-53 282-520	221-361	77-310	87-204 306-346	328-529	187-418
Chap. III Monopolization, Attempt to Monopolize, and Predatory Pricing	447-608	99-281	152-221 674-701	311-456	347-385 603-713	57-204	597-778
Chap. IV Vertical Integration and Vertical Mergers	806-822	832-842	1009-1074	457-466	857-876	251-263	779-839
Chap. V Tie-Ins, Reciprocity, Exclusive Dealing, and the Franchise Contract	686-784	627-703	702-785	551-660	777-856 876-902	665-760	500-597
Chap. VI Resale Price Maintenance and Vertical Nonprice Restraints	609-685	523-627	580-673	457-510	205-261	585-664 761-797	419-500
Chap. VII Refusals to Deal	332-367	383-426	362-481	42-43 166-167	714-776	530-584	368-416
Chap. VIII Horizontal Mergers	822-863	750-814	867-968	661-700	347-505	205-250 323-327	809-880
Chap. IX Conglomerate Mergers	864-900	815-831	968-1008	701-733	505-532	269-322	880-902
Chap. X Price Discrimination and Differential Pricing Under the Robinson-Patman Act	901-965	713-736	1221-1308	-----	943-989	871-934	919-969
Chap. XI Jurisdictional, Public Policy and Regulatory Limitations	106-137	416-425	1075-1221	12-76	990-1054	798-870 1070-1167	969-1067
Chap. XII Enforcement, Procedure & Related Matters	54-105	855-869	98-151	733-815	35-86 291-305 533-602	-----	69-186

GLOSSARY

A

Active Supervision. A requirement that before private conduct will found to qualify for the "state action" exemption to the federal antitrust laws, the conduct must be actively supervised by the state itself.

Actual Potential Entrant. A firm that might enter a concentrated market with high entry barriers **de novo**, were it forbidden to enter by merger. The doctrine is sometimes used to condemn potential competition (conglomerate) mergers under § 7 of the Clayton Act.

Antitrust Injury. A requirement assessed by the Supreme Court that a private plaintiff seeking damages not merely be injured by an antitrust violation, but that it be injured by the **anticompetitive effects** of the violation.

Arbitrage. The act of purchasing and reselling a product. Arbitrage can often frustrate price discrimination when a purchaser who pays a low price for a product resells the product to someone from whom the seller had asked a higher price.

Areeda-Turner Test. A legal test for predatory pricing, which generally condemns a price lower than average variable cost, provided that the firm charging the price is a monopolist. Under the test a price above average variable cost is generally legal.

Articulation (Authorization): A requirement that before a governmental subdivision's regulatory policy will qualify for the "state action" exemption to the federal antitrust laws, the policy must be authorized by the state itself, and the authorization must be "clearly articulated."

Asset Acquisition. A merger by acquisition of a firm's assets, rather than its stock.

Attempt to Monopolize. The offense of trying to acquire a monopoly by illegal means. A violation of § 2 of the Sherman Act.

Average Cost. Sometimes called Average Total Cost. The sum of all a firm's costs, both fixed and variable, divided by its output. In order to be profitable, a firm must sell its output at an average price equal to its average costs.

Average Fixed Cost. The sum of all a firm's fixed costs (i.e., costs such as the investment in the plant, which do not vary with output), divided by the number of units produced.

Average Variable Cost. The sum of all a firm's variable costs (i.e., costs such as utilities and raw materials, which vary with output) divided by the number of units of output.

B

Barrier to Entry. Some factor in a market that makes operation more expensive for new entrants than it is for established firms. To the extent entry barriers exist, the firms established in a market may succeed in charging monopoly prices without causing new entry.

Basing Point Pricing. The act of charging freight rates from an arbitrary "basing point," rather than from the location where the product is actually shipped. If basing point pricing is used by several firms in a market, it can facilitate collusion.

Bathtub Conspiracy. See intra-enterprise conspiracy.

Before-and-After Method. A method of estimating a private plaintiff's damages by looking at its profits or the price it paid before and after an antitrust violation occurred, and comparing with the violation period.

Brand Specific Product. A product that bears some unique characteristics placed in it by its particular manufacturer. For example, although Chevrolets, Fords, and Chryslers are all automobiles, and all compete in that market, they are nevertheless distinguishable from one another. As a result, some customers may prefer one over another.

C

Capacity. The number of units a plant is capable of producing when it is operated at its most efficient production level.

Cartel. An association of two or more firms who would otherwise be competitors, for the purpose of fixing prices and reducing output.

Celler-Kefauver Amendments. The 1950 Amemdments to § 7 of the Clayton Act, which expanded the statute to apply to vertical as well as horizontal mergers, and which revealed Congress' concern for the protection of small businesses from larger, more efficient competitors, particularly if those larger firms were the products of one or more mergers.

Clayton Act. The second federal antitrust law, passed in 1914. § 1 of the Clayton Act defines relevant antitrust terms; § 2, as amended by the Robinson–Patman Act, prohibits certain instances of differential pricing (called "price discrimination" in the Act); § 3 prohibits certain tying arrangements and exclusive dealing contracts; § 4 creates a private action for treble damages; § 5 provides for the relationship between public antitrust suits and subsequent private suits and governs several procedural matters; § 6 grants labor a partial exemption from the antitrust laws; § 7 prohibits certain mergers and acquisitions; § 8 prohibits certain interlocking directorates; § 16 provides for injunctive relief from an antitrust violation; § 20 augments the labor exemption.

Colgate Exception. A carefully controlled exception to the **per se** rule against resale price maintenance (RPM) for a supplier's "unilateral" announcement that it will not deal with resellers who deviate from its stipulated resale prices.

Concentration. A term that describes the relative number of firms in a market, and their relative sizes. A market that contains a small number of relatively large firms is said to be "concentrated."

Concerted Refusal to Deal. An agreement among two or more firms not to deal with some firm who is not a party to the agreement, or to force others not to deal with that firm.

Conglomerate Merger. A merger of two firms that are not actual competitors, and which do not stand in a buyer-seller relationship with one another; that is, a merger that is neither horizontal nor vertical.

Consignment Agreement. An agreement for the resale of a product under which ownership of the product and risk of nonsale remains with the supplier (consignor) untill the dealer (consignee) makes the sale. To be distingushed from a sale-resale contract.

Constant Returns to Scale. An industry characterized by costs that do **not** decrease as output increases; that is, an industry which enjoys **no** economies of scale.

Consumer Goods Pricing Act of 1975. A federal statute that abolished state authorized "fair trade," or legalized resale price maintenance. The statute also expressed Congressional approval of the current rule of **per se** illegality for resale price maintenance.

Consumer Welfare Principle. The principle, not entirely uncontroversial, that the goal of the antitrust laws is to provide consumers with the highest possible output of quality goods at the lowest possible price.

Cross Elasticity of Demand. A measurement of the rate at which consumers will switch to one product in response to a price increase in a different product.

D

Deadweight Loss. The social loss that occurs when the monopolist reduces output and raises the price of its product. The deadweight loss is a substantial part of the social cost of monopoly.

Delivered Pricing. A sales mechanism under which the cost of delivery is built into the price. The result may be that people who are located close to the seller pay the same delivered price as people who live much further away, and for whom the costs of delivery are much higher. Delivered pricing can facilitate collusion.

Differential Pricing. Charging different customers different prices for the same product. Under the Robinson–Patman Act this practice is characterized as "price discrimination," although in fact it is not the same as economic price discrimination. See "price discrimination."

"Direct Injury" Test. A test for plaintiff standing in antitrust cases that purports to measure whether the plaintiff's injury was a "direct" or "indirect" consequence of the violation.

Direct Purchaser. A person who deals directly with a monopolist or member of a cartel.

Disfavored Purchaser. The purchaser in a price discrimination scheme who is asked to pay the higher price for a commodity or service, or who produces the larger rate or return to the seller.

Divestiture. A firm's act of selling off one or more of its parts, such as a subsidiary, a plant, or certain assets that create productive capacity. Divestiture is sometimes mandated by the courts in merger and monopolization cases.

Dual Distribution. An arrangement under which a supplier distributes a portion of its product through independent dealers, and the rest through dealerships owned by the supplier.

DuPont Fallacy. The fallacy of concluding that a relevant market necessarily concludes all products for which the cross elasticity of demand is high at **current** market prices. Since a monopolist generally prices in the high elasticity portion of its demand curve, the demand for a monopolist's product may frequently appear to be quite cross elastic with other products. This is so because the monopolist is **already** charging a monopoly price.

E

Economic Profits. The same thing as monopoly profits. Any amount of profit in excess of that necessary to maintain investment in the industry.

Economy of Scale. Any factor in a market that causes cost per unit produced to decline as output is increased.

Eight Firm Concentration Ratio (CR8). A measure of market concentration that consists of the sum of the market shares of the eight largest firms in a market.

Essential Facility Doctrine. A doctrine that a monopolist who controls a qualifying "essential facility," such as a natural monopoly, a subsidized facility such as an athletic stadium, or perhaps a regulated monopoly has a duty imposed by § 2 of the Sherman Act to share this facility with rivals.

Excess Capacity. Plant capacity in a market in excess of the amount that will satisfy consumer demand when price equals marginal cost.

Exclusionary Practice. Technical term for practice by a monopolist designed to prevent competitors or potential competitors from increasing their output or entering the market.

Exclusive Dealing. A form of vertical integration by contract under which a buyer agrees to purchase all its needs of a particular product from the seller—i.e., the buyer agrees not to deal in the same product with a different supplier. Exclusive Dealing can be a violation of § 3 of the Clayton Act.

Efficiency. Efficiency, for antitrust purposes, means two different things. **Productive Efficiency** is a ratio of a firm's output to its inputs—e.g., a firm that produces outputs valued at $10.00 with inputs costing $7.00 is more efficient in this sense than a firm that produces outputs valued at $10.00 with inputs costing $8.00. **Allocative Efficiency** refers to the welfare of society as a whole. A practice or rule is efficient in this sense if the total of all gains it creates is larger than the total of all losses.

Elasticity of Demand. The rate at which demand for a product changes in response to changes in the market price. If a small price increases causes a large drop in demand, demand is said to be "elastic." If even a relatively large price increase causes only a relatively small decrease in demand, demand is said to be "inelastic."

Elasticity of Supply. A measure of the rate at which other firms will increase their output or enter the market in response to a firm's price increase.

Equilibrium. A situation in which the status quo will remain unchanged as long as it is not affected by any force imposed from without. For example, when a market is in equilibrium supply and demand are in balance. The equilibrium can be destroyed, however, by some externally imposed changed, such as a change in consumer tastes, a war or famine, a new invention that greatly reduces the costs of production, or many other things.

F

Facilitating Device. A device, such as basing point pricing or "most favored nation" clauses, that can make either tacit or express collusion in a market work better.

Failing Company Defense. A defense that sometimes permits a firm to acquire a failing firm about to go into bankruptcy, even though the acquisition is illegal under general Clayton Act standards.

Fair Trade. The exercise of resale price maintenance, pursuant to state enabling statutes that once were authorized by federal law. In 1975 Congress passed the Consumer Goods Pricing Act, which repealed the legislation authorizing state's to enact Fair Trade laws.

Favored Purchaser. The purchaser in a price discrimination scheme who pays the lower price, or who produces the lower rate of return to the seller.

Federal Trade Commission Act. A statute passed in 1914 that created the Federal Trade Commission and condemned unfair methods of competition.

Fixed Cost. A cost, such as investment in the plant, which does not vary with a firm's output.

Four Firm Concentration Ratio (CR4). A measure of market concentration consisting of the sum of the market shares of the four largest firms in the market. The CR4 has been widely used in antitrust analysis, although now it is being replaced by the Herfindahl–Hirschman Index.

Franchise Agreement. Generally, an agreement between a supplier of a good or service or an owner of a desired trademark or copyright (franchisor), and a reseller (franchisee) under which the franchisee agrees to sell the franchisor's product or to do business under the franchisor's name.

Free Rider. A firm that takes advantage of a product or service offered by someone else without paying for it. Resale price maintenance, vertical nonprice restraints, and many joint ventures are undertaken by firms in order to solve free rider problems.

Fungible Product. A product which has no important characteristics that identify it as coming from a particular supplier. If a product is perfectly fungible consumers will not know who the particular manufacturer of the product is; or, if they do know, they will not care.

G

Geographic Market. That part of a relevant market that identifies the physical area in which a firm might have market power.

H

Hart-Scott–Rodino Antitrust Improvements Act of 1976. A procedural statute that gave states attorneys general the right to sue as **parens patriae** for injuries suffered by consumers in the state, provided for premerger notification, and generally strengthened the antitrust enforcement powers of the Department of Justice.

Herfindahl-Hirschman Index (HHI). An index of market concentration that consists of the sum of the squares of the market shares of all the firms in a market. The HHI is the index used in the 1992 Justice Department Merger Guidelines, and is achieving some acceptance by courts.

Horizontal. Pertaining to a relationship among competitors—e.g., an agreement among competitors is called a horizontal agreement.

Horizontal Merger. A merger of firms that were competitors before the merger occurred.

I

In Pari Delicto. A common law defense that prohibited a plaintiff from suing if it had been a participant in the contract or conspiracy that led to the violation of law at issue. As a general rule, the defense of **in pari delicto** is not recognized in the antitrust laws.

Indirect Purchaser. One who dealt only indirectly with a monopolist or cartel member.

Industrial Organization. The study of how the structure of the business firm and the market are determined.

Interbrand Competition. Competition among sellers of different brands of a particular product.

Interlocking Directorates. The presence of the same person on the board of directors of two or more corporations. Sometimes a violation of § 8 of the Clayton Act.

Intrabrand Competition. The competition that occurs among the sellers of the same brand of a product.

Intra-Enterprise Conspiracy. A "conspiracy" alleged to occur between two subsidiaries, divisions, or other parts of the same firm. Sometimes called "Bathtub Conspiracies."

J

Joint Venture. A combination of two or more firms for the carrying on of some activity that each firm might otherwise pursue alone. Joint ventures may result in substantial economies. However, they may also facilitate collusion.

L

Leverage. In traditional antitrust theory, a mechanism, such as vertical integration or tying arrangements, by which a monopolist seeks to enlarge its monopoly by extending it into a market previously not monopolized. Today it is generally believed that a monopolist cannot enlarge its monopoly profits through leverage, expect perhaps by price discrimination.

M

Marginal Cost. The additional costs that a firm incurs in the production and distribution of one additional unit of output. In a perfectly competitive market price equals marginal cost.

Marginal Revenue. The additional amount of revenue that a firm, particularly a monopolist, makes when it produces and sells one additional unit of output. The monopolist's profit-maximizing price is located at the intersection of its marginal cost and marginal revenue curves.

Market Power. The power that a monopolist or dominant firm (or a cartel) has to make a profit by reducing output and charging a price higher than marginal cost.

Market Share. A measure of a firm's relative size in relation to some relevant market. Properly measured as the output of the firm in question divided by the sum of the firm's output and the capacity of other firms in the market. Often measured by courts, however as the output of the firm in question divided by total market output. Market share is often used by courts as a surrogate for market power, which cannot be measured directly in litigation.

Merger. The acquisition by one firm of all or part of the stock or assets of another firm.

Minimum Efficient Scale (MES). The same thing as "minimum optimal scale."

Minimum Optimal Scale (MOS). The smallest plant capable of realizing all the economies of scale available in a particular industry. Any plant smaller than such a plant will have somewhat higher costs.

Mobility Barrier. The necessity of a long period of time between a firm's decision to enter a certain market and the day when it actually begins production. If a market contains substantial mobility barriers, then the incumbents in the market may be able to earn monopoly profits while outsiders are gearing up to enter the market.

Monopolist. A single firm that controls a sufficiently large share of the output in any market that it can effectively control the total market output, and therefore increase its profits by reducing production.

Monopoly. A market dominated by a monopolist.

Monopoly Power. A high degree of market power. As measured by the proxy of market share, generally a firm with at least 70% of a relevant market.

Monopoly Price. The same as the profit-maximizing price.

Monopsonist. A monopoly buyer rather than seller.

Most Favored Nation Clause. A clause in a contract that gives the purchaer the retroactive advantage of any price cut later offered by the seller, generally within a specified time period. Widespread use of such clauses can facilitate tacit collusion.

N

Natural Monopoly. A market in which costs declining continuously as output increases, all the way to the point that demand in the market is saturated. As a result, the market may operate most efficiently only if it is occupied by a single firm which sells at a price equal to its average costs. Such markets are prime candidates for traditional price regulation by a regulatory agency.

Network Industry. A market, such as professional or intercollegiate sports, where agreements among the competitors in the market are absolutely essential to the functioning of the market. For example, professional basketball teams must agree with each other about when games will be played, how many games will be played per season, and how the income from a particular game will be divided.

***Noerr-Pennington* Doctrine.** A doctrine that generally exempts petitioning activities directed at a government entity from the antitrust laws.

No Fault Monopolization. A theory frequently discussed but never adopted by either the Supreme Court or Congress, under which certain monopolists would be condemned even if they had not engaged in any impermissible exclusionary practices.

Nondiscriminatory Profit–Maximizing Price. A monpolist's profit-maximizing price, assuming that it cannot engage in price discrimination. Often called simply the monopolist's "profit-maximizing price."

O

Oligopoly. A concentrated market in which firms might be able to reach certain understandings concerning price and output without formally or expressly coming to any "agreement."

P

Parens Patriae Action. An action for damages brought by a sovereign in behalf of its citizens. Parens Patriae actions by states are authorized, subject to certain limitations, by the Hart–Scott–Rodino Antitrust Improvements Act of 1976.

Per Se Rule. A rule under which the court will not consider elaborate arguments that a particular practice is actually procompetitive, but will condemn the practice without taking these arguments into account. The rule is applied to a practice only after long judicial experience has convinced the Supreme Court that a certain practice is virtually always anticompetitive. The purpose of the rule is to avoid expensive litigation in areas in which it is not likely to be fruitful. Currently the **per se** rule is applied to horizontal price fixing, horizontal territorial or customer division, vertical price fixing (resale price maintenance), and some concerted refusals to deal and tying arrangements.

Perceived Potential Entrant. A firm that is perceived by incumbents in a concentrated market to be a likely entrant. As a result, the firms in the market keep their prices lower in order to discourage the perceived potential entrant from entering. If the perceived potential entrant merges with a firm already in the market, then its status as a perceived potential entrant ends. This rationale is sometimes used to condemn certain potential competition (conglomerate) mergers under § 7 of the Clayton Act.

Perfect Competition. A situation in which a large number of sellers each sell a relatively small percentage of a perfectly fungible product. Under perfect competition no seller individually can control total market output, and price will equal marginal cost.

Persistent Price Discrimination. The monopolist's systematic policy of obtaining different rates of return from different groupings of sales.

Predatory Pricing. The attempt by one firm to drive one or more other firms out of business by temporarily charging very low prices; so that the predator can charge monopoly prices later. Analyzed by courts as an attempt to monopolize under § 2 of the Sherman Act, or occasionally as a violation of the Robinson–Patman Act.

Price and Supply Squeeze. The monopolist's attempt to force subnormal returns on vertically related independent companies by charging them a high price for an input product (such as raw aluminum) but selling the output product (such as fabricated aluminum) through its own vertically related subsidiaries at a very low price. The result is that the independent firm is "squeezed" between its high costs and a low market price.

Price Discrimination. The sale or lease of products to two different purchasers at two different rates of return. More technically, two sales that yield different ratios of price to marginal cost. Price Discrimination should be distinguished from differential pricing, which is the sale of the same product at two different prices.

Price Theory. The study of the price and output decisions of the firm.

Primary Jurisdiction. A doctrine under which the courts will defer to a regulatory agency with respect to questions of antitrust violations in the market regulated by the agency. However, the courts will be able to enforce the antitrust laws if they find that the agency's evaluation of the issue in question was superficial.

Primary-Line Robinson–Patman Violation. A violation of the Robinson–Patman Act in which the victims are the violator's competitors.

Problem of Characterization. The problem, often very difficult, of deciding whether to apply the **per se** rule or the rule of reason to a particular practice.

Product Standardization Agreement. An agreement under which a group of firms in a market attempt to produce more uniformity in the product the market produces. Such agreements may give consumers better information about what they are buying; however, product standardization agreements can also facilitate collusion.

Producers' Surplus. The amount a producer earns in excess of the minimum amount required to maintain investment in the industry—i.e., earnings in excess of a competitive rate of return.

Product Differentiation. A situation in which products that compete with each other in the same market can nevertheless be distinguished from one another in the eyes of consumers. As a result, some customers may prefer one brand to another, and be willing to pay a higher price for it.

Product Market. That part of a relevant market which identifies the product or service at issue.

Profit-Maximizing Output. The output level at which the firm, particularly the monopolist, will maximize its profits. The profit-maximizing output level is determined by the intersection of the monopolist's marginal cost and marginal revenue curves.

Profit-Maximizing Price. The price at which the firm, particularly the monopolist, will maximize its profits. It is determined by the intersection of the monopolist's marginal cost and marginal revenue curves.

R

Raising Rivals' Costs. A series of strategies by which a dominant firm might make it more expensive for rivals to do business, thus giving the dominant firm an "umbrella" under which it can raise its own prices.

Reciprocity. An agreement under which one firm will purchase from a second firm only on the condition that the second firm purchase something from the first firm in return; or alternatively, that one firm will sell to a second firm only if the second firm will sell something in return. The legality of reciprocity agreements under the antitrust laws is analyzed in much the same way as the legality of tying arrangements.

Recoupment Theory of Predatory Pricing. A theory of predatory pricing under which a large firm that operates in several geographic markets drops its price in the target market in order to drive a competitor out of business, and raises its price in other markets in order to subsidize this predation.

Relevant Market. A grouping of sales for which the elasticity of supply and the elasticity of demand are sufficiently low that if a single firm controlled all the sales it could profitably reduce output and charge a price higher than marginal cost.

Requirements Contract. A contract under which the buyer agrees to take all its requirements of a certain product from the seller, and the seller agrees to supply them. See exclusive dealing.

Resale Price Maintenance (RPM). Sometimes called "vertical price fixing." An agreement between a supplier and a dealer that the dealer will resell the supplier's product at a stipulated price. Since 1911 RPM has been **per se** illegal under the Sherman Act, subject to some very important exceptions.

Reservation Price. The highest price that a prospective purchaser is willing to pay for a particular product or service.

Restrictions on Distribution. A generic term that refers to the various restrictions that a supplier might impose on its dealers. These include tying arrangements, exclusive dealing, resale price maintenance, vertical territorial and customer restrictions, vertically imposed location clauses, and perhaps others.

Robinson-Patman Act. Really § 2 of the Clayton Act, as amended in 1936 by the Robinson–Patman Amendments. The act prohibits certain instances of differential pricing (i.e., charging two different buyers different prices for goods of like grade and quality). Differential pricing is called "price discrimination" in the Robinson–Patman Act and the cases that apply it.

Rule of Reason. A method of antitrust analysis in which the court is permitted to make a detailed inquiry concerning the effect on price and output of a certain practice. The alternative to the Rule of Reason is the **Per Se** Rule.

S

Secondary-Line Robinson–Patman Violation. A violation of the Robinson–Patman Act in which the victims are the violator's customers.

Sherman Act The first federal antitrust law, passed in 1890. § 1 of the Sherman Act prohibits contracts, combinations and conspiracies in restraint of trade. § 2 of the Sherman Act prohibits monopolization, and attempts and conspiracies to monopolize.

Social Cost. The cost to society as a whole of any particular practice or rule. A social cost should be distinguished from a mere wealth transfer, which is a payment from one person to another, but which leaves the welfare of society as a whole unaffected.

Sporadic Price Discrimination. The sales of products at different ratios of price to marginal cost (or in other words, at different rates of return to the seller) that occurs constantly in changing, competitive markets. **Sporadic** price discrimination is random as to each buyer, as opposed to **persistent** price discrimination.

State Action Exemption. A limited exemption from the antitrust laws for activities that are 1) either compelled or authorized by the state, 2) for which the state has articulated a policy of displacing antitrust with some form of regulation, and 3) which the state actively supervises (or, if municipal conduct is being challenged, which the municipality actively supervises).

"Sunk" Cost. A cost that is irreversible, in the sense that a firm that invests in the market will not recover this cost in the event of failure; industries with high "sunk" costs are therefore considered to have high barriers to entry.

Supply. The amount of a good produced at a given price.

Supply Curve. A line on the price-output graph that shows the cost of production in a market at any given output level. The supply curve is the vertical sum of the marginal cost curves of the individual firms in a market.

T

Tacit Collusion. Collusion that exists among competitors even though they have not explicitly or formally created a cartel. Similar to Oligopoly.

Target Area Test. A test for private plaintiff standing in antitrust cases which attempts to determine whether the plaintiff was in the "target area" of the violation.

Tie-in. See Tying Arrangement.

Transaction Costs. The costs of using the marketplace.

Tying Arrangement. A condition imposed by a seller or lessor that a buyer or lessee may obtain a desired product (the "tying" product) only if it also agrees to take an additional product (the "tied" product), which may or may not be desired. Some tying arrangements violate either § 3 of the Clayton Act or § 1 of the Sherman Act.

V

Variable Cost. A cost such as utilities or raw materials, which varies with a firm's output.

Variable Proportion Tying Arrangement. A tying arrangement in which different buyers use different amounts of the tied product in proportion to their use of the tying product. For example, an arrangement in which the lessor of photocopy machines requires all lessees to purchase their photocopying paper from the lessor. Commonly used by lessors as price discrimination devices.

Vertical. Pertaining to a relationship between a buyer and a seller—e.g., an agreement between a supplier and a retail dealer is called a vertical agreement.

Vertical Integration. What occurs when a firm performs for itself some activity that it could otherwise purchase in the marketplace.

Vertical Merger. A merger of two firms that stand in a buyer-seller relationship.

Vertical Nonprice Restraint. A vertical restriction imposed by a supplier on its dealers, which does not govern the resale price.

Vertical Price Restraint. A vertical restriction imposed by a supplier on its dealers, which governs the price at which the product can be resold.

Vertically Integrated Firm. A firm that operates in two or more production or distribution levels in a partcular production and distribution chain. For example, an oil refinery that also owns and operates its own retail gasoline stations is vertically integrated.

Y

Yardstick Method. A method of estimating antitrust damages by finding a market similar to the one in which the antitrust violation occurred, and making a comparison of prices or profits between the two markets.

APPENDIX E

TABLE OF CASES

APPENDIX F

INDEX

(Capsule Summary and Appendices are not Indexed)